A ROYAL AIR FORCE PILOT

1st Edition

Published in 2013 by
Woodfield Publishing Ltd
Bognor Regis PO21 5EL England
www.woodfieldpublishing.co.uk

ISBN 1-84683-152-0

Printed and bound in England

Typesetting & page design: Nic Pastorius
Cover design: Klaus Berger

A Royal Air Force Pilot's Tales

A personal reflection on 30 years' service with the RAF ~ 1950-80

Harry M. Archer

Woodfield

Woodfield Publishing Ltd

Bognor Regis ~ West Sussex ~ England ~ PO21 5EL
tel 01243 821234 ~ **e/m** info@woodfieldpublishing.co.uk

Interesting and informative books on a variety of subjects

For full details of all our published titles, visit our website at
www.woodfieldpublishing.co.uk

For Jean

Preface

This book was originally written in about 1982, not with any view to publication, but rather as a record for my son of what life was like in the service in 'my day'.

Since retirement, I have devoted myself to golf, kung fu and tai chi. My son went on to an excellent career in the service as fighter pilot and test pilot. I believe we are the only father/son combination to have graduated from any test pilot school. He is now Chief Test Pilot of FRAviation.

My RAF career in brief

1945	Joined RN (Fleet Air Arm). Took voluntary discharge May 1946
1947-50	Edinburgh University
1950	Joined RAF
1951	Basic and Advanced flying training at RAF Thornhill in Southern Rhodesia
1952	UK familiarization, jet conversion, and fighter Operational Conversion. RAF Middleton St George
1953	Central Flying School for training as jet flying instructor. RAF South Cerney & RAF Little Rissington
1953-55	Instructing on Meteors at 203 Advanced Flying School. RAF Driffield
1955	Conversion to Canberras, RAF Bassingbourn
1955-56	27 Squadron as Squadron Training Officer and Instrument Rating Examiner RAF Waddington
1957	Empire Test Pilots School, RAE Farnborough
1958	Aeroplane and Armament Experimental Establishment, Boscombe Down – 'D' Squadron
1958-60	Aeroplane and Armament Experimental Establishment, Boscombe Down – 'B' Squadron
1960-63	Air Force Flight Test Center, Edwards AFB
1964	RAF Staff College, Bracknell
1964-66	Ministry of Defence Operational Requirements Branch
1966	Refresher flying, conversion to Victor B2 RAF Manby & RAF Wittering
1966-68	Commanded 100 Squadron RAF – Victor B2/Blue Steel RAF Wittering
1968 -71	Ministry of Defence Operational Requirements Branch
1972	Air War College followed by RAF Strike Command
1972-74	RAF Strike Command as Group Captain Ops (Offensive)
1974	Refresher flying, conversion to Nimrod MR1 RAF Manby & RAF St Mawgan
1974–76	Officer Commanding RAF St Mawgan
1976-80	Ministry of Defence Operations Branch and Central Staff
1980	Retired

Hours Flown – approx. 7,000
Aircraft Types Flown – approx. 170

SUMMARY OF AIRCRAFT TYPES FLOWN

FIGHTERS	TRAINERS	BOMBERS	TRANSPORTS	COMMUNICATIONS	MARITIME	MISCELLANEAOUS	HELICOPTERS	GLIDERS
ATTACKER	ATHENA	A-5	ARGOSY	ANSON	ATLANTIQUE	APACHE	BELVEDERE	OLYMPIA
BEAUFIGHTER	BALLIOL	B-17	BAC 1-11	AUSTER	GANNET	AVRO 707	BRISTOL 192	SEDBERGH
F-100	BULLDOG	B-25	BELFAST	BEAVER	GOOSE	BLACKBURN B2	DRAGONFLY	SKY
F-102	CHIPMUNK	B-29	BEVERLEY	BEECHCRAFT E18	NEPTUNE	BONANZA	H-21	
F-104	FOUGA MAGISTER	B-47	BRITANNIA	DEVON	NIMROD	CESSNA 152	H-37	
F-106	HARVARD	B-52	C-118	DOMINIE	NORD 262	CESSNA 170	H-43	
F-4	JET PROVOST	B-57	C-119	Fi-156 STORCH	PBY-5A	CESSNA 310	SEA KING	
F-5	MAGISTER	B-58	C-123	HS 125	SEAFIRE	EP 9	SKEETER	
F-80	MORANE SAULNIER 760	BRIGAND	C-130	ISLANDER	SEAMEW	EXTRA 300	SYCAMORE	
F-86	PRENTICE	CANBERRA	C-135B	Me-108	SHACKLETON	GANNET	UH-1D	
FIREFLY	PROVOST	He 111	C-140	OXFORD	SWORDFISH	K-13	WESSEX	
GNAT	PT-13	LANCASTER	C-54	PEMBROKE	WYVERN	KINGAIRE	WHIRLWIND	
HORNET	SAAB J105	LINCOLN	C-82	PIONEER		LASA 60	YH-23	
HUNTER	T-28	MOSQUITO	COMET	PROCTOR		PIAGGIO 166		
HURRICANE	T-33	VALIANT	DC-3	T-28		PIONEER		
JAVELIN	T-37	VICTOR	ELECTRA	T-29		RYAN MONOPLANE		
LIGHTNING	T-38	VULCAN	FOKKER F27	T-39		SILVAIRE		
Me-109	TIGER MOTH		FREIGHTER	TWIN BONANZA		SKYVAN		
METEOR			HASTINGS	TWIN PIONEER		TIPSY B		
P-38			HS 748			TIPSY JUNIOR		
P-51			Ju-52			TRAVELAIRE		
SCIMITAR			KC-135			TWIN BONANZA		
SEA HAWK			KC-97			U-10B		
SEA VIXEN			MARATHON			U-2		
VAMPIRE			VALETTA			U-3A		
VENOM			VARSITY			X-14		
			VC-10					
			VISCOUNT					

CHAPTER 1

I CAN'T REMEMBER A TIME when flying wasn't the most important thing in my life. My earliest childhood memory is of late 1936, at the time of the abdication of King Edward VIII. I can remember quite clearly the excitement of the adults in the household, the comings and goings of neighbours anxious to discuss the crisis and the tension among the grown-ups huddling around the radio for news bulletins as the situation developed. The occasion sticks in my recollection not because of the gravity or, indeed, the events of the crisis which, to be honest, I didn't understand at all, but rather because an uncle had given me a Dinky toy lead model of the de Havilland Comet in which Scott and Black had won the 1934 MacRobertson air race to Australia. I can see that little model in my mind's eye today as clearly as if I held it now. It was a brilliant red colour, with the registration letters G-ACSS in white on wings and fuselage. It had the name 'Grosvenor House' in tiny letters on the nose and the race number, 34, on the tail. I can recall the feel and weight of it and the two two-bladed propellers which would whirl around when I blew on them I don't doubt that, by modern standards, it was a thoroughly bad toy to give to a nine year old child – all sharp edges and lead paint – but I played with it and cherished it for more years than I care to remember. When it finally went the way of all toys, I felt as if I had lost an old and trusted friend.

Around this time, I started to become fascinated by aeroplanes. It was the period of frantic and belated rearmament prior to World War 2 and the popular press reflected a growing national awareness of aviation and aviation personalities. Amy Johnson, Jim Mollison, Amelia Earhart, Wiley Post and Alan Cobham were almost household names and the Empire Air Days at Hendon were widely reported in the newspapers and by the Pathé and Movietone newsreel programmes in the cinema. I can remember watching a Saturday show in the Bungalow cinema in Portobello for hours just to see the Pathé News report of one Hendon display. It only ran for a matter of seconds, but the flickering images of the squadron formations, the giant Heyford heavy bombers and the tied-together aerobatics made a very deep impression on me. In a child's way, I began, then, to develop the feeling that this was the world I wanted to be in and be a part of, when I grew up.

Just shortly after this extended attendance at the cinema – for which I was soundly chastised when I eventually got home – there was great excitement when an aeroplane was reported to have landed near Joppa, a mile or two distant from Portobello. I remember rushing to the reported scene after school, pedalling my bicycle furiously, my heart in my mouth lest the visitor should have managed to get away before I arrived. It hadn't. It was a Hawker Hart of one of the Auxiliary squadrons, which had experienced engine trouble en-route to Edinburgh Turnhouse and had made a forced landing on the beach. It was the first real aeroplane I had ever seen close up and it was the most beautiful thing I had ever experienced. So fragile looking and yet so purposeful. It was finished in glittering silver all over, with a red flash down the fuselage and the squadron crest painted large on the vertical fin. The pilot was there when I arrived, white-overalled, helmet and goggles casually in hand, chatting to a policeman and looking like a visitor from the Gods. I stayed on the beach until it was quite dark, just happy to be near a real aeroplane until, reluctantly, I had to return home – to another frosty reception for staying out too late. I have a feeling that my model Comet was withdrawn for a time in retribution, but I didn't really mind. The real thing had been immeasurably better and more than worth it.

In the years up to the outbreak of World War 2 in 1939, I read just about everything I could lay my hands on which had any sort of connection with flying. Through Captain W E Johns and his creation Biggles, I relived the World War 1 air campaigns until the aircraft, the personalities and the tactics of that period were more familiar to me than my daily schoolwork. The fascination of that era led me into the biographies of the early 'aces' – Mannock, McCudden, Ball, Rickenbacker, Immelmann and Richthoffen. I knew that they had been participants in a long and terrible war – how terrible I knew from my uncles, both Seaforth Highlanders who had been in the trenches in France from 1914 to 1918 – but these flying men seemed, somehow, to have been above the meanness and misery of the trenches. Air warfare had been in its infancy and there had been about these pioneer air fighters something of the glamour and chivalry of mediaeval knights in their one-on-one, man-to-man, combats in the sky.

My reading about the early days of air warfare led me to develop an interest in the aircraft of the period. Although all of my knowledge came from books, I felt that I knew them all, their good points and their shortcomings. The performance capabilities and handling qualities of the Camel, the Spad, the Bristol Fighter, the Albatross, the Pfalz and the Fokker, were as familiar to me as if I had spent hours in their cockpits. I knew all about the smell of hot castor oil, the spray of it that misted up the goggles and the torque spin engendered by the rotary engines. From this interest, it was a short step to building and flying models to see why aeroplanes performed as they did. Initially, my attempts at model building were simple in the extreme – fairly primitive hand-launched gliders – and generally unsuccessful; they crashed. But the urge to know why they flew – or, more generally, didn't fly – in a particular way was insistent and led me to studying, at a relatively early age, some quite advanced textbooks on aerodynamics and aircraft design. As I became more experienced, my models became more ambitious. I progressed from basic box structure gliders, covered with tissue paper tautened by water spray from my mother's scent atomizer, to shaped fuselage, rubber band powered models, silk covered and tautened by the application of real aircraft dope which turned my head every time I used it. I remember how I loved the drum-like tautness of a well doped, fabric covered, model. By 1939, when materials for model construction became hard to obtain, I had a number of quite complex models flying, including one with all-balsa sheeted fuselage and wing coverings and a tiny petrol engine power plant. I had one model for which I designed interchangeable wings so that I could experiment with the effects of different design features such as wing camber, aspect ratio and taper, on the models flight characteristics. I was about eleven or twelve years old then and it depresses me to think that I would have quite a job to produce anything like that model today

In retrospect, it is astonishing how much I learned in that period without, in any way, being conscious that I was learning anything at all. I was interested in aeroplanes and I enjoyed playing about with my models. It was only years later, when I had to get down to the business of learning about aerodynamics in earnest, that I realised how much was already locked away in my consciousness from that early interest in the subject.

It was about this time, too, that I came across two books which fascinated me more than any of the others I had read. Oddly enough, both were written by American authors. The first was 'I Wanted Wings' by Lt Beirne Lay Jr, United States Army Air Corps – the same man who, later, as General Beirne Lay Jr, United States Air Force (Retd) established himself as a bestselling author and Hollywood scriptwriter, responsible for the screenplays of such outstanding film productions as 'Twelve O'clock High' and 'Command Decision'. 'I Wanted Wings' was Lay's account of his entry into the Army Air Corps, his training and eventual graduation as a bomber pilot. His book introduced me to a very different sort of flying world centred on Air Corps training at Kelly and Randolph Fields in Texas. The world he wrote of was a strange one, the images of the aircraft, the people and the places, different and somehow brighter and sharper than the ones with which I was then familiar. Even the language – of 1930s America – seemed crisper and more expressive than anything I had read before. Although I didn't realise it at the time, the story of Lay's personal odyssey was a fascinating, first hand, insider's account of the early days of the United States Air Force when people like Hap Arnold, Tooey Spaatz, Ira Eaker, Curtis LeMay and Billy Mitchell were relatively junior officers just beginning to make their marks in the emerging world of American military aviation.

The second book was by an author whose name I have since forgotten. It was called 'Dive Bomber' and was a story not dissimilar to Beirne Lay's except that the author entered the United States Navy as an aviation cadet and subsequently graduated to fleet service in the old USS Saratoga. The flying parts of the book were absorbing – training at Pensacola in the SN-J, fighter conversion at Charleston, Texas, to the original Grumman biplane fixed undercarriage version of the F-4F, then operational conversion to the retractable undercarriage Grumman F-9F, the "hottest pursuit ship in the fleet." Equally absorbing was the author's account of life as a carrier borne fighter pilot in the United States Navy in the mid to late 1930s. The life depicted was fascinating – squadron re-assignments to San Diego, to Norfolk and to Hawaii, goodwill cruises all over the world, annual fleet exercises in the Pacific, parties, good comradeship and, as an ominous backdrop, the sense of all of this taking place in the shadow of the war clouds which, even then, were quite clearly evident on the horizon.

When the war that had seemed inevitable finally arrived, it was not long before Edinburgh got its first taste of what so many were to experience during the next six years. Within a month, German bombers launched an attack on elements of the Royal Navy at Rosyth causing some damage. The raiders were intercepted by fighters from 602 and 603 squadrons of the Royal Auxiliary Air Force and two bombers were shot down. In the course of this engagement, one of the German aircraft was chased at rooftop height right over the middle of Edinburgh with a couple of fighters in hot pursuit. I watched them from the promenade at Portobello, wildly excited at the breakneck dash out to sea, the chatter of the gunfire and the tiny puffs of smoke from the fighters' wings as they fired. It never occurred to me to try to get under cover until it was all over. The whole thing was simply too fascinating not to have watched it out to the end. I don't know whether the raider I saw was one of the two shot down, but he would have had to be very lucky to have got away unscathed. A Fettes schoolboy of the time, who also witnessed this engagement, wrote to the Secretary of State for Air that the boys of the school "remained unconvinced of the horrors of war." I know that I felt exactly the same.

The war years fanned my interest in flying as probably nothing else could have done. Hardly a day went by without some aspect of military aviation being reported in the papers or on the radio so that there was a wide availability of information on the subject. More importantly, perhaps, the war years provided the opportunity for a much closer involvement, at a personal level, in the service side of aviation. I can't remember when the Air Training Corps was started as a sort of pre-Service training organization, but I remember being among the first to join. I loved every minute of my time in the corps, the drilling, the classroom work, the occasional camp at a nearby service aerodrome and the practical exercises on antique pieces of service equipment that were provided for cadets to learn on. I became something of an expert in aircraft recognition and, as a result, was led into lecturing my fellow squadron members on the subject. Able-bodied 'real' lecturers were in short supply at the time and any cadet who showed aptitude in a subject was encouraged to try his hand at teaching his fellows. Although dreadfully embarrassing to begin with – we were all about 12 to 15 years old at the time – lecturing was invaluable experience for those of us who had to do it. Over a period of time, one developed the confidence to stand up in front of a class and just get on with the teaching, without being overly self-conscious about the experience. It also taught the very worthwhile lesson that anyone who presumes to teach had better know his subject inside out, or one of his 'pupils' can be counted on to make him look and feel, like an absolute idiot.

I remember two incidents from my ATC days with some pleasure. At first, I had great difficulty with sending and receiving Morse code – even at the modest eight to ten words a minute standard we were supposed to attain. Because my wretched performance was a continual source of comment from my instructors, I scraped together the materials to build a simple, battery-operated, Morse key and buzzer. With this piece of home-made kit, I spent hours practicing in my bedroom until the sound of the Morse code characters became as familiar to me as the spoken alphabet. I suppose I was learning early the essence of the philosophy attributed to Ben Hogan when that great American golfer was supposed to have remarked, "If you can't outplay them, outwork them." The upshot of my hours of solitary practice was an award from the Edinburgh ATC Wing Headquarters as one of only two cadets who achieved a standard of twenty-five words a minute at the annual proficiency assessments. To this day, I am still childishly proud of that award because I feel that I put in the time and the effort to earn it.

The second incident, which I recall with mixed feelings, originated in the ATC's predilection for involving the cadets in physical activities. Most of the games and sports in which we were expected to participate were familiar to me from school and I enjoyed them. Boxing, however, was a very different matter. It had not been part of the school sports curriculum and, moreover, as an only child, perhaps overly protected from the hurly-burly of too active participation in any sport 'with the rough boys', I was singularly ill-equipped psychologically for the ring. While the rest of my fellow cadets were cheerfully knocking spots off each other in bouts which, on the whole, were characterized more by enthusiasm than skill, I generally managed to find some craven excuse which would keep me on the outside of the canvas. The Squadron Commander was a kindly man and I believe that he was well aware that I was, in point of fact, scared stiff. Inevitably, however, this situation could not go on forever and the time duly arrived when I had run out of reasons for non-participation. In the event, on the night in question, I was paired with a newcomer to our squadron, a very slight small boy who was, I believe, put in with me purely because we both had red hair. I was not in the least looking forward to the encounter, but I did cheer up a bit when I saw my opponent stripped for action. He was at least a head shorter and a stone or so lighter and looked, at face value, even less of a boxing prospect than I did.

It pains me now to recall that his appearance somewhat encouraged me and I began, unkindly, to think that I might cut something of a figure by giving him a sound drubbing. In this unchristian frame of mind, I advanced from my corner at the opening bell, we touched gloves and that was my last conscious recollection until I was being brought round on my stool by the inexpert application of smelling salts and wet towels. The whole engagement – including the count – had lasted for something like twelve seconds. Some time later, I learned that the puny opponent I had so confidently expected to knock over was Ronnie Muir who had been an amateur boxer of some note with the Leith Sparta Boxing Club practically since he could walk. Ronnie later went on to win a medal at the Commonwealth Games in Australia and had a distinguished career as a professional before he hung up his gloves. Although the bout was an absolute debacle, I must confess to having, in later years, made some capital out of the encounter by remarking airily, "Oh, I don't do it anymore, but when I was younger I went in with Ronnie Muir."

While I was in the ATC, I volunteered for the Fleet Air Arm under the 'Y' scheme, which was supposed to provide preferred entry to pilot training in the Navy. When the time for my call-up came, the war was over and the Navy had more pilots and aircrew than it knew what to do with. At the time, it was rightly more concerned with the problems of demobilization and resettlement of its returning servicemen than with the starry ambitions of youngsters who had not been available for the main event. Nevertheless, it was with high hopes that I set out in January of 1946 to report to HMS Royal Arthur for processing prior to flying training for the Fleet Air Arm. Right at the outset, I encountered a certain amount of difficulty in even reporting in on time. As I remember, I went by train to Grantham where I had to change for Skegness. On arrival at Grantham, I enquired of a porter when the next train for Skegness was due and was somewhat discountenanced to learn that "it went on Thursday." Since this exchange took place on a Sunday, it appeared that I was in for something of a record wait between trains. Further enquiry, however, made it clear that it was my misunderstanding of the Lincolnshire dialect which was at fault. What the porter had tried to convey was that I should "change at Firsby," and a train to that destination did, in fact, depart somewhat sooner than I had at first believed.

When I finally arrived at HMS Royal Arthur – the pre-war Butlins Holiday Camp at Skegness – the conditions were generally pretty chaotic – understandable perhaps at the time when a great many serving personnel wanted out and there seemed to be little or no interest in those of us who wanted in. After a few days, I was called to see the Unit Medical Officer and bluntly told that I was suffering from tuberculosis and would, accordingly, be discharged from the service immediately. While I was doing my best to cope with this shattering piece of information, I contrived to steal a glance at the X-Ray plate, which the doctor was flourishing. It was, beyond doubt, a picture of somebody's chest but, if the name on the plate was to be believed, that somebody wasn't me. When I made this point to the doctor, he was much put out and insisted on me having yet another set of X-Rays to satisfy him. I got the feeling that I had really ruined his day by not having tuberculosis. Happily for me, the re-test and another which I had prudently arranged at a local health clinic for my own peace of mind, proved to be negative and the immediate discharge was quietly forgotten about. The incident was very quickly resolved, but it left me with a profound distrust of service medicos, which I carry with me to this day.

Much as the event had agitated me, I soon had enough other problems to worry about. It was very quickly becoming apparent that the Navy had more pilots and other aircrew than it would usefully be able to employ over the next few years, even taking into account the large numbers who had opted to leave the service. The prospects for new pilot training courses were slim in the extreme and seemed to be becoming slimmer each day. Eventually, the day arrived when those of us who had arrived as 'Y' scheme entrants were assembled to learn the Admiralty's decision on our situation. There was, we were told, to be no new pilot or other aircrew training courses for at least one year. If we wished to remain in the service until the courses restarted, we could, as an interim measure, re-muster to either cook or gunner, which would at least keep us out of mischief while we waited. Alternatively, if we could not accept the prospect of the years wait, we were to be allowed to take an immediate honourable voluntary discharge. Since I had always had difficulty in boiling an egg competently, I had no hesitation in discarding the option of re-mustering to cook – a decision from which countless matelots have almost certainly benefited unknowingly. Equally, while life as a seagoing gunner did have a certain appeal, it wasn't flying and flying was what I wanted to do. In the event, then, I opted for voluntary discharge and left the Royal Navy in the middle of 1946 without ever having really got used to the feel of the uniform.

When I arrived back in Edinburgh, my dreams of a life in the flying world were at a very definite end. I quickly learned that the RAF was in precisely the same situation as the Navy. Even with my expertise in aircraft recognition, my twenty-five words a minute Morse and my ring experience with Ronnie Muir, my prospects of becoming a pilot had come to zero. I had reached the end of the aviation road.

In the circumstances, I had to decide and decide quickly, what I was going to do with my life in place of the career I had wanted so badly. Because I had unwisely left school early, my educational qualifications were minimal and would certainly have made little impression on any prospective employer. Again, at this fairly critical period, I found that I was being strongly influenced by a book I had read, a book that had made a deep impression on me at the time. This was Edward Marjoribank's 'Life of Carson', the biography of the great Irish lawyer and states-man. In spite of my minimal educational qualifications, I determined to get myself to university and become a lawyer. Quite clearly, lacking the requisite qualifications, even getting to university was going to present something of a problem. The only possible route to admission lay in sitting the university Prelim-inary Qualification Examination and successfully achieving passes in seven subjects, four at the lower level and three at the higher level. This represented a fairly daunting task, particularly since the examination, preparatory to the next university entrance date, was to be held within a matter of some six to seven months. This was not an ideal situation but, like it or not, it was the situation which existed. It left me with something like seven months to tackle five years of schoolwork in seven subjects, some of which I had never even studied before.

I will pass very quickly over that period prior to sitting the Preliminary Exami-nation. Every day, I worked on the textbooks I had acquired; often well into the early hours of the morning, weekends included. No sport, no recreation, no amusement. I simply couldn't afford the time for any distraction from the primary objective. In the end, the effort – and it really was an effort – was justified. I ob-tained the requisite passes in all subjects and was accepted by Edinburgh University. There are a number of ways by which a candidate can get to a universi-ty and my heartfelt recommendation to anyone contemplating such a course is to avoid, like the plague, the approach into which I forced myself. That really was doing it the hard way.

From the time I got into university, I lived the relatively carefree life of a stu-dent at one of the most delightful institutions of higher education in the United Kingdom. The work was there to be done, but the pace was what you wanted to make it and there was plenty of time for more pleasurable diversions. I played a lot of soccer which I loved without ever being particularly good at it and did some sprinting at any length up to 440 yards. With a bit of time to call my own, I fre-quented the local dance halls of the time, the Cavendish in Tollcross, the Plaza in Morningside and the Palais in Fountainbridge. I liked dancing and, like many others of my age I suppose, probably imagined myself to be something of a dash-ing fellow on the floor. The reality was probably painfully different. Nevertheless, it was fun and for me, as for most of my generation, the dance hall was a hugely important element in the social life of the time

In this way, I passed three years looking forward to graduation and a future within the legal profession. All thoughts of flying had long since been pushed very firmly to the back of my mind. And there they stayed, quietly forgotten, until one Saturday in 1950, when the casual remark of a friend in the middle of Princes Street irrevocably changed the course of my life.

CHAPTER 2

DURING THE LATE 1940S and early 1950s, Edinburgh had two very good football teams and it was my habit to go to either the Easter Road or Tynecastle grounds on Saturday afternoons to watch one or other. Because the University team played its fixtures on Saturday mornings, it was the practice for those of us going to the afternoon match to have a quick snack lunch in one of the Princes Street restaurants en-route from the University ground. After one such snack, a friend and I were walking along Princes Street on our way to Easter Road when an aeroplane flew over quite low. My attention must have wandered while I was watching it because, quite suddenly, my friend grabbed me by the arm and remarked jokingly, "It's not Easter Road you should be going to, Harry, it's in there." When I turned round to see what he was talking about, I found him pointing to a shop window a few doors along from the corner of Castle Street. The premises had been taken over as a RAF Recruiting Office and, in the middle of the window display, among models and photographs of service aircraft, was a very large poster the wording on which ran: DO YOU WANT TO FLY? IF SO, COME INSIDE.

I can remember vividly being quite shaken by the message. I had always wanted to fly. Four years earlier, I had tried as hard as I knew how to get the chance to fly. I hadn't made it and had done my best to put the desire out of my mind and concentrate on other things. In the split second of looking in that window, however, I knew that the desire was still there, as strong as ever and maybe even stronger and would probably always be there no matter what else I tried to do to replace it. I excused myself from my friend, pushed open the front door and, melodramatic as it sounds, walked straight into a new and altogether different, life.

I have often thought about that incident during the intervening years. It arose out of the purest chance and yet it determined the next thirty years of my life for me. At the end of the day, I suppose that it all comes down to a matter of luck, which has a way of evening itself out over the long run. When I had tried to get into the Fleet Air Arm in 1945, the time had been wrong and, in that sense, the luck had gone against me. Now, in trying to get into the RAF in 1950, with the Korean War providing the impetus for rebuilding the strength of the Armed Forces, the time was right and the luck was running with me.

After the initial interviews and medical examinations, I had to wait for some time before being called down to the RAF Aircrew Selection Centre at Hornchurch for aptitude testing. There were about three days of academic, co-ordination and leadership tests before I was informed that I was considered suitable for aircrew training in the Pilot/Navigator category. I was to return home to await formal notification. Some time later, I was called back to the Recruiting Office in Edinburgh and informed that the RAF were prepared to accept me for pilot training on a Short Service Commission which, if I remember correctly, was an engagement of something like twelve years. I knew that I was at a crossroads – I didn't have too long to go before my final degree examinations and I was fairly confident that I could get a pass. I had the prospect of employment in the firm with which I was doing my law apprenticeship and I liked the work that I was doing. I could have been perfectly happy as a lawyer and made for myself quite a reasonable and useful life in Edinburgh. But it wasn't flying and flying was what I had really wanted to do ever since I could remember. I couldn't tell whether I was doing the right thing, or making the most ghastly blunder, but I did know, beyond any possible doubt, that if I didn't take the chance while it was there, I would regret it for the rest of my life. When the man put the form down in front of me, I took a deep breath, reached for my pen and signed on the dotted line.

The wait between formally committing myself and receiving orders to report seemed interminable but, in due course of time, official notification arrived that I was to report to Number 1 Induction Reception Centre at RAF Cardington, near Bedford, to be enlisted into the Service. I travelled south in the highest of good spirits and, on the tenth of December 1950, I raised my right hand and swore the Oath of Allegiance to become a member of the Royal Air Force.

At long last, I was in.

The recruit draft of which I was a part was not kept long at Cardington – just long enough to be kitted out with uniforms and equipment and to fill in what seemed to be an endless succession of forms providing details of religion, next of kin, person to be advised in case of death or accident, educational qualifications, sports, hobbies and a host of like details. After five days of this, we were taken down to the railway station and dispatched to the Aircrew Transit Unit at Driffield in Yorkshire. Just before we left Cardington, I was asked by a fatherly old Flight Sergeant where we were being sent. When I told him Driffield, he sucked his teeth meditatively, and then remarked, "Two places you want to avoid in this 'ere Air Force Sonny, Yorkshire and Lincolnshire. Don't you forget that" I didn't. I had plenty of time not to since I spent quite a bit of the next few years at various units in both counties – and loved every minute of the time I spent in each of them.

I don't think I will ever forget my first impression of Driffield. We arrived there in the early evening of 15 December and the whole place was knee deep in snow. Service transport couldn't use the roads, so we had to pick up our bags and march, or rather stagger, the two or three miles to the Station. Our route took us right through the main street and I remember thinking that the whole scene was exactly like something out of a Christmas card. First impressions last and I have always felt that Driffield was one of the nicest places I have ever been to.

The Aircrew Transit Unit was simply a large holding camp where drafts of potential aircrews were held until the time came for them to be slotted into a course at one or other of the Initial Training Schools. We were given a lot of lectures mostly, as I recall, on the dangers posed to young men like us by women "of a certain type." One got the impression that women of this type were lying in wait in droves somewhere outside the main gate just waiting to pounce on us unsuspecting victims. I regret to have to say that, during the month I was there, I remained resolutely un-pounced on and I don't believe that any of my colleagues fared any better. Attempts were made to give us some preliminary 'square bashing' but, since the parade ground was about a foot deep in snow and had a surface like a skating rink, this initiative was not altogether successful. Great importance was attached to teaching us how to salute correctly and we had the traditional service litany "longest way up and shortest way down" thoroughly dinned into us.

We became obsessed with saluting and, after a matter of days, were saluting everything in sight quite indiscriminately, much to the delight of the station permanent staff airmen, who were unused to this sort of greeting from anybody. Most of our time, however, was spent shovelling snow in clearing the roads of the camp. I very quickly discovered how effete I had become at University when I had to wield a shovel for a couple of hours. The snow was probably a godsend to the permanent staff, since it gave us something to do and so eased their burden of filling in our time. Since it snowed and snowed heavily, practically every single day that we were there, the staff were not overly taxed by our presence.

We were at Driffield over the Christmas and New Year holiday periods – not that anybody save the Scots seemed to bother much at New Year. I had become friendly with a New Zealand colleague on the same draft and a family he had met in the village invited us for lunch on Boxing Day. It was a very kind gesture on their part because I believe that it was the first Christmas either of us had spent away from home. After the meal, we all went along to the Bell Hotel where the local Hunt was to commence its Boxing Day meet. I could hardly believe the scene – it really was straight out of a Christmas card. The horses stamping, their breath condensing in the cold air, the dogs yapping and sniffing everywhere, the riders scarlet-jacketed, drinking the stirrup-cups provided with grave formality by the landlord of the hotel. I had never seen anything like it. When the hunt had gone, to the accompaniment of much horn blowing, stamping and wild hallooing, the bar of the hotel, warmed by a blazing log fire and gleaming with copper and brass tankards and harness pieces, was the perfect place to finish off a memorable day. I remember thinking that, Edward the First notwithstanding, the English might not be such a bad bunch after all.

While on the subject of the English, I recall an incident at Driffield, which introduced me to my first real experience of the urbanity and self-confidence that characterises at least one of the social classes. One of my co-cadets was the son of a Belgravia family of some note, a thoroughly charming, cultivated and witty individual who, in spite of a complete willingness to undertake any task set for him, seemed constitutionally incapable of adjusting to the fairly hectic pace of life, which was the norm for our situation. In the mornings, when the rest of us were frantically rushing about preparing for first parade, which took place at some ungodly hour before breakfast, Michael would languidly draw on his silk dressing gown prior to testing whether the hot water was at precisely the temperature required for his morning shave and bath. Since these operations seemed to take an eternity to complete, he was frequently late for first parade, or missing altogether. When the NCOs went apoplectic at his late or non-arrival, he would enquire of me, quite seriously, "but surely they can't expect a chap to turn out before he's prepared himself properly for the day." My advice that the situation should simply be accepted rather than rationalised had little or no effect and he continued on his completely individualistic way throughout all of our stay at Driffield – much to the astonished admiration, I might say, of the rest of us conformists.

Towards the end of our time at Driffield, Michael announced that, when the postings came through, he would host a party at the Bell to which all ten or so of us on the draft were invited. When, in fact, the postings did arrive, we had about three days' notice of the move and Michael, reminded of his promise, was, inevitably, out of money. For anyone else on the course, I believe, that would have been the end of the matter, but not for Michael. "Oh, that's all right," he remarked airily, "I'll borrow a quid or two from Attila." Attila, I should explain, was the Sergeant Drill Instructor who had run our work parties and broken us in, none too gently, to the 'square'. The nature he deployed to us was not, to say the least, loveable – perhaps best characterised by his oft-repeated assertion, "I like young aircrew cadets – soft boiled with mushrooms on the side." The very thought of speaking to him, much less trying to tap him for a loan, would have terrified most of us. In the event, however and to our utter stupefaction, he coughed up like a lamb and the party, at which Attila was an honoured and lively guest, went ahead most successfully. Afterwards, in the NAAFI, Attila 'fleshed out' our service education by himself rendering several choruses of all-time favourite Air Force ditties such as 'Shaibah Blues', 'Leaving Khartoum' and 'Lloyd George knew my Father', as well as some delightful and unprintable parodies of a number of other choice selections from 'Songs My Mother Didn't Teach Me'.

My own posting, to which I reported on 12 January 1951, was to Number 3 Initial Training School at Royal Air Force, Cranwell. Everybody in the service knew Cranwell, the Air Force counterpart of the Army's Sandhurst and the Navy's Dartmouth. The Cranwell cadets were and I think rightly, the elite of the service, carefully moulded by their four-year course into highly competent, dedicated, professional military officers. In the course of my career, I was to meet and work, with, many old Cranwellians and the overwhelming majority, by their first class performance in the job, were living testimonials to the excellence of their training at the College. The whole ambience of the place, dominated by the graceful College buildings, was redolent of professional quality and service tradition.

Almost needless to say, it was not to this part of the Cranwell complex that Flight A1 of Number 4 Wing of the Initial Training School was assigned. We were, if you like, the down-market side of the station, accommodated in bare wooden huts characterised by acres of gleaming linoleum which required endless polishing and heated – very inadequately heated I may say – by black, sinister looking stoves which put out little in the way of heat since, for most of the time, the fires had to be out to permit the stoves, too, to be polished. In fact, practically everything that was a part of our everyday life had to be polished – boots, rifles, floors, bed frames, stoves, buttons, shovels. Daily, every item received its allotted quota of polish, Brasso or Blanco. Very early on in my career, I learned the truth behind the old Service adage, "if it moves, salute it: if it doesn't move, polish it: If it can't be polished, paint it white."

The six-month course on which we were embarked was designed to provide for us the transition from civilians into servicemen. Every day started with drill, with or without arms, on the main parade square – an hour of non-stop marching, wheeling, about turning, advancing to the front in review order, saluting on the march and so on. These activities were conducted to the constant accompaniment of fortissimo comments from the troop of 'drill pigs', the hard working drill instructors, whose function was to knock us into some semblance of military shape and whose injunctions, hallowed in the service since the days when Pontius was a pilot, were designed to keep us in a state of perpetual dread of making some foolish error. "Am I hurting you lad? No? Well, I should be, I'm standing on your bloody hair." – "Did you shave this morning Lad? You did? Well, put a blade in the razor tomorrow." – "Get in step Lad, you're poncing about like you've got two left legs." – "Did you break your mothers' heart, Sonny? Well, you bloody well won't break mine!"

There was an apocryphal story at the time of the cadet who wandered past a barrack room in which a Corporal DI lay sleeping. Greatly daring, the cadet yelled through the open window, "Atten-SHUN." Whereupon, so the story goes, the Corporal, still sleeping, responded by yelling back, "STAND STILL!"

It might not seem like the greatest fun in the world to be subjected to this sort of activity at seven in the morning of a bitterly cold Lincolnshire winter day, but I must be honest and say that I loved every minute of it. Numbed fingers and screaming instructors notwithstanding, there was a tremendous satisfaction in being part of a well-drilled unit on the square, everybody alert, disciplined and responsive. On very rare occasions, we had a band to accompany us and I can still remember the exhilaration of drilling well on a cold, crisp morning to the strains of the RAF march-past. Not everybody's cup of tea, maybe, but I liked it.

After the drill sessions, most of the day was taken up with classroom lectures on a wide range of service topics. Air Force history, basic mathematics – cunningly disguised as preliminary navigation – theory of flight, theory of engines, Air Force law, Air Force organisation, rank structure and a host of other subjects. We participated in endless initiative tests and had an early introduction to small-scale 'Escape and Evasion' exercises, designed – we often felt bitterly – to muck up our uniforms and equipment and ensure that the night would be spent restoring them to pristine condition for the following days inspection. There was little or no time to spare in each day and, after we had done our stint of polishing everything in sight – in what was, theoretically, our spare time – there was seldom time for much in the way of personal activity before 'lights out'.

It is all too easy to look back now and laugh at the system that kept us on the hop for most of the waking day. Certainly, there were elements of the training which were childish and the 'bull' could never really be justified in itself. The odd thing, however, was that the system worked. It weeded out the few who really couldn't conform to the new way of life and conditioned those of us who stuck it out to abide by the old maxim, "no matter how daft the order, obey it first, then argue about it afterwards." In spite of ourselves, we did shed our civilian skin and, although very far from the finished service product, we did become, each in his own individual way, more coordinated, more self-reliant, more disciplined and more adaptable. It is the oldest cliché in the world to say that the services turn boys into men but it is, nonetheless, true for all that. At any rate, the system of that time certainly did.

Towards the end of our time at Cranwell, the postings for our flying training assignments were published. Craning through the crowd around the notice board, I made out the entry that concerned me most – 'Cadet Pilot Archer to Number 3 Flying Training School, Feltwell'. After the formal passing-out parade and a round of farewell parties, I packed my bags for my first leave since I joined and headed north to Edinburgh for some well-earned relaxation, prior to starting the real business of the job in earnest at Feltwell.

CHAPTER 3

MY LEAVE IN EDINBURGH was supposed to last for three weeks, to fit in with the assembly date of the next scheduled pilots course at Feltwell. In the event, it lasted for something like ten days. I arrived home late one Saturday night to find a telegram waiting for me with orders to report back to Cranwell 'immediately'. There was no explanation given for this recall and I immediately started to have all sorts of depressing thoughts about what could possibly have gone wrong to justify my being pulled back so abruptly. I repacked hastily and caught the first available train south early next morning.

When I arrived at Cranwell, I found that my posting to Feltwell had been cancelled and that I, with twelve others from Cranwell and the Initial Training School at Jurby, were to be formed into a small draft being put together to make up a shortfall in numbers on Number 5 Pilots Course at Number 5 Flying Training School at Thornhill, in Southern Rhodesia. I never did discover, either then or later, how the Air Force had selected the thirteen individuals to make up the shortfall on the course scheduled for Rhodesia. There seemed to be no logical common factor amongst us. We were not linked alphabetically by name, we had all finished in different order of merit in our ITS courses and we were not even remotely in one age category. After many years, I have come to the conclusion, odd as it may seem, that we really were just selected absolutely at random – probably with a pin – from personnel assigned to the next courses at the UK flying training schools.

Regardless of how the selections were, in fact, made, I was delighted to find myself on a draft for the last overseas country to operate flying training schools under the old Commonwealth Air Training Scheme. By some unfathomable quirk of the posting system, I had wound up scheduled for what amounted to an overseas posting with just about six-month's total service under my belt. I didn't know much more about Rhodesia than I could remember from school geography classes, but I did know that the weather – always an important factor in flying training – was likely to be considerably better than that in Norfolk. That made the posting thoroughly acceptable to me.

The next few days at Cranwell were spent in a flurry of kitting-out with tropical uniforms and equipment and with inoculations and vaccinations for what seemed to be every complaint known to medical science. Like many another serviceman bound for foreign parts, I learned, at first hand, the extremely unpleasant effect of the TABT 'jab'. Given the choice – which we were not – I think that most of us would have opted to risk the Typhoid or Paratyphoid. If their effects are worse than the effect of the immunisation, they must be very unpleasant indeed.

In due course, armed with all of the paraphernalia deemed essential to support the British in foreign climes, we were transported to London Airport and embarked aboard a British Overseas Airways Boeing Stratocruiser for the flight to Africa. This was the Johannesburg flight with scheduled refuelling stops at Tripoli, Kano, Brazzaville and Livingstone, which was, in fact, to be our destination.

Although most of us had been airborne for short flights at one time or another during our time in the cadet forces or at the Initial Training Schools, the long flight out from London was probably our first taste of anything other than 'up and down' air experience flying. Also, for most of us, it was our first journey outside the UK. Understandably, we were all pretty excited about the prospects of what lay ahead for us, so that we got precious little rest during the trip. None of us wanted to miss any of the sights en-route; the Alps, the Mediterranean, the first view of the African Continent and the Sahara Desert. We must have driven a patient flight crew to the edge of distraction by trooping up to the flight deck in relays, to have all the instruments and controls pointed out to us. I can remember thinking that cockpits had obviously changed quite a bit since the days of the Camel and the SE5. The layout of the Boeing looked dauntingly like the console of a Wurlitzer organ and I am sure that many of us wondered if we would ever possibly learn and remember what all of the dials, knobs, switches and levers were for. Mention of the Camel reminds me that I saw one – the four-legged variety, that is – from the airport restaurant during our refuelling stop at Kano. This particular animal was proceeding sedately and with its characteristic expression of disdain, along a dusty road just outside the airfield boundary. I don't know why I should have been so taken by the sight but, to be fair, camels on the hoof are not exactly an everyday sight on the streets of Edinburgh.

With the novelty and excitement of the journey, we were all pretty tired when we finally disembarked at Livingstone in the early hours of the morning. Fortunately, Headquarters Rhodesian Air Training Group had correctly anticipated that we would not arrive in best fettle for an immediate onward train journey and had arranged a blank day for us at the Victoria Falls Hotel, some little way from the airport, to recover from the effects of our travels. I remember very clearly that first day on African soil – inevitably, none of us wanted to sleep now that the opportunity to do so was available. We spent much of the day relaxing in the grounds of the hotel, sampling our first taste of local products which were to become very familiar to us – Castle Lager and, for the more sophisticated, South African brandy at, as I recall, ninepence a glass. We gasped our way through our first C to C cigarettes – Cape to Cairo was their official brand name, but they were known somewhat cynically throughout Southern Africa either as Cough to Consumption or Camel to Consumer. Heedless of the blistering sun, we swam in the hotel pool, the fair skinned amongst us rapidly taking on the colour of freshly broiled lobsters and ensuring at least a couple of days of quite unnecessary discomfort when the inevitable sunburn set in.

Even while we were enjoying ourselves during that first day in the familiar surroundings of a modern hotel, it was impossible not to be aware of the world which lay all around us outside – so obviously completely different from anything we had ever known. I was very forcibly struck by two features of the place which left one in no doubt that we were a long, long way from home. One was the apparent emptiness of the landscape to eyes more accustomed to the UK countryside, which seemed to have something different to look at every couple of hundred yards. Here, around the hotel in every direction, stretched the characteristic scrub, semi-desert of Central Southern Africa, sandy-brown, flat, dotted with what looked like badly stunted trees and apparently limitless. It was easy to imagine that the cloudless blue sky, the blazing sun and the empty land, shimmering in the heat, had been like this, unchanged and indifferent to the existence of man or beast, since the beginnings of time.

The other feature which was immediately noticeable was the absence of any significant background noise. Maybe it was there to those who were familiar with the environment but, to us newcomers, fresh from the highly urbanised life of the UK, the relative silence of the countryside was something quite new. It was particularly marked in the evening, during our first experience of the very short tropical twilight, when the flaring sun was sinking rapidly below the horizon. Sitting on the hotel verandah, as the daylight turned swiftly into night, we all felt the sudden and absolute silence, as if the whole world outside our little encampment was holding its breath. Later, when the night sounds began – all of which we took, somewhat fearfully and probably quite incorrectly to be the cries of lions and other ferocious beasts of prey – the strangeness of our surroundings was even more pronounced. Steely-eyed aviators though we might have fondly imagined ourselves to be, we were, none of us, keen to go for a moonlight stroll in the hotel grounds that first night.

On the following morning, prior to our departure for Gwelo, the nearest town to Thornhill, we were lucky enough to have sufficient time available to take advantage of a hotel organised outing to Victoria Falls. Even though all of us had some idea of what to expect from magazine photographs and from the newsreels, the reality of the spectacle was still awesome. Before seeing the real thing, it is just impossible to conceive of the sheer volume of water – about 150 million gallons a minute – thundering over the mile wide, 300-foot drop. The spray from the Falls rises hundreds of feet into the air and is visible for miles around and the booming roar of the cataract can be heard from a long way away. The local natives, we were told, call the Falls 'Mosi o Thunya' – The Smoke that Thunders – and it is a name that exactly captures the feel of the place.

After this memorable experience and feeling that we were really 'getting our knees brown', we were soon on our way to our final destination. RAF Thornhill lay a matter of a few miles outside Gwelo, which is itself located just about bang in the centre of Southern Rhodesia. Although small by European standards, Gwelo is an important population centre on the road between Salisbury, some 150 miles to the North East and Bulawayo, about 100 miles South West. It had, at the time, a population of about forty thousand, including about nine thousand of European descent. It was the manufacturing, light industry and distribution centre, for the many small mining towns in the area and for the large mixed and tobacco farming communities throughout the district. It boasted at least one good hotel – inevitably, the Cecil – one cinema, known locally as the Bioscope, a very large open-air swimming pool and a golf course. I often used to wonder what the Edinburgh University Golf Team would have made of Gwelo's contribution to the Royal and Ancient game. Not a blade of grass on the greens, or, rather, browns – which were covered with oiled sand – and precious little on the fairways, which were rock hard and intersected by numerous 'dongas', deep gullies which carried away flood water during the rainy season.

Immediately before we had left UK, there had been a change in the policy relating to the rank of aircrew under training. Previously, all aircrew had been ranked as Cadet Pilot or Navigator or whatever and had worn airmen's uniform with white discs behind the cap badge to signify their status. Literally a couple of days before we left, it was decided that all aircrew should be commissioned at commencement of flying training so that, overnight, we all became Acting Pilot Officers on Probation, resplendent in brand-new officers uniforms happily provided, within a matter of hours it seemed, by Moss Bros or the Forty Gieves. Now, on arrival at Thornhill, we discovered that one by-product of the new policy had been the very rapid construction of a new Officers Mess – No 2, or the Cadets, Mess – where we would live in splendid and enforced isolation from the 'real' officers of the permanent staff. Acting Pilot Officers we might have been in the eyes of God and the Air Council but, at Thornhill, we were cadets and cadets we would remain until that coveted brevet was pinned on. Still, we did get batting service – courtesy of the personnel of the Rhodesian African Rifles – and we no longer had to wash our own dishes and cutlery, so we were all quite happy with the situation.

Our first few days at Thornhill were taken at a relatively slow pace – doubtless to give us a chance to become acclimatised and get used to our surroundings. We started our ground school programme of lectures and – a great moment this – drew our first issue of flying kit. We must have been one of the last flying courses in the RAF to be issued with the Sidcot jacket and the old fur-lined flying boots – not as daft as it sounds, since the early mornings and nights in Rhodesia can be quite cold. I am not sure whether 'bone-domes' had even been invented then, but they were certainly not on our scale of kit. Instead, we drew old leather helmets and goggles, which made us look like something out of a Western Front photograph, circa 1917. We were taken over the aircraft we were to fly – the much loved Tiger Moth, on which countless thousands of RAF pilots had trained – and were instructed in the art of hand swinging the propeller. This was an activity which filled me with dread, as I could just visualise myself making a botch of the operation and finishing up in a number of very small pieces distributed across the airfield. I was relieved to learn that 'hand swinging' was purely a precautionary measure in case we ever came down away from the airfield and had to get the thing going again. For our normal, day-to-day operations, the gallant ground crew would do the job for us.

Eventually, after what seemed like an eternity of waiting, the great day at last arrived for our first exercise in the air. We sat about in the crew room, nervously drinking coffee and smoking too many cigarettes, until our turn would come to shoulder our parachutes and set off for our first flying exercise of the course. No doubt about it, we were all very nervous. Not so much of the actual flying, which was, after all, what we desperately wanted to do, but rather of the potential for failure at this early and critical stage. Would we be airsick? Would we remember all of our careful briefings? Would we be able to remember which way to move the controls? Would we freeze up and muff our chance? We had all heard the horror stories of students who had failed to make the grade in these early flights and had been unceremoniously 'chopped' from progressing further with their training. Up to this point, I suppose that all of us had been secretly a little smug about having attained the standard to be accepted for flying training. Now, the time had arrived for us to justify that assessment of our potential.

When my turn came at last, I walked slowly out to the flight line with my instructor, Flight Lieutenant Denis Darney, a short, stocky, cheerful individual who, I later learned, was generally assigned the borderline students because of his calm and encouraging method of instruction. Denis never raised his voice in the air and his strongest criticism of a recalcitrant student was invariably a quiet, "come on now, you know you can do better than that." I liked him from the very start and felt that if anybody could get me through the course, he was the man to do it.

As we went through the simple ritual of the pre-flight check, I tried very hard to keep my mind on what I was actually doing rather than on what I might very shortly be doing. Then it was into the rear cockpit, strap in, helmet and intercom on and follow Denis through the time-honoured ritual of "Switches Off: Suck in," a couple of swings of the prop to prime the engine, then, "Switches On: Contact." A firm swing of the prop, the engine fired at once and the whole little aircraft seemed to come to life. We taxied slowly away from the flight line, Denis demonstrating how to swing the nose on bursts of engine against the deflected rudder, in order to maintain a clear view ahead. Then he talked me into duplicating, or at least attempting to duplicate his performance myself. Awkwardly at first, prone to overdo the bursts of throttle and rudder, then with increasing confidence, I edged the machine slowly round the perimeter of the airfield towards the Air Traffic Control caravan positioned at the downwind end of the landing strip. Thornhill had no runways, so that we generally had the advantage of taking-off and landing directly into the prevailing wind. Just short of the caravan, we halted, slightly angled across wind to give a view of the approach path and began the routine drill of engine checks and pre-flight vital actions. Both of these routines were simple in the extreme. The Tiger Moth had only one engine, one fuel tank, no pneumatics, no hydraulics, no propeller constant speed unit and precious few other frills. The main checks were that the engine had warmed up to normal operating temperature, that the oil pressure was normal, that the flying controls moved freely within their limits and that there was nobody on the approach likely to land on your neck when you moved into position for take-off,

All being well, Denis took control of the aircraft and, instructing me to follow him through on the controls, taxied out to line up for take-off A thumbs-up to the caravan Controller, formally replied to by a green Aldis lamp and I felt the little throttle starting to move gently forward. The aircraft responded immediately and, light as it was, gathered speed very quickly. I felt the control column move very slightly forward to raise the tail and a gentle pressure on the rudder to counter the propeller torque. Then, a tiny backward pressure on the stick – almost imperceptible – and we were off, our shadow racing across the ground with us, before we eased into a slow climb to our operating height. I have often read the accounts of others of their first flight, their intoxication with the new sensations and their feelings of exaltation and freedom. Prosaic as it may sound, I honestly felt none of these high-flown emotions – I was simply too busy trying to follow Denis Darney's methodical demonstrations of the effects of the flying controls. Stick back, nose up; stick forward, nose down; stick left, bank left; stick right, bank right; rudder left, nose left; rudder right, nose right; throttle forward, nose up; throttle back, nose down. In each case, Denis followed the traditional training system that the RAF had employed successfully for years. Demonstrate the exercise with the student following through on the controls. Describe your actions and point out how the aircraft responds. Let the student try to duplicate the action until he absorbs the feel of what he is doing and how the aircraft is reacting. Make the student repeat the exercise until it is ingrained in him and his performance is smooth, relaxed and confident. Then go on to the next exercise.

After what seemed like a very long time at these simple initial exercises, it was back to Thornhill for a demonstration of the circuit joining and landing procedures. Start the re-join a thousand feet above circuit height on the 'dead' side of the airfield – the side away from circuit traffic – keeping a sharp lookout for other aircraft. Let down to circuit height and position yourself at the upwind end of the downwind leg at a thousand feet and at such a distance that the wing-tip appears to be running down the landing strip. Carry out the pre-landing checks and assess the strength of the wind to determine the position from which to start the cross-wind turn. For an average wind, start the crosswind turn when the airfield boundary appears from under the trailing edge of the lower port mainplane, thirty degrees of bank, throttling back gently to settle down at initial approach speed. As the extended centreline is closed, bank again to arrive at a position for a straight-in approach for the last two or three hundred feet. As the touchdown point approaches, throttle back gently and raise the nose to reduce to touchdown speed. Just before touchdown, close the throttle and keep raising the nose until the aircraft settles smoothly in the classic 'three-point' landing, when the two main wheels and the tailskid make a simultaneous and velvety contact with the ground.

When the chocks were being replaced back at the flight line, I glanced at my watch and was dumbfounded to realise that the whole flight had lasted barely twenty-five minutes from take-off to touchdown. I was soaked in perspiration from the concentration that had been called for and I felt that I was ready to retire exhausted for the rest of the day. In fact, I was airborne again within a matter of an hour or two for the next series of exercises.

That night, I made the first entry in my brand-new Royal Air Force Pilots Flying Log Book: 'July 13; Tiger Moth No LSS55; Aircraft Captain, Fl/Lt Darney; Pupil, Self; Duty, Exercises 1, 2, 3 – ground handling, effect of controls, circuit procedure'. There seemed to be an awful lot of blank pages still to be filled in, but I was more than content. I had made a start.

CHAPTER 4

FOLLOWING ON OUR INTRODUCTION to the air, we started work in earnest on the exercises necessary to prepare us for our first solo experience. Daily, we went through the stalls, spins, engine failure and engine fire drills and forced landing practices, which we had to master before we could be considered safe to be sent off on our own. I remember that Barry Gould was the first of our course to solo and, as the days passed, those of us who had not yet done so began to experience a recurrence of the nagging doubt – which was never far away – as to whether we were going to make it or not. In due course, both Andy Anderson and Mike Jenkins, my co-students with Denis Darney, successfully made their first solo flights and I began to be seriously concerned that I was falling behind my colleagues. I was only too well aware that I had not made satisfactory progress with my three-point landings. Try as I might, I could never seem to get the hang of settling into the right position during the flare-out to achieve that gentle simultaneous contact of the main wheels and tailskid all together which is the hallmark of the true 'three pointer'. In an attempt to avoid the worst effects of the bone-shattering arrivals to which I seemed to be prone, I had developed a technique of 'wheeling' the aircraft in – touching down slightly fast on the main wheels and then allowing the tail to sink gently as the speed fell off. Quite rightly, Denis Darney disapproved of this technique, pointing out that it would not do me a lot of good if I ever had to make a forced landing into any restricted space.

As the days went by, I became unhappily conscious that Denis was giving me more and more time in the circuit, with particular emphasis on my touchdown technique. Every sortie we flew seemed to wind up with a succession of 'touch and go' landings and I was becoming really worried. My worst forebodings seemed to be only too well justified when, for one sortie, I found that I was to be flying, not with Denis Darney, but with one of the Squadron check pilots. I was convinced that this was the dreaded 'chop' check, which constituted the end of the flying road for so many aspiring pilots. Nor was my depressed mood lightened by the awareness that the instructor I was due to go with had a reputation for being something of a three-point landing purist. I pondered gloomily what he would make of my arrivals. Safe they might be; classic they were not.

In the event, the shortness of the flight that we made confirmed my worst fears. One stall, one spin, one overshoot, then in for the final landing. Perhaps inevitably, with one technique in my mind and another in my hand so to speak, I made an absolute Grade A hash of the final round-out. I got the power-off too early it seemed and I was too high in the flare. Dreading the shattering arrival I felt to be imminent, I hauled back desperately on the stick in a forlorn attempt to cushion the worst of the impact. To my utter stupefaction, the little aircraft whispered gently on to the grass like a butterfly with sore feet. It touched down so gently that, for a second or two, I didn't even realise that we were on the ground. When we got back to the flight line, with me still somewhat stunned by the unexpected turn of events, the instructor left the engine running, climbed out of the front seat and yelled in my ear, "OK, just one overshoot, then come in for a final land-ing. And for God's sake try to get the bloody thing down in one piece." I could hardly believe it. He was actually sending me solo. I was going to make it. My relief and elation was inexpressible and the actual first solo flight was something of an anti-climax. I have heard it said that a pilot's first solo is generally the safest flight he ever makes – because he's too frightened to do anything stupid. There may be something in that. I know that I took Tiger Moth L6151 through that ten-minute flight as if there were a crate of very fragile eggs in the front seat. Later, when I was being debriefed, with Denis Darney hovering about to catch every word, the instructor with whom I had flown remarked, "By the way, that was a very nice landing. First decent three-pointer I've had from your lot." Denis's face was a study. I learned, there and then, that, in the flying business, it is sometimes better to be lucky than good.

While those of us who had managed to go solo were rejoicing that we had cleared that particular hurdle, there were, unhappily, a number who did not. Apart from the chronically airsick, most of those who failed to survive to the solo stage would, quite probably, have made the grade had the time been available to afford them further dual instruction. Unfortunately, in the service, the flying hours available to reach any particular standard are strictly limited and the train-ee either attains that standard within the allotted number of hours, or he goes. It was very depressing to see ones colleagues, some good friends among them, pack their bags and leave – some tearfully, some with forced bravado, all with the in-tense hurt of seeing their dreams crumble about them.

After this nerve-jangling period, the course settled down to a fairly steady rou-tine. We did ground school one day and flew the next. One of the great benefits of our location was that we worked tropical hours so that, on ground school days, we started work at 6am and finished at 1.30pm. It would have been counter-productive to have tried to work on in a classroom through the heat of the after-noon. The flying days were even better since, as in most tropical locations, the air is much smoother in the mornings. Later in the day, as the increasing ground temperature triggers off the thermals, it becomes progressively more turbulent. If we were scheduled for the first sortie of the day, we would be wakened by the batman with a steaming mug of hot tea at about 5am. Then, it was down to the flight line by 5.30 to brief and do any necessary flight planning prior to first take-off at about 6am – just as the sun came over the horizon. Real Dawn Patrol stuff. Then, after the flight, it was back to the Mess for a good breakfast and a bit of relaxation before the next sortie was due.

As a result of this routine, the bulk of the afternoons were free time. In spite of the heat, we played a lot of sport; soccer, rugby, tennis and cricket and were ac-tively encouraged to do so in order to maintain our level of physical fitness. Many afternoons were spent in the open-air swimming pool in Gwelo and some of the golfers among us tried out our skills on the local course, where we quickly discov-ered a new variety of golfing hazard. The course was pitted with quite small holes slightly smaller than rabbit holes – and, at first, we used to reach down and feel about to retrieve any ball which rolled into one. Later, after a caddy had pointed out that they were snake holes, we tended to treat any ball that rolled into one as very definitely 'lost'. Occasionally, to provide a change from the Mess, some of us would have dinner at the Cecil Hotel – a cool, spacious structure straight out of Somerset Maugham. We tried some of the local dishes, mainly fish like kingclip and the oddly named 99, a small, very tasty variety. The crayfish, I remember, were very good too. The four-course a-la-carte dinner was a first class meal by any standards. As I recall, it cost six shillings.

As we settled into the routine of our working life, we started to take the opportunity of seeing something of Rhodesia beyond the confines of Thornhill and Gwelo. Most of us contrived to acquire some sort of second hand – or, more accurately – twenty-second hand transportation and many and weird were the vintage cars which daily accumulated in the parking area of No 2 Mess. I purchased a part share of a Morgan two-seater, a lovely little car that was a joy to drive except in the rainy season, when its lack of a roof proved something of an inconvenience. I remember that we always carried an umbrella in the boot – just in case. Thus equipped, we set off, on our free weekends, to explore the world about us. Right from the start of my time in Rhodesia, I was fascinated by the strange sounding names of the small towns and mining communities in our local flying area. Gatooma, Que Que, Mvurna, Shangani, Shabani and Selukwe were already familiar landmarks on our local flights and I visited them all. I remember being in a cinema in Selukwe, during one of these trips, when a sudden torrential rainstorm, drumming on the tin roof of the Bioscope, totally drowned out the soundtrack of the film. Apparently thoroughly used to this sort of thing, the whole audience trooped out of the cinema into a bar directly across the street, where we sat drinking tea or beer or whatever until the rain ceased. At this point, we all downed drinks, trooped back into the cinema and the film restarted from the point where it had been interrupted.

In due course, I ventured further afield. Salisbury, very English looking somehow, with a quaintly old fashioned atmosphere; Bulawayo with streets wide enough to permit an ox team and wagon to turn completely around between the pavements; the simple site of Rhodes' grave in the Matopos; and, near Fort Victoria, the ruins of a long-forgotten and untraceable civilisation at Zimbabwe.

One of the highlights of this early exploring was a visit to Umtali, on the eastern edge of the country quite close to the border of what was then Portuguese East Africa. This is a heavenly spot, set in a bowl in a range of three thousand year old granite hills that constitute the Eastern Highlands. Here again, the place names are delightful. To the south of the town is Danganivuru – The Place Where The Rain Is Born – and, to the east, Mubvunibi – The Mountain Of Drizzle. During my first visit, I was told a story of the area which stuck in my mind. I had been playing golf at Leopard Rock with a Lodge Warden whom I had met in the hotel the previous night. After the game, we were sitting on the verandah of the club with a cool beer when he asked me if I knew much about the area. When I replied that I was making my first visit, he leaned back and told me the story of The Old Man of Tshinyakweremba.

About four hundred years ago, so the story goes, the area was occupied by the J'indwi tribe. On the slopes of Mubvurnbi, a village flourished at Tshinyakweremba – The Place Of Tired Feet. One day, an old man, weary and decrepit, arrived in the village seeking hospitality. A local festival was in progress and the villagers, drunken and boisterous, rejected the old man and drove him away. One woman felt sorrow for the stranger and followed him with food and drink. To her, the old man revealed that he was a spirit from the paradise of ancestors, returned to ensure that the tribe were maintaining their ancient customs and traditions. Enraged at his rejection, he vowed to destroy the village that night. The woman, however, would be spared if she left at once. On her return to the village, the woman told of the stranger's warning, but the inhabitants laughed her tale to scorn. That night, fleeing alone, the woman looked back and saw, at the top of the mountain, the old man summon up the forces of nature against the village. Thunder crashed, tempests blew and torrents of rain fell until, finally, a huge bolt of lightning struck, with fearful force, against the mountainside, which collapsed on to the village obliterating it utterly. "If you look hard," said my companion quietly, "you can still see the bloodstains of the villagers to this day." I followed his pointing finger and there, at the spot he indicated, were scattered patches of a tiny blood-red flower which grows nowhere else in that entire range of hills.

Next day, I made a point of visiting the supposed site of the village. Now, it is a forest of surpassing beauty where trees, bushes and flowers of every type and colour abound. But, directly above the forest is a six hundred foot precipice, as sheer and clean as if it had been cut from the mountain with a knife. In the forest, in the soft whisper of the wind and the calls of wood pigeon and other birds at night, it is said that it is possible to hear the muffled cries of the long dead villagers buried by that awful landfall. I didn't stay long enough to find out but, in that quiet, beautiful, melancholy place, I could well believe it.

When we were not exploring the countryside, we progressed steadily with our ground school and flying programmes. In the air, we started our first instrument flying exercises – with a canvas hood strapped over the rear cockpit to shut out the outside world. We were introduced to cross-country flying, when we religiously and meticulously planned sorties during which we could see Thornhill almost every mile of the way. We started our aerobatic training and spent hours looping, rolling, stall turning, and, in many cases, recovering from the stalls and spins which attended our initial efforts. Even that early on, it was drilled into us that we were not being taught aerobatics because they were fun, or exciting, or looked good during air displays, but because every operational pilot has to be capable of flying his aircraft into any attitude necessary to complete his assigned mission – and then flying it safely out again.

With the increasing purposefulness of our flying, there arose a rash of nonsense brought about by us trying to conform to our slightly dotty ideas of what 'real' aviators were like. Pilot Officer Prune moustaches appeared all over the place, wild, unshackled growths which had to be stuffed inside the face mask whenever we had to converse with our instructors in the air. Everyone had his picture taken in the classic big-time aviator pose – foot on the port wheel, hand resting negligently on the engine cowling, square jaw and steely eyes riveted into a 'Wild Blue Yonder' expression. I still have one myself. It looks like something out of Fred Karno's Flying Circus. Scarves – either blue polka-dot or plain white silk – became an essential element of our flying kit. One enterprising student, I recall, upstaged us all by suddenly sporting a silk stocking as a neckpiece. Unkind – or, perhaps, envious – colleagues averred that it was one of a pair of nylons he had surreptitiously purchased at a Gwelo haberdashery, but he stoutly maintained that it was the genuine article, given to him by an admirer he was too much of a gentleman to name. Whatever the facts of the case, we all wished secretly that we had thought of it first.

In all of this very pleasant existence, there was one major shortcoming. Since our first arrival in Rhodesia, we had lived in an entirely male world and, in spite of determined efforts by a number of individuals to do something about it, few of us had any contact with girls of our own age. There must have been plenty of them about the place, but they all seemed to disappear whenever a Thornhill contingent arrived on the scene. Rumour had it that certain wartime trainees at Bulawayo had pursued the local lasses with a touch more robustness than was acceptable – at least to the parents concerned. Be that as it may, our social life was very definitely on a very low gas. We did, of course, have a lot of Mess parties, official and otherwise, but these were strictly stag affairs. It was, in fact, a projected party – an official one – which brought the situation to a head. The permanent staff officers laid on a party night to which, they announced, they would be bringing their wives and to which we were invited to bring our girl friends. Since I don't think any one of us even knew a girl locally, much less had one as a friend, the occasion held every promise of turning out to be the social debacle of the year.

It was at this point that I had what amounted to a brainwave – a brainwave which established for me an unsought and thoroughly undeserved, reputation as a ladies man and general sophisticate. Reckoning that our chances of rounding up some twenty-five or so girls on an individual basis in time for the party were next door to zero, I phoned the Matron at Gwelo Hospital and asked her if she had twenty-five nurses on her staff who might care to join us for the event. When the Matron recovered from her initial shock, she said that she would put the word about within the Hospital and let me know if there should be any response. Well, believe it or not, there was. On the night, twenty-five nurses duly turned up in their party dresses and a rip-roaring good time was had by all. Shortly afterwards and to the envy of every other course at Thornhill, we were invited back to the hospital for a sundowner party. There, we met some of the British South African Police and local schoolteachers and invitations began to be exchanged with them. Our social life was off and running and we never looked back thereafter.

Mention of Gwelo Hospital reminds me of the most embarrassing incident I suffered during my time in Rhodesia and which I cringe to recall even now. It happened somewhat later in the course and all began at a sundowner party at the Hospital. During the course of the evening, one of our party had hoisted rather too many whisky sours and was beginning to feel the effects. To avoid any unfortunate social gaffe, he was hurriedly hustled out of the company and dumped into the first available car outside. It happened to be mine and, in due course, I was deputed to run him back to Thornhill. As we approached the Main Gate of the Camp, I suddenly realised that something was very wrong. At this point, I should explain that, years previously, I had broken off my two front teeth in an overly ambitious piece of ice-skating at Murrayfield Ice Rink in Edinburgh. Since then, I had worn a small denture plate with the two front teeth on it. I had worn it for so long that I never even noticed its presence. I noticed it alright that particular night however – or, to be more accurate, I noticed its absence. I swear that I was as sober as any judge but, where my front two teeth had been, there was now only a gaping void.

Unceremoniously dumping my now insensible companion, I went over the car with a fine tooth comb – and with no success. Desperate now, I phoned back to the Hospital and whistled a plea for an immediate search of the premises – a request which met with a great deal of hilarity and not much else. I never did find those two teeth and, even today, when I see pictures of African warriors in all their finery, I take a good hard look at the necklaces they are invariably wearing – all teeth and two of them could well be mine. In due course, the Unit Dental Officer made me up a replacement plate, but not before I had endured endless painful witticisms on the subject. You would hardly believe it, but there was a popular song of the time entitled 'All I Want for Christmas Is My Two Front Teeth'. I got it everywhere I went, until I became almost afraid to show my face outside my room. If I never hear that particular ditty again, it's going to be much too soon.

Following the, by now, thorough familiar sequence of dual instruction, solo practice and check flight, we worked our way steadily through the remainder of our basic flying training phase. The hours recorded in our log books increased slowly but surely as the end of our Tiger Moth flying neared. Since those days, I have often looked back and given thanks that I was lucky enough to have found my feet in the air in that particular aeroplane and in that particular location. In later years, on visits to Flying Training Units, I used to watch the young trainees, trussed up in leg restraining belts, oxygen masks, bone domes and a mass of other essential kit, on their way out to the jet trainers which later became standard – aircraft with relatively high performance, retractable undercarriages, pressurisation, a host of cockpit controls, closed canopies, radio aids – and all their flying being undertaken in the densely populated and tightly controlled airspace of the UK. I used to feel really sorry for them. It seemed to me that they would never know the sheer fun of flying as we had known it in those early days. No radio, no airways, no controlled zones, no restricted areas. Just the open cockpit, the wind singing in the wires, the cloudless blue sky, God in his Heaven and all well with our world. Truly, as the poet put it, in those golden days we really did 'slip the surly bonds of earth and dance the skies on laughter silvered wings'.

Just before the end of our Tiger flying, I had an experience which jarred me out of any sense of complacency I might have felt about my increasing competence. I was detailed for an instrument flying check with the Squadron Instrument Rating Examiner – the holder, I remember, of a Master Green Instrument Rating which, to us unrated students, ranked him just slightly below the Holy Ghost in order of precedence. At the time, I had a grand total of less than thirty hours in the air, of which something like two hours had been 'under the hood'. Right from the start of the sortie, the instructor, who was no Denis Darney, left me in absolutely no doubt that my performance fell a long way short of his expectations. His non-stop biting comments on my every shortcoming very soon had me completely on edge and, in the state of nerves to which I was rapidly reduced, I probably performed much worse than I might have done otherwise. In all truth, I probably wasn't as good as he might have expected but, to be fair, the Tiger wasn't the best platform in the world for precise instrument flying. It was light and rocked about in every bump and its instrumentation was primitive – no artificial horizon and no gyro compass, only the old P Type magnetic compass which rolled about drunkenly in its alcohol filled case. We never had to practise 'limited panel' flying in the Tiger – a limited panel was all we had to start with.

The check lasted an hour and ten minutes and every minute of it was sheer purgatory. When we got down, I was told very bluntly that my performance was unacceptable, that my instrument flying ability was non-existent and that, if I had any visions of completing the course, I had better get my finger out pretty smartly. I was absolutely shattered and it took a couple of sessions of Denis Darney's gentle encouragement to rebuild anything of my self-confidence again. Still smarting from the experience though, I resolved there and then that nobody would ever again find any justification to criticise my instrument flying. I obtained permission to put in extra hours in the Link Trainer and took every opportunity I could find to cram in time in that excellent training aid. I put in an awful lot of lonely afternoon and evening hours in that machine, when all of my friends were away enjoying themselves at Gwelo Pool or elsewhere. When, much later, I finished the course at Thornhill, I had a total of 187 hours in the air – and over 400 in the Link Trainer. In my final gradings, I was assessed as 'above average' in instrument flying – and I never held a lower assessment for as long as I wore the RAF uniform.

When, at long last, we survived the Squadron Commanders Final Handling Check, we had formally completed the forty-odd flying hours which constituted the basic phase of our training. Of the twenty eight who had started out with such high hopes, nineteen made it through to face the next stage, a sobering fact which made us all very conscious that we were engaged in a serious business which would demand from us our very best efforts if we were to meet the challenges which lay ahead. For the moment, that challenge was the advanced phase of the course and the conversion to the North American Harvard Mark IIB. Three times the weight of the Tiger Moth, the Harvard had four times the power. It climbed twice as fast, it flew twice as fast and it could fly more than twice as far. It had an enclosed canopy, retractable wheels and a propeller constant speed unit. To our somewhat awed eyes, it really did look like the original 'hot pursuit ship' – and we couldn't wait to get our hands on it.

CHAPTER 5

AS IS NORMAL WHEN converting to a new type of aircraft, the first week of our advanced flying phase was taken up with learning the 'nuts and bolts' of the new machine. At the time, the Harvard represented a very considerable jump in complexity and sophistication and introduced us to many systems and procedures which were quite new to us. We put in hours and hours poring over the Pilots Notes, sat through endless lectures on the operating systems and spent a lot of time in the cockpit familiarising ourselves with the layout of the various controls. In pairs, we tested ourselves in blindfold cockpit drills, when one student would name a particular switch or control and his partner, blindfolded, would have to reach out instantly and place his hand unerringly on the nominated item. Eventually, after a series of tests by the various systems specialists, we signed reams of formidably official looking forms swearing blindly that we had studied – and now thoroughly understood – the engine system, the fuel system, the hydraulic system, the pneumatic system, the electrical system, the airframe limitations, the engine limitations and Heaven knows what else. We blithely swore blind that we knew more about the aeroplane than the men who designed and built it.

On top of all this, we had to learn the checks. The Harvard was big-time stuff and there seemed to be a check list for every conceivable eventuality. Pre-flight checks, pre-start checks, post-start checks, pre-taxy checks, pre-take off checks, post-take off checks, climbing checks, pre-joining checks, pre-landing checks, post-landing checks, shutdown checks. And, to top it all off, there were periodic in-flight checks designed, presumably, to ensure that the mental effort of remembering all the other checks hadn't tired us out so much that we might inadvertently doze off. All of these checks and all of the emergency drills, had to be committed to memory. If something were to go wrong in the air, there was unlikely to be time available to pull out Pilots Notes and start a leisurely perusal of the relevant chapter. So, again in pairs, we went through many sessions of testing ourselves out on all of the checks, drills and procedures we would have to be familiar with in the air. I know that some of us began to doubt whether we would ever manage to find the time actually to fly the wretched aeroplane with all of the checking, drilling, proceduring and system managing that we seemed to be expected to cope with.

To help us through this welter of memorising, we were introduced to the use of mnemonics which were supposed to make the retention and recall of lists of actions somewhat easier. Strictly speaking, we had got on to this technique somewhat earlier in the course during our navigation studies, when the procedure for getting from compass heading to true heading was commended to us in the form C-D-M-V-T (compass-deviation-magnetic-variation-true). This was drilled into countless RAF aircrew as 'Cadburys Dairy Milk Very Tasty' and remembered by countless others in another, quite unprintable, version. I never really found these mnemonics to be of much value. I soon discovered that I could forget the mnemonic as readily as the check itself. One notable exception, however, was the

Harvard pre-take off vital actions check. I forget now what the official version was, but there was an unofficial version, of a quite surpassing vulgarity, that I confidently expect to be able to recall instantly to my dying day. The drill was T (Trim), M (Mixture), P (Pitch), F (Fuel), F (Flaps), G (Gills), G (Gyros), H (Hydraulics, H (Hood) and H (Harness) and nothing would induce me to repeat the ingenious and unrepeatable word play which etched that particular check so indelibly into my memory.

When, after all this, we did finally manage to get into the air, we found that the Harvard was an absolute delight to fly – straightforward, practically viceless and, in spite of everything we had led ourselves to believe, very simple to operate. It did, however, introduce us to one or two slight problems for which all of our lead-in work had not prepared us fully.

The first problem arose when we set about trying to get the engine started. It very quickly became apparent that, during this operation, one hand was needed to hold back the control column to keep the tail firmly on the ground, one hand was needed to operate the fuel 'wobble' pump to build up fuel pressure, one hand was needed to operate the engine primer pump to get starting fuel into the engine cylinders and one hand was needed to make the selections on the inertia starter. Four hands – and all with something to do at the same time. To get around our shortage of available limbs, the technique adopted was to hook the left leg around the stick to hold it back, 'wobble' furiously with the left hand, prime like mad with the right hand and delicately make the starter selections with the right big toe. Absolutely true, I swear it!

The other problem, which should never have arisen but not infrequently did, stemmed from the fact that the Harvard had three fuel tanks which were selectable. In the Tiger Moth, with its single tank, you simply turned on the tap at start up and that was it. The fuel flowed until you landed or the tank ran dry. In the Harvard, in order to check proper fuel feeding, the drill was to start up on the reserve tank, taxy on the port tank and take off on the starboard tank. In this way, you ensured both that there was actually fuel in all tanks before you got airborne and that all of the tanks were feeding the engine properly. Almost needless to say, this system caught some of us out, particularly during the early solo flights when it was only too easy to forget to make the fuel selection changes. One would be flying along, happy as could be, when, without any prior warning, the engine would suddenly stop. Fortunately, there was never any real problem in this situation. All it took was some lively 'wobbling' and priming and a bit of fiddling with the propeller pitch control and then a gentle dive would get the warm engine going again. Oddly enough and, I believe, much to our instructors disappointment, this sort of thing very rarely occurred during a dual sortie when we were probably much more meticulous in our observance of the checks.

For my advanced stage flying, I was again lucky in being assigned to another instructor in the Denis Darney mould – Flying Officer John Grant, a quiet, dryly humorous, Scot who had the knack of making his students feel relaxed and confident. Under his gentle prompting, I soloed without any problems and started in to the more rigorous flying exercises of the advanced phase.

Although it was tremendous fun, the advanced phase was deliberately designed to become progressively more and more demanding and we had to work hard to keep ourselves up to the mark. With a full blind flying panel now available, we were introduced to instrument pattern flying using two ground marker beacons around which we flew increasingly intricate timed manoeuvers, aiming always to hit the 'overhead' at one or other of the beacons on a precise heading and at a precise height. Using the new, to us, VHF (Very High Frequency) radio – a simple four channel version – we tried our hand at controlled let-downs, talked to the overhead on radio bearings taken by the Ground Controller on our radio trans-missions. At overhead, a turn on to an assigned outbound heading, a let-down to half your height plus two thousand feet, a procedure turn and then follow the controllers directions until you were told to look up. At this point, down would come the blind flying screens and there would be the airfield – hopefully, dead ahead.

On navigation exercises, our cross-countries started to take us further and further afield. Although map reading was really very easy in Rhodesia, we tried hard not to fall into the trap of navigating from ground to air – a procedure which, in the UK, will almost certainly guarantee that anyone other than a real expert will get himself lost very quickly. Instead, we conducted our pre-flight planning with real care in working out the effect that the forecast winds would have on our pro-gress and then, in the air, sweated to hold course and airspeed as accurately as we could, as we progressed from turning point to turning point. In theory, this tech-nique guarantees arrival dead on time at the final destination. In practice, however, winds are seldom exactly as forecast and rarely constant over the period of a ninety minute flight, so that, throughout the flight, we had to make continu-ous re-calculations of the adjustments to heading and airspeed necessary to arrive at destination on track and on time.

If we ever found ourselves uncertain of our position during these flights – no self-respecting pilot is ever 'lost' – we could always fall back on a radio bearing from Thornhill or from Heany, the other Rhodesian Air Training Group airfield near Bulawayo. In a situation of 'navigational uncertainty', the plot of the radio bearing on the chart at least told you that you were on that line – somewhere. A match with some of the ground features then visible would generally fix your position fairly accurately and allow you to proceed, with renewed confidence, to the next crisis point.

In our aerobatic work, we repeated all of the manoeuvres from our Tiger Moth days and were introduced to some new ones calling for more precision and smoother aircraft handling. We started sequences of manoeuvres, when we would link a number of individual aerobatics into a coordinated sequence, aiming to exit from one element at precisely the speed and altitude required to enter directly into the next. This called for the development of the capacity to execute one part of a sequence accurately while, at the same time, thinking ahead to getting properly set up for entry into the next element.

During these more advanced exercises, we began to get our first experience of 'black out' when the 'g' or gravity forces drain the blood temporarily from the upper body to 'pool' in the lower half of the frame. The result is generally a short loss of vision although, if the 'g' is sustained overlong, unconsciousness can re-sult. We were taught to yell like mad during any manoeuvre likely to lead to 'black out' since the tensing of the stomach muscles helps to minimize the effects. On dual sorties and with the instructors' eardrums in mind, the courteous student would remember to switch off his intercom microphone before commencing this uninhibited bellowing. If he didn't remember to do so, he generally got a good bellow right back to remind him of what it was like to be on the receiving end.

Our formation flying, too, became more and more demanding as we progressed from simple joining and station keeping to position changing, formation manoeuvres and, best of all, tail chases when we would career wildly about the sky in loose line astern, trying desperately to keep the aircraft in front right in the top centre of the windscreen and never knowing whether you were upside down or right way up so hard were you concentrating on holding position. We learned to take up and hold station by lining up features on the airframe of the lead aircraft and holding on to that position regardless of what the leader was doing. Climbing, diving, looping, rolling, right way up, or upside down, if you hold the leader in the same relative position, you are flying good formation.

With these sorts of exercises to fill our days, we gradually accumulated our first forty or fifty hours on Harvards, by which time it was mid-November and the time had arrived for our fourteen day mid-course leave.

CHAPTER 6

WHEN THE OCCASION OF our leave arrived after four months of quite intensive effort, everyone on the course was ready for a break in the proceedings. We had been required to work hard right from the start and we were now ready to get away from it all for a spell and really let our hair down. While some were quite happy to take their relaxation in Rhodesia, others aimed rather further afield. One group, undaunted by the distances involved, set their sights on Cape Town – something like twelve hundred miles away in a straight line and considerably further by either road or rail. For my part, I joined with five others in setting our sights on Durban in Natal as our destination.

The first problem to be overcome was the acquisition of a vehicle likely to last the roughly two thousand miles involved in the round trip we planned. Certainly, none of the ones we had would have been a good bet to get us to Durban and back. Eventually, we got hold of a venerable Dodge roadster which looked as though it might have spent its early years roaring about Chicago with gangsters blazing away from its windows. Second gear couldn't be engaged which made for some very fancy driving on the hills, but it was big, comfortable and would just about take the six of us with light luggage. Thus equipped, we duly launched forth on our great trek south.

Almost at the start of our journey, we had a stroke of good fortune although we didn't realize it at the time. About forty miles from Beitbridge on the southern border of Rhodesia, we lost all of our cooling system water when a hose burst – inevitably, right out in the middle of nowhere, with not a car, village, or sign of civilization in sight in any direction. After a time, a car appeared heading south and, on learning of our problem, the middle-aged driver very kindly offered to drive on to Beitbridge, pick up a replacement hose and brings it back. It really was extremely kind of him and, after he had completed his eighty mile round trip, we proceeded together to Beitbridge. There, over a drink, we learned that he was a resident of Durban and we invited him to call any of us at the South African Air Force Mess where we would be staying, so that we could thank him properly for his kindness. Saying that he would do so, he went off on his way.

Fully mobile again, we set off across the Transvaal to Johannesburg where we had arranged to stay with the family of one of the South Africans on the course. As we passed through Pretoria, I had wanted to visit the Voertrekker Memorial since my great-grandfather had, in fact, been one of the original trekkers from the then family home in Graaf Reinet up to the Orange River. On the day we passed through Pretoria, there was a National Voertrekker festival underway and it became quite clear that 'Brits' were not in the least welcome to join in the festivities. Memories of the Boer War seemed to have died very hard in that part of the world and I never did get out to the Memorial on that occasion. I did make it on the way back, though.

From Johannesburg, we pressed on through Pietermaritzburg – which I remember for the masses of brilliant flowers which seemed to burst out of every garden – to Howick from where we began the long descent towards Durban and the Indian Ocean beyond.

The time we spent in Durban far exceeded our wildest expectations. Our SAAF hosts, in whose Mess we had been allowed to stay, could not have been friendlier or more hospitable. We were invited to join a group from one of their fighter squadrons in their exhilarating sorties 'downtown'. We swam, duly mindful of the sharks, in the warm sea, we lost our bets at the racecourse, we played golf at Royal Durban – on real grass – and we partied at the George Hotel, the Louis Hotel, the Cosmo Club and anywhere else where a party could be generated. We visited Mngeni – The Valley of a Thousand Hills – Ixopo and Umshlanga Beach where, I remember, the entire night staff of the George Hotel, including the band, joined us after closing time for an impromptu cook-out and jazz session which went on until after daybreak.

In the midst of all this mad, gay, social whirl, I was dressing one night for a party when a telephone call came in for any member of the visiting RAF party. When I answered, it was our knight of the road from Beitbridge, taking us up on our invitation. Everyone else had long since departed to the fleshpots downtown, so it fell to me to do the honours. I arranged to meet our friend for dinner together with his wife and their son and daughter. The son and daughter, of about our own age, knew every spot in Durban worth knowing and, for the remainder of our visit, involved us in what seemed like a 24-hour round of non-stop entertainment. The prices in Durban seemed to be very low and, although we were far from well paid in those days, what money we had seemed to go a very long way.

When the time finally came for us to pack our bags and head north again, I don't think that there was any one of us who hadn't had the time of his life in a delightful city, full of people who had, it seemed, gone out of their way to make sure that we had a leave to remember.

On the way back, we followed generally the same route by which we had come south but, having seen a lot of Zulus in Durban and visited the tribal lands around Mnengi, we did make one major detour to visit the site of Isandhlwana which was the scene of one of Britain's heaviest ever military defeats during the Zulu War in the late nineteenth century. At this desolate spot in the shadow of the brooding mountain, a complete British field army was wiped out, almost to the last man, by Cetaweyo and his warriors. At the actual battle site, I was strongly reminded of the melancholy atmosphere of Culloden and it was not difficult to imagine the terrifying sight of the thousands of Zulu in their traditional fighting buffalo battle formation bearing down on the hapless defenders of the British camp. Close by, we also visited the small community of Rorke's Drift where, only days after Isandhlwana, a few survivors from that battle and a small detachment of South Wales Borderers, stood off the ceaseless attacks of the Zulu impi in an engagement in which not a single man of the British force escaped some wound and eleven Victoria Crosses were won during the battle.

When, in due course, we struggled back to Thornhill from all points of the compass, the staff, very sensibly, took things very quietly and slowly for the first few days to give us time to get over the excitement of our leave and come gradually back to reality. Quite rightly, they wanted us to have our minds fully back on the job when we started back into the air after the break.

CHAPTER 7

BEFORE LONG, WE HAD all had a check flight preparatory to going solo again and the second half of our advanced training started in earnest. Just a couple of weeks after our return, I achieved my first hundred hours in the air – heavily underlined and exclamation marked in my Log Book. A real milestone event, I felt. Soon afterwards, we started night flying and this brought a totally new dimension to our flying experience. The familiar airfield suddenly seemed to be a totally different place at night and we had to become familiar with taxying between the flares which lighted our way to and from the landing strip. For runway lighting, we had gooseneck flares every fifty yards or so and we learned to judge our approaches by the perspective of the rows of flares as viewed from the cockpit – too high and the flares looked far apart; too low and they looked like two unbroken lines. We quickly got used to the eerie glow of the cockpit lighting and we learned to keep an even sharper look out at night for the navigation lights of other aircraft going about their business. I liked night flying from the start. One had the feeling of doing the job in a private little world of one's own.

So the weeks went by, with the hours accumulating in our Log Books and the exercise accomplishment board in the squadron crew room gradually filling up. At this stage, we were doing more and more solo sorties and dual flying was becoming limited to progress checks and the odd revision flight. Perhaps inevitably, it was around this time that the spate of accidents and incidents, avoidable and otherwise, which seem to attend every flying course, began to catch up with us. Some of the incidents were just plain daft, like the student dive bombing the crocodiles at a pool near Selukwe who delivered his 'bomb' – a half brick he had smuggled aboard – straight into his propeller. Some were due to growing overconfidence – normally easily identified by bits of trees and bushes unknowingly picked up during unauthorized low flying. Some were down to plain stupidity, like the student who called for a true bearing (from Thornhill) when what he really wanted was a course to steer (towards Thornhill). In spite of Air Traffic's pleading, he stubbornly flew away from base until he ran out of fuel and had to force land well on his way to Bechuanaland. Some were due to bad luck, like the student who followed the traditional practice of sneaking up behind another aircraft approaching Thornhill at night and then switching on his landing lights to scare the wits out of the pilot in front, only to discover, to his cost, that the other pilot was the Air Officer Commanding the Rhodesian Air Training Group up on an unannounced visit from Heany.

My own contribution to this sorry catalogue was, I'm happy to say, completely unavoidable. I was doing some local flying at about five thousand feet one night when the propeller suddenly parted company from the engine. Oddly enough, this incident, which was caused by shearing of a lock bolt, really brought home to me the value of the training we had been given. Almost without thinking, I started into the drill I had done so often with John Grant and in solo practices. Locate a high key position; set up a gliding pattern to get there at the right height; plan to hit low key on the correct heading and height; wheels down on the hydraulic accumulator; flaps down on the hand pump. Final flap setting when you're sure – really sure – of making the field. Then, just put it down. No problems and just like we'd practiced it.

Not long after this incident, John Grant was posted back to the UK and I was assigned to another instructor with whom I didn't get on too well. On our first flight together, with me 'under the hood', he put me through a mental dead reckoning navigation exercise. With no flight planning and only the morning 'met' briefing to supply wind information, all headings to steer and airspeeds had to be worked out in the head. After a few fairly short legs around the local area, during which I was struggling to keep a mental plot of our position, I was directed to fly to the Ngamo Dam which would be our destination for the purposes of the exercise. Working hard to fly steadily and accurately, I counted off the minutes to our Expected Time of Arrival. When our arrival time came, I was told to stow the blind flying screens and look outside. When I did, I was frankly astonished to find myself right over the middle of the lake and about three quarters of a mile from the dam itself. I could hardly believe it. About forty minutes on pure mental dead reckoning and we'd got there well within a mile. While I was quietly congratulating myself on this performance, my new instructor started giving me merry hell for not being able to find my way around the local countryside. I bit my lip very hard and doubted whether we were going to get along together.

Worse was to come when we flew together again on a night cross country to Heany where we were to make a touch-and-go landing before the return leg. The wind at Heany that night was almost directly across the runway and I was following the standard procedure of 'crabbing' in, with the nose pointing off into the wind preparatory to kicking off the drift with a bootful of rudder just before touchdown. This is a manoeuvre which calls for pretty exact judgment and timing. Too early with the rudder and you simply start drifting off the runway line again; too late and you have already touched down going sideways. I thought that I had got it judged just about right and was actually on the point of taking off the rudder to bring the nose straight, when the instructor, without the mandatory "I have control," grabbed the controls and threw in a real bootful of rudder himself. At this point, my foot, which was still pushing on the rudder, slipped straight past the pedal. When the instructor tried to straighten up for the touchdown, he trapped my foot between the pedal and the side of the aircraft. That really put the cat among the pigeons. With almost full rudder applied one way and drifting quite markedly the other, there was no way that he could now put down safely. Full power went on at once as we roared off into the night skewing across the airfield like a drunken duck. It took some time, at a safe height, to get my foot disentangled. On the way back to Thornhill, I flatly refused to take over control of the aircraft from him and, when we landed, I marched straight in to the Squadron Commander formally to request a change of instructor. I was re-assigned to a different instructor next day.

This little unpleasantness soon forgotten, I carried on with the remaining course exercises until, quite suddenly it seemed, the daily flying program started to include the various final check flights which would constitute the effective end of our training. Final Handling Test with the Squadron Commander, final Instrument Flying Test with the Squadron Instrument Rating Examiner and final Navigation Test with the Squadron Navigation Officer. In my turn, I sweated my way through these final hurdles, then sweated even more until the results were announced. When, at long last, the results were posted, I was delighted to see that I had been rated as average as a pilot under training and above average in both instrument flying and navigation. I was even more delighted to find that I had taken the Ground Studies award and had tied for top place on the course with Barry Gould who took all the flying awards. This happy circumstance could only have been achieved as a result of some fairly judicious fiddling of the final marks, but neither Barry, who thoroughly deserved his placing, nor I, who didn't, was about to argue the point. At that time, the top student on every flying course was eligible to be offered a Permanent Commission in the service – an opportunity to make a full time career as a professional Royal Air Force officer which many much more deserving aspirants would have given their right arms for. Now, after about fifteen months total service, we were having this golden opportunity handed to us on a plate. I think that both of us took all of ten seconds to make up our minds before we accepted the offer with almost indecent haste – before the 'powers that be' had a chance to change their minds.

After the final flying checks, the atmosphere on the course became noticeably more relaxed. We all knew that we were through and we were simply keeping our hands in in the air during the two or three weeks which remained before the course Passing Out Parade at which we would be formally presented with our wings. Many of us scrounged passenger or dual trips in the station Anson – our first taste of multi-engine flying – and in the brand new Chipmunks which were replacing our much loved Tiger Moths. We spent more time than we liked on the 'square' in preparation for the final parade. Qualified pilots we might nearly be, but we still had to be able to carry off a parade as if we knew what we were doing. Preparations were made for the end-of-course party and it was wisely decided to stage this event after the passing-out parade had been held. This decision stemmed from the experience of earlier courses when the events had taken place the other way around. Time and again, we had watched people hobbling out on crutches, or with their arms in slings, to receive their flying badge. On one famous occasion, a graduating student had even insisted on taking part in the bath chair to which his energetic partying the night before had consigned him. Bath chair or not, he was not going to miss his big moment. I can remember him vividly, resplendent in best uniform and brand new wings, with his splinted leg sticking out straight in front of him, coming smartly to the salute as he was solemnly wheeled past the reviewing stand. When our own turn came, I believe that we were the first Thornhill graduating course, when every single man got to the ceremony under his own steam and without visible signs of self-inflicted injury.

Eventually, our great day came and, one by one and bursting with pride, we stepped forward to have our wings pinned on by the Air Officer Commanding. It would be quite impossible to describe our emotions. Of the original group, sixteen of us saw it through to the culmination of our hopes and dreams. I remember returning to my room after the parade and hanging my uniform up on the wardrobe. The brand new wings seemed to be absolutely huge. As I stretched out on the bed to give myself a chance to admire them, I felt an overwhelming sense of pride and elation that I was now privileged to wear the same flying brevet as had been worn with such distinction by all of the greats of the service past; Mannock, McCudden, Finucane, Malan, Bader, Gibson, Cheshire. By the grace of God and a lot of luck, I was now a very humble member of their company. I was and I had the wings to prove it, truly a pilot at last.

CHAPTER 8

ON THE 23RD MARCH 1952, absolutely exhausted by their round of formal and informal farewell parties, Number 5 Pilots Course from RAF Thornhill piled themselves and their belongings aboard a Transport Command York for the flight back to the UK. During the long flight, there was little of the eager-eyed goggling at the sights en-route which had characterised the journey out. We were all simply too tired and the flight provided a heaven sent opportunity to catch up on some of the sleep we had missed during our last days at Thornhill. I do, however, recall one moment of magic which I was lucky enough to experience on the way. Our take-off from Entebbe in Uganda was scheduled for dawn and I had wangled a seat on the flight deck to watch the proceedings from 'up front'. The take-off path led directly over Lake Victoria, a vast expanse of water dotted about with innumerable islands of every shape, size and height. Drifting lazily over the surface of the water, in the stillness of that early morning, there was a thin, milky-white layer of low mist, through which the tops of the many islands stood out, black and festooned with wraith-like streamers of mist. As we took off, the sun emerged slowly over the eastern horizon and, as it rose, the mist on the surface of the lake became tinged with uncountable shades of red, from palest pink to deepest scarlet. The whole prospect was exactly like a scene from one of Walt Disney's films, the black islands and the drifting, rosy-tinged background. I had never seen anything like it before and I have seen nothing like it since. In some of our journeying through Africa, I had seen some instances of the harshness and even ugliness of nature. At Entebbe, that morning, I was given a glimpse of its occasional breathtaking beauty.

Arriving back in the UK to the very forcible reminder of how cold mid-March can be, particularly after nearly a year in the sun, we split up for a couple of weeks leave before reassembling, as a course, at Number 1 Flying Training School at Moreton-in-the-Marsh, not too far from Cheltenham, for acclimatisation to the very different flying conditions of the UK. The acclimatisation process only took two weeks and was spent mainly in cross-country exercises, to accustom us to finding navigational features seemingly every ten yards or so along route and to help us adapt to the much more tightly controlled airspace in which we would be operating. The airways, control areas, control zones, restricted areas and danger areas were all quite new to us and took some getting used to.

The course passed off without any major problems, although we did get one telling demonstration of how easy it was to be caught out by the new and unfamiliar conditions. One night, while we were debriefing in the crew room after some cross country flights, a somewhat white-faced Sergeant came in and asked who had been flying one particular aircraft. When the pilot was identified, the Sergeant asked if he had noticed anything odd about his aircrafts performance. The pilot could think of nothing out of the ordinary, although he did admit that the machine had seemed to drag a bit during his taxying back to the flight line. He thought that the brakes might have been binding slightly. When, on the Sergeants invitation, we all went out to have a look at the machine, we could hardly believe the state it was in. There were no flaps, no tailwheel, the engine cowling was filled with twigs and small branches and some of the lower aerials had been torn off. It looked like a classic case of unauthorized low flying except that, inexperienced as we were, none of us was stupid enough to have tried that sort of trick at night. The pilot was completely baffled by the state of the aircraft and, quite sincerely, could offer no explanation.

Next morning, the solution to the mystery became evident. Wheel marks in the field short of the runway showed quite conclusively that the pilot had touched down a couple of hundred yards short of the airfield, barged through a five foot thicket fence and finally ended up on the runway. Although he'd felt the landing to be a bit on the bumpy side, he had simply put that down to loss of touch caused by the lay-off during his leave.

Improbable as the story seemed, I had a fair measure of sympathy for the unfortunate pilot involved. In Rhodesia, we done all of our night circuit flying with only two rows of goose-neck flares to mark the runway. Now, in the UK, we had approach lighting, full runway lighting, airfield beacons, angle of approach indicators, full taxiway lighting and hazard warning lights all over the place it seemed. Until we got used to it, it often seemed that the approach to land was being made down the middle of Blackpool promenade – during the illuminations.

Towards the end of our acclimatisation, the postings came through for our next assignments. Since Moreton had really only been a temporary interlude, these were the ones we had been bursting to see ever since we left Rhodesia, because they would, in large measure, determine the pattern of our future careers. When the list finally went up on the Notice Board, we found that we were being split up and distributed throughout a variety of different units. Some were assigned as co-pilots to Bomber, Coastal, or Transport Commands. Some went to communications squadrons, some to air experience flights and some went back to holding units to wait for a suitable slot to come up. Four of us, to our unspeakable delight, were assigned to jet conversion, with orders to report forthwith to Number 205 Advanced Flying School at Royal Air Force Middleton St George near Darlington.

CHAPTER 9

ALTHOUGH JET AIRCRAFT HAD come into service with the RAF in 1944 with the Meteor Mark 1, they were by no means a common sight in the Service in the early 1950s. There were about fifteen squadrons of Meteors in Fighter Command and a small number in various test and research establishments. Outside of the personnel at these units, there were relatively few pilots who had ever even seen a jet, much less flown one. The early Meteors were fairly typical of first generation jet aircraft. They were underpowered and suffered from stability problems at high transonic speeds. The aircraft experienced large trim changes, high stick forces and a self-sustaining yaw instability (snaking) due to airflow separation over the thick tail surfaces.

With a distinct feeling that we were entering a very new sort of flying world, my companions and I reported into Middleton to become part of the twelve strong Number 35 course. We were quite right – it was a different sort of world. If the Harvard had seemed like a big jump from the Tiger Moth, the big, brutal-looking, eight ton Meteor represented a really staggering performance enhancement. Virtually overnight, the top speed available to us jumped from 205 mph to 585 mph; service ceiling went up from about twenty thousand feet to something nearer forty five; rate of climb became about five times what we had been used to; and endurance came down from about three hours to about forty minutes – which was about how long it took the Meteor to get through its three hundred and twenty five gallons of aviation kerosene. We had four months to learn all that there was to be learned about flying it.

Following the pattern with which we were familiar, the course got under way with a couple of weeks of very intensive groundschool. No afternoons off now! Quite apart from familiarization with the aircraft systems, checks and operating procedures, we had to learn a number of subjects which were completely new to us: theory of jet propulsion, the aviation medicine implications of high-speed, high-altitude flight and the aerodynamics of flight at speeds approaching the speed of sound. We learned a whole new vocabulary in which compressibility, Mach Number, decompression, barotrauma, flame-out and asymmetric flight became the familiar terminology of our jet-age environment.

It would be difficult for any pilot to forget his first experience of jet flying, particularly in those days when the machines were nothing like as refined and sophisticated as they were to become. At Middleton, we had the Mark 4 Meteor for our solo work and the two-seat, slightly higher performance Mark 7 for our dual sorties. The initial start-up introduced a touch of drama early on in the proceedings. With the engine being turned over on power from an external trolley accumulator, the fuel high pressure cock was gently eased to the half open position to introduce fuel into the combustion chambers and the ignition button pressed. If this operation was timed correctly, light-up occurred and the fuel cock could be opened fully to sustain combustion. Too slow and the engine simply wound down to a standstill; too fast and you were liable to get 'torching' when the excess fuel would erupt from the tail end of the jet pipe in a great sheet of flame accompanied by a terrifying 'whoosh'.

Taxying in the new aircraft was delightfully simple. With no engine in front of the cockpit and a tricycle undercarriage, the view forward was superb and eliminated the requirement to swing the nose from side to side which we had been used to in order to see where we were going. At first, the closeness of the cockpit to the nose of the aircraft was slightly disconcerting in that one got the impression of sitting in front of the aircraft rather than inside it. Without turning the head, one couldn't see anything of the airframe at all, except the very short nose section in front.

At take-off, the initial sensation was somewhat disappointing. I suppose that it was natural to expect a jet to rocket away at the start like a bullet from a gun. In fact, the initial acceleration was rather sluggish. To minimize the likelihood of engine compressor stalling, or overhigh jet pipe temperatures, the throttles had to be opened carefully until the engines picked up speed. And, of course, there was no propeller to provide an immediate 'grip' on the air. As a result and quite unlike the Harvard which fairly leaped away at the start, the Meteor started its take-off run trundling sedately along the runway, with the pilot gingerly inching the throttles on until the engine revolutions built up, the jet pipe temperatures stabilised and it was possible to get the power on in earnest.

Once the throttles were fully open, the whole tempo of events started to pick up. At about 70 knots, a slight backward pressure on the stick lifted the nose-wheel off the runway and set the aircraft in the flying attitude. At something like 90 to 95 knots, the main wheels left the runway and one started to feel the acceleration of which the aircraft was capable. In the early stages, we had to be quite nippy to apply the wheel brakes and get the undercarriage up before we reached the wheels-down limiting speed. In next to no time, it seemed, the Air Speed Indicator reached 290 knots, our initial climbing speed and the nose would be raised to settle into the climb. If the nose wasn't raised pretty smartly, the speed would go on building quite alarmingly. Once settled into the climb, the ground below fell away at an awesome rate as the clouds above seemed to come rushing down to meet you. The needle of the Climb and Descent Indicator was hard up against the upper stop and one really got the impression of going upstairs in something of a hurry.

At altitude, unless there was some cloud about and there generally wasn't much at our operating altitudes of between thirty and forty thousand feet, there was little enough impression of speed. Far below, the patchwork quilt of towns, fields and open spaces seemed to drift slowly by and it was only by checking the flight instruments that one realized how fast the aircraft was traveling. Up high, we flew speed on the Machmeter which told us how fast we were flying in relation to the local speed of sound. This gave us a much more meaningful indication of our speed than the Air Speed Indicator which was affected by the reduced air density of the upper altitudes. At forty thousand feet, the ASI would read roughly half the airspeed at which the aircraft was actually moving.

The other piece of instrumentation which we learned to monitor very closely indeed was the fuel gauges. The twin Derwent engines of the Meteor went through fuel at what seemed to us to be a horrifyingly fast rate. Some students swore that, at high power settings low down, when fuel consumption was at its highest level, you could actually watch the fuel gauge needles move. Right from the start of our flying, it was stressed that we should always aim to be back in the circuit and preparing to land by the time the gauges read 40/40 – forty gallons left in each of the main tanks. Inevitably, occasions arose when for one reason or another, we didn't make the safety of the circuit by the time we were down to that fuel state. Believe me, at 30/30 or 20/20, you really could see the needles move and the most welcome sight in the world was the two thousand yards of Middleton concrete just waiting for you to set down. As a semi-emergency measure, we were taught to shut one engine down when we got low on fuel. At half power, with the live engine operating more efficiently at the higher power necessary to maintain speed, the fuel consumption was somewhat reduced. Of course, flying the thing on one engine was quite a bit trickier. Still, better to have slightly more difficult flying and a few more minutes to make it back to base, than no fuel and a desperate search for somewhere to put the thing down or, even worse, a rather slower return to earth by parachute.

I suppose that I was lucky at Middleton. I took to the Meteor as a duck takes to water. In spite of its brutal, almost ugly, appearance, it was an absolute thoroughbred to fly. It had no nasty tricks or unpleasant surprises up its sleeve and was docile as a lamb throughout its operating envelope. It was so docile, in fact, that if a ham-fisted student ever got it into a spin, all he had to do was take his hands and feet off the controls and leave the aeroplane to its own devices. Almost invariably it would recover smartly after a couple of turns.

Getting to have more affection for the 'meatbox' day by day, we went through our first solos on type, had our introduction to asymmetric flying – flying on one engine with the other shut down – and made our first tentative forays into the regime of high subsonic speeds. Asymmetric flying wasn't easy in the Meteor. With one engine out, full rudder deflection was required at low speeds to hold the aircraft straight and the leg loads were very heavy indeed. The trick was to wriggle yourself into a position such that the leg could be locked at the knee with full rudder applied. After a few minutes of this, every muscle in the leg would be twitching uncontrollably and many students developed 'asymmetric leg' – manifested by spasmodic jerking of the affected limb during the walk back to the crew room after landing. Since the objective of our asymmetric training was to enable us to get down on one engine, a lot of our work was done at low speed in the circuit. Asymmetric leg became a very common affliction, particularly if the instructor put you through a few full power overshoots. I used to dread overshoots on the port engine. The starboard engine ran the aircraft hydraulics so that, with the starboard engine running, the landing gear and flaps could be raised normally. With the starboard engine shut down, no hydraulic power was available and during the overshoot with your left leg twitching and jerking all over the place, you had to raise the wheels and flaps on the hydraulic hand pump. I forget how many strokes of the pump it took to get everything up but it was an awful lot and the aeroplane had to be flown left-handed because you needed your right hand to operate the pump. After a session of this sort of flying, all you wanted to do was go and lie down quietly in a darkened room.

The high subsonic speed flying was much more agreeably exciting. The Meteor had none of the design features which minimized the effects of compressibility for later aircraft. Basically, the problems of compressibility occur when the airflow over parts of the aircraft structure reaches supersonic speed. This can happen when the aircraft is, itself, flying well below the speed of sound, because any curved surface on the aircraft, such as a cambered wing or a cockpit canopy, accelerates the airflow well above the general flight airspeed. In the Meteor, high Mach number flight produced an almost textbook demonstration of the effects of compressibility – much better than any modern high performance aircraft can produce. As speed built up, there would be a general slight loss of effectiveness of the controls, primarily the ailerons and the aircraft would start a sort of mildly drunken motion, wallowing about in all axes of movement. The nose would pitch gently up and down, the wings would rock in gentle banking and the aircraft would yaw mildly left and right. As the Mach number increased, the oscillations would become wilder as the controls became less effective. Close to the Mach limit, there was a very sudden onset of buffeting and banging – known as the 'cobblestones effect' – and almost exactly like driving a car without springs or shock absorbers at high speed over a heavily rutted road. Finally, as the ailerons lost effectiveness completely, one or other wing would drop irrecoverably and the aircraft would fall away totally out of control.

Although we did fly into the loss of control situation to familiarize ourselves with what it was like, we normally initiated recovery action before all control was lost. The recovery was simplicity itself: close the throttles gently and 'pop' the dive brakes – retractable flat plates on the top and bottom surface of each wing which extended into the airflow and really slowed you down in a hurry. There was a rumour in the service around that time that, when Gloster began design work on any new aeroplane, they started with the airbrakes and designed the rest of the aeroplane around them. Certainly, the airbrakes on the Meteor and on the Javelin, another Gloster product which I flew much later, were about the simplest and most effective I ever used. In the Meteor, with throttles closed and airbrakes extended, it was possible to lose height at almost thirty thousand feet a minute. That was really coming down like a brick.

CHAPTER 10

AS WE PROGRESSED STEADILY through the course, the emphasis shifted gradually from the straightforward conversion to a new aircraft type to an introduction to the sorts of techniques we would be using in the fighter squadrons for which we were destined. Tail chases became more like dogfights, navigation became more a matter of area recognition rather than the identification of individual ground features and formation sorties started to include some, probably quite unauthorised, attempts at 'finger four' battle formation when the spacing between individual aircraft was much wider than we were used to and station keeping that much more difficult.

Towards the end of the course, we were introduced to operations under control from one or other of the Fighter Sectors, when the ground controller, working from his radar plot, would vector us on to non-existent targets to familiarise us with the techniques and procedures of ground controlled interceptions. It was very exciting, particularly at night, to follow the controllers directions as he manoeuvred us into position behind a 'bandit' before he advised, "target dead ahead now, three hundred yards, look up and engage visually." Invariably, we would look up and scan desperately about the empty sky for the bandit which we had become convinced was really there.

One night, we were given the opportunity to participate in one of the air defence exercises, when we would be vectored on to real targets provided by Bomber Command and various Training Command multi-engine training units. During this particular exercise, one Middleton student was vectored on to a Training Command Varsity at about eight thousand feet somewhere north of Tees-side. When he was finally told to "look up, target dead ahead," he peered through the windscreen and there, sure enough, there it was, engine exhausts glowing red in the night sky, a couple of hundred yards dead ahead. Caught up in the excitement of the occasion, the student closed slowly on the target. At something like a hundred yards, he flicked the firing button from 'safe' to 'fire' – we never carried ammunition on any sortie at Middleton – and gently squeezed the button. Instantaneously, there was a blinding flash from the port mainplane of the Varsity just inboard of the port engine. A raging fire erupted which quickly engulfed the whole port wing and the stricken aircraft plunged earthward to crash, in a shattering explosion, on the dark moors far below.

The poor student was absolutely appalled. He was convinced that, by some incredible mishap, his guns had, in fact, been loaded and that he had shot the other aircraft down. When he got back on the ground, he was practically hysterical and it took some time to convince him that the taping over the gun ports of his aircraft was unbroken and that his guns could not possibly have been fired. Later, we found that the Varsity had experienced an engine fire which the crew thought had been extinguished. They had declared an emergency on the distress channel and had been heading towards Thornaby for an emergency landing. Unhappily, the fire had not been completely extinguished and, at the precise time of the simulated attack, had reached the port mainplane fuel tank with disastrous results. After that incident, I don't think that any of us ever handled a weapon control light-heartedly again.

All in all, Middleton was a very happy unit, at which we were encouraged to re-gard the Mess not only as our home, where we lived, ate and slept, but as the centre of our social life. As a result and at a time when few of us had much money and equally few owned a car, our Mess life was very lively with many parties of one sort or another. These were the days when high-spirited young pilots – and some not quite as young – indulged whole-heartedly in the sort of potentially hazard-ous Mess games which would turn any present-day Station Commanders hair white. 'Mess Rugby', 'Zulu Warriors', 'Are You There, Moriarty' and 'High Cockalo-rum' fairly knocked the stuffing out of us and the Mess furniture and fittings. Daft and dangerous it may have been, but the Station authorities had rightly decided that, if had to blow off steam, we were better doing it where they could keep an eye on us and prevent us from getting into any real trouble.

Occasionally, a sortie would be made into 'downtown' Darlington. There was an old variety theatre – I think it was called the Theatre Royal – which was a great favourite with our course and where we passed quite a few Friday evenings. By this time, of course, variety had become something of a dead art form and the acts which we watched in the half- empty theatre were the last hardy survivors of their tradition. Madam Zelda and her Performing Pekinese, someone playing all-time favourites on a musical saw and the inevitable siffleur whistling, equally inevita-bly, 'In a Monastery Garden' were the sort of performances we cheered and stamped for. I like to think that the gallant performers appreciated our support. One who probably didn't was the star of a balancing act who performed prodigies of equilibrium, juggling with one hand, twirling hoops with his feet, playing a mouth organ – and all balanced on one hand on the back of a chair of which three of the legs were tilted off the ground. He drew polite applause; to his obvious chagrin, his assistant, a shapely and scantily clad young lady, who did little but hand him his props, brought the house down in a storm of appreciation. Ah well, that's showbiz!

Because of Darlington's location on the main railway route between North and South, many of us took the odd weekend at home. One snag was that the Station Commander had a predilection for Saturday morning parades, which meant that, immediately after the parade, there was a breakneck dash into Darlington to catch the train, still in uniform and with week-end civvies stuffed into a traveling bag. On one memorable occasion, following a particularly robust Mess party at which we had both suffered minor injuries, a friend and I were standing on the platform at Darlington station when we were approached by a charming, white-haired, elderly lady. Eyeing the sling supporting my friends arm and the sticking plaster on my forehead, she enquired gently if we were involved with "those noisy aeroplanes at Middleton." On being assured that this was indeed the case, she delved into her purse, presented each of us with a half crown and said, "you are both dear brave boys and I do hope you are fully recovered soon." I was absolutely flabbergasted, but my colleague, to his eternal credit, gravely accepted the coin, gave her a dazzling smile, thanked her sincerely for her thoughtfulness and de-parted with a salute and half bow that would have gone down well in any

Ruritanian operetta. Nobody has ever believed this story, but it is absolutely true. It really did happen.

On a personal note, Middleton marked the beginning of what was eventually to prove to be a permanent change in my status. During the Christmas I had spent in Rhodesia, I had bought a packet of cards to send to the family and some friends at home. The packet contained one more card than I actually needed. Reluctant, in spite of my sound Scottish upbringing, to save the spare card until next year, I sent it off to an attractive young lady in Edinburgh with whom I had often gone dancing in my student days. Before long, she wrote back and we began a correspondence during my time overseas. Back home again, we renewed acquaintance during various leaves and grew increasingly close. By the time Jean came down to Middleton for the end-of-course Ball, it was tacitly understood that we were unofficially engaged and would marry as soon as I had completed all my training and settled down on a squadron.

With all of this in mind, I waited impatiently for the postings to come through. We knew that we were all scheduled for Fighter Command and that our next stop would be the Operational Conversion Unit at Stradishall, prior to our squadron assignments. We all knew it, but we wanted to see it down in black and white.

In due course, the postings did come through. The postings were to Stradishall. Everyone was delighted. Except me! No Stradishall for me! Instead, I was to go to the Central Flying School at South Cerney to learn how to be a flying instructor.

CHAPTER 11

TO SAY THAT I WAS disappointed would be a massive understatement. I was appalled. At first, I couldn't really believe the posting notice. I was certain that there had been some mistake and that I had been issued with a posting rightfully meant for someone else. After all, Central Flying School was where all of the Qualified Flying Instructors of the RAF were trained and considerable experience and proven ability were the prerequisites for selection to the courses there. I had only just finished my own flying training, my experience was low – barely two hundred and eighty hours – and, while I could get up and down reasonably competently in the few types of aircraft I had flown so far, I had not had the opportunity to demonstrate any ability outside of the well-supervised training environment. What's more, I didn't want to be a flying instructor – not yet anyway. I wanted to be a fighter pilot. All of the training I had been through had been leading up to that role and I was hanged if I could see why I should miss out now when I was so close to reaching a squadron.

Righteously indignant and armed with all of these good reasons why my posting should be changed, I phoned the personnel staffs at Group, at Command and finally, in desperation, at Air Ministry. I might as well, as they say at home, have saved my breath to cool my porridge. All I got for my pains was a flea in the ear for having the temerity to question a posting notice and an assurance that my assignment constituted a 'career' posting for which I should be duly grateful. Years later, I learned that, in the jargon of the personnel staffs, a 'career' posting is one that THEY persuade YOU to accept so that they will have better prospects of advancement in THEIR careers. I was gravely advised that there was a serious shortage of jet qualified instructors and that I would be doing my duty for the greater good of the RAF if I would just get on with it and help to redress the shortage as soon as possible. As a cunning sop, I was told that the tour of duty for people in my situation would be two years to the day, after which we would be assured of preferred postings to the Command of our choice.

With the posting staffs' words of comfort still ringing in my ears, I duly reported in to join Number 148 Flying Instructors Course at Royal Air Force South Cerney. Right from the start, it was apparent that Central Flying School was an organisation quite different from any I had previously served at. It is, I believe, the oldest flying instructor training organisation in the world, with an unparalleled record of achievement in all aspects of the art of teaching in the air. Nearly every Air Force shapes its training systems around the teaching methods and procedures first formulated at CFS and, to this day, it is the final and absolute arbiter in every phase of pure flying techniques throughout the RAF. Only one standard is acceptable at CFS – the best. This uncompromising approach applies both in the air and on the ground. In fact, I had an excellent demonstration of CFS standards during the first evening I was there. In the Mess bar, after dinner, a small group were chatting away quietly when one among them attempted to flick the ash from his cigarette into an ash tray on the bar counter. He missed. Before the Barman could do anything about it, a tall distinguished-looking gentleman at the end of the bar absolutely exploded at this "slovenly and careless behaviour, unbecoming to users of the Mess of the Central Flying School" The distinguished-looking gentleman was, I learned later, the Commandant of the establishment and his displeasure was unmistakably manifested when the bar was closed, on the spot, for three days.

Uneasily beginning to feel that I really had no right to be where I was, my doubts were compounded when I met the ether members of the Course. There were pilots from every operational command of the RAF and they all seemed to have years and years of flying experience and thousands and thousands of flying hours. There were three or four who had just returned From Korean war service with the Sunderland flying boat unit based at Iwakuni in Japan and I listened quietly to their shop talk of sorties flown during their time there. Ten and twelve hour patrols seemed to have been commonplace and I gloomily calculated that, at that rate, any one of them could have run up my entire total of flying hours in a couple of months. There was, however, one bright spot, in that I was one of only two on the course who had any sort of jet experience. The other was an engaging young fighter pilot called Alan Brindle who had flown Spitfires and Meteors with 66 Squadron and who, like me, would clearly rather have been in Fighter Command than where we were.

The course on which we were engaged was to be undertaken in two parts. The first phase, to be conducted on the Percival Prentice at South Cerney, would introduce all members of the course to the techniques of teaching the exercises involved in basic flying training to ab-initio students. In the second part of the course, to be conducted at the other CFS airfield at Little Rissington, we would be taught the techniques involved in taking students through the exercises of the advanced and applied stages of flying training. At Rissington, the student instructors destined for piston-engine training units would do their airwork in the Harvard; those destined for jet-equipped units in the Meteor.

From the very start of the course, we were required to familiarise ourselves with the CFS 'bible' – The Royal Air Force Manual of Flying Instruction. This Air Publication is continually updated by the Staff of the CPS Examining Wing – the dreaded 'Trappers' – who have the responsibility for standardizing and categorizing all flying instructors in every Command of the RAF worldwide. The manual contains the specialised knowledge accumulated over many years of experience in the art of teaching people how to fly, distilled into chapter after chapter on individual training exercises and covering the briefings required, the techniques and procedure involved in the airwork and the post-flight debriefings which are used to drive home the lessons learned in the air. Rumour had it that the first edition of the Manual was received by the first Commandant of the School from the same source and at about the same time, as Moses got his orders at the top of the mountain.

In our airwork, we followed the instructions of the Manual to the letter. For each exercise, we were required to develop a 'patter' which incorporated all of the instructional points to be made during the demonstration part of the sortie. Each exercise was conducted at least three times. First, the staff instructor, acting the instructor part, would conduct a thorough ground briefing of the course member, playing the student, take him through the air demonstration of the techniques and procedures involved and talk him through duplicating the performance. On landing, a detailed ground briefing would follow to reinforce the air instruction and to clear up any points of doubt or difficulty. Afterward, the roles would be reversed and the course member, this time in the instructor role, would repeat the performance with his own instructor acting the part of the student. Finally, course members would be paired up for 'mutual' sorties, during which they would, in turn, patter each other through the particular exercise.

From day one, we had the importance of accurate flying drummed into us. It was continually stressed that there was no point in demonstrating circuit flying at a thousand feet to a student if the altimeter was, in fact, registering nine hundred and ninety nine, or a thousand and one, feet. For every single manoeuvre in the syllabus, the demonstration had to be given at exactly the altitude, airspeed and angle of bank specified. Near enough was simply not good enough. At no time during the entire course, were we allowed to get by with a reasonably good performance. At CFS, that constituted a bad and unacceptable performance. The pressure to attain absolute precision in everything we did, in the air or on the ground, was totally unrelenting. It was manifested, too, in our instructors' insistence that, at all times, the aircraft should be properly 'trimmed-out'. This involved almost non-stop manipulation of the trim controls to relieve any residual forces on the primary flying controls. At any time in the flight, we could be required to release the controls completely and woe betide any student if the aircraft then started to deviate from its flight path. "Out at trim" the instructor would scream, making the offense sound like the aviation equivalent of genocide. There was a rueful joke at the time which ran, "You are demonstrating looping to the Queen. At the top at the loop, Her Majesty falls out of the aeroplane. What is your first action?" The correct, if somewhat callous, answer was, "re-trim to compensate for the change in weight"

Hardly surprisingly, the general standard of our flying improved quite dramatically in a relatively short space of time. We learned to keep one eye en the instrument panel virtually constantly, so that we would instantly pick up the minutest divergence from the desired flight condition and be making the necessary correction almost before the indicators had a chance to register the deviation. If we didn't, the Instructor could be relied upon absolutely to start into his "speed, height, heading, bank, trim" song and dance.

One day, I had a quite dramatic demonstration of the improvement in my own ability and confidence. I had been flying a 'mutual' low-level circuits sortie at Kemble airfield with a Lebanese student as my partner. He was flying the return to South Cerney in fairly poor weather conditions, with me happily relaxed and looking forward to the post-flight cup of coffee. Suddenly and without a word of warning, my partner hauled back on the stick, pushed on full power and rocketed into the cloud layer right over our heads. After a second on two, he seemed to lose interest in the proceedings and more or less left the aircraft to its own devices. At this point, with the attitude indicator 'toppled' and swimming about uselessly, l grabbed the controls and started into the standard procedure for 'recovery from unusual attitude on limited panel instruments'. Seconds later, with me very white and shaken, we broke out of cloud again, very nearly under full control and still in one piece.

Back on the ground, l demanded, in extremely forthright terms, to know what on earth he had been playing at. My co-student had an imperfect command of English but, from what I could gather, he had just felt like doing a loop at the time and he couldn't see what all the fuss was about anyway, since Allah had undoubtedly been watching over us. I was forced to inform him, very bluntly, that regardless of his personal arrangements with the Almighty, I was not entirely sure that my adherence to the Church of Scotland really qualified me for Islamic protection. I made it crystal clear that, if he ever pulled a trick like that with me again, intensely painful and very personal retribution would speedily follow the event.

Somewhat older and wiser after this little piece of nonsense, I carried on to the end of our training at South Cerney. Although I thoroughly enjoyed the course, the value at which was clearly evident in the much enhanced standard of my own flying, I must he honest and admit that the Prentice was not really my idea of a stimulating airplane. Underpowered and with a fixed undercarriage, its performance was insipid at best and its handling qualities were once accurately described by an ex-Bomber Command student as "not much different from a Lancaster on one engine." Up until then, all at the training aircraft I had flown had tandem cockpits, with one seat behind the other. I never did like the Practice's side-by-side seating, which displaced you from the aircraft centre line. In fact, I never did like any side-by-side trainer I ever flew. As the end of the basic stage grew near, I could hardly wait to get back into the Meteor again.

CHAPTER 12

WHEN, AT LAST, the first part of the course was completed and we moved to Little Rissington, climbing back into the Meteor again was just like meeting up with an old and trusted friend. Even though most of my flying was now being done from the back seat, with its more restricted forward view, it was a real joy to be back in an airplane with a bit of performance in it. The course itself followed the now familiar pattern into which we had been introduced at South Cerney, only now we were tackling the more interesting and demanding training exercises of the advanced and applied stages.

Our move to Rissington took place during the first week in December 1958 and, fairly soon afterwards, there was to be a very large pre-Christmas party to be held in the Town Hall in Cheltenham. I can't remember now who was the sponsor of the event but, by all accounts, it was to be the social occasion of the year in the local area, with dancing till the early hours, buffet supper, cabaret acts, tombola and all round general merrymaking. A number at invitations came to the Mess and, because a majority of the 'living-in' permanent staff officers were away on Christmas leave, course members – who didn't qualify for leave during their courses – fell heir to a few of the available places. I was one of the lucky ones and arranged to travel to Cheltenham with a colleague in his Triumph Roadster. I mention his car deliberately because its type had some influence on the subsequent events of the night.

On the night at the party, immaculate in evening wear, my colleague and I duly presented ourselves at the Town Hell and launched ourselves forth upon the festivities. It was a very good party indeed, non-stop dancing to two bands, seemingly unlimited food and drink and a packed throng of guests who were all hell-bent on making the occasion one to remember. During the course of the evening, my friend and I met up with two young ladies, instructresses from a riding school near Evesham and happily settled into a foursome with them. Much later, as the last waltz was being announced, my colleague asked the girls how they were planning to get back to Evesham. They were, it transpired, to phone a colleague at the riding school who would then come over to collect them.

At this, my colleague, sensing that opportunity was not so much knocking as forcibly kicking the door down, gallantly offered to run our charming companions home. Thus, in due course, at some unearthly hour in the morning, with snow falling heavily in a biting cold wind, we left the Town Hall to make our way to Evesham. It was at this point that the make of my friends' car started to assume real significance. The Triumph roadster was a very fine motor car, very sporty, with a long bonnet and two enormous headlights. It was, however, very definitely a two-seater, with a tiny 'cockpit' into which two adults could just about be squeezed. To get four of us into it was plainly a physical impossibility

Nothing daunted by this apparently insuperable problem, the proud owner raised the rearward opening panel of the hoot to reveal a tiny space into which two adults could just about be fitted – provided they were on fairly close, not to say intimate, terms with one another. As he remarked, it wasn't far to Evesham and we'd be there before we knew it. Had any of us been fully sober, I doubt whether we would have entertained the idea for a minute but, at the time, it didn't seem to be an entirely unacceptable proposition. As my lady friend and I wiggled into the cramped opening, which seemed only marginally larger than a good-sized suitcase, I gallantly offered my overcoat to her to supplement the thin stole she had draped around her. If gallantry was to be the order of the day, I was going to get my contribution in too.

Notwithstanding the proximity at my delightful companion, it was not long before I began to feel the effects of the extremely cold, snow laden, night air. The space available to us was so limited that it was virtually impossible to snuggle down out of the slipstream and the fact that the boot cover opened to the rear effectively removed any protection from the full force of the icy blast. In very short order, the top half of me acquired an over-all covering of driven snow, while the temperature of all parts of me fell to hitherto unexperienced levels. Matters were not significantly improved by the dawning realisation that the short journey to Evesham seemed to be taking an unconscionably long time to complete. The minutes dragged by as I edged closer and closer to the borders of hypothermia. As we roared endlessly on, I began to wonder bitterly if "just North of Evesham" had not been a polite euphemism for "just South of Carlisle."

After what seemed like an eternity, we finally drew up in front of a large country house. By this time, I was so cold that I was unable to stand unaided because of cramp, I was shivering uncontrollably in every limb and my teeth were chattering like castanets. Even inside the house, with a large whisky inside me and positioned perilously close to a large open fire, I still couldn't get the numbness and shivering out of my bones. When it became clear that I really was very badly chilled, it was suggested that a hot bath might affect some improvement and I was duly immersed in a steaming hot tub to thaw out. This was certainly a step in the right direction, in that my skin temperature returned to something like normal, although I was still a very long way from feeling warm.

at this point, there was a consultation between our hostesses, as a result of which a tub of yellowish cream was produced which, they averred, was the complete answer to my problem, absolutely guaranteed to remove all traces of cold or chill from the system. Modestly attired in a towel, I was duly treated to a thorough rub down with this preparation, which certainly seemed to be very effective. Within a very short space of time, I started to feel myself returning to normality so, re-dressed and spruced up, I hastened back to re-join the party. For a while, everything went swimmingly. Close to the fire and with a drink in hand, I had almost completely thrown off the effects of the exposure I had sustained. There were now quite a few people in the room, other girls returning with their escorts from nights out and odd members of the riding establishment. Records were being played, furniture had been moved aside to provide some space and a few couples had started dancing.

It was not too long, however, before I started to detect that, almost imperceptibly, the others in the room were congregating in little groups leaving me increasingly isolated by the fire. Every time I engaged someone in conversation, they would seem to have to replenish their drink, or suddenly see a long-lost friend, or have to leave the room. A sort of sterile area was opening up around me, making me feel more and more like the only drunk at a teetotallers convention. When, in some sort of desperation, I managed to pin my course colleague in a corner to try to get an explanation from him, he wrinkled his nose in distaste, leaned well back and confided in me, "It's that stuff you've got on you. It must have come out of the stables. Honest to God, Harry, you smell like a b..... Derby winner."

I hadn't noticed it before but, now that he mentioned it, I did seem to be carrying around a fairly obvious aroma of the Wintergreen variety – an aroma which, stimulated by a few stiff whiskies and the heat of an open fire was becoming perceptibly stronger by the minute.

The rest of the occasion was a nightmare. The pungent smell of the rubbing lotion became more and more overpowering. I formed the unhappy impression that strong men were paling at my approach and all the girls in the place looked to be ready to faint. Eventually, when the situation had clearly become quite intolerable, my colleague was forced to take me away. He was, I remember, extremely bitter about it all and vouchsafed me absolutely no sympathy whatsoever. In fact, his mood became positively savage when he found that we had to make the drive back to Rissington with all the car windows wide open. It was very uncomfortable, but the cold was much the lesser of two evils.

It took ages for the effects of that rub-down to wear off. Every morning and every night, I would have a hot bath and a vigorous scrub down with carbolic soap, followed by an all-over application of a well-known brand of aftershave but, as I recall, it was the better part of two weeks before anyone would sit with me at mealtimes, or invite me to join them in the bar.

As the Meteor phase progressed, Alan Brindle started to intrude more and more significantly into my daily activities. Although he was much more experienced than I, we had a jet background in common, we were among the younger members of the course and we seemed to hit it off well together. Alan made an early impression on the Rissington scene when he was called before the Commandant at the end of the first month to explain why all of the Meteor Flights in his log-book had been entered in the column reserved for single-engine entries. "Oh well, Sir," he explained airily, "I'm really a Spitfire man and I didn't want to spoil a good logbook." The new Commandant, Air Commodore 'Bill' Coles was a pilot with a long and distinguished record of bomber flying behind him and this sort of explanation was not one calculated to appeal greatly either to his reason or to his sense of humour. I was not present at the subsequent exchange of views which, I suspect, were somewhat one-sided, but I did notice that Alan's Meteor flights thereafter were meticulously logged in the multi-engine column of his Flying Log Book.

On formation flights together, Alan used to scare the daylights out of me. It wasn't so bad when he was leading, when I could pick my own discreet distance from him, in spite of his constant bleating for me to close up. When I was leading, however and in spite of my careful briefings for him to stay on his own side of the runway, I used to catch terrified glimpses of him roaring across the runway, as soon as we started moving, to lock in with his wing-tip just about scratching my ear. Thereafter, no matter what I did to try to ease away from him, he would stay, tucked in, absolutely relaxed and clearly enjoying himself hugely. He explained that this was the normal Fighter Command technique, which caused me to conduct a serious review of my plans for the future. After a while, I just gave up watching him. Without fail, a glance outside the cockpit scared me stiff.

On one memorable occasion, Alan led two of us in a formation sortie and, on return to Rissington, called for permission to execute a low break. I should explain that, in the circuit, the Harvards flew at one thousand feet and the Meteors at two thousand feet. At Rissington, a low break was from the height of the Harvard circuit up to the Meteor level. At least, it was to Air Traffic Control. But not to Alan. About five miles out, he put us into echelon starboard and took the formation down until the trees flashing by started to look uncomfortably close. Howling in at something approaching 450 knots, we screamed over the runway caravan and executed the classic fighter circuit re-join. Air Traffic Control went absolutely berserk, yelling "abort" instructions over the air, flashing red Aldis lamps in every direction and firing off red Verey cartridges that looked just like so much flak. Alan affected not to understand all the fuss. He'd called for a low break and a low break was what he'd done. Doubtless, he made his point at the subsequent interview with the Commandant, but he was very quiet for a time thereafter.

Even without Alan to lead me astray, I managed to get myself into one scrape which I would just as soon have passed up. At that time, it was possible to get the use of a Harvard for a week-end sortie away from base – it counted as a land-away cross-country – and I had determined to try to get one for a week-end in Edinburgh. I hadn't flown a Harvard for nearly a year but, after the initial contacts had been made, I arranged with the Harvard Flight Commander that he would give me a quick 'once around the circuit' check on the Saturday morning before my departure.

When Saturday morning arrived, things started to go slightly awry. The weather was not particularly good, in that there was quite a strong wind blowing and odd bits of low cloud around the place. The Harvard Flight Commander with whom I had concluded the arrangements was not available and his Deputy was clearly not over-enthusiastic about undertaking a piece of extra-curricular dual revision. "I mean," he asked me plaintively, "it can't be all that long since you flew one of these." In a flash, I saw the entire week-end going swiftly down the drain, at which point I stuttered something about, ..". ..month or two at least." "Oh well," came the rejoinder, "you're practically current. No check required"

Strapping myself hastily into the aircraft, before he had a chance to reflect on the matter, I was approached by a young WAAF from the Signals Section who was trying to get to Glasgow. Could I give her a lift with me? I started on about parachutes, R/T and all the rest, but she had come fully prepared, parachute at the ready and swearing that she had been fully briefed by the Safety Equipment Section for every possible eventuality. Anxious to get away, l told her to climb in to the rear seat and get strapped in.

After narrowly missing beheading one of the ground crew on start up because I'd set the parking brake improperly, we lurched out to the end of the runway with me quickly re-learning that the wheel braking system was a lot different from that on the Meteor. Inevitably, the wind was almost directly across the runway and getting stronger by the minute – and I'd forgotten how quickly a piston-engine aircraft would swing when the power was poured on too rapidly. Weaving an eccentric path down the runway, I finally managed to get it off the ground in one piece – seemingly travelling mainly sideways, I admit, but at least safely airborne.

Eventually settled down at about eight thousand feet, I relaxed somewhat for the leg up to Dishforth in Yorkshire, where I had planned to refuel. I was beginning to get the feel of the Harvard again and confidence was slowly ebbing back when it happened. Sudden deathly hush as the engine stopped. Yes, the old bugbear from Rhodesia had caught up with me. I was still on the reserve tank which was, by now, bone dry. It took me a couple of seconds to remember the little matter of changing tanks and, in the interval, I automatically set up an emergency landing pattern to an airfield which was conveniently situated a mile or two off to port. When it dawned on me what the problem was, I started the wobbling and priming necessary to get the engine going again. While thus engaged, I became uncomfortably aware that it had suddenly become extremely cold and draughty in the cockpit. Investigating this latest development, I discovered that my WAAF passenger had clearly decided that this was the end of the flight as far as she was concerned. She had the hood back, straps undone and was standing up in the rear cockpit apparently on the point of imminent departure from the scene. Frantically, I hauled back on the stick as hard as I possibly could, whereupon she collapsed into the back seat in a heap. I yelled back at her that everything was under control and, for God's sake, to stay where she was till I got things sorted out.

When I finally did get the engine going again and the intercom back in operation, I assured her that this was just a trifling problem and nothing to get alarmed about. I'm not sure that she was entirely convinced, but at least she did get strapped in again.

It took a lot longer to get up to Dishforth than I had expected and I decided that the winds must have been somewhat stronger than forecast. The accuracy of this assumption became evident when I raised Dishforth on the radio. In response to my request for joining instructions, I was politely advised that landing at Dishforth was not permitted as the airfield was experiencing surface winds of seventy to eighty knots. At first, I thought that they were joking but, when it became clear that they were quite serious, I asked for clearance to any nearby diversion airfield with rather better weather conditions. After a slight delay, I was informed that the gale-force wind conditions were prevalent over pretty much all of the UK and particularly over the eastern part of the country.

By now, I was really in a fix. I didn't have enough fuel to divert to any distance and I was going to have to get down reasonably soon before the Harvard turned into a glider. On the other hand, my final approach speed was around the eighty knot mark and, if the wind got any stronger, I'd probably finish up having to make my final approach to land flying backwards. After some discussion with Dishforth Air Traffic, I was cleared to enter the circuit and land. In what I assumed was an attempt to encourage me, they advised that they would have a party of airmen on the end of the runway to catch me as I touched down.

The runway at Dishforth lay parallel with the A1 trunk road and, as I started a long straight-in approach, I was uncomfortably aware of northbound cars whizzing past me on the road below. Even with no flaps down and a fair bit of power on,

I seemed to be hardly moving. Eventually, as we crawled over the end of the runway and the wheels met the concrete, I closed the throttle and came to a complete stop in something like thirty yards. Men now appeared from everywhere, grabbing on to the wings and tail to hold the aeroplane down on the ground. In that sort of wind, it could easily have got airborne again without any help from me.

After we had been manhandled into a hanger, I was met by the Station Commander who advised me most earnestly to reconsider any plans I might have had to continue with the flight north. In his considered judgment, such an undertaking would have been "injudicious." After what I'd been through just to get that far, I was happy to agree with him.

Now, I knew that we are not supposed to get eighty knot winds in the UK. All I can say is that the inhabitants of Canvey Island in particular will have cause to remember that week-end, when gales and high seas lashed the entire east coast of England and inundated large areas of the Dutch coastline. For me and my unfortunate WAAF passenger, that was the end of our week-end in Scotland. I remember that we made the best of a bad job by going in to Harrogate for dinner and a cinema show, so the trip wasn't a total write-off. When we got hack to Rissington on the Monday morning, the look of relief on the Harvard Deputy Flight Commander's face was mute testimony to the worrying week-end he had put in.

Not long after this best forgotten incident, I discovered that my instructor seemed to be giving me more and more time on aerobatic exercises. I hadn't been worried about my performances up until then, but I couldn't help remembering Denis Darney and the sudden burst of work he had put in on my three-point landings. Eventually, after quite a few sorties of hard aerobatics, one after the other, I asked my instructor directly if I was not making the grade. He was quite put out. "Certainly not," he replied testily, "matter of fact, I'm thinking of putting you up for the Brabyn Trophy." I was dumbfounded. The Brabyn Trophy is awarded to the winner of the course jet aerobatics competition, held just before the official end of course ceremonies. I had never even dreamed of being selected to compete and I worked really hard at the subsequent practices, each one being flown at a progressively lower height down to the display altitude.

When the day of the competition arrived, I went through my well-rehearsed sequence without a hitch. So also, it seemed to me, did the other competitors. At the end of the day, I discovered, to my utter disbelief, that I had won. I should stress that this disbelief was not due to any sense of false modesty, but simply to the realistic recognition of the fact that I was not the best aerobatic pilot around. I was reasonably good, but there was at least one I knew to be better. Alan Brindle had also competed and I knew, from having flown with him, that he was far and away a better aerobatic pilot than I was. However, I hadn't been doing the judging and I was more than happy to accept my unexpected moment of glory.

As the end of course results were published – no slip of paper on the Notice Board this time, but a formal promulgation in Air Ministry Instructions – I discovered that, in addition to winning the Brabyn Trophy, I had been awarded an immediate B1 instructors category in place of the more usual B2 and had graduated with a distinguished pass – one of six conferred. I was very proud my these achievements, particularly in the light of my relatively limited experience and I felt that I had gained tremendously from the course. At the course graduation dinner, I was seated next to a tall, dark Wing Commander who was wearing an odd looking medal with a dark-red ribbon ahead of the Distinguished Flying Cross on his mess kit tunic. After we had left the table, I asked a colleague to identify the medal for me. "You dozy b......," he exclaimed, "don't you know a Victoria Cross when you see one." Well, I had thought I would have known one, but that was the first Victoria Cross I ever saw worn. My dinner companion had been Wing Commander Leonard Trent, VC, DFC, RAF.

CHAPTER 13

WITH THE COMPLETION OF the CFS course, I came to the end of the time in my flying when I could be regarded as a 'student' pilot. Strictly speaking, I suppose, the end of formal training had occurred earlier, on graduation from Middleton St George but, even though CFS should, more accurately, have been regarded as 'role conversion', to me it had simply been a continuation of the training routine I had been a part of since I started flying and I had continued to regard myself very much as a student. Now, with my brand new instructors category, three hundred and eighty hours in my log book and a posting to Number 203 Advanced Flying School, RAF Driffield, in my pocket, I was about to start the productive phase of my flying career – and, incidentally, start producing some return to the service for the massive investment they had made in my training.

When I reported in at Driffield, I found that there had been a great many changes since I had last been on the unit waiting to go to Initial Training School. The entire Station was now exclusively dedicated to the operations and support of the Advanced Flying School, which operated as three separate training squadrons, each with about a dozen or so aircraft and about the same number of flying instructors. Each squadron had its own hanger which provided administrative offices, working accommodation, crew rooms and safety equipment section, as well as first line servicing facilities for its own aircraft.

At any one time, there were about four student courses in residence, each at a different stage of the training programme. Additionally, there were a number of occasional special courses designed to provide jet familiarisation and/or conversion for senior officers, staff officers and selected pilots from industry. The resident living-in population was large and continually changing and the delightful old pre-war Mess was pushed to cope with a living-in population considerably larger than had been anticipated when it was built.

The whole atmosphere about the place was one of continuous bustle and activity. The flying went on day and night and, because the sorties were generally of quite short duration – about thirty five to forty minutes on average – the circuit seemed always to be filled with aircraft taking off or landing. The noise of jet engines was virtually continuous and the slightly sickly smell of aviation kerosene all-pervading. In later years, as aeroplanes became more and more expensive and the cost of operating them ever higher and higher, the amount of flying available to stations had to be curtailed somewhat, purely on the grounds of cost. In the early 50s, such restrictions were not major factors and the amount of flying which pilots could get was limited more by the necessity to avoid fatigue than by anything else. People often flew three, four, or five sorties a day so that, even at forty minutes a time, monthly totals of forty, fifty, or even more hours were not uncommon.

When I started work as one of the instructors in Number 3 squadron, I was sent off on a number of sector reconnaissance flights to familiarise myself with the local flying area, on weather checks and on a number of flights as either formation leader or instrument safety pilot. The idea was to get me used to the station and its flying procedures as quickly as possible, so that I would be thoroughly familiar with the environment when I was allocated a student and started work in earnest. This preliminary shake-down flying took place during ten days in February 1953 and involved thirty seven flights in a relatively short period. With that sort of start, I just knew that I was going to love the place.

In due course, I had my acceptance check flight with the Wing Commander Flying and was allocated my first student. I found the work absolutely absorbing and did make a conscious effort to remember how I had felt when I had been going through the mill myself. There is an old truism that new instructors learn more from their students than the students learn from them and there may be something in that. I learned, very early on, that most students react better to a gentle approach, in which the instructor tries to build up their confidence, than to any other. I also learned to appreciate the value of the CFS insistence on absolute accuracy in our flying. When you are demonstrating same particular exercise and the student is simply following through on the controls you can practically feel his eyes on the instruments just waiting for you to deviate from the flight conditions you have told him you will fly.

Some few students require a more authoritarian approach than I would generally regard as desirable. I remember, early on, flying with one who really was a most excellent 'stick-and-rudder' pilot. Not a good pilot overall – he had too much confidence for his experience level – but a good handler of the aeroplane. During our aerobatic sorties, his safety checks were not carried out conscientiously and his awareness of other aircraft in the vicinity was poor, but he reeled off manoeuvre after manoeuvre pretty well as capably as I could have done myself. In an attempt to make him realise that he didn't know it all, I decided to demonstrate to him a very gradually tightening level turn which I had been shown by Johnny Severne at CFS and, during which, I had quietly blacked-out. I started the turn just above a thin layer of cloud to provide us with a good height datum and gradually wound up the turn tighter and tighter. When I was just about at the greying-out stage myself, with my student exhibiting no signs of distress whatsoever, the aircraft dipped ever so gently into the top of the cloud. Immediately, I relaxed the back pressure on the stick and eased off fractionally on the bank. The results were spectacular in the extreme. We couldn't have been in the cloud for more than a second or two at the very most but, whereas we entered the cloud in a very tight turn to the left, we came out in an equally very tight turn to the right. A very good trick indeed – or it would have been if I'd been trying to do it. The effect on my student was electric. On the totally inaccurate assumption that the manoeuvre had been intentional, he leapt immediately – and erroneously – to the conclusion that my aerobatics were something really special. For the rest of his course, he begged me daily to show him how to do the instantaneous turn reversal I had demonstrated. Daily, I responded that he'd have to show me a much higher standard of safety procedures and airmanship than he had so far, before I could even consider leading him into such advanced techniques. I might say that I tried for years – on my own – to duplicate the performance and never managed it once.

I did two years to the day at Driffield – exactly as the posting staffs had promised when I was posted from CFS – and I often look back on that tour of duty as the happiest I ever had in the Service. At the time, all I wanted to do was fly and flying was there to be enjoyed in abundance. In my two years, I logged just under eight hundred hours – seven hundred and eighty seven to be exact – and packed into that flying more experience than it would have been possible to accumulate in any other flying assignment anywhere in the RAF. In 3 squadron, I was in daily contact with other instructors of very considerable flying and instructional experience. The Squadron Commander was Squadron Leader Robert (Steve) Carson, MC, whose exploits with the Dutch Resistance after he had been shot down in 1944 were recorded in Paul Brickhill's book 'Escape or Die'. I remember the 'Boss' remarking feelingly once on the subject of strafing runs, "Once is fine; twice is pushing your luck; three times and you deserve all that's coming to you." He was shot down during his third pass at a German troop train. When he hit the ground, he found that a number of the Wehrmacht who had been on the train were extremely keen to offer him their viewpoints on his recent activities.

Another of the squadron pilots was Jerry Sodek, a Czech, who had fought right through the war in a number of air forces. Jerry used to tell me about his training in pre-war Czechoslovakia when the instructors would fill the fuel tanks with just sufficient petrol to do a thirty minute exercise. When the fuel ran out, the student was expected to be somewhere in the vicinity of the airfield so that he could 'dead-stick' it back in again. Jerry said that, since those days, he had never been worried about the thought of an emergency landing. For the first year or so of his career, EVERY landing had been an emergency landing.

On the squadron, too, was Flight Lieutenant Mike Levy, unquestionably the unluckiest Flight Safety Officer of all time. I was actually in the squadron office on the day Mike took over the job. At almost precisely the same instant as he put his signature on the chitty to take on the job formally, there was a tremendous bang outside. Rushing to the window, we saw a Meteor 7 disintegrating into a heap of wreckage in the middle of the runway. When we arrived at the scene, we found an extremely bewildered instructor and student sitting on the grass beside the wreckage, utterly bemused by what seemed to them to be a totally inexplicable crash. The instructor had been flying a tight circuit from the rear seat and, just before touchdown, the whole aeroplane had simply seemed to fall to pieces for no good reason that they could think of. While Mike Levy was trying to calm them down sufficiently to get a coherent story out of them, we were all utterly thunderstruck to observe yet another pilot staggering unsteadily out of the wreckage. In all the excitement, nobody had noticed that there was rather a lot at wreckage about – more than just one Meteor could reasonably have provided. In fact, two aircraft had been involved and one – the tight circuit exponent – had actually landed on top of the other – a solo student who had been landing off an instrument approach. The solo student was even less coherent than the other two. He kept on repeating that he'd just put the wheels on the ground when the sky seemed to fall in an him and the next thing he knew was hearing all the argument going on outside – at which point, he thought he'd better unstrap from what was left of the cockpit and get his tuppence worth into the conversation. Incredibly, all three pilots get away without even a scratch.

Just days later, Mike Levy was reaching for his Incident Report pad again, when an instructor – who should have known better – allowed a student to stretch his glide during a simulated forced landing. Students always felt that they would make it to the field long after it was obvious that they were going to come up short. On this occasion, the instructor was determined to drive home to the student that he would not make it, so he let him carry on down to about a couple of hundred Feet, still something like half a mile short of the runway. When it was obvious, even to the student, that they had no chance of making the field on the glide, the instructor ordered him to overshoot. The standard overshoot procedure on the Meteor was to apply full power and then to raise the wheels and flaps. On this particular occasion, the student, possibly unsettled by his misjudged approach and the proximity of the ground, reversed the procedure and started his overshoot by retracting the flaps. This ill-judged move lost him a large proportion of the lift that was keeping the aeroplane in the air. Before the horrified instructor could even get his hand to the throttles, the aircraft came down like the proverbial lift into a field some way short of the airfield boundary. Again, nobody hurt, but another full day for the poor Flight Safety Officer.

That was one of the problems of instructional flying. Because of their lack of experience, students were quite likely to fly you into situations which could be quite tricky to fly out of, yet they had to be allowed to make their mistakes in order to learn their lessons. The good instructor would always assume control of the aircraft before the situation became really dangerous, but sometimes it was not all that easy to decide on the precise moment to intervene. Too early and the student would probably never even appreciate that he had been approaching a critical flight situation; too late and you were likely to have trouble getting out of the situation without bending the machine.

About six months into my tour, I was talking a student through his first high-speed run after my demonstration of compressibility effects and the standard recovery. We were close to our Mach limit at around thirty thousand feet, with the aircraft lurching about all over the place in the cobblestones effect, when I ordered him to recover. The standard recovery technique was to by close the throttles and extend the air-brakes. I felt the throttles come back all right and was just waiting for the deceleration from the air-brakes when, without any warning whatsoever, the aircraft hood opened. My recollection of the next few seconds is extremely hazy, but I do remember the aircraft going through a series of manoeuvres quite new in my experience. The hood on the Meteor 7 opened sideways and the aerodynamic effect of the large canopy being suddenly displaced off to the right side of the fuselage played absolute havoc with the flight characteristics and handling qualities of the aircraft.

In some confusion, we fell through about fifteen thousand Feet, all the time yawing and rolling violently to the right. Without the protection of the canopy, the noise level was unbelievable and, in the back seat and with no windscreen in front of me, I was very badly buffeted about by the airflow. My goggles were blown back over the top of my flying helmet and I could barely see what was going on.

Eventually, as we got lower and the controls became more effective again, I managed to get the aeroplane under some sort of control. The problem was the opened canopy which could not be closed from inside the cockpit and could not be jettisoned from the open position. The aerodynamic side force from the canopy was continually trying to drag the aircraft into a violent diving turn to the right and I was having to hold on almost full left rudder and aileron just to stay straight and level. There was almost no control movement available to get the aeroplane to turn left. The noise in the cockpit was so bad that I couldn't use the radio to contact Driffield and I could barely make out the students' calls on the intercom.

After a bit, I found that by using differential throttle – carrying more power on the right engine than on the left – I could achieve some limited directional control and coax the aircraft into a slow and somewhat unwilling, turn to the left. I descended carefully to about five thousand feet and, very gingerly indeed, started to slow down to check the low speed handling. Finding that I had just about adequate control left at some twenty knots over the normal approach speed, I lowered the wheels and worked myself into a position about ten miles from base on the extended runway centreline. I didn't try lowering any flap, as I wasn't sure what the result might be and I had no desire to push my luck any further. I could get down without flaps if I had to and I didn't know what effect the extra drag of the flaps might have on the limited control I had.

Keeping an extra sharp look out for other aircraft in the circuit area, I dragged the aircraft in towards the runway in a long low 'bomber' type of approach. I kept the speed well up, on the premise that going off the runway at the far end is generally a better proposition than coming down short and out of control. As the wheels hit the concrete, I popped the air-brakes to kill the wing lift and slammed down full flap, to get as much drag as possible. The Meteor settled down gently and rolled on smoothly down the runway just as if everything were perfectly normal. I didn't even have to use much braking to slow down well before the end of the landing strip.

Back in the crew room, filling out one of Mike Levy's' Incident Reports, the cause of the difficulty we had experienced became clear. In the Meteor, there were two levers, one above the other, on the left side of the cockpit. The lower one was the air-brake lever; the upper, the canopy opening lever. In the excitement of his first high speed run, my student went for the wrong lever. I learned something that day about the principle of good cockpit design and, thereafter, kept my left hand very firmly on the canopy opening lever during all student high-speed run recoveries.

That particular little piece of drama introduced me to one part of instructional technique which hadn't been taught at CFS – the good instructors' cockpit posture. This involved the instructor adopting a sitting position of absolutely minimum comfort, but which permitted him to have the right hand nestling lightly on the stick, the left elbow on the air-brake lever, the left hand on the flap lever and the left knee wedged under the undercarriage lowering lever. This posture would not have done much for the students' confidence, had he been able to see us but, at least, it gave the instructor a fighting chance to nip in the bud his students' more obvious attempts to wreck the machine. Maybe that's why I never did like side-by-side cockpits in training aircraft.

CHAPTER 14

IN ADDITION TO rapidly expanding my experience in the air, Driffield provided a very swift introduction to my other duties as an Air Force officer in a more general sense. Orderly Officer was a regular chore which, oddly, seemed to come round a lot more frequently for the new boys than for the more established hands. I never could understand why. I soon learned that there was more to the job than simply going round the Airmen's Mess at meal times with the traditional "any complaints?" Like all young officers, I learned how to deal with the Saturday night drunks as they rolled back on to base from the local pubs – never, ever, get involved in arguments with them, otherwise they might light-heartedly hang one on you and compound a simple offence of drunkenness into the more serious 'striking a superior officer'. The trick, as I remember it, was to get someone else to guide the offender away to bed, while you lurked about in the shadows. The idea was, presumably, that if he belted the duty Corporal or the Duty Fireman, the offence was somehow less heinous and, anyway, there was a fair chance that, once away from prying eyes, they would belt him right back. I did my turn at pay parades, solemnly counting out the weeks earning on to the table, while the NCO in charge droned through the ritual of "serial number; cap off; cap on; salute; next." Under instruction, I sat in on a number of Squadron Commanders Orderly Rooms when defaulters were dealt with. One, which I recall with much pleasure, involved an Irish airman who was charged with overstaying his leave. This particular airman had never assimilated the idea that leave was awarded for a given number of days – to him, a leave lasted for as long as his money held out. Regularly he arrived back late, was charged, cheerfully pleaded guilty and was duly chastised – although it is only fair to point out that he came back early just as frequently as he came back late.

On the occasion in question, the hearing of the charge proceeded as usual until, to the absolute consternation of all concerned, the accused pleaded not guilty. This was unheard of; he always pleaded guilty. The hearing was thrown into some confusion, until the Squadron Commander gently elicited the reason for this unprecedented plea. Apparently, the charge read that the accused had overstayed his leave to attend the Irish Shinty Cup Final. In fact, as he indignantly advised the hearing, he had been attending the Irish Grand National at the time. To the swiftly amended indictment, he pleaded guilty as usual. Such was the relief of all concerned, that he was discharged with a simple admonition – a disposal of the case to which he responded by inviting all concerned to take note that the Squadron Commander was "a true Christian gentleman, by God." On this elevating note, the proceedings ended as he was almost flung out of the room bodily by the officiating Flight Sergeant who appeared to be on the verge of a stroke.

Another routine chore of the time involved taking Church Parades on Sunday mornings. In those days, Roman Catholics and Jews were allowed to dismiss from the parade to attend their own services – a system which, I might say, led to the profession of either the Catholic or Jewish faith by a surprisingly large number of highly unlikely candidates. The drill was for the parade NCO to bellow the order "fall out the Roman Catholics and Jews," at which point those individuals fell out to the sidelines, while the rest were marched off to Church. At Driffield, the order was invariably followed by the station wags' sotto-voce aside – audible to the entire parade – "plus all Hindus, Hottentots, Voodoo Bashers and Sons of Witch Doctors." This sally never failed to reduce the parade to near hysteria and it was a hard job to get them under control again for delivery to the Padre in a suitably reverent frame of mind.

The various ground duties which a young officer is required to undertake are an essential and extremely important part of his general service training and experience. They provide him with a frequently essential reminder that his primary employment is not – as he often fondly imagines – as a pilot, but as an officer of the Royal Air Force. piloting is simply his trade. Moreover and equally importantly, they provide him with close contact with the airmen for whom, in later years, he will bear direct responsibility. If he is sensible and observant, he will learn the one great lesson of command in any military force, namely that any commander is only as good as the men who serve with him and that they are the ones who actually do all of the work for which, if he's lucky, he will take the credit.

It can be, I admit, somewhat difficult to hold these lofty ideals in the forefront of your mind, when you are tied up in some particularly dreary piece of necessary ground administration. As the Americans so colourfully put it, "sometimes it's difficult to remember that the objective is to drain the swamp when you're up to the ass in alligators."

On one occasion at Driffield, another instructor and I had a contest to see which one of us could accumulate most flying hours in a month. I forget the results now, but we both certainly did much more flying than was good for us. When the Wing Commander Flying got our logbooks for signature at the end of the month, he read us both the Riot Act, grounded us for two weeks on the spot and ensured that we would be kept out of mischief by ordering Tammy Sime to check the spare parts stores inventory and ordering me to review the station key inventory. Until then, I had no idea of the number of keys held on a station. When my grounding was over, I had checked less than a quarter of the inventory and it took me a very long time indeed to get through the remainder.

I suppose that my most obvious piece of learning by doing (incorrectly) occurred with the moving of the Station ensign. Every morning, there was an ensign raising parade conducted by the duty Orderly staff and attended by any defaulters there happened to be. At the end of the working day, there was a repeat performance, at which the ensign was ceremoniously lowered and put to bed for the night. On one Saturday afternoon when I was doing Orderly Officer duty, I was rung up by the Orderly Corporal with the news that the ensign was still on the station parade ground where it had been run up that morning during a full scale Station Commanders parade. He advised me that it would be necessary to get it back to its normal location outside the Guard Room in time for the late afternoon lowering ceremony.

Blissfully ignorant of the welter of Service ceremonial associated with flags in general and the RAF ensign in particular, I airily instructed the Corporal to get himself down to the square, run down the ensign and then run it up again on the flagpole outside the Guard Room. During the execution of this directive, the Station Commander happened to pass by the parade square on his way back to his quarters from the Mess. On the carpet, in his office, first thing on the following Monday morning, I learned that he had not been pleased by what he had seen. I learned, further, that there are very many ways of handling the movement of a service ensign and, somewhat painfully, that getting the Orderly Corporal to conduct a one-man lowering and raising on his own is not one of the approved options. The lesson was driven home by an assignment to check the inventory of fire extinguishers on the Station. There are nearly as many of them as there are keys.

In between these assorted secondary duties, I still managed to get my fair share of the flying that was going. It was still possible, in those days, to persuade misguided friends at other units to let you try your hand on their aeroplanes. I very much doubt if there would be much chance of that today. I was quite lucky in having some colleagues whose misplaced trust in my capability allowed me to put the Provost, the Meteor NF11 – the night-fighter variant – the Meteor 8, the Vampire and the Venom in my log-book. It was all excellent experience and made a beginning to providing me with some sort of yardstick for comparing the characteristics of one sort of aeroplane with another. All of these trips were 'scrounged' at other units and all went off without a hitch.

Around this time, I was flying a fair number of week-end Staff Continuation Training cross-countries up to Edinburgh, an activity which finally resulted in Jean and I setting the date for our wedding for the end of June. Alan Brindle was to be best man. On the Saturday of the ceremony, when Alan was due to fly up, all of Yorkshire was under a thick blanket of fog and there was no way that he could get airborne. When he called me with the news, I was left with a wedding due in three hours and no best man available. At this point, I ran across an old friend whom I hadn't seen for years. His plans to attend a football match that afternoon were very swiftly modified to permit his attendance at the Church at which, for the second momentous time in my life, I happily signed on the dotted line and said, "I do."

CHAPTER 15

WHEN JEAN AND L ARRIVED at Driffield to settle down to married life in the service, we set up home initially in a self-contained flat in a large country house in the village of North Dalton. Shortly afterwards we were offered one of Driffield's married quarters and, in due course, moved on to the 'married patch' on the Station.

In those days, life in the Service – and particularly married life – vas very different from what it became in later years. For a start, the job was relatively poorly paid – I can remember chatting to a workman one day while he was mixing concrete for a repair to part of the runway and discovering that his weekly pay was almost exactly the same as my monthly salary, including flying pay. In the circumstances, the social life of any unit was very much an in-house affair centred around the station Mess and the Married Quarters area. House ownership was almost unheard of and most married couples lived either in the station married quarters – if they were lucky – or in local hirings, if they were not so fortunate. The week-end exodus from the station, which later became so common as a result of more widespread car ownership, was quite unknown, and, on Saturday and Sunday nights, station messes were packed from wall to wall with married officers and their wives and the station bachelors and their girlfriends. The Mess was the station club and social centre and was almost continuously in use for some function or other. The result was that everybody on a unit very quickly got to knew everybody else and a very strong social spirit was engendered and fostered.

In addition to the Mess activities, there was a set pattern of social exchanges in which all officers on the station were expected to participate. In many ways, this was a hangover from the pre-war service and it later died out almost completely. 'Calling' was very much a requisite and cards would be left at the homes of various unit executives at the prescribed hour. In return, a card would be received advising when the hostess would be 'at home'. This, in turn, would lead to a 'call', during which coffee and sherry would be decorously sipped to the exchange of local chit-chat. Later, after a decent interval, the call would be returned, to be followed by invitations for drinks, or dinner, or whatever, at which time one was fully launched into the social swim. I have often heard the system dismissed disparagingly as hopelessly antiquated and outrageously snobbish. In my own view, it was nothing of the kind. In the circumstances of the time, it was a civilised and entirely enjoyable, method of arranging a social structure within what was virtually a closed community and it provided an opportunity for people to get to know one another better than has ever been the case since. In particular, for young officers, whether married or single, it provided a social life which would otherwise have been unavailable and which ensured that no one was ever left feeling out of the activities of the unit.

One at the slightly unusual aspects of our social life at Driffield involved a roadside cafe called The Four Winds, which was situated just outside the airfield boundary virtually at the end of the main runway. It was owned by a relatively young couple, the husband Italian and the wife Irish and, being within a couple of minutes' walk from any at the hangers, it operated during much of the day as an unofficial crew room where people would drop in for a coffee or a chat. For station permanent staff personnel and for countless students passing through, it provided what was virtually a Number 2 Mess which seemed to be open for business whenever an out-of-hours meal was required. I have often been in a party at the Bell Hotel in Driffield, from which, at closing time, a quick call to The Four winds would ensure that a meal was waiting by the time we got there. For students, the owners operated a system of never presenting a bill after the twentieth of the month. If the customer had any money, he would ask for the bill; if not, it quietly went on the slate, to be settled at the end of the month. It was like settling a second mess bill. I can only hope that the young owners realised the affection in which they were held at Driffield and how much their unfailing kindness and consideration were appreciated. Many years later, I made a refuelling stop at Driffield on my way to the north and spent most of my time on the ground back in that well known cafe. It was a real pleasure to meet those good friends again.

Away from the social side of things, I found myself becoming involved in what was virtually a one-man fighter pilot conversion course. Because of the ready availability of flying, instructors used to do a lot of SCT flying – Staff Continuation Training – during which you were expected to practise and perfect your own flying techniques, without having to worry about a student in the front seat. Using these SCT sorties, Alan Brindle set about sharpening me up for fighter flying in preparation for my posting at the end of my instructional tour. Whenever we had the chance, we would launch off as a pair to practise formation climbs and descents, battle formation and cross-over turns, high-quarter attack passes and, most exciting and demanding of all, dog-fighting. Alan's whole career had been spent in this environment and he was an excellent teacher. He used to demonstrate and drive home, the lessons I had read about so many years ago in the books I had acquired about World War 1. Although the performance of our aircraft was so much higher than the primitive machines of those days, the basic principles of air combat remained the same. See the enemy before he sees you; never fly straight and level for any length of time; try to attack out of the sun; never let your opponent get a height advantage; always break into your adversary when jumped; and, most important of all, keep a constant lookout – a real lookout – every single second of the time. I used to think that I kept a conscientious scan of the sky going – until Alan started to jump me without warning at every opportunity. In very short order, I learned to scan quickly, systematically and thoroughly, so that I wouldn't have to face the embarrassment of suddenly finding him sitting on my wing, grinning all over his face and giving me the thumbs-down for lookout. After a while, I seemed to be doing all of my flying in a continuous corkscrew weave, with my neck on a perpetual swivel and my eyeballs sticking out like organ steps. I felt as though I was developing goitre, but at least he didn't catch me out quite so often.

The dog-fighting was tremendously stimulating. I can't think of any other exercise in the flying world more calculated to flood the system with adrenalin and tune-up the reactions to concert pitch. Alan and I always started at about twenty to twenty five thousand feet in line abreast at normal cruising speed of about 250 knots and, if possible, heading directly into the sun. On the command 'go', we would each break outward through ninety degrees and fly away from each other for twenty seconds. At the end of the twenty seconds, it was on with full power, reef the aircraft into the tightest climbing turn possible and start scanning desperately for the opponent. When you saw him, you were closing very rapidly head-to-head and had to decide which way to turn to achieve a firing position. If both of you turned in the same direction, the engagement would become the classic 'tail-chase', in which the only possible winner is the one who can sustain a tighter turn than his adversary. Even a seconds worth of slackened turn can be fatal, giving the opponent the chance to cut inside your turn and bring his guns to bear. This sort of engagement is a high rate of turn, high 'g', full power manoeuvre, conducted on the very edge of blacking out. After a minute or two of this, you are wringing wet with sweat, your arms feel like lead weights and your pulse rate hits unprecedented levels. In two identical aircraft, the engagement generally ends in a draw with neither pilot able to gain a firing position. It took me many weeks before I even came close to getting a draw.

In the other case, when the two aircraft turn in opposite directions, the manoeuvring is even more exciting. Again, the initial turn back brings you head-on to each other, so that you close rapidly in a maximum 'g' climbing turn. As soon as you pass, you have to guess which way your opponent is going to turn back. Turn the same way and you are into the tail chase; the opposite way and it's into the 'yo-yo', a high 'g', max rate climbing turn manoeuvre. It sounds fairly straightforward but, in the heat of the engagement, with every nerve straining for the slightest advantage and your heart banging like a drum, it is the most physically and mentally demanding exercise imaginable. And that's only simulated combat! What it must have been like in the real thing, with the opposition shooting live ammunition at you and life and death the literal stakes of the contest, is almost impossible to imagine. I always landed from one of my battles with Alan absolutely drained. He, damn him, always looked as if he were quite ready to re-fuel straight away and have another go.

On as many occasions as we could contrive, we would try to jump some of the other aircraft using our bit of the UK airspace. There were something like seventy plus squadrons of fighters in the UK at that time, so we had plenty of opportunity to try our luck. The front line squadron pilots were always driven to fury if they were jumped by a yellow-banded Training Command Meteor and they would do their damndest to make you pay for the presumption. In our 'offensive patrols', we mixed it with the Fighter Command Meteors, Vampires and Hornets, with the USAF F-84s and F-86s and with the Navy's Attackers. It was one of the latter's Flight Commanders who came up with the definitive jet age put-down during a wild melee just north of Hull one day. Observing his Number Two run into compressibility trying to outrun a Meteor in a dive, he remarked languidly, as the unfortunate Attacker flicked onto its back quite out of control, "Doctor Mach, I presume."

When he was not leading me into this sort of mischief, Alan was always capable of getting into hot water on his own account. One day, he and another ex-Fighter Command instructor got into a great argument about which of their two late squadrons could scramble their aircraft more quickly. Eventually, it was decided to resolve the issue by having the two of them perform a two-man, no-notice, scramble from the crew room on a signal from an independent referee. The winner was to be the one whose wheels left the ground first. As a concession and to allow for the fact that our Meteors didn't have ejection seats, they were permitted to place their parachutes in their aircraft in advance. When the 'alarm' finally came, Alan was airborne before his rival had barely cleared the squadron dispersal area. In fact, the loser was so far behind that he didn't even bother to take off, but simply taxied back to dispersal in disgust. Everyone was very impressed with Alan's performance – particularly the Wing Commander Flying who had happened to be in Air Traffic Control while it was taking place. Alan collected a month's Orderly Officer as his prize and, even at that, felt that he had got off lightly.

At about this time, the whole Station was afflicted with a craze for doing slow loops. This can be a very effective display aerobatic, but it is also extremely dangerous, as the low speed 'over the top' can bring you very close indeed to the limits of control. The normal entry speed for a loop in a Meteor was 290 knots and, over a period of time this was brought down and down until, having hit a new low of 215 knots one day, I decided that, for me at any rate, the competition was ever. Alan was away on leave while all this took place and on his return, I was giving him his re-familiarisation check when, very ill advisedly, I told him what had been going on during his absence. "How low did you get?" he enquired casually, as he lowered the wheels in the downwind leg of the circuit prior to landing. Blissfully ignorant of the trap I was walking into, I replied proudly, "215 knots." The words were hardly out of my mouth when I felt the throttles slam open, the wheels and flaps came up and the stick come hard back. I sat rigid while he calmly looped out of the circuit, popped the airbrakes during the recovery, dropped the wheels and flaps again for the landing and strolled casually away from dispersal, whistling to himself. The maximum speed for lowering the undercarriage in the Meteor was 175 knots and we had certainly been below that when we pulled up. If I hadn't sat through it – however unwillingly – I simply wouldn't have believed it.

It was something of a relief to discover that pilots a lot more experienced than I was could find themselves being led into silly situations by others. On one occasion, we were lounging about the crew room, when a Meteor almost took the roof of the hanger off in a low 'beat-up'. When we rushed outside to find out what was going on, it was to discover that the aircraft – a brand-new Mark 7 ~ was being delivered to the station by one at the Gloster test pilots who was something of a display ace. He certainly gave the place a thorough going over as he went through the whole range of low level display aerobatics before he concluded his exhibition with a dazzlingly original manoeuvre that none of us had ever seen performed before. Coming in very low and fast, he seemed to throttle back abruptly as he pulled up into a beautifully smooth straight loop. As he started the pull up, a thin trail of what seemed to be black smoke poured back from each engine to etch the whole path of the loop clearly in the sky. We were all very impressed and very keen indeed to discover how he had achieved this spectacularly novel effect.

When we had a chance to chat to him, we discovered that his technique was to start the loop with plenty of speed in hand and immediately select the fuel high pressure cocks to the off position to shut dawn both engines. He then selected the fuel cocks on again to induce a stream of unburnt kerosene – the black trail we had seen – to pour out of the engine tailpipes. As he came back into the level position during the pull out, he pressed the engine relight buttons to fire up the Derwents again and carried on with the rest of the display. Very simple and very impressive.

Among the audience listening to this explanation of how to execute the manoeuvre was the station individual aerobatic display pilot. He was very much taken with the idea of being able to incorporate the new 'paraffin loop' into his own display sequence and he couldn't wait to try it out. Next day, he did – with somewhat unfortunate results, having overlooked one or two minor differences between the brand-new Mark 7 Meteor the Gloster pilot had flown and the old, tired, much-used Mark 4 in which he attempted to reproduce the manoeuvre. The Mark 7 was brand-new; had a special ante-chamber relight system; had high energy ignition; had a new 28 Volt electrical system; and had the relight buttons on the end of the high-pressure cocks. The Mark 4 was a long way from being new and incorporated none of these refinements.

The actual 'paraffin loop' which he performed was every bit as impressive as the original. The problems came during the recovery, when the fiddly, old-fashioned relight system completely failed to get the kerosene-soaked engines to light-up again. Very fortunately, his exit speed from the loop was high enough to let him zoom up to a couple of thousand feet, from where he was able to execute a glide approach back to the airfield for a safe landing. In some ways, his display was even more impressive than the Gloster pilots had been, but it was some time before he tried a repeat performance. Some time later, when I took over the job of display pilot, I did a few paraffin loops myself, but only when I was safely strapped into a new Mark 7 equipped with all the 'goodies' to get the engines going again. Even at that, I always made sure that I came out of the loop fast and going up – just in case.

CHAPTER 16

ROUND ABOUT THIS TIME, formation aerobatic teams became something of a craze throughout the RAF. Formation aerobatics were nothing new but, in the past, they had generally been performed exclusively by squadrons which had been allocated an official commitment to undertake display flying for occasions such as Battle of Britain Day, Farnborough Air Show, or various 'Open' days. I remember that 54 Squadron were one of the leaders in jet formation aerobatics – they had been engaged in display flying since the days of the old Hendon shows and had a great deal of experience in the art. Now, all of a sudden, every unit that could get a few aeroplanes into the air together started to field its own display team. Not to be outdone, Driffield assembled its own team, for which I operated as spare man, filling in when one of the regulars was on leave, or otherwise unavailable. The team was led by 3 Squadrons new Commanding Officer, Lieutenant Commander Des Russell RN, whose manipulation of the leave system was already something of a legend at Driffield. It seemed that every time Des needed a day off, the occasion coincided with some great event in naval history, for which sailors were entitled to a holiday. Nelson's birthday, the anniversary of some long-forgotten naval battle, even the launching of the Ark seemed to constitute day-off entitlements for the "dark blues." The RAF hierarchy were suspicious, but none of them knew enough about naval tradition to argue the point.

Des drove the Driffield team to a very high standard of performance and we gave displays all over the country. He was a first class formation leader, always thinking well ahead so that nobody in the formation was ever required to do anything out of the ordinary to hold position. This is by no means as easy as it sounds, in that the leader has to position his team in such a way that the whole display is executed in front of the spectators and, at the same time, ensure that, in all the turns and rolls, the outside man is not having to bend the throttles to keep up, nor the inside man having to judder about close to stalling speed. Formation leading is a real art and display formation leading demands the very highest standards of capability in that art.

Even with a good leader, formation aerobatics is a very demanding exercise. From the second the team starts its take-off roll, the eyes of the formation members are locked on to the lead aircraft to the total exclusion of everything else. They never notice anything of the display, the ground, the spectators, or the sky – only the leader, held always in the same relative position. Everything inside the cockpit is done by feel – no looking for controls or anything else; every ounce of concentration is focused totally on the leader – and on nothing else. On occasions, this can lead to difficulty since, if any minor problem does occur, attention cannot safely be diverted to deal with it. In fact, even without any problems, it is still possible to get into difficulty.

On one occasion when I was flying number two in the team, we concluded our display with a three-plane formation landing – number four, the man in the box position, having broken off to land independently. A very tight circuit was flown, landing gear and flaps lowered by feel and we were about fifty feet off the ground when Des decided that he wasn't happy with the final approach and ordered a go-around. As I stretched out my hand to raise the wheels, I discovered, to my horror, that they were still up. Somehow or other, I had missed lowering them during our approach. In my position on the right of the leader, I had been blanked out from the sight of the runway controller and he had not been able to see that I was still 'clean' until we were almost down. Another second or two and I would have concluded our display with a spectacular belly landing, which would have done nothing to enhance my popularity within the team, or my professional reputation overall. I will never know what made Des Russell decide to go round again at the very last minute, but I have fervently thanked my lucky stars ever since that he did.

Away from these rather more exotic bits of flying, I was kept busy with my routine instructional duties. As I built up experience, I became more and more confident in the job and felt that I was becoming increasingly able to get my students through the syllabus without too many difficulties. In due course, I became an Instrument Rating Examiner and undertook all the Instrument Rating Tests in the squadron. I liked this appointment because I had always had a feel for instrument flying and felt that I was reasonably good at it. I always believed that the ability to fly safely and accurately on instruments was a pilot's best safeguard against ever being caught out by the weather. It seemed to me rather like an insurance policy where the premium is the amount of practice you put in. If I was ever caught out in a bad weather situation and had to get down from an instrument approach in marginal conditions, I wanted to have plenty of practice – and confidence in my own ability – under my belt.

In point of fact, to describe the Driffield bad weather recovery procedure as an instrument approach is probably something of an overstatement. We had no true landing aids as they are understood nowadays, no Ground Controlled Approach, no Instrument Landing System, no radar. We could get a VHF radio homing to the approximate overhead, followed by a procedural let down, during which the controllers used radio bearings to get us headed back towards the airfield. Although this system was, strictly speaking, an airfield approach aid rather than a landing aid, some of the controllers became very adept at interpreting the radio bearings to line you up pretty well with the runway and it became a matter of professional pride for them to position you sufficiently accurately for you to land straight in off the approach. In later years, people used to laugh at the antiquated kit we used then, but I can honestly say that I have done many approaches in poor weather conditions, under the guidance of a controller using only VHF bearings, which were a lot better than some of the GCA approaches I was later talked through. Primitive the system may have been, but it was all that we had – and it worked.

Quite apart from the official approach aids, everyone at Driffield was very familiar with the unofficial – and very effective – bad weather approach aid provided, all unknowingly, by a combination of nature, the Air Ministry, British Railways and the Yorkshire County Council Health Board. If one ever did get caught out in bad weather, the drill was to head east until you were certain of being over the sea. When safely clear of land, a slow let down was made until cloud was broken. It is very seldom that cloud extends right down to sea level, so this was a reasonably safe procedure. Once below cloud, you turned west and headed back in towards the mainland until land was sighted. If the first sighting revealed a rocky coastline of cliffs and crags, you were north of Flamborough Head; low, flat, sandy beaches put you south of Flamborough. In either case, you then turned towards Flamborough until the Head came in sight, at which point you started to edge round to the south side to pick up Bridlington and then Carnaby runway – a very long landing strip built during the war for the recovery of damaged bombers staggering back from Germany. Once Carnaby was in view, you aimed to pick up the railway line from Bridlington to Driffield which you followed to the village of Burton Agnes. Here, you lowered the wheels and transferred your attention to the A166 which paralleled the railway at Burton Agnes and which led you straight to Driffield Hospital. At Driffield Hospital, wheels and full flap were selected, a turn made on to 240 degrees and, in a matter of seconds, there was the runway, dead ahead. Simple, effective – and, again – it worked.

One Saturday morning, we had good cause at Driffield to bless that unofficial 'get-you-back' route, when we launched a Station 'Balbo' in weather conditions that were far short of what they should have been for such an exercise. I should explain that a Balbo is a mass formation flight, named after the eminent Italian Admiral who first started the idea. In the '50s, it was quite common for RAF Stations to launch Saturday morning Balbos, in which as many aircraft as were serviceable were put into the air in a sort of local 'show the flag' exercise. On one memorable occasion, something like fifty fighters from Linton-on-Ouse did a low-level Balbo right over the middle of York – at almost exactly the same time as the visiting Archbishop of Canterbury was rising to give his sermon in York Minster. His Grace was, to use the classic expression, not exactly gruntled by the coincidence.

In the case of the Driffield fiasco, the starting weather was really quite poor, with low cloud and a lot of scudding rain. Quite a few people didn't even turn up for the briefing, on the grounds that it was sure to be cancelled and, even when the thirty five or so of us who did turn up actually taxied out, the general feeling was that it would all be scrubbed before we ever got airborne. In the event, it wasn't. The Station Commander launched and, like a bunch of dutiful sheep, the rest of us launched with him. I was somewhere down the back of the formation, flying number two to one of our Sergeant Pilot instructors, 'Timber' Wood and it seemed to me that we went into cloud almost as soon as our wheels left the runway. It was very bumpy in the cloud and the visibility was so poor that even Timbers' aircraft kept disappearing momentarily. I blessed Alan Brindle for the hours he spent forcing me to fly tight on him during our many sorties together. Eyes glued to my leader, I stuck to him like a corn plaster until, after what seemed like an age, we all broke through the overcast into the brilliant sunshine on top – miraculously, all still there and all still in tight formation.

While we were still heaving a collective sigh of relief at getting up safely, it became clear, from the radio exchanges with Air Traffic Control, that the weather was not getting much better and there might well be elements of interest in getting back down through the cloud again. There was no possibility of Air Traffic controlling individual let-downs for the number of aircraft we had airborne, before the tail-enders would be very short of fuel indeed. Eventually, after it had been decided that even section formation controlled let-downs would probably take too much time, it was decided to let the whole lot down, still in formation, out to sea and come back in by the Carnaby bad weather route.

When we did break cloud on the descent, after a fairly nerve-wracking tight formation let-down, we shifted into echelon starboard for the low-level recovery back to Driffield. And it really was low-level – the whole formation couldn't have had much more than seventy or eighty feet to spare as we swept in over Flamborough Head. When we did, at last, pick up the airfield lights and the flares they were firing to guide us in, it felt as if we were almost scraping the tree tops. Once back in the circuit, it was a hair-raising experience to get back on the ground again. We had to land in pairs in order to get the formation down as quickly as possible and each section was flying as tight as they could on the section in front. At times, it felt as if your aircrafts nose was liable to get stuck in the jet pipe of the aircraft in front of you. The jet wash from seventy-odd engines in the same crowded piece of sky was worse than I had ever experienced and all the aircraft behind the lead section were bucking about violently in the turbulence. At slow speed and with wheels and flaps down, it felt even worse, but the section breaks and the subsequent split into pairs on the downwind leg, went like clockwork. Touchdown was made still formating in pairs and the whole formation was safely recovered within a couple of minutes of reaching the airfield.

Afterwards, there was very little discussion of that particular Balbo. We all knew that it had been a mistake to go on with it in the weather conditions which existed, but we got up and down again without any more than a touch of reasonable anxiety. In a sense, I suppose, it could be regarded as a tribute to our training and discipline that we got away with it. I know that there had been a few moments when I would just as soon have broken off from the formation and made my own arrangements to get back down. But you are trained to trust your leader and to stick with him come what may. And that is precisely what we did. I might say that the next Driffield Balbo was deferred until there wasn't a cloud in the sky anywhere within a hundred miles of Yorkshire.

CHAPTER 17

WHEN, IN APRIL 1954, Carol Anne Archer appeared upon the scene – I was airborne at the time and got the good news over the R/T – I was well into the second year of my instructional tour. I was enjoying it as much as ever and developing the confidence to tailor the training of my students to accord with their individual requirements, rather than just slavishly expounding the gospel according to CFS. Somehow or other, I always seemed to have good students to work with, keen, eager to learn, aggressive and full at character. One I remember with particular pleasure was a New Zealander, Sandy Burns, who was one of the best I ever had. Sandy was one of a group of New Zealanders who went through Driffield together and a nicer, livelier bunch would have been hard to find. I have known a lot of New Zealanders in the Service and I have yet to come across one whom it was not a pleasure to know. If the ones we get in the Royal Air Force are representative of the rest of the population, then New Zealand must be a delightful country indeed.

Sandy was a very determined pilot who revelled in all the fighter-orientated parts of the course like formation and aerobatics. In particular, he loved tailchases, which were supposed to be fairly mild 'follow-my-leader' exercises in long-line astern to accustom the student to following his lead aircraft through any sort of manoeuvre. With Sandy, every tail-chase developed into a virtual dogfight, with me pulling out everything I knew to shake him off. More often than not, he hung on through everything I could throw at him, even including, on one ill-judged occasion, a vertical dive from about thirty five thousand feet, when we came down so fast that we both hit compressibility and both lost control. When I recovered, he was still there on my tail, stirred perhaps, but not noticeably shaken.

As I came up towards the end of my tour, I had a couple of uncomfortably close calls which reminded me – if I ever really needed reminding – that you can never afford to get casual in the air – not ever. On the first occasion, I was in the front seat when a student became suddenly disorientated during a climbing turn in cloud following an instrument take-off and allowed his airspeed to build and his bank angle to fall off. When I quietly advised him to watch his speed, he over-controlled violently to try to get back to the required flight datum – so violently, in fact, that we executed what amounted to a sharp flick roll and wound up in a very high speed dive, upside down. The situation was not unlike my previous experience with my Lebanese co-student at CFS, but this time, when we came out of cloud, we came out inverted and at about four times the speed. As we did, we were headed straight at one of the little villages on the wolds to the north of Driffield and, specifically, almost straight at the local church tower. As we missed it, I swear that I could see every detail of the clock face from the very closest of close ranges. When I got home that evening, my mother, who was staying with us, asked me if I was feeling unwell. I was, she said, "as white as a sheet."

The second near miss happened during an Open Day at Hooton Park, near Manchester. I was scheduled to do the solo aerobatics display which I had performed many times before. On the day, I started, as usual, with a low inverted approach to the airfield, to be followed by a hesitation roll back to the inverted position for the fly-away to the next element of the display. When I had almost finished the roll and was coming back to the inverted level position again, I suddenly wondered what the altimeter was reading. Why, God alone knows. I was upside down, flying very fast and very low and that is no situation for having your eyes anywhere but outside the cockpit. Anyway, I snatched a quick look, during which the aircraft dipped out of the roll and hit the runway with the starboard wing-tip. There was a very spectacular shower of sparks as the concrete took off six or seven inches of the wing, before I wrenched the aircraft back into a steep climb to a safe altitude. That was the end at my display for the day – not overlong, but a very hard act to follow. I never looked inside the cockpit again during a display.

During the last couple of months of my time at Driffield, the unit title was changed to Number 8 Flying Training School, as part of a re-organisation of Flying Training Command. We had a lot at personnel changes, including quite a rapid turn-over in Commanding Officers. One of these changes in command provided an incident which beat hollow anything Mack Sennett could have ever dreamed up and became a much cherished part of Air Force legend.

Normally, when one Station Commander hands over command to his successor, the exercise is conducted in the Commanding Officers office in Station Headquarters. The incomer checks the books, counts the cash and signs for one RAF Station in good working order. From that moment on, he's in command.

One of Driffield's commanders decided that this sort of procedure was a touch too informal for his liking and arranged with his successor that command would be handed over formally at a full station parade. Since the CO designate was learning to fly Meteors at Worksop, it was arranged that a Mark 4 would be flown down there and left for him to make his arrival on to the Station in style. Better and better! Since the new CO would be flying himself in, why not hold the parade on the operational readiness pan at the end of the main runway? The new man could then step straight from his aircraft to take the salute, accept command and get down to business straight away.

Came the day and everything was arranged as per the master plan. The entire station strength on parade, resplendent in best blue and medal ribbons, the ensign bravely fluttering and the band, as usual during waiting time on parades, providing excerpts from 'Lilac Time' and 'The Merry Widow'. Eventually, a lone Meteor was seen to join the circuit, lower its wheels and set itself up on the final approach.

As the Meteors wheels hit the concrete, two events happened simultaneously. First, the parade was brought to the 'General Salute'; second, every pilot present realised that the touch-down had been too fast and too far down the runway. While we remained rigidly at the salute, the tortured screams of the brakes were clearly audible, followed by a couple of loud pops as the main wheel tyres burst. At this point, the aircraft came directly past the front of the parade, nose wheel still in the air and still going at a fair old lick. Every eye on the parade swivelled automatically to follow the Meteor as it went off the end of the runway, across the overshoot area, through the airfield boundary hedge, across the main Bridlington road and into a field beyond, where it disappeared in an enormous cloud of dust. After a moment of stunned disbelief, the whole parade simply broke up, as the emergency crews and crash rescue personnel raced off to their vehicles – the only time in my entire service career when I was part of a parade that was not formally dismissed. As a postscript to the story, I should add that the new Commanding Officer was uninjured, the aircraft was virtually undamaged except for the burst tyres and the official hand-over of command took place, somewhat later, in the Station Commanders office.

During the last few weeks of my tour at Driffield, I did everything I could to ensure that my posting to Fighter Command would proceed without any possible snags. Mindful of the posting staffs' assurance that assignment to the command of my choice would be available, I made it quite clear to anyone who would listen that the posting of my choice would be to Fighter Command. I didn't want a repeat of the situation which had arisen when I left Middleton St George. Much as I had enjoyed my instructional tour and much as I realised its value to me, I felt that the time was long overdue for me to get into the front line of the Service and get settled into an operational squadron.

In this instance, I really had everything in my favour. I had finished my full instructional tour, I held an A2 instructor category, a Green Instrument Rating, an Instrument Rating Examiner qualification and an above average assessment across the board. Moreover, this time I had friends in high places – former colleagues, with whom I had craftily kept in touch, were now holding the posting staff appointments at both 11 Group and Fighter Command. Contact with them left me assured that my next posting was a mere formality. On all counts, it seemed to me, I had it made.

When I actually got the formal posting notice in my hand, I couldn't believe it – again! With everything in my favour and nearly a thousand hours on the current type of front-line fighter, how could I possibly be posted to the Bomber Command Bombing School at Lindholme? for the second time, I went back up the posting chain, only to discover that all of my friends in the appointments staffs were completely powerless to do anything about the situation. The posting, I was told, came directly from Air Ministry and the staffs at Group and Command had no power at all to intervene.

Greatly daring, after the wigging I had received from them last time, I contacted the Ministry staff again. As on the previous occasion, I got very short shift and absolutely no sympathy. Bomber Command, I was informed, was in the process of expanding their Canberra force markedly and they were desperately short of jet qualified instructors to fill the Training Officer slots in the squadrons. I was ideally qualified for this sort of assignment, so to Bomber Command I would go. When I pointed out that I had no instructional experience on Canberras, I was told that very few people had – that was why there was a shortage. When I recalled their promise of a preferred posting, I was informed – as if it were not already abundantly evident – that things had changed a lot over the past two years and, anyway, the chap who had told me that had recently left the job – to take up my posting to Fighter Command, I would have bet. This time, there was no carrot of good things to come at the end of my next tour. Instead, there was some evidence of the stick, as I was reminded that I had just finished a full flying tour and was, in fact, due for a ground tour as station adjutant or some other such appointment.

In the light of all the circumstances, there wasn't anything I could do about it. I was disappointed, but at least I was going to be carrying on flying. I packed my bags and headed for Lindholme.

CHAPTER 18

THE COURSE AT LINDHOLME lasted for all of nine days during which I made four flights in a Lincoln and two in a Varsity – all bombing runs, either visual or radar, over one or other of the Bomber Command bombing ranges. To this day, I don't know what the course was supposed to teach me, other than what it was like to be in a bomber while the bomb aimer went through his "LEFT, LEFT; RIGHT; STEADY; STEADY; STEADY; BOMBS GONE" routine. Anyone who had ever been to the cinema is totally familiar with the routine from any number of war films and the pilots only involvement – so far as I could gather – was simply to fly the aircraft in response to the bomb aimers directions. Since this only involved very small heading changes at a set height and airspeed, I couldn't really see that it should have taken about thirty hours of flying to get the message across. After the forty minutes duration of the Meteor, the sorties seemed endless. We carried up to twenty four 25 pound practice bombs, released one at a time and each individual run seemed to take forever. After about six or seven runs, everyone in the aircraft was bored to distraction and a little voice inside your head seemed to be repeating insistently, "God Almighty, another seventeen or eighteen runs to go." After twenty runs, you felt that you had been through a gruelling operational tour. After twenty four, you were tottering on the edge at battle fatigue. You ate innumerable sandwiches you didn't want, sucked sickly sweets, drank gallons of coffee and smoked far too many cigarettes. Anything to get your mind off the tedium of the sortie. I began to understand why Bomber Command was known throughout the service as 'Eating Command' and why there were a large number of substantially built aircrew in its ranks.

To be fair, I did enjoy the experience of flying the Lincoln and the Varsity. They were the first really heavy aircraft that I had ever flown and I particularly liked the feel – and the sound – of the Lincoln. The Merlin engines had a very characteristic deep growling pitch which I found very mellow after the high pitched whine of the Derwent jet engines I was more used to. Nevertheless, the flying was sedate and unexciting and the bombing exercises dull in the extreme. If this was what Bomber Command was all about, then I really wasn't looking forward to a lot more of it at all.

When the unutterably dull Bombing School course eventually dragged to a close, any change had to be a change for the better. Accordingly, it was with a sense of real relief that I reported to Number 231 Operational Conversion Unit at Bassingbourn in March 1955 to commence my conversion to the Canberra. Bassingbourn officers mess was quite famous throughout the Air Force for having the best and biggest bar in the service. During World War 2, Jimmy Stewart, the American film star, had flown B-24s from the base in the course of a distinguished operational career. After the war, he had a 'Hollywood' type bar – all chrome, teak and quilted fittings – flown across for installation in the Mess; a gesture much appreciated by all later converts to the Canberra.

The Canberra was one of the great success stories of the post-war British aircraft industry. Test flown by Wing Commander Roland Beaumont, it first flew at Warton in May 1949 and entered service with 101 Squadron at Binbrook in May 1951. In the Mosquito tradition of light bombers, it was unarmed and relied on its very high performance to escape interception. During the early part of the 1950s, it could certainly outfly anything else in the sky. It cruised comfortably at 45000 Feet at a Mach number of around 0.8 – about 530 mph. Its range was more than two and a half thousand miles and it was remarkably manoeuvrable – a well flown Canberra would give an aerobatic demonstration that had the fighter display pilots of the day looking to their laurels. In fact, it was Roly Beaumont's ability to demonstrate the Canberra which made it the first British post-war aircraft to go into service with the United States Air Force. In a competition fly-off against the three-engined Martin B-51, Wing Commander Beaumont's superb display of the Canberra's capabilities and performance sold the aircraft to the Americans who accepted it into service as the B-57.

I found the Canberra a beautiful aircraft to fly – at the time, a real Rolls Royce of the air. It handled superbly, had a much better performance than the Meteor and was practically viceless. Its 'goldfish bowl' canopy gave a magnificent all round view although, being a fixed canopy, it caused the cockpit to heat up uncomfortably on the ground during hot weather. The only access to the outside world through the canopy was by a very small "'clear vision' panel about the size of a saucer.

The only feature I never did like about the Canberra was the flap system. In most aircraft, the flaps can be lowered and raised in stages; in the Canberra, they were either fully up or fully down – no intermediate selection was possible. I never liked this feature from the standpoint of asymmetric landings, when you had to be that much more careful with the timing of flap selection than would have been the case with a 'staged' flap system. Moreover, the trim change on lowering or raising flap was very pronounced – by far, the most marked of all the aircraft trim changes. As flaps were lowered, the nose of the aircraft tended to rise quite sharply and it took all – or very nearly all – of the available elevator trim to keep the aircraft in a trimmed-out condition. To this day, I have never understood why the designer didn't go for a more conventional system.

Flaps apart, I came to like everything about the Canberra. It was quite reasonably stable in flight, so that accurate flying – either for navigation work or bombing runs – was not difficult. It was very responsive and it handled beautifully at low speed – it was very simple to make landing touchdowns into real 'greasers', when the tyres whispered gently on to the concrete. All in all, a real thoroughbred.

At the time my conversion course started, it was Bomber Command policy to operate the Canberra with a two-man crew. Before too long, this policy was changed because of the workload on the poor navigator who had to do all the navigation, operate the radar, take all the sextant shots for the astro-navigation phases and do all the bombing, both radar and visual. The navigator in those days was generally the thin one in the crew! At Bassingbourn, there was no formal system for constituting crews from the pilots and navigators on the courses. Instead, during the ground school phase, each category surreptitiously sized the others up so that, somehow or other, by the time the flying stage approached, people had paired off into prospective crews who would be able to operate together in the air.

Towards the end of the ground school phase, I found myself more and more paired with a tall 'Geordie' from Gateshead, Ken Mason. I liked his methodical approach to his job – quiet, efficient, endlessly checking everything he did. Not the type ever to make a careless mistake. When the flying assignments finally came out, Ken and I were a crew and we stayed as a crew for all the time I spent in the Canberra force. We did have a minor problem during our early days together, in that we both had what could be described as fairly pronounced regional accents. It was all right on the ground but, in the air, with the distortion of the intercom system, there were times when we couldn't understand each other too well. We got over that problem by hardly ever using the intercom at all: instead, we passed handwritten notes to each other.

During our early solo conversion flights, I was utterly distrustful of having anyone else navigate me around the place. I had done my own navigation for years without ever getting lost – well, not too lost, anyway – and I found it hard to simply sit back and let Ken get on with the job which was his professional specialty. I was forever passing him useful fixes – or so I thought – quite ignoring the fact that, from forty thousand feet, it is almost impossible for any pilot to fix his position visually within twenty miles – you simply can't see straight down because of the aircraft structure. Ken was very patient until, one day, he was forced to point out that he was navigating to limits of accuracy that my visual fixing simply couldn't match and that we would really get along a whole lot better if I simply flew the aeroplane as accurately as I could and left him to get on with the job of getting us from A to B on time. After that, while I still kept my own flight plan and maps, I kept my mouth shut. Experience proved that Ken was doing the job effectively and that I could rely on him. Although I wasn't smart enough to realise it at the time, this reliance is what flying as part of a crew is all about. You do your professional job as well as you possibly can and you rely on your colleagues to do the same. If they do, the crew functions like a smoothly meshed piece of machinery. If they don't, you start looking for a new crew.

While on this general subject of crew flying, it might be relevant to touch on the vexed question of aircraft captaincy. At the time, the Air Force regarded all multi-discipline crews as Captains and others. The pilot was invariably the Captain and the other members of the crew were regarded and referred to, not as Flying Officer Smith or Pilot Officer Jones, but as 'so and so's crew'. This applied even when members of the crew outranked the pilot. In our early transition flying, when we had an instructor on board, Ken and I had to operate the standard intercom system of calling each other by our crew function, "Navigator to Captain" or vice versa. When solo, we invariably used first names.

I never really understood the obsession of the Service with aircraft captaincy. In a good crew, the real captaincy of an aircraft varies throughout the course of a sortie. On take-off or landing, effective captaincy is vested in the pilot, the professional specialist in that field. In route flying or cross country work, effective captaincy is in the hands of the navigator. Similarly with bombing and the bomb aimer, or electronic counter measure work with the air electronics operator. I have never known a case where somebody in the crew asked the pilot whether he was lined up with the right runway or whether he ought to have his flaps down or not. These issues are the pilots' job. Equally, I have never known a pilot, told to steer 317 degrees on a navigation leg, who asked the navigator whether it shouldn't be some other course to steer, or who asked the bomb aimer, in the middle of a bombing run, whether he was quite sure he meant LEFT instead of RIGHT. In such circumstances, a crew simply could not operate at all much less operate effectively.

I recognise that, to some people, emergencies constitute a case for having a captain to determine the course of action to be followed. To my mind, however, the same situation applies as in any other flight situation. Any emergency involves one or other area of crew specialisation and, purely on the grounds of specialist knowledge if for no other reason, the appropriate crew member becomes, effectively, the crew captain in redressing the situation. Like any other pilot, I had to cope with a number of emergency situations during my flying career. Two of them were resolved by my asking the Navigator what to do – and doing it – and one was resolved by a Flight Engineer. In these cases, those crew members effectively captained the aircraft back to safety – I simply did as I was told.

In any event, with only two of us in the crew, Ken and I didn't have to bother ourselves overmuch with problems of captaincy. For the better part of two months, we flew our way through the Canberra conversion programme, doing our cross-country navigation exercises around the UK, dropping our practice bombs visually or by radar at Theddlethorpe and Chesil Bank ranges and carrying out simulated radar attacks on targets in Aberdeen and other towns and practising the new range of airfield and landing approaches made possible by the availability of aids such as Ground Controlled Approaches (GCA), Instrument Landing System (ILS), GEE, BABS, Radio Compass and Rebecca/Eureka.

At the time when we had almost reached the end of the course, there was a change in Air Ministry policy with regard to the constitution of Canberra crews. The workload on the single navigator had at last been recognised and it was decided to bring in another navigator to share the work. One of the two would act as Navigator/Plotter – the man who runs the pure navigation side of the flying – and the other would be the Navigator/Radar – responsible for radar fixing, radar and visual bombing and sextant operation.

As a result of this change in policy, Ken and I had to cast about for a new crew colleague from among the spare navigators on the unit. Eventually we fixed on Al Naismith, a plotter with a quietly professional air of competence about him and a very pleasant easy-going personality. Al had been on the previous course at Bassingbourn, from which his pilot had been suspended, so that he was waiting to be crewed-up again on the next available course. So it came about that we all got together and Ken and I had found ourselves a plotter. At least, that's what I thought at the time. Years later, Al confided to me that the selection had, in fact been entirely the other way around. After his experience with his first pilot, who had been suspended for sheer lack of ability, Al had not been at all keen to link up with another beginner. He had known Ken Mason from Navigation School and, as he put it to me, "I was looking very carefully for a pilot who wouldn't scare me out of my pants every time we got into the aircraft. I wanted someone a bit older, with a bit of experience, preferably a QFI, preferably married and preferably with a family. You were tailor made." In any event, we all did one flight together just before the course ended and we were then formally constituted as a crew and pronounced ready to launch ourselves on Bomber Command proper. We were to join Number 27 Squadron at RAF Scampton.

CHAPTER 19

NUMBER 27 SQUADRON, Royal Air Force has had a long and distinguished history in a variety of roles from the time of its formation in November 1915. Sent to France as a fighter unit, its original equipment, the Martinsyde G100 'Elephant', soon proved to lack the performance required for air combat duties, with the result that the Squadron was converted to the bombing role. In this capacity and operating the G100 and the DH4, it participated in virtually every major campaign on the Western Front until the Armistice in 1918. Disbanded in January 1920 the Squadron reformed three months later at Mianwali, India, in which country it operated its DH9 and Wapiti aircraft in the campaigns on the North-West Frontier during the twenty years up to 1939. In the Second World War, the Squadron operated Blenheims in Malaya and Java and Beaufighters and Mosquitos in India and Burma. Disbanded in 1946, the Squadron reformed a year later as part of 46 Group Transport Command, equipped with Dakota aircraft and participated in the Berlin Airlift of 1948. Disbanded again in 1950, the Squadron reformed yet again in June 1953 at RAF Scampton in Lincolnshire, as one of the front line Canberra units of RAF Bomber Command.

It was to this distinguished Squadron that Al and Ken and I attempted to report on the 6th of June 1955 after a month's leave following our graduation From Bassingbourn. I say 'attempted' advisedly, since even as simple a procedure as reporting in to our new squadron turned out to be somewhat less simple than we had at first innocently assumed. We assembled in the imposing entrance hall of the Officers Mess at Scampton, flanked by the portraits of the stations wartime VCs – Nettleton, Hannah and Gibson – and set off together for the squadron offices. Right away, we ran into our first snag; 27 Squadron was no longer at Scampton. During the period of our leave, the Squadron had been moved to nearby Waddington, some ten miles away on the other side of Lincoln. Apparently, Scampton was due to have extensive work carried out on the runways and the Squadron move to Waddington had taken place the week before we were due to report in. What a way to start a Squadron tour! A bomber crew that couldn't even find their Squadron!

When we were able to round up some transport and get ourselves across to Waddington, we went through the usual administrative arrival procedure, read all of the appropriate Order Books, drew flying kit and were duly marched in to be officially welcomed to Number 27 Squadron by the Commanding Officer. This was to be our first exposure to one of the most remarkable and complex, officers with whom I ever had the good fortune to serve.

Squadron Leader P W Helmore, DFC, AFC – known throughout the Service as 'Peter Willie' or 'PW' – was a lean, dark man of about medium height. An ex-Cranwell cadet and the son of the inventor of the Helmore light, he had flown 102 operations in Bomber Command during the height of the bomber war over Germany – including operations as a Master Bomber in the Pathfinder Force. He had about him a peculiar intensity of manner – something like a coiled spring, or a volcano on the very verge of eruption. He was urbane, charming and thoughtful and, at almost the same time, dictatorial, explosive and thoroughly unreasonable. He was a bomber man to his fingertips and ran his squadron on the premise that the enemy – any enemy – was likely to appear on the crest of the Lincolnshire Ridge first thing tomorrow morning, if not sooner. There is a tired old Air Force joke that, on any squadron, there are three ways of doing things: the Air Force way; the common sense way; and the Squadron Commanders way. On 27 Squadron, things were done Peter Willie's way – all the time and every time!

Whether he recognises it or not, every Squadron Commander develops certain minor eccentricities in dealing with the affairs of his command. In most cases, these individual idiosyncrasies are no more than minor personal foibles which, as the man in command, the Commander is relatively free to indulge. The squadron personnel simply learn to live with the Boss's way of doing things. One Squadron Commander I knew had a 'thing' about his place at the Mess Bar – a spot at the end, which was always left clear for him. On one occasion, he returned from leave to find that a glass display cabinet for sundries had been erected during his absence at the precise spot at which he was wont to hold court. Without a word, he left the Mess, to reappear, minutes later, armed with a large hammer and a saw. With these implements, he proceeded to demolish the display cabinet, the broken remains of which he pitched straight into the rubbish container. Then, back in his accustomed spot, he settled down contentedly with his drink.

Like any other Squadron Commander, Peter Willie had his share of personal idiosyncrasies. Two, in particular, had a profound influence on the way that the Squadron operated. He had a 'thing' about timekeeping – particularly with regard to take-off times – and he had a 'thing' about bringing bombs back to base. In regard to these two issues, Peter Willie went far beyond the boundaries of reasonable personal foibles; with him, the subjects could accurately be described as full-blown, almost manic, obsessions.

At Bassingbourn, I had always attempted to make my take-offs at the time scheduled in the flying programme, but the achievement of a precise time was never regarded as a 'life or death' issue. Given that Bassingbourn was a conversion unit and not the front line, anywhere within ten minutes either way was held to be quite acceptable. On a front line squadron, one would reasonably be expected to do better than that – say, within five minutes either way. On an individual sortie, five minutes could fairly easily be made up en-route to the first turning point.

Regardless of how any other squadron might have viewed the matter, in 27 Squadron a take-off time was meant to be achieved exactly; not within a few minutes either way, but absolutely precisely – to the second. Strictly speaking, even that standard wasn't good enough for Peter Willie. To him, an eight o'clock take-off didn't mean that you started your roll at eight o'clock. To him, it meant that your wheels left the ground at eight o'clock on the dot and woe betide anyone who failed to meet that standard.

For every single flight, we used to calculate, from the performance charts, the exact time required to get from the start of the take-off roll to unstick, given our aircraft weight, fuel load and bomb load and the prevailing weather conditions. Then, we would sit on the end of the runway with the navigators eyes glued to the second hand of his watch – checked within an hour of take-off with the BBC time signal – until he called, "x seconds to unstick, brakes off"; "y seconds to unstick, power up"; and then, as the second hand ticked round to the top, "unstick" – the last frequently in a sort of strangled shriek if we looked like being a second or two out. At this point, the pilot hauled back and attempted to get the aircraft into the air – however unwilling it might be at the time.

On any occasion when Peter Willie wasn't flying himself, he could be absolutely counted on to be sitting in his Land Rover, just off the runway at somewhere around the unstick point, with his own watch – also checked against the BBC time signal – in his hand, logging the exact time that your wheels left Mother Earth. Within five seconds and you would probably get away with an offhand remark about getting the navigators watch replaced; outside five seconds and it was a full scale crew dressing down; outside ten seconds, it was a 'stand to attention on the carpet' professional reprimand; outside fifteen seconds and you got the impression that you had undermined the integrity of the Squadron, Bomber Command and the Royal Air Force, made a signal contribution to the downfall of the British Commonwealth and, almost single handedly, destroyed the moral fabric of the Western democratic way of life. You almost expected to be offered the opportunity to 'do the honourable thing' with a service revolver somewhere in a quiet part of the Mess gardens.

Regardless of how one regarded this particular mania, it certainly made every crew in 27 Squadron into excellent timekeepers. Day in and day out, we made our take-offs and landings with a precision that would have made any commercial airline green with envy. This strict – not to say obsessional – punctuality meant that we were generally the first Bomber Command squadron to get airborne for our routine daily bombing runs. We were generally over the ranges, carrying out dummy runs, when the ranges came on the radio and announced that they were ready for business. This call was invariably followed, almost instantly, by a call from a 27 Squadron aircraft, "running up for first attack," and the first bomb would go down within a matter of minutes. Most of the other squadrons hadn't even thought about getting airborne by then.

Peter Willie's other mania concerned bringing bombs back from a sortie. I always wondered if some incident in his operational career had led him so utterly to reject the idea of ever returning to base with an unexpended store still on board. On some occasions, it was downright difficult to get rid of all your bombs, but no explanation or excuse ever came near to placating 'PW'. One got the impression that if it were ever a choice between dropping bombs anywhere over the United Kingdom, or bringing them back to Waddington, then it was going to be a case of 'look out below'.

Our big problem in this connection was bomb bay icing. After the Canberra had been at altitude for any length of time, the bomb bay became very cold indeed – the temperature at 45000 feet, according to the International Standard Atmosphere, is minus fifty-six and a half degrees Centigrade. In such conditions, it was not uncommon for ice to form between the bomb and the retaining crutch. When the release button was operated, the release micro-switch and bomb hook would function normally and the bomb would be 'released' – but it would remain firmly in place, iced-up solidly to the retaining crutch. There was no way for the crew to know that this had happened and the Range could only report, "no bomb observed." Later when the aircraft descended into warmer air, the ice would melt and the bomb would fall off and roll about in the bottom of the bomb bay. Sometimes you could hear it, or even feel it, but there was nothing you could do about it anyway, since there was no access to the bomb bay in flight.

The problem didn't normally arise during our multiple-run practice attacks on the bombing ranges, because the aircraft was generally relatively warm at the start of the practice and we were not usually at altitude for long enough for internal icing to form to any significant extent. On 'first run' attacks, however, we flew a whole high altitude navigation profile before we went in to drop our one and only bomb. Worse still, on this sort of sortie we generally let down directly from high altitude into the circuit for landing – giving little time for the warmer air at lower levels to affect the temperature in the bomb bay. On such occasions, if you did have a hang-up, the first you knew of it was when you shut down in dispersal. On opening the bomb bay doors, either the bomb fell out, causing alarm and despondency all round, or it would still be there on the crutch surrounded by a mess of rapidly thawing ice. When this did happen, Peter Willie would erupt from his office at high speed in a towering fury, bearing down remorselessly on the ashen faced crew huddled beside the evidence of their infamy. Then it was another 'striking at the roots of democracy' performance.

Most of us quickly developed a quite unofficial technique to fall back on in the event of a suspected hang-up. If we had sufficient fuel – and we generally had – we would let down over the sea and then fly about at high speed for ten minutes or so at low altitude to warm the aircraft up. Then we would open the bomb doors and throw the aircraft about fairly violently to dislodge anything that might still be stuck on in the bomb bay. I know that I got rid of at least a couple myself this way. Not in accordance with Bomber Command procedures perhaps, but I didn't want to take any chance of a face-to-face confrontation with 'PW' with a hang-up still on the aircraft or, worse still, lying on the ramp.

In the event of failure of the radar during radar-bombing attacks, we adopted a 'fall-back' technique – or, at least, I did. In these cases, I would listen out on the range radio frequency for another aircraft on its way in to attack, then position myself to fly close formation behind it. When its bomb doors opened, ours opened: when its bombs left the aircraft, ours were right behind them. Sometimes I felt that the range were a bit suspicious about two "bombs away" calls coming so close together, but the technique got the job done – even if you seldom got even a decent result out of it. You got the bombs within the range area and that was all that mattered. Oddly enough, one of the few direct hits I was credited with came as a result of this technique. It was on a night exercise first run attack with one live thousand pounder on a range at – well, I'd better not say. I had lost most of the electrics, including the radar, en-route to the target. With about a hundred miles to go, I picked up an aircraft heading for the target area and locked on to the jet efflux from its engines. Closing up, I could just about make out the bomb doors in the faint moonlight. When he bombed, we let ours go. His bomb was reported as an undershoot; ours a direct hit. As soon as he called "bombs gone," I realized that I had been formating on 'PW' himself. Later, having congratulated me on a good attack, he added, frostily, "you must have been ahead of time; you were almost right up my back at the release point. You really must watch this timing more carefully." I was almost tempted to tell him that I got a better result out of his bombing run than he did himself.

In later years, I often used to wonder how much of Peter Willie's eccentricities were a true part of his character and how much was assumed as an aid to him getting the job done the way he wanted it to be done. At the time when he assumed command of the squadron, Bomber Command had experienced some nine years of peace and, inevitably, some elements of a 'peace-time' atmosphere had got into the way of doing things. Not for 'PW' though. His way was to run a Squadron that was always prepared to go to war – and to go to war efficiently. Not tomorrow or next week, but now, immediately, this very minute. At the end of the day, it is results that count and which demonstrate how well or how poorly a Commander is doing his job. During Peter Willie's time, 27 Squadron consistently flew more hours, dropped more bombs and achieved better results than any other squadron in the Command. Eccentric in some respects it may have been, but Peter Willie's way wasn't such a bad way after all.

Very shortly after I had arrived on the Squadron, I was involved in two incidents which brought home to me very forcibly the unpredictability of Peter Willie's response to any given situation. On the first occasion, I was flying an eight bomb visual drop sortie at a barge target at Wainfleet Range in the Wash. We had got one bomb away and were having great difficulty in getting our second run completed. First, the range radar went unserviceable for a time. Then, there was trouble with the range radio and then there was difficulty with the bomb plot system. It seemed that every time we got into our run-up, something or other would go wrong to force an abort. Even when everything was working perfectly, some aircraft on a first run attack – which carried priority on the ranges – would appear to send us round again on yet another dummy run. We went round and round, again and again, in a dispiriting sequence of one abort after another.

At the time, I suppose that I was still consciously resentful of having been sent to Bomber Command instead of to fighters. I missed the variety and excitement of Meteor flying, compared with which the bomber routine of long, straight line, high altitude, cross-countries and interminable bombing practice seemed, to me, to be tedious and uneventful in the extreme. As we droned round and round the range and one unfinished attack succeeded another, I slipped all too readily into the state at mind when I was almost looking for some way to relieve the monotony by some act or other which had a bit at spirit in it. While I was brooding in this somewhat rebellious mood, the Range came up on the radio to call me in for my next attack. Fatally, the controller added, "please try to make it snappy. We have a lot of aircraft waiting to use the range."

For me, that last remark did it. Snappy he wanted; snappy he'd get. Disregarding Kens' directions, I dropped down to a couple of hundred feet and pushed the speed up to something over three hundred and fifty knots as we tore in towards the target. As the barge flashed by under the nose, I hauled the Canberra up into a slow loop, topping out at about three thousand feet. Coming over the top into a vertical dive, with the barge target directly underneath, I popped the dive-brakes and opened the bomb doors and, at the very last minute before I had to start the pull-out, punched the pilots' bomb release button to let all seven remaining bombs go at once. Although I say it myself, it wasn't too shabby for a first-time dive bombing attack. Much later, I learned that three of the seven bombs actually impacted on the target.

I didn't see anything of the result of my attack. I was far too busy pulling out of the dive and getting the aircraft back to altitude. The thrill of the dive attack was fading very fast and I was, even then, uncomfortably aware that I had gone rather too far with my uncharacteristic impulsiveness – a viewpoint which seemed to be confirmed when the Range Controller came up on the radio with a direct order to "clear the range at once and return to base IMMEDIATELY." I had little doubt that his next conversation was going to be with the station authorities at Waddington.

During the flight back to Waddington, I had plenty of time to consider just how far I had overstepped the mark. Whatever else might have been said about Bomber Command, it was a highly disciplined organisation and it was unlikely that my exploit – which amounted to rank flying indiscipline – would be treated lightly. I was uncomfortably well aware that pilots had been court martialled for less. More immediately, however and infinitely more terrifying, I knew that I would have Peter Willie to contend with when I got down. He would go absolutely hairless when he learned what I had been up to. Bad enough for one of his squadrons pilots to have been guilty of flying indiscipline – but to have deliberately flouted Command, Group, Station and Range Safety Orders into the bargain! The prospect didn't bear thinking about.

Somewhat to my astonishment, I was not immediately carpeted when I got back on the ground. Instead, Eric Senior, the Flight Commander, told me to go home at once – Jean and I were living in Married Quarters at Scampton at the time – and to report formally to the CO at ten o'clock the following morning. I spent a thoroughly miserable night at home, gloomily reflecting that 'PW' was probably giving himself time to prepare my discharge papers before he had me in.

At ten the following morning, in best blue uniform and quaking in my shoes, I was formally marched in to face PW. He had me sit down – which surprised me – then told me that I must have been well aware that my exploit at Wainfleet would, inevitably, be reported back to Waddington. As a result of his discussions with the Station Commander, he had been directed to deal with the matter – at least initially – at squadron level and to take such action as seemed to him to be appropriate in the circumstances. I braced myself. "I have decided," he said quietly. "to take no further action. Everybody is entitled to one piece of stupidity in their time – and you've had yours. As far as I'm concerned, the matter is now closed."

I could hardly believe what I was hearing. He was letting me off the hook. I nearly collapsed from the sheer relief!

Leaning back in his chair, Peter Willie went on in the same quiet, level tone, "Harry, I didn't decide lightly to let the matter drop. I knew that your preference was to go to fighters rather than to Bomber Command. I know that you've been involved in a lot of display aerobatics and formation team flying. More importantly to me – and to this Command – I know from your records that you have ability and experience in jet flying – more jet experience than a lot of the pilots in Bomber Command just now. I could use your experience and I could use your ability – but only if I could count on them being applied one hundred percent to the role for which this squadron exists."

"If I can't rely on that, then all the experience and ability in the world is of no value to me."

"I hope that you didn't think," he went on, "that anybody here was going to be impressed with your little bit of fancy flying. We're not. What impresses us here is navigation accuracy, bombing accuracy, timing accuracy – the things that really matter to this squadron. If you could show us better results in these areas than anybody else, then we might be impressed. Not otherwise"

He paused for a moment or two to let his point sink in, before he continued, "what you have to do now is think very seriously about what you want to do with your flying. As I've said, I could use your experience here and I'd be happy if you could feel that you wanted to stay. But, if you do, I'm going to need a total commitment from you to the role of this Squadron – and, to that role alone. If you honestly feel that you can't give me that commitment, then I will personally see to it that you are posted immediately to Fighter Command for the next conversion course at Stradishall. Now, take as long as you need to think things over and then let me know what you want to do."

When he had finished speaking, my mind was in an absolute turmoil. I had come into the office fully expecting to be roasted and probably severely disciplined, for what I now recognised as a rather silly piece of bravado. More than anything else, I felt genuinely ashamed – ashamed of behaving like some small, spoiled child, stamping and kicking up a fuss to draw attention to himself – showing off, really. Perhaps more importantly, I had also had a chance to recognise something of the quality of the man on the other side of the desk. Peter Willie knew me a lot better than I knew myself. If he had stormed at me, I was just stupid enough to have stormed back – and that would have been the end of my career, right there and then. Instead, he had got me off the hook on which I had hung myself and simply given me a chance to look at my behaviour fairly objectively – and I wasn't very proud of what I saw.

Maybe I hadn't wanted to come to bombers, but that was no excuse for not giving it my best shot. Even as I digested PW's staggering offer to have me posted to Fighter Command, I realised that I could never take him up on it. It would have smacked too much of the easy way out – dodging the gentle challenge he had hung out to prove myself capable in the bomber business. Maybe I never would impress him or anybody else with my results on the squadron but, even if I didn't, the least I could do was ensure that it wouldn't be for want of trying. I stood up and said firmly, "Thank you, Sir. If you'll have me, I'd like to stay."

As I left the office, my whole attitude to Bomber Command had undergone an abrupt, complete and permanent change. In the course of that one short interview, I had become what I was to remain for the rest of my flying days – first and foremost, a bomber pilot. I owe it to Peter Willie Helmore that I ever had the chance.

CHAPTER 20

NOT VERY LONG AFTER this incident, I was detailed to fly an Air Commodore, who had been visiting the station, back to his home base at another airfield in the South of England. He was a qualified Canberra pilot so, as a matter of courtesy, he was allowed to fly the aircraft on the trip down. Although I was the designated captain of the aircraft, I rode in the folding 'rumble' seat in the aisle to the right of the pilots' ejector seat. The flight down passed off uneventfully but when we got into the circuit at our destination it became obvious that the Air Commodore was somewhat out of practice and was having real difficulty in getting us on to the ground. The runway was relatively short for a Canberra and there was a gusty crosswind blowing quite strongly.

On the first two approaches, the Air Commodore never really got the aircraft set up properly to 'crab' in to the runway centreline. We did a lot of last minute weaving about as we approached touchdown, with the speed getting altogether too low for my peace of mind. When we did actually get on to the centreline, we were too far down the runway to have landed safely and we had to go around from both attempts. On the third approach, I had to point out urgently that the speed was again dangerously low and suggest that we overshoot once more. On the fourth try, we were again drifting very markedly across the runway as we entered the pre-touchdown phase. If we had touched down, we would have been quite likely to write off the undercarriage, so I told him quite bluntly to go around yet again.

As we got back to circuit height, I honestly felt that I couldn't let him go any further with his attempts to land. The four tries he had made had convinced me that I simply could not have any confidence in his ability to get us down safely in the prevailing circumstances. I tried to sugar the pill by suggesting that he might not be used to our particular mark of the Canberra and that I would take over for the landing. The Air Commodore didn't like this idea one little bit and made his views on the matter abundantly clear. He was in the drivers' seat and he would do the landing. At this point, I was left with no choice. I felt that he was simply not capable of making a safe landing in the conditions and the safety of the aircraft – and the crew – was my responsibility. I swallowed hard and said firmly, "Sir, as the captain of this aircraft, I am assuming control on an issue of flight safety. Please be good enough to change seats."

Fortunately for me, the Air Force orders on responsibility in the air are absolutely unequivocal. Regardless of the rank of any person on board, the authority of the designated aircraft captain is paramount and unchallengeable. It was my trump card and I had absolutely no hesitation in playing it. After all, I was strapped into the aeroplane too. There was nothing the Air Commodore could do. Obviously very angry, he got out of the seat and, in a very strained atmosphere, I got myself strapped in and went on to make the landing. When we got to the flight line, the Air Commodore climbed out without a word, threw his luggage into the staff car waiting for him and drove off, very tight-lipped.

On the way back to Waddington, I was really concerned at the unfortunate turn of events. I knew within myself that I had been right; I had been forced into the only course of action open to me. At the same time, I knew equally well that, in any head-to-head confrontation with an Air ranking officer, a Flying Officer is going to have to be very right – and very lucky – to come out unscathed.

When I landed, I went in to inform Peter Willie of what had happened. While I was in his office, the telephone rang – the Air Commodore on the other end of the line. Although I couldn't make out any of the conversation from the other end, I could hear that what was being said was being said loud enough to indicate that the speaker was pretty well steamed up. Peter Willie heard it out to the end before he spoke himself. Then, very quietly, but very succinctly, he replied. "Air Commodore, I very much regret that this incident ever occurred. However, I must make it quite clear to you that I have absolute confidence in Flying Officer Archer's judgment on any matter relating to the safety of his aircraft. If he says there was a flight safety hazard, then there was – and that is all there is to it. I entirely endorse his action in assuming control of the aircraft and I have nothing further to say on the matter." Quite calmly, he then replaced the telephone receiver, dismissed me with a nodded, "that's all, Harry," and bent back to the paperwork on his desk.

I never heard another word about the affair. Peter Willie's immediate and unqualified backing of my action probably nipped any potential problems in the bud. I learned something about command that day. Peter Willie knew perfectly well that he could be bringing a lot of trouble on himself by backing my action so unreservedly – even Squadron Leaders don't lightly enter into confrontations with Air Commodores. In spite of the possible consequences, he backed me unhesitatingly and to the hilt. For him, loyalty really was a two-way principle. When one of his Squadron needed it, it was there. Peter Willie was an undoubted character and he often did things in ways that seemed to the rest of us to be maddening, unreasonable, or even just plain daft. But, none of us ever doubted his quality, or his integrity. We were lucky to have him as the Boss.

CHAPTER 21

AFTER OUR INITIAL INTERVIEW with Peter Willie, Al and Ken and I got down to the task of bringing ourselves up to operational standard on the Squadron. In those days, Bomber Command operated a Crew Classification Scheme by which crews were allocated a Command Category appropriate to their demonstrated ability and experience. At the bottom of the Classification ladder were the new crews – like ourselves – who had not been in the Command long enough to produce sufficient results for assessment. At this stage, the crew was rated as 'non-operational' and was very much on probation in the Squadron.

When sufficient routine training and participation in the Commands periodic exercises, had been completed to permit analysis of the results achieved, the crew would be formally examined by the Bomber Command Standardisation Unit which was responsible for the implementation of the Classification scheme. If the appropriate standards were achieved, then the crew would be categorised as a 'combat' rated crew. Thereafter, assuming that results continued to improve, a crew could, with increasing experience, continue up the classification ladder through 'combat star' and 'select' to the pinnacle of demonstrated professional capability at 'select star' rating – a classification held by very few crews indeed and them the acknowledged 'aces' of the Command.

In addition to the crew rating, each individual crew member was categorised in his own professional specialty. No crew could hold a crew classification higher than the category of its lowest rated member. In some ways, this was considered to be unfair, in that it was theoretically possible to have two crew members rated at, say, 'select' or even 'select star', while the overall crew classification was set at 'combat' – the category held by the third and least capable, member of the team. Moreover, while it was relatively difficult to go up the ladder by consistently achieving the higher standards required, it only took one bad result, or a single below par performance by one man during a standardisation flight, to bring you down the ladder again.

While the system was often criticised, it did achieve two very worthwhile objectives. First, it provided the planners at Bomber Command with a very accurate and proven, assessment of the true operational capability of the crews in the Command. Second, it provided every squadron member with a very strong incentive to work for the highest standard he could possibly attain in his own area of specialisation. No one ever wanted to be the one who let the crew down. In a very real sense, the crew became more important than the individual.

Because of the nature of Bomber Commands operations, with its constant emphasis on crew performance, the individual crew members were drawn together in a very special way. They trained together, planned together, flew together, played together and partied together. Inevitably, they grew very close. Because, quite literally, their lives depended on one another, they developed fierce and unquestioning crew loyalties, bred out of many working hours in the air together and nurtured by a hard-earned confidence in each other's ability. You can't 'talk a good game' in the air flying with a crew. Pilot, navigator, or whatever, you have to prove your ability and earn the respect and trust of your fellow crew members by your performance – and by your performance alone. There is simply no other way.

Right from the start of our tour, I was very conscious that I had been lucky indeed to have got myself crewed-up with Al and Ken. Although we were, in some respects, very different personalities, we seemed to have much the same basic approach to the job. Quite simply, we aimed to be methodical, thorough and painstaking – a way of going about the job that suited our working personalities. At all times, we did everything we could to eliminate mistakes in our work – particularly mistakes which could be avoided by cross-checking each other. In flight planning, for example, it was Al's responsibility to produce the navigation flight plan, Ken's to produce the radar fixing and astro navigation schedule and mine to produce the fuel and aircraft performance planning. While most crews were happy to leave each man to look after his own area of responsibility, it was our invariable practice to produce duplicates of each planning element. I prepared a duplicate navigation plan, Al a duplicate radar and astro schedule and Ken a duplicate fuel and performance plan. In this way, we could compare the two independently produced copies of each planning document and ensure that the figures in each tallied exactly.

Some other crews used to think that we were mad to load ourselves with this extra work, or that we really didn't trust each other. We didn't see it that way at all. On ninety nine point nine percent of occasions, the two versions came out identical, so that, in one way, you could say that the work had been wasted. But we were looking for the one case in a thousand when the two versions didn't agree – and, in that case, we had avoided getting into the air with an error in our planning. We will never know whether, if we had used a different system, we would ever have got airborne with an error and, if so, whether that error would have got us into difficulty. What we do know, however, is that we didn't and, at the end of our squadron tour, we walked away to our next postings still in one piece and functioning reasonably normally. To me, at any rate, that fact justifies our way of doing things up to the hilt.

For much the same sort of reasons, we backed each other up in the air by cross-checking our performance as much as we possibly could. Al and Ken monitored each other and they both monitored me. On instrument approaches, for example, Al used to maintain a continuous quiet readout of our airspeed from his indicator and Ken did the same for our altitude. Other pilots who flew with us used to laugh that I was 'navigator-ridden', but I liked to feel that we were all involved in getting down safely and I found the back-seat monitoring a valuable back-up to my routine scanning of the blind-flying instrument panel. I was confident of my ability to fly accurate instrument approaches, but I was very well aware that a bad weather approach for real often involves coping with combinations of unpleasant conditions – rain, low cloud, turbulence and cross-winds. In these circumstances, with the aircraft lurching about all over the place and the ground getting closer by the second, I was always happy to use all the help that I could get.

Still on instrument approaches, at night I always used to have Ken come forward and sit beside me on the 'rumble' seat, so that he could look out for the approach lights and leave me free to concentrate exclusively on the instrument panel. In the latter stages of a bad weather approach, as you near break-off altitude, there is an almost irresistible temptation to come off instruments for a quick peek ahead for a sight of the approach lights. If you do this a few times, alternating between the instrument panel and the world outside, it is not difficult to become somewhat disorientated – and any disorientation can be downright dangerous in such a situation. With Ken up front to do the lookout for me, I could stay very firmly on instruments without any temptation to look up until he called "approach lights clearly visible." Then I could look up to pick up the lights and go ahead with a straightforward visual landing.

We developed a lot of our individual crew techniques during our initial squadron flying, when we were trying to put together the results necessary to qualify us for an operational crew classification. During our first six weeks, we flew off the required sorties until, in due course and with satisfactory results posted on the squadron crew record board, we were duly examined by the Standardisation Unit and rated as a 'combat' category crew. With our formal certification, we became an operationally qualified crew in the front line main force of Bomber Command and our squadron tour started in earnest.

With classification, we entered into the day-to-day routine of main force operations. We flew long range navigation sorties, sometimes ranging far afield over Norway or Germany. To simulate possible operational conditions, we frequently made these navigation sorties using only limited navigation aids, or by fixing our position solely by astro-navigation. It took real concentration to fly a Canberra steadily enough to give the navigator a chance to get a good star 'shot' with his sextant. Even very slight deviations from the set heading or airspeed could throw the resultant fix miles out of position. I got a very pointed lesson in how important accurate flying was to the navigator when Ken had me take a few sextant shots myself – firmly on the ground, with the sextant immobile on a fixed mount in the Mess gardens. Out of eight tries at star shots, I got only one which put us in Lincolnshire!

We continued our standard practice bombing exercises on visual and radar ranges all over the country. With eight twenty five pound practice bombs aboard, it could take quite a long sortie to get all eight runs in – particularly on radar attacks when we might be starting our run-in from as far away as a hundred miles from the target. We did a lot of simulated attacks on real target complexes in various towns – Aberdeen docks, I remember, seemed to be a favourite target location. In these attacks, the aircraft position at the instant of bomb release was very accurately recorded by one of the ground radar bomb plot units, so that it was possible to calculate fairly precisely where your weapon would have impacted. On return to base, you would find your impact point plotted on a photograph of your target. Somehow, these simulated attacks always seemed more realistic to me than our routine range exercises when we were actually dropping real bombs – perhaps because it was easier to imagine attacking this sort of target for real, rather than the barges or simple geographic locations that we bombed on the ranges.

With increasing experience, we practised more and more first run attacks, when you flew a long navigation leg before going in to deliver the one and only bomb on board. These first run attacks could be quite demanding exercises. Any error during the navigation stage and you could be pushed to be in position to make your attack precisely on time: any slip during the final run-in to the target and you could completely negate the couple of hours work that had got you to that point. The aims of the exercises were always the same: accuracy in track keeping; accuracy in timing; and accuracy in weapon delivery.

As we became more and more familiar with the operational routine, we worked up to flying sorties at our full war mission all-up weight – with a capacity fuel load on board and six live one thousand pound bombs in the bomb bay. Periodically, we carried out live drops at selected ranges. If the weather conditions were favourable, you would sometimes see the flashes as the weapons detonated far below. At all events, you could always feel the characteristic lurch as the bombs left the aircraft – when all six were dropped together in one stick, the aircraft became instantaneously something like three tons lighter.

The basic techniques which we used and, indeed, the whole operational concept of the use of the bomber force stemmed from the experience gained by Bomber Command over Germany during World War Two. In the face of determined and effective defences, it was learned that any prolonged stream type of attack could – and probably would – incur unacceptable losses. To minimize the attrition rate, it became necessary to saturate the target defences by pushing as many aircraft as possible through the target area in the shortest possible time. By day, this could be done by flying in tight formations – as the United States Air Force did – but, at night, or in adverse weather conditions, this tactic was simply not possible. The only way to achieve the objective was to co-ordinate the flight plans of all the individual aircraft involved, so as to form them into a tightly packed 'box' and then to have each aircraft hold its allocated position in the box by rigid adherence to its assigned track, height and timing. In exercises, we often operated as part of a force several hundred aircraft strong. When one considers that Bomber Command did it under real war conditions with a thousand or more aircraft on a raid, one gets some idea of the rigid flying discipline and accurate flying that made the technique work.

I vividly remember our first participation in a major night Command exercise when the whole of the main force was involved. We took off in a squadron stream to head towards the force assembly area, at which point, in accordance with normal procedure, we switched off our navigation lights, Thereafter, we were completely on our own, in our private little piece of the night sky, with no sign of any other aircraft about us. At the end of the sortie, as we approached the Force Dispersal Point, dawn was just about breaking. As it slowly became lighter, I began to make out the shapes of other aircraft flying close beside us – at first, only one or two, then more and more by the minute; ahead, behind, above, below and off to both sides. Very soon, I could see that I was right in the middle of the biggest Balbo I had ever flown in – each aircraft operating completely independently, yet held safely together purely and simply by the crews ability to fly their flight plan tracks and timings accurately. After that experience, nobody ever had to convince me that our practice sorties were worth the effort.

One of the few perks of being an operationally qualified crew was that you became eligible to be allocated an occasional 'Lone Ranger' flight. These were overseas navigation exercises during which you were allowed to spend a few days at your destination before returning to the UK. Apart from providing a useful opportunity for the crew to gain some experience of overseas deployment and operating from an unfamiliar base, they were a very welcome break from the daily training routine. As a combat category crew, we qualified for Ranger flights to Germany and to Malta. 'Combat Star' and other higher category crews were eligible for destinations such as Cyprus and other more exotic locations.

The Malta Ranger, which provided a welcome opportunity to soak up some sunshine and warmer weather, was always a favourite with the crews. In those days, the whole economy and life of Valetta, if not the entire Island, seemed to revolve around the servicing of the ships of the Mediterranean Fleet. When the Fleet was in town and the Jolly Jack Tars came ashore in force, Valetta became a very lively spot indeed. The cafes and bars were packed to overflowing, impromptu street parties were in full swing all over the town and the night life was brash, noisy and non-stop.

On more sedate occasions, I used to like the Phoenicia hotel at the top of Kingsway and the City Gem restaurant in Sliema, where the proprietor always had a bit of a soft spot for the RAF. I had many very pleasant dinners on the open-air terrace dining room of the Phoenicia, looking out over Grand Harbour, with all the running lights of the ships in the port twinkling in the darkness. We also did the standard 'tourist' visits – to Rabat – there was a very good restaurant there called the Griffon, – to St Pauls Bay, to Melheia Bay and to the small island of Gozo off the North coast. We played golf at the Marsa and wasted our money backing losers at the racecourse there.

Every now and again and always against our better judgment, we became involved in a nights foray to Strait Street – an area of very dubious night club establishments just off Kingsway and known throughout the service world as 'The Gut'. Definitely not the sort of place to take your maiden aunt. A night out in the Gut for us started almost invariably at the Rexford at the top end of the street, where the girls wore evening dresses and didn't actually molest the customers physically. From there, as the night progressed, you went down – literally as well as metaphorically – to take in such other more robust establishments as The Egyptian Queen and The New Life, where the girls didn't and did. At the bottom end of the Gut, there were only two rules to be observed by the prudent visitor: keep your eye on your drink and your hand on your wallet. Anyone who didn't stood a better than even chance of returning to consciousness sometime next day in thoroughly unfamiliar surroundings, very drunk, very ill and very, very, poor. I regret to have to say that the experience was not entirely unknown.

With these sorts of activities to fill our days, we worked our way steadily through our squadron tour of duty. I came to love crew flying passionately and to appreciate the level of skill and commitment that was necessary to make every flight go off smoothly and produce good results. To operate as part of a good crew is, I believe, one of the most rewarding experiences in flying. Obviously, in most cases, the job could be done by any three aircrew arbitrarily lumped together for the occasion. But to do the job with real finesse, to plan and operate to the best of your individual capabilities and to deal effectively with the difficulties and problems which arise From time to time, you really have to know your fellow crew members and their way of working, as they have to know you. Oddly enough,

Strategic Air Command of the United States Air Force went through a period when they actively discouraged the formal constitution of crews. Their experience led them to the view that crew members could become emotionally over-dependent on one another to the detriment of mission accomplishment and they preferred to make up crews from the available squadron personnel on a strictly ad-hoc basis.

I believe, personally, that they were wrong and I am very glad that the RAF never adopted the idea. If we were ever to get ourselves into any sort of difficult situation in the air, I always wanted to feel that I would know and be able to rely on, the ability of my colleagues to do their part to get us out. You don't develop that sort of confidence and trust flying with relative strangers – no matter how good they might be. It is knowing them – really knowing them – that makes the difference.

I have often been asked what sort of work we actually did on a squadron to fill in our time. Everybody knows that flying was the primary occupation but, to be fair, you can't spend every minute of the day in the air. I have often run across the impression that our non-airborne hours were spent lounging about the crew room, playing cards, drinking coffee and generally revelling in the joys of idleness.

Needless to say, it wasn't quite like that. It is difficult to arrive at a figure of working hours available because, by the very nature of the job, squadrons don't work rigidly set hours. Nevertheless, if one works on an average of eight hours a day for five and a half days a week, there would be something like a hundred and seventy six working hours to be filled during the average month. We flew about fifteen sorties – or something like forty five flying hours – most months when the weather was reasonable – and, with our radio and radar aids, the weather could be regarded as reasonable most of the time. Hence, there were – at least on the face of it – about a hundred and thirty hours of non-flying time available during the average month.

Of course, such a simplistic assessment takes no account of the fact that any flying sortie actually takes up much more time than that spent in the air. Long before take-off time, you have to attend for mission and weather briefing. Then, you have to complete your mission planning during which every aspect of your projected sortie has to be prepared in meticulous detail – routeing, timings, navigation fixes, navigation aids, navigation and radar bombing fix points, star selections for astro work, signals and communications channels and frequencies, fuel load and projected consumption rates, best aircraft cruising altitude and other performance parameters, diversion airfields and a host of other essential planning elements. That done, you have to draw and check your flying clothing and personal safety equipment, get a bite to eat if you're lucky – if not, you're stuck with sandwiches and chocolate bars in the air – and get out to the flight line. There, you go over the relevant documentation to check the aircraft service-ability record and current outstanding 'snags', confirm the fuel and weapons load and assure yourself that all the trades involved in preparing the aircraft for flight have signed-off for their work. If all is well, then you can actually get out to the aircraft to conduct your external pre-flight inspection – a miserable task on a wet and windy night – after which, you are free, finally, to climb aboard.

Once aboard, you begin the systematic check of the aircraft equipment and controls. If anything is not functioning properly, this is the time to find it out – not when you're at forty thousand feet on a dark and dirty night. Every system and every piece of operational equipment that can be tested on the ground, is gone over carefully to ensure that it is working correctly. Any snag is immediately tackled by the specialist ground crew to attempt 'on-the-spot' rectification and a prudent aircrew will always get to their aircraft early enough to allow plenty of time for such last-minute rectification work to be completed in time to make the scheduled take-off.

When, at last, you are actually ready to start engines and get the flight underway, you will probably have already put in something like three to four hours at work – and all of it work that has to be done carefully and thoroughly – to prepare for the sortie properly. In pre-flight preparation, any sloppiness or short-cutting is fraught with potential danger.

Even after you land, the sortie is far from over. The ground crew have to start preparing the aircraft for the next flight, so it is essential to review with them every detail of the aircrafts performance and the functioning of the equipment. Every snag has to be carefully defined so that they can have a clear idea of the problem when they set about rectification. Moreover, every ground crew I have ever known have a real pride in 'their' aircraft and it is little enough reward for their hard work for the aircrew to take time to involve them in the results of the sortie.

Back at the squadron, you are debriefed on the sortie in great detail and conduct a preliminary assessment of your results. You check back with the meteorological section to advise them of the weather conditions actually experienced during flight, so that they can, if necessary, re-assess and update their forecasts. When your debriefing sequence is complete, you are free to shower and change, get something to eat if the Mess is still serving meals, have a beer to help you unwind and, finally, call it a day. If, at that point, you check your watch, you will probably find that you have been on the go for something like nine or ten hours.

On days when you are not scheduled to fly, there is generally plenty to do to keep you out of mischief. You spend a lot of time in the flight simulator, flying practice sorties and practising the sort of emergency drills which you can't reasonably carry out in the air – engine fire drills and explosive decompression are good examples. You practise ejection seat operation – sometimes on the rig which fires you up a ramp on a much reduced cartridge charge. You practise crash landing and ditching drills in a cockpit rig and you practise sea survival – getting rid of your parachute and harness and operating your one-man dinghy – in a local swimming pool. Periodically, you are sent to Plymouth to be thrown off a launch into the English Channel to rehearse these drills in a real sea environment. Almost invariably, it seemed, these exercises were conducted in the middle of winter, when the shock of going off the launch into a very cold and unfriendly sea could be absolutely numbing. Even after you got into the dinghy, the cold and the non-stop rolling motion ensured that you were miserable beyond words. You were wretchedly and comprehensively seasick and you learned the hard way just how difficult it is to get yourself organised and operate your survival equipment when you feel that oblivion would be a merciful release. The only thing I have ever experienced worse than a one-man dinghy is a multi-crew dinghy in which, apart from being unutterably miserable yourself, you have to watch your companions being ill all over the place non-stop. Very few people indeed have the stomach for that sort of experience.

Away from the flying side of things, most of the junior members of a squadron are assigned some station or squadron secondary duty, to enable them to gain experience of the running of the service in a wider sense. These secondary duties are very important to a young officer's career, in that they often provide the only opportunity for his flight and squadron commanders to assess his capability and commitment in a non-flying activity. With detailed formal assessments being completed annually on his performance as an Air Force Officer overall and not only on his performance in his specialist aircrew capacity, the secondary duty is an important part of the young officers responsibility and provides him with the opportunity to demonstrate his adaptablity and capability in a wider context. Performance in secondary duties is invariably taken very seriously into account by promotion boards when assessing a junior officer's suitability for advancement.

In addition to secondary duties, all young officers of those days had to make themselves eligible for promotion by sitting various promotion examinations which were held twice a year. As I remember, the 'B' examination qualified you for promotion to Flight Lieutenant and the 'C' to Squadron Leader. Additionally, by the time you made Flight Lieutenant, you were probably starting to think ahead to Staff College, for which you had to undertake the 'Q', or Staff College Qualifying, Examination. Of course, success in the appropriate examinations was not, in itself, any guarantee of promotion. All it did was make you eligible for consideration by the Promotion Board. If your annual assessments were not up to the mark, then there would be no promotion – no matter how many examinations you had passed. Promotions were promulgated twice yearly and each list normally provided at least a couple of people on a station with good cause for a celebration party. Unhappily, because the number of promotion candidates always far exceeded the number of promotion vacancies at any rank level, there were always many more people destined to have to fall back on yet another 'Feast of The Passover' party.

With all of this sort of activity going on, it is fair to say that we were kept fairly well occupied during our squadron tours. Obviously, spare time was available and we did lounge about crew rooms, we did drink coffee and we did play a lot of cards, chess and other games – I became quite a useful crew-room bridge player on 27 Squadron – but there wasn't nearly as much unoccupied time as outsiders seemed to imagine. And, when you were working, you were working fairly hard, so that you seldom had any compunction about having an hour or two off when it was available. Rightly or wrongly, you felt that you had earned it.

CHAPTER 22

I SUPPOSE THAT IF YOU collected together all the members of a squadron who had served together at one time and then asked them for their recollections of the period, you would get as many different answers as you had people assembled. Apart from the really major issues which affected everyone, you would find that each person remembers most vividly those events which involved himself, or the crew of which he was a part, or those occasions which, for one reason or another, were important to them as individuals. In this respect, looking back on the time I spent with 27 Squadron, I am in no different situation.

I remember those years, first and foremost, as a very happy time. We felt that we were doing a worthwhile job in an honourable profession and we derived real satisfaction and fulfilment in carrying out our various duties to the best of our ability. We were serving on a good squadron and we all felt – doubtless, exactly as they did in every other squadron – that we were the best in the business. Morale was high and was sustained by lots of parties to hold the squadron together as an entity. To be fair, most of the social events were successful as a result of – as one writer put it once – high, rather than potent, spirits, but they were fun and maintained the feeling of unit integrity and comradeship which is so vital to any Service organisation.

Inevitably, each generation of squadron members produced its own characters whose exploits – often highly coloured – pass, in due course, into squadron legend. My generation was no different. Quite apart from the Boss – a genuine character in his own right – we had a number of others who would readily have stood out in any crowd. Perhaps because of his incorrigible sense of fun, I remember particularly vividly Flight Sergeant Eddie Kelly, who was Peter Willie's navigator. Eddie was a very experienced navigator indeed, who had served in many bomber squadrons before he came to 27. The Boss was always sending him off to he commissioned and Eddie was always coming back before the course had got very far underway. He would cheerfully explain that he didn't want to be an officer. He had started out as a NCO and, if he had his way, he was going to finish up as one too. Eddies' aim in life was to get the maximum possible fun and enjoyment out of whatever he was doing at the time and he carried everyone he was with along with him. A born storyteller and practical joker, he was a great man to have around when the pressure was on and everyone was starting to become a bit intense. In such situations, he could always be relied on to find something to make the rest of us laugh and come back to normal. He was worth his weight in gold to the squadron for his infectious personality alone. Many years later, I met Eddie when he was, I believe, the senior Master Navigator in the RAF. He knew practically every Air Marshal on the Air Staff on first name terms, having served with most of them when they were very junior. When he came to the end of one tour, he would go down to the Ministry of Defence, have a chat with Air Marshal X, whom he had served with in Y squadron and fix himself up with the next flying tour of his choice.

One of the Flight Commanders was Squadron Leader Eric Senior who was a notable RAF cricketer – I believe that his brother was too. I remember Eric telling me once of going to play an away match in his earlier days at, I think, Dishforth, where they were supposed to have a young fast bowler who was knocking wickets over twenty to the dozen. Eric said that the young bowler, a fairly strapping fellow, retired so far away to start his run up that he appeared to be coming from somewhere in the next county. When his first ball was delivered, it flew past Eric at such a rate that, as he used to remark plaintively, "I never even saw the bloody thing." In a matter of a few overs, this fearsome new bowler had skittled out the visitors, leaving a succession of white-faced and badly shaken batsmen to totter back to the pavilion. The young bowlers name was Fred Trueman and, according to Eric, every batsman in the RAF was mightily relieved when he completed his National Service and departed to terrorise batsmen elsewhere.

Another of our characters was Flight Lieutenant 'Jock' Kennedy, just back from an exchange tour as a transport pilot with the Royal Australian Air Force. I think that I was the only one on the squadron to call him by his proper name of Tom. Jean had an absolute thing about 'Jock' as a nickname. I used to get it myself until she very firmly put an end to it. Rumour had it that Tom had taken a number of chorus girls off on an unauthorised joyride in a Dakota while with the Australians and had been forced to make an emergency landing with the thing at Alice Springs after a malfunction. No one was hurt, but you can just about imagine the reaction of the authorities to the spectacle of a bevy of pretty chorus girls extricating themselves daintily from the aircraft. Whatever the truth of the story, it obviously didn't hurt Tom's career in any way – maybe the Australians are a bit more open minded on these matters. Tom was another ex-Cranwell cadet who exemplified all the best qualities fostered at the College. He retired quite recently as Air Chief Marshal Sir Thomas Kennedy, latterly Air Member for Personnel.

I remember, too, Master Pilot Johnston, another very experienced Bomber Command hand, who had served with Eddie Kelly previously on Lincolns. He was a Pole, with a last name so unpronounceable that he was forced to adopt his wife's maiden name when he settled here. He had come out of Poland twice to the west and was very set on not having to do so a third time. On one of our Squadron deployments to Wunsdorf, quite close to the East German border, nine of the ten aircraft carried out the standard Wunsdorf let-down, outbound towards the East. The tenth, piloted by 'The Master', let down westward on his own highly individual – and completely unauthorised – approach. "I had to run away from there twice," he explained later, "and I'm getting too old to have to do it any more." In crewroom bridge games, he was a careful, cautious player, usually partnered by Eddie Kelly who bid as if he were playing poker rather than bridge. On one occasion, following a spirited and disastrous, overbid by Kelly, 'The Master' accosted him seriously, "One more overbid, Kelly and I strike you." Next hand, after Master Johnston had opened one of something, Kelly leapt straight to a grand slam in diamonds. As the Master reached purposefully across the table, Kelly very hurriedly spread his hand – a stone cold thirteen trick certainty against any lead. He survived to overbid again another day.

Along with the people, I recall some occasions which will stay with me for as long as I am able to remember. One Saturday night, on a Command Exercise, we took off for a routine first-run attack sortie against a target in Northern Norway. It was a dreadful night, dark and miserable, with low cloud and teeming rain. Because of the static interference, I turned the volume on the Radio Compass – tuned to the BBC Light Programme for time signals – right down. We climbed up and up through very heavy thunderstorm clouds until, quite suddenly, we burst through on top into a sort of valley among the upper clouds. The scene was unforgettable. On all sides, bathed in brilliant moonlight, the piled banks of cumulonimbus clouds towered high above us, like mountains of cotton wool. In the unusually bright conditions, the whole force ahead of us was clearly visible, threading their way in and out of the clouds ahead.

As we broke through into clear sky, I reached out mechanically to turn up the Radio Compass volume – right on cue to catch the broadcast of the last night of the Proms from the Albert Hall. At the precise instant that we topped the clouds into the overwhelming skyscape above, the orchestra struck up the opening bars of Elgar's 'Pomp and Circumstance'. I called Al and Ken up front to view the spectacle around us and the three of us huddled uncomfortably in the cramped cockpit, silently spellbound by the emotion of the wonderful music and the awesome panorama of the heavens about us. I don't know how many people were in the Albert Hall audience that night, but I can guarantee that not one of them heard, or savoured, the Elgar as we did in our intensely private and majestic world above the clouds.

I remember other occasions landing back at Waddington in the clear, soft light of early dawn on a summer morning, with the dew heavy on the grass and not a breath of wind stirring. Tony Lawrence, our Squadron adjutant was a bit of an expert on edible fungi and, after debriefing, we would often go out on to the far side of the airfield to collect hatfuls of 'plate' mushrooms – huge things, about three or four inches across. Then, back to the house to have Jean fry them up with eggs and bacon and lashings of hot tea and toast. I have never had mushrooms like that since – they had more taste than any others I have ever eaten.

Mention of the domestic side of things, reminds me that the squadron wives didn't always have the easiest time of it. They were generally quite young, with young children to cope with and they had to do most of the coping on their own. With exercises and deployments and working all sorts of odd hours, the husbands were frequently away when they were most needed about the home and the poor wives were simply left to get on with things as best they could. They were generally far from their families and home friends and they were frequently far out in the country, away from towns and good shopping, in the sort of isolated locations so beloved of Bomber Command. Even the various social events tended to engender a great deal of shop talk and I heard more than one wife remark feelingly, that, "the hanger doors never seem to close."

To keep themselves in touch with some sort of social life, the squadron and station wives used to have quite a lot of coffee mornings, when they would get together to discuss something other than last week's bombing results, or tomorrows flying programme. During one of these occasions when Jean was hostess, some twenty or so ladies were chatting away happily in our lounge, when the back boiler of the coal fire burned through. In a flash, gallons and gallons of water from the heating system cascaded out from the back of the fireplace, carrying a sooty, coal dust laden, flood into the room to a depth of an inch or two. The carpets and rugs were ruined in an instant, to say nothing of some twenty pairs of shoes. Not a very pleasant occurrence for the hostess who had put a lot of effort into arranging a relaxing social occasion and especially since – in my absence in the air – she was left get on with arranging the repairs and organising the clearing up.

I don't think that the service wives have ever got anything like the credit they richly deserved. Outsiders often have the impression that they spent most of the day swanning about like something out of a Noel Coward musical comedy, sipping cocktails and arranging flowers. The reality was very different – running a home and looking after a family in difficult conditions – and with precious little help from hubby or anyone else. No wonder they looked forward to leaves. In many ways, the wives experienced all of the disadvantages of being in the Service, without any of the compensating advantages.

I remember one occasion when Jeans normally equable disposition was stretched dangerously close to breaking point. I had been at a Squadron dining-in night during which I had – not to put too fine a point on it – taken rather more to drink than was strictly wise. I would hesitate to say that I was blind drunk, but my condition at the conclusion of the proceedings may be gauged from the fact that the colleague who insisted on seeing me safely home did so without his trousers – these having been discarded during some light-hearted activity earlier in the night. When we arrived at my quarters, my helpmate propped me up against the front door, rang the bell and, in a sudden burst of discretion, made off at high speed. When Jean arrived to open the door, I pitched headlong into the hall and, so I was later informed, went off into fits of uncontrollable laughter.

By the time Jean had managed to manhandle me upstairs to the bedroom, the racket had wakened Carol Anne who, not to be outdone in the noise making stakes, immediately set to bawling as loudly as she was able. When Jean dashed off to attend to her, I opened the bedroom window to let in some air and, having done so, collapsed insensible again at the side of the bed. Hearing the crash, Jean immediately abandoned Carol Anne to her howling and rushed back to see what was happening to me. From the door, she couldn't see me, prone behind the bed. Seeing only the wide open window, her immediate conclusion was that I had taken a header into the garden and she rushed downstairs again to try to put the pieces together. When, in due course, the situation was sorted out and I was found to be still intact, Jean suffered a total and dramatic, sense of humour failure. I got a verbal roasting that would have sobered up a boatload of drunken sailors on the spot and it was a very, very long time, believe me, before I had one over the eight again.

On a less emotionally charged occasion, I remember an odd incident when I checked out in the Station Oxford. After a twenty five minute 'round the circuit' jaunt, I was signed off as Oxford qualified and detailed to fly an airman up to Edzell on compassionate leave. Although I had flown a few other types of aircraft on 'one-off' trips, most of my flying had been in Meteors and Canberras and I was still a bit wary of aircraft which were new to me – particularly if they had piston engines and conventional tail-wheel landing gear. Feeling my way around the cockpit fairly gingerly, I managed to get my passenger up to Edzell without any great problem and was actually lining up for take-off on the way back when I suddenly experienced an instant and thoroughly unexpected, feeling of total confidence – an experience I have never been able to understand or explain to this day. Literally in a flash, I knew that I could fly the Oxford without any problem at all – it wasn't just a feeling of 'thinking' that I could; it was something that I suddenly 'knew' as a matter of absolute certainty. Moreover, I knew, with equal certainty, that I could fly anything else that had wings on it, as long as it had a stick and rudder in the cockpit. It was a very odd sensation indeed but, since that day, I never had a single qualm about any aircraft I was ever asked to fly. Whatever the shape, size, or performance, I simply knew that I would be able to cope.

Sometime in late 1955 or early 1956, an article in the Daily Telegraph created absolute turmoil in the squadron. The papers' correspondent 'Peterborough' recorded in his column that 12 Squadron – whose emblem was a fox – had recently been presented with a live Fox and that 9 Squadron – whose emblem was a bat – had, equally recently, been presented with a live bat. Both of these squadrons were part of the Canberra force at RAF Binbrook, near Grimsby and, in Peterborough's article, he went on to note something like, "near neighbours 27 Squadron at Waddington have been somewhat upstaged by these events." Our squadron emblem, stemming from the units first operational aircraft and its long service in India, was an Indian elephant.

Peterborough's mild journalistic witticism positively galvanised Peter Willie into activity. Never one to hide his squadrons light under any bushel, he clearly regarded the comment as a challenge to be met and matched. During one of his earlier postings in Singapore, he had met the legendary 'Elephant Bill' and, in very short order, a personal letter was winging its way eastward to that worthy with a request to remit, more or less by return of post, one Indian elephant, 27 Squadron, for the use of.

When word of this initiative reached the ears of the Station Commander, he is supposed to have asked PW what on earth he proposed to do with an elephant at Waddington. A bat or a fox might not be too unreasonable: but a fully-grown elephant! PW's response, so the story goes, was that the elephant would be well accommodated and looked after in the squadron hanger and that it would be very useful for towing Canberra's around the airfield during the winter when snow and ice made things difficult for the tractors.

At first, the reaction of squadron members to all this was one of mild amusement. Very quickly, however, when it became obvious that PW was taking the whole thing deadly seriously, a measure of consternation set in. Particularly with Brian Winkworth who found himself nominated as Officer-in-Charge (designate) Elephant – a secondary duty to end all secondary duties and one, I can confidently attest, without precedent in Air Force history.

In the event, the whole thing fell through. Elephant Bill wrote back to say that, in his view, a fully-grown Indian elephant could not reasonably be expected to prosper in the Lincolnshire environment. Brian Winkworth heaved an immense sigh of relief and PW fell back on borrowing an elephant from a circus which was visiting Lincoln and bringing it up to Waddington for a squadron photograph. During this photographic session, with the elephant in centre-stage pride of place, the wretched beast misbehaved itself disgracefully, noisily and continuously. If elephants are like this all the time, then we did very well to avoid getting one on the squadron as a permanent fixture.

Oddly enough, as a result of all the comment generated by the business of the elephant, a London Brewery – whose trade mark was a red elephant – got to hear of the affair and very kindly offered to provide us with our very own, uniquely 27 squadron type, elephant. Subsequently, at a delightful and very 'wet' presentation ceremony, their directors presented PW with a beautiful model elephant, painted in the green of our squadron emblem and furnished with a green silk saddlecloth bearing the squadron crest, intricately worked in gold thread. So, we got our elephant after all and a collective 27 Squadron snook was cocked at Peterborough, the Daily Telegraph and all their works and pomps. Incidentally, Brian Winkworth had to live with 'Sabu' – after the distinguished actor who had starred in the film 'Elephant Boy' – for the rest of his time on the squadron.

In the middle of 1956, at a time when the Squadron was starting a series of low-level formation flying rehearsals in preparation for a fly-past to mark Her Majesty the Queen's Review of Bomber Command at Marham, I went off on a Lone Ranger to Malta, in the course of which I was persuaded to accompany Al and Ken on an outing to Melheia Bay. It was a very hot day and, since I have the sort of colouring which can't take too much exposure to the sun, I let Al and Ken get on with the sunbathing, while I relaxed on the beach with a long drink under a large sun umbrella. In due course, I fell sound asleep and, while I was still sleeping, the sun moved round sufficiently to leave me unprotected by the umbrella. When I finally wakened, I knew at once that I had incurred a bad case of sunburn. I had gone a bright shade of lobster pink, my skin was hot and tingling and I felt that every part of my outer covering was stretched, just about to its limit, over my bones.

Next morning, as we prepared to fly back to the UK, I knew the worst: I had to be carried out to the aircraft as the tops of my feet were so badly burned that I couldn't bend them to walk. My flying suit felt as if it were made of emery paper and my shoulders, back and chest were so sore that I couldn't bear to do up the shoulder-straps of my parachute or safety harness. It was all I could do to buckle up the safety harness lap-strap. I spent a thoroughly uncomfortable three hours en-route back to Waddington before hobbling in to see Peter Willie to ask for a few days off to recover. But PW had problems of his own. "You see, Harry," he explained, "we're right in the middle of our flypast rehearsals and I simply don't have the time to train anyone else to take your place. If you bung on plenty of Vaseline or sun-tan lotion, you'll be fine."

The next week was an absolute nightmare. We flew every day in tight squadron formation at a thousand feet bumping and lurching about in the mid-day turbulence. I simply had to strap in – and strap in tightly. I went through the tortures of the damned as the straps bit into my shoulders as if they were brands of fire. At night, Jean consigned me to the spare room, after having to use the vacuum cleaner to clear the bed of the skin I was shedding. Day after day, soaked in Calamine Lotion, Nivea Cream, Johnsons Baby Cream and anything else I could get my hands on, I stuck in the number three position through every agonising inch of the rehearsal route. When, at last, we actually flew the real thing – coincidentally, my six hundredth hour on Canberras – my relief was inexpressible. No disrespect to Her Majesty, but I have never been so glad to get a flight over with in my life. I need hardly add that I have never been caught out in the sun since.

As I started to come within sight of my tour-expiry date, I began to do some serious thinking about what I should be doing when it came time for me to move on. I knew that I was long overdue for a ground tour of some sort, but I had no intention of coming off flying unless I was absolutely forced into it. The new four-engined V-Bombers were just starting to come off the production lines and would soon replace the Canberras as the front-line equipment of Bomber Command. The Valiant was already in service and Waddington was starting to set itself up as the Operational Conversion Unit for the Vulcan. I had seen a Vulcan flown into Waddington by Roly Falk, then Chief Test Pilot of A V Roe and had been much impressed by its obvious performance and by its very striking appearance – with its huge delta wing, it looked for all the world like a great white bat. I knew that the Command would be looking for its most experienced and highly qualified aircrew to man the new V-squadrons and I didn't rate my chances of selection highly.

One day, leafing idly through a copy of Air Ministry Orders in the Squadron Crew Room, I came across an item which caught my eye. It was an entry drawing the attention of all personnel to the existence of the Empire Test Pilots School at Farnborough and inviting suitably qualified individuals to consider submitting applications for the next course due to assemble in February 1957. At the time, I had only the very vaguest idea of what test flying was all about. I had seen a Clark Gable movie once in which his test flying technique seemed to have been simplicity itself. You climbed the aeroplane as high as it would go and then, at full throttle – and to the accompaniment of suitably stirring background music – dived the thing headlong at the ground. If, during the subsequent pull-out, the wings came off, the aircraft had clearly failed the test. If not, you landed to thunderous applause from the assembled ranks of senior officers and a rapturous welcome from the leading lady.

When I did a little checking up on Farnborough, I found that the Clark Gable technique seemed to have gone out of fashion. The Empire Test Pilots School – known, less formally, as 'ETPS' – was, I found, one of four Service Schools which existed to train pilots in the art of evaluating aircraft performance and handling. The United States Air Force had one at Edwards Air Force Base in California, the United States Navy one at Patuxent River, Maryland and the French Air Force had the rather splendidly titled "Ecole des Filots d'Essais de Vol" at, I think, Istres. The objective of each of these establishments was twofold: to teach pilots enough of the aerodynamics and physics of flight to enable them to communicate intelligently with the aircraft designers and engineers and to learn something of the principles of aircraft design and system operation. Of more immediate practical interest to me, the School gave pilots instruction in and practical experience of, the flying techniques used in flight test programmes.

The course at Farnborough lasted eleven months and, from what I could find out, the academic syllabus was fairly daunting. Calculus seemed to feature largely in the scheme of things, which I found somewhat off-putting. At the time, the sum total of my knowledge of advanced mathematics could have been written in large capital letters on a postage stamp. On the other hand, the School was said to

operate a fleet of some fifteen or so different types of aircraft, from gliders to supersonic fighters, from heavy bombers to helicopters and it was very tempting to
think of having the chance to get one's hands on such a variety of aircraft types.

I talked it over with Jean to find out how she would feel about me putting in an
application for the course. She had been with me through the better part of two
flying tours, we had a family to consider and we both recognised that there could
be a higher than average risk factor in the sort of flying that I was now considering. To her eternal credit, she didn't hesitate for a second. "If this is what you want
to do," she told me stoutly, "go ahead and send in your application." Accordingly, I
obtained an application form from the Administrative Section, had it vetted by
'PW' as my Squadron Commander and sent it off. I didn't know whether I would
even be considered as a suitable candidate, but I felt that I had at least done
something positive as far as my next posting was concerned. Now, all I could do
was wait to see what would develop.

CHAPTER 23

WHILE I WAS WAITING FOR my application to grind its way through official channels, more serious events in the world at large started to intrude forcibly into our squadron life and, very soon, drove all thoughts of next postings out of my head – and everyone else's, for that matter. This was during late 1956, when events in the Middle East – and in Egypt, in particular – began to assume the proportions of a genuine international crisis. The nationalisation of the Suez Canal seemed to bring matters to a head, as far as political activity and military preparedness was concerned. When, a matter of a couple of months later, Israel attacked Egypt, the Middle East fat was well and truly in the fire.

As luck would have it, 27 Squadron was one of two Bomber Command squadrons that carried a commitment to Operation Alacrity – the reinforcement of the Middle East garrison in time of emergency. As I recall, 61 Squadron was the other designated reinforcement bomber unit. During October, we did relatively little flying, but a great deal of work seemed to be going into getting every squadron aircraft into absolutely top-line condition. Every day, a new rumour of impending departure to some base in the Middle East would flash around the squadron, only to be replaced next day by another, even wilder, flight of fancy. Quite obviously, something pretty significant was afoot but, at working level in the squadrons, we didn't have much idea of what it was, or how we might be involved. Eventually, the word came through that Operation Reinforced Alacrity had been called and we were briefed for deployment to Nicosia in Cyprus to fulfil our commitment to the Operation. On October 1st, Peter Willie led the first four squadron aircraft off to Malta en-route to Cyprus. Two days later, I was one of the second wave of four to lift-off from Waddington heading towards what looked – with increasing certainty – to be a very probable war situation. For 27 Squadron, the Suez Campaign was underway.

In the thirty years that have elapsed since the Suez Campaign, enough has been written of the events of the time to provide a reasonably clear picture of the political machinations which led up to the Anglo-French intervention. Needless to say, few, if any, of the personnel actually involved in the operations had any idea of the realities of the political background. As far as they were concerned, this was simply the latest of a number of crisis situations which had arisen in the Middle East and their involvement stemmed purely and simply from the directives of their political masters in Whitehall. It is the essential reality of military service in any country, anywhere, that when the Government of the day says jump, you jump.

At this point, it might just be worth enlarging very slightly on the general reaction of military personnel to the prospect of their impending involvement in real live operations. Whatever may be the situation elsewhere, the personnel in the UK Forces are a long way from being simple-minded automatons, with no views of their own on political or international affairs. On the contrary, they are just about as representative a cross-section of the community as it would be possible to assemble – and, for the most part, a highly intelligent and involved cross-section. The very nature of their job encourages a lively interest in and awareness of, international affairs in the world at large. Just like most other members of the community, they have their own views on world affairs – views which are probably rather better informed than the average. Hence, when any crisis situation emerges, there are probably as many personal opinions on the issues within the services as there are in the country as a whole.

The difference between the service personnel and the rest of the population is that the serviceman has freely and without compulsion or coercion, accepted a way of life by which he has obliged himself to obey the orders of the reigning Sovereign, her Government and its Ministers. He has taken the Queens shilling and he is, or ought to be, unreservedly the Queens man. In these circumstances, the serviceman – whatever his personal views on a situation, or however strongly those views may be held – adheres to his contract of service and obeys all lawful orders fully, immediately and to the best of his individual capability. If an individual cannot, in conscience, live with this concept – which, in days gone by, went by the name of 'duty' – he should not be in the service in the first place. In the Armed Forces, duty is the essence of the whole way of life.

I have often been wryly amused – when I wasn't being frankly appalled – by the viewpoint that the average serviceman is absolutely itching to get his country into a war somewhere or other, so that he can get the chance to do for real what he spends so much of his time practising. You could sometimes get the impression that we went about the place with the blood lust red in our eyes and considering the day wasted if we hadn't actually had the chance to bomb or napalm some helpless village or other. The reality, I can state with some conviction, is quite different. In any front-line unit, you live with the certain knowledge that, if some act of war does occur, you are booked for very early participation in the event. Not the politicians, not the mass of the population, not even loved ones back home, but you – personally! You also know that, whoever the enemy might turn out to be, he is going to be fairly ill-disposed to you – also, very personally! Not to split hairs, he is going to do everything he can to kill you. In my experience, this simple fact provided the most excellent reason for servicemen to do everything they could to keep their country OUT of any war. Whatever the rights or wrongs of the situation, it was them who were going to be shot at first. Certainly, if a conflict does arise, it is your job – and your duty – to fall-to and fight, but you would have to be pretty half-witted to actually relish the prospect, or be involved, in any way, in bringing it about.

In the case of 27 Squadron – and, I suspect, the vast majority of the servicemen involved in the Suez Campaign – the operation started off being regarded almost as a deployment exercise – the sort of overseas reinforcement which is a routine peacetime commitment for most front-line units. A fairly predictable political response to a crisis situation – show a bit of armed strength, wave the flag, rattle a few sabres and wait for the situation to calm down. That was largely what I was thinking as I winged my way across the cloudless Mediterranean towards Cyprus. I suspect that there were many others who shared my complacency. If there were, then they, like me, were very shortly due for a rather rude awakening.

When we actually got on the ground at Nicosia, it was to find ourselves in the middle of an absolute hive of military activity. While the airfield had a two thousand yard runway, so that aircraft operation presented no problems, the place had never been expected to have to cope with the sheer numbers which Alacrity had brought in. By the time we arrived, the base already housed something like eight bomber squadrons, six transport squadrons and two fighter squadrons – not to mention the Army detachments, the Paratroops, the French Foreign Legion and God only knows what else.

Our immediate impression was that everything looked very 'operational' – all the aircraft we could see had 'wasp-band' stripes – three yellow and two black – painted round the fuselage and on each mid-wing section. Bomb dumps and armament stores were sited on every piece of spare ground, guns and ammunition of all shapes and sizes were littered everywhere, the camp roads were chock-a-block with officious-looking Jeeps and Land Rovers racing about in all directions and there were more military personnel than I had ever seen assembled in one place. Perhaps not surprisingly, the accommodation situation was chaotic.

The Mess had been designed to house something like a hundred officers all told, so that, for the great majority of junior ranks on the Base, operational accommodation was the order of the day – Nissen huts or tents. When we finally got to 27 Squadrons' part of the field – sandwiched between the Paras and the Foreign Legion – we found a somewhat inexpertly erected Operations Tent, beside which were our crew tents – waiting for us to put them up. Outside the Ops tent, I remember, was a boldly lettered sign which proclaimed "WELCOME TO CYPRUS – THE GIRLS WEAR NO NICOSIA." I always suspected Kelly of involvement in this piece of bawdy humour, but I could never get him to own up to it.

My first 'active service' duty was to carry out an order to "do something about these b..... tents." Quite clearly, the personnel of 27 Squadron – too used to comfortable Mess life – wouldn't have made the reserve team in a Boy Scout tent raising contest. Recognising my own lamentable lack of capability in this sort of enterprise, I immediately resorted to low cunning and made a surreptitious approach to the Regimental Sergeant Major of one of the Army units. After a degree of haggling, I arranged for two barrels of beer to be delivered to our gallant brothers-in-arms, following which a small body of soldiers descended upon us and, in what seemed like a matter of minutes, erected every tent in sight to the very highest standards of military precision. Not only that, they actually laid out paths, marked them off with ropes and stakes and generally got the place looking something like a military encampment. As Jean often says, it pays in the long run to get an expert in. The cost of the beer was debited to Squadron Funds and I don't think that we ever made a better investment. When PW got back from Force Headquarters, he was actually quite impressed.

For the first couple of days in Cyprus, our flying was limited to familiarisation with the local area, the airfield and the airfield let-down procedures. We did get in one fairly long night cross-country by way of Crete, El Adem and Tobruk, during which we could see the running lights of what looked like hundreds of ships far below us on the Mediterranean. By day, with the US Sixth Fleet in the area and all of our transports and supply ships, the place must have looked like Henley Regatta.

It is difficult now to recapture the feeling of general confusion that existed at Nicosia during the four days before the balloon went up. The only news of events which we had come from the BBC Overseas Service, from whose broadcasts it was clear that the Israelis and the Egyptians seemed to be hell bent on fairly major conflict. What was considerably less clear – at least, at working level – was where exactly we stood. The sheer scale of our presence demonstrated that we were very likely to become involved, but few, if any, of us seemed to have any idea of whether we would be going in to join the Israelis to overthrow President Nasser and re-take the Suez Canal, to join the Egyptians to hold the Israelis back, or simply take on everybody in sight, in order to take over Egypt again. On top of all of this confusion, there was the additional problem that Cyprus was right in the middle of a bitter and bloody, terrorist campaign to achieve 'Enossis' – political union with Greece. Every Greek-Cypriot had to be regarded as a potential terrorist and there were hundreds of them working on and around the airfield.

On October the 30th, the situation became somewhat clearer with the announcement that Egypt had rejected the Anglo-French ultimatum to both Israel and Egypt to withdraw their forces ten miles from both sides of the Suez Canal and allow Anglo-French forces to occupy the Canal Zone temporarily as a neutral formation. With that rejection, all possibility of a peaceful resolution of the crisis vanished and Operation 'Musketeer' – the occupation of the Canal Zone by Anglo-French forces – was launched.

The RAF operations began on October 31st with the primary objective of neutralising the Egyptian Air Force. The Egyptians had been supplied with Mig fighters and Ilyushin bombers by the Warsaw Pact countries and it was anticipated that the fighters, at least, might well be piloted by Russian or Czech instructors. Accordingly, at dusk on the last day of October, the first RAF strikes were flown against a number of Egyptian airfields.

Even at this very early stage in the campaign, the element of near-farce, which characterised much of the events of the time, was strongly in evidence. The RAF strikes were mounted from both Cyprus and Malta – the Valiants and longer-range Canberra Mk 6s from Malta and the shorter-range Canberra Mk 2s from Cyprus. One of the targets for the combined Malta/Cyprus force was Cairo International airport where there was supposed to be a detachment of Mig Fighters. After the Malta Force had launched, it was discovered that an American transport aircraft was actually on the ground at Cairo International in the process of evacuating American civilians from the area. When news of this situation reached the War Room in London, an immediate order was passed to Musketeer Force Headquarters to avoid, at all costs, bombing Cairo International. Unfortunately, by the time this order was received, the Malta-based bomber force was already airborne en-route for Egypt.

The situation was resolved by having the leader of the Cyprus-based Canberras which, being much closer to the operational area, took-off later than the Malta force – call the Malta Force leader on the radio – in clear – with the anguished order, "Do NOT, repeat NOT attack Cairo; your target is now Almaza repeat Almaza. What Bomber Command of 1939-45 would have made of this sort of carry-on doesn't bear thinking about. The poor crews briefed for the attack on Cairo International were now well and truly out on a limb. All their careful flight planning and target study had, in a second, become so much wasted time. Few of them had anything other than the vaguest idea of where Almaza was, much less what was there worth bombing. While everyone was frantically trying to locate Almaza on their maps, a new voice came on the radio – strength ten – to announce, "This is Almaza Radio, Almaza Radio. Aircraft calling Almaza, your course to steer is...." Incredible but it happened – probably the only time in military history that an attacking force was homed to the target by the target itself!

27 Squadron was not involved in the first night of operations. At the time, we were briefing for an attack to be carried out at dawn next morning on the Ilyushin bomber base at Inchas. In some ways, the briefing for our first operational participation was exactly the same as many other briefings we had sat through for exercise raids. The weather, routes, heights, timings, target details, aiming points and recovery procedures were all covered in precisely the same way as we had heard them covered many times before. The difference from our routine exercise briefings was, however, sharply highlighted when the briefing staff got around to dealing with the defences we would be likely to encounter and the procedures to be followed in the event that we had to bale-out or crash land somewhere 'over there'. It was during these phases that throats started to get a bit dry and palms a bit sweaty and cigarettes were being lit up two and three at a time.

The enemy, the Intelligence Officer advised us earnestly, could be expected to deploy his high performance fighters behind a flak belt just south of the coast. This flak belt featured a mix of Russian-built Surface to Air guided missiles and Radar Directed Anti-Aircraft Artillery, both assessed as being accurate up to forty thousand feet and both assessed as being lethal, given a missile or shell detonation anywhere within the general vicinity of the target aircraft. At this point, pulse rates were going up fast all round. If we were to be shot down, continued the Intelligence Officer imperturbably, we were to make our way to a particular spot in the desert and remain out of sight until a rescue aircraft – operating on a once-a-week basis – would fly in to pull us out.

With possible survival in the desert in mind, I asked whether we would be issued with side-arms. After all, if you have to survive, it's a lot easier to shoot your dinner, whatever it might be, than trying to run it to earth. "Ah, well now," came the response, "we don't think that would be a very good idea. If you did happen to come down wearing a revolver and the civilian population got to you, they might think that you were behaving in a hostile manner." Well, I was glad that I had got that one cleared up. You go out and drop six thousand pounds of high-explosive on some poor unsuspecting civilian and he only gets the idea that you are being hostile when you come down with a service revolver strapped to your hip!

After the flak belt, went on the Intelligence Officer remorselessly, we would expect to run into the Migs – possibly piloted by Russian or Czech Instructors, who would be pretty capable individuals. This was really cheerful news for us – going in at twenty six thousand feet in an unarmed bomber and certain to be silhouetted against the dawn sky. A fighter pilots dream come true! The wretched man was scaring our pants off.

When the briefing was over and we went off to get our gear together, I think that it would be true to say that we were all pretty frightened. For most of us, this was our first experience of a war operation and the briefing hadn't done a lot to cheer us up. Peter Willie, however, was absolutely on top form. I always had the feeling that, after a hundred and two operational raids over Germany, he couldn't take the Egyptian defences seriously and was quite prepared to go and do any little bombing jobs that might be required, completely on his own. His eagerness to get going and his obvious enthusiasm to get into the thick of it, did a lot to bolster our unsteady spirits.

when we lifted off the runway at Nicosia in the early hours of the morning of 1st November, I remember very vividly watching the coastline of Cyprus slip away behind us and wondering to myself if we were going to be seeing it again in a couple of hours' time. Like many another at that moment, I metaphorically squared my shoulders, set my jaw and headed off for the flak and the Migs.

From that point onward, the whole raid was a huge anti-climax. Apart from a moments tension when Al quietly came up with Bomber Commands hallowed "Enemy Coast Ahead," we flew what was virtually a routine training sortie to In-chas, dropped our bombs and flew back. No missiles, no flak, no fighters! Here we were, nerves screwed up to the hilt to do or die for Queen and Country and it all turned out to be about as exciting as a trip to Wainfleet Range.

Back on the ground at Nicosia again, we discovered that the Egyptians had re-acted very quickly to the threat to their Air Force elements and had moved their bomber force well away from their Northern bases to Luxor in the south. We were told later that this move was based on their assumption that, since Cyprus was out of range of their bombers operating from Luxor, then Luxor ought to be out of range of our Canberras operating from Cyprus. After our debriefing, we were put on stand-by for operations that night against their new 'hidey-hole', to demon-strate that their assumption was altogether unfounded.

The raid on Luxor airfield that night was another thoroughly unexciting and uneventful mission – again, virtually no opposition, although one or two crews reported seeing sporadic anti-aircraft fire in the target area. I didn't see any myself or, if I did, I didn't recognise it as flak. This raid was my first experience of operat-ing with a pathfinder force and there were so many flares, target indicators and bomb flashes in the target area that I was hard pushed to identify the lights that really mattered.

I remember being very impressed by the pathfinders operations that night. They were from 139 Squadron and led by a very experienced New Zealander who had served with 617 Squadron during the 1939-45 war. On our way to the target, it was as black as sin outside all the way down to Luxor, until Al remarked that, by his watch, the pathfinders should just be approaching the target area now. As he spoke, the first lead-in flare burst in the sky some thirty or forty miles directly ahead of us. Thereafter, the lead-in flares went off in a continuous stream point-ing the way directly to the target. As we got closer, we saw the first ground-flares and target indicators go down, followed by the detonations of the bombs from the first aircraft of the attack force. As fires developed and spread among the hangers and airfield buildings, we heard the voice of the Master Bomber, calmly directing each aircraft in turn to attack a specific aiming point within the target complex. "Bomb two hundred yards north of the green marker": "More markers west of the hanger area": "Aim at the secondary fire near the red marker." It was like a textbook demonstration of how to get the maximum effectiveness out of the attack force available.

In our turn, we went in and bombed our assigned aiming-point and turned away for the long flight back to Cyprus, leaving Luxor Airfield and the bulk of the Egyptian Ilyushin force, in a fiercely blazing ruin behind us. The Ilyushins, which had always constituted a real threat to the Anglo-French forces, took no part in the subsequent campaign.

With two raids under our belts and no opposition encountered, we were beginning to get a taste for this sort of operational flying. As long as the opposition isn't actually shooting at you, war isn't such a frightening proposition after all. Now that we knew what it was all about, we had all become heroes overnight!

Our new-found heroism received a rude shock on our second day of operations when we were assembled for briefing for a raid in which only 27 Squadron was to be involved as the attack Force. The target was Cairo Radio Station and the attack was to be conducted at low-level. Peter Willie, by now absolutely in his element, told us that he had volunteered the squadron for this mission which, he went on absolutely straight-faced, might incur heavy losses. In the circumstances, only volunteers would go on this one. It was all like something out of some bad Hollywood movie. Our new-found heroism evaporated on the spot and the pulse rates went sky high again. Nevertheless, everybody volunteered – just like in the movies – all of us feeling, I might say, like a collection of prize idiots. Eventually, with the dramatics over, PW got on with the briefing.

The big problem for us was the very low altitude attack we were to carry out. Virtually all of our visual bombing experience was from something like 25 thousand feet and we had no experience of doing the job really low down. Instead of the bomb aimer having his sight angle tilted a few degrees away from the vertical, he could almost expect to be somewhere in the back of the aircraft trying to get it raised high enough to get the target in his sights. And at high speed and in bumpy conditions at low level, it wasn't going to be easy to get bombs on target.

In the event, Cairo Radio was attacked and, after the attack, Cairo Radio was off the air. On that basis, I suppose that the sortie could be considered a success. But, to be honest, the result was achieved more by good luck than good bombing. To hit a pin-point target with the equipment we had at the time was almost an impossible proposition. Our whole method of operation was based on the premise that if you dropped a whole lot of bombs on a target area, there was a statistical probability that some of them would actually hit the target. The more bombs you dropped, the higher the statistical probability. This system works perfectly well against area targets such as airfields, marshalling yards, barracks areas, dock facilities, or groups of factories. It is, however, much less likely to be successful against individual targets, particularly small ones, when you have to drop an awful lot of bombs to give yourself any sort of reasonable probability of actually hitting that one, specific, target. Using an unfamiliar technique, at low-level and high speed, it was asking a lot to expect 27 to take-out a point target such as Cairo Radio.

As things turned out, the bombing was even harder to do than had been anticipated. 139 Squadron had been ordered to mark the target for the attack – why, Heaven only knows! Cairo Radio was a large white building, standing on its own, that was clearly visible to the attack force practically from the Egyptian Coast. In broad daylight, it stuck out like a sore thumb. Nevertheless, the target was to be marked and 139 Squadron duly did their stuff with their flares, target markers and target indicators. By the time they had finished, there was so much smoke and dust raised in the area that the target was completely invisible and the attack force had to drone about the place waiting for the obscuration to clear before they went in. In fact, the smoke and dust never did look like it was going to clear and the attack had to be made with the target still half hidden in the murk. After the first few thousand pounders went down, still more smoke and dust – this time accompanied by sand – arose to blank the target almost completely. It was virtually blind bombing and very few of the attackers really had any idea of whether they had hit the target or not.

At the end of the day, however, Cairo Radio was off the air and that had been the objective of the exercise. 27 Squadrons' dare-devil exploit had not been in vain. Some time later, when the muck had subsided sufficiently to allow post-strike target photography, it was noted that several hits had, in fact, been achieved. The only sour note came from an Intelligence Officer who gave it as his view that Cairo Radio had ceased to broadcast, not because of any damage to the installation, but because one of the bombs had overshot the target far enough to hit an approach road, under which ran the main power supply cable. The resultant crater had, he alleged, broken the cable and deprived the installation of all electrical power. So much for heroics!

Only three more raids were made by 27 Squadron before the 5th November, when the first airborne troops landed on Egyptian soil. On the night of 2nd November, three aircraft paid a return visit to Luxor, on the 3rd, we attacked the railway marshalling yards at Ismailia and on the 5th, we attacked the tank assembly facilities and fuel storage depots at Huckstep Barracks, just north east of Cairo. During one of these two latter raids – and, for the life of me I can't remember which – a navigator on one of the other squadrons claimed a high-altitude operational bagpipe playing record by regaling the force with 'Scotland the Brave' before he was forcibly silenced.

When, on the morning of the 5th November, the airborne forces went in, the RAF's bomber participation in the campaign was over, although the huge transport effort went on for some time and fighter cover sorties for the ground forces were flown by both RAF fighters and RN carrier-borne aircraft.

It is all too tempting now to look back on the whole Suez campaign as an absolute debacle from beginning to end. Undoubtedly, it was a political miscalculation of the first magnitude. From the military standpoint, however, it did demonstrate the value of the training of the personnel involved. The RAF bomber force had the job of ensuring that the Egyptian Air Force took no part in the campaign and that objective was achieved. Our operations went off exactly the same as our routine training exercises and, apart from non-standard aberrations like the raid on Cairo Radio, our results tallied almost exactly with the results we achieved on the ranges at home. Admittedly, there was no opposition to speak of – in spite of Eddie Kelly's expressed concern, en-route to Ismailia at forty thousand feet, that "some of those b..... spears are coming up fifteen feet." My own belief is that, opposition or not, the results would have been the same. We were trained for the job and we would have got it done just the same – regardless.

After operations in Egypt had finally ceased and the withdrawal had got underway, most RAF units remained in Malta or Cyprus until about the end of November, when they started to return to the UK. 27 Squadron stayed on a little longer than most and didn't actually start homeward until late December. In the interval, we filled in our time with navigation exercises and quite a lot of fighter affiliation sorties – flown mainly to give the fighter squadrons on the Island a chance to keep their hands in.

During this period, there took place a round of celebration parties such as, I am sure, Nicosia Officers Mess had seldom, if ever, experienced before. One of the more memorable was organised by Number 1 Fighter Squadron – whose Hunters were based at Nicosia -for their colleagues of, I think, 8 Squadron from Akrotiri. On the day when this blast was underway, Al and Ken and I were strolling down to the Mess for a quiet drink when the front door crashed open and three of the fighter aces hurtled down the steps to fling themselves bodily into the goldfish pond in the courtyard. We three were somewhat taken aback by this over- exuberance and it was only when the bodies failed to reappear from the pond that we felt that we ought to do something about it. By the time we got to the courtyard, the three loonies in the pond had come quite close to drowning themselves. We hauled them, gasping and spluttering, out of the water and spread them out on the ground to recover. They were, quite clearly, so stupendously drunk that discussion of their idiocy would have been quite pointless.

Inside the Mess, the situation was almost indescribable. The bar was packed from wall to wall with a seething mass of howling fighter pilots – all of them literally roaring drunk and some of them being prevented from falling down only by the sheer press of the bodies around them. Many were wearing Service revolvers – issued because of the terrorist activity – and indiscriminate and highly lethal shots were being loosed off at various bar fittings and through the windows. There was hardly an unbroken windowpane in the place and the poor bar staff were absolutely white faced with terror. The whole mob were in the grip of patriotic fever: 'Rule Britannia', 'Land of Hope and Glory' and 'There'll Always be an England', being rendered *molto fortissimo* and to the accompaniment of glasses, tumblers and beer mugs being hurled into the fireplace at the conclusion of every chorus. Bets were being taken on who could hang on to the ventilator fans longest. With squadron pride at stake, various idiots hung on grimly, bodies virtually horizontal as the fans were turned up to full speed, until their grip was lost and they were flung off to crash insensible on top of their cheering colleagues.

Heaven only knows what the repairs must have cost the squadrons, to say nothing of the damage to the individuals themselves – one fighter acquaintance of mine was having pieces of glass removed from his rear end for some weeks afterwards. The fighter contingent was very subdued for some time after the event but, to be honest, I must give them credit. I've been to a good few uproarious parties myself, but I must reluctantly concede that 1 Squadron really set an all-time standard at Nicosia. It might well be argued that the famous Bomber Command dinner at Scampton could stand comparison, but there wouldn't be a lot in it and, anyway, that's another story.

CHAPTER 24

ONE OF THE PILOTS of the fighter element involved in the proceedings was Derek Bryant, who had been one of my best students at Driffield. During the party, he had attempted to drink me under the table – unwisely, as it turned out. I selected whisky, which was then my standard tipple. Derek, more used to beer, collapsed quickly and comprehensively. Before he passed out, he mentioned that he was quite keen to have a quick trip in a Canberra, so I smuggled him aboard on one sortie for a bit of familiarisation with the serious side of the Air Force. Derek and his squadron had been in Cyprus for considerably longer than we had, so when the prospect of a crew Lone Ranger to Gibraltar came up, I offered him an unofficial ride with us, provided he could square his absence with his Squadron Commander and provided he could keep the whole enterprise strictly between ourselves.

On this particular Lone Ranger, we had arranged to take one of our ground crew through with us to give him a bit of a break from Cyprus. With Derek now surreptitiously added to the crew, that made a total of five on board – just right for the Canberras oxygen system which provided five supply outlets: one at each crew ejection seat, one at the rumble seat and one 'wanderlead' at the bomb aimers station down in the nose.

When we taxied-out for the trip to Gibraltar, we slowed down on the taxyway to pick up Derek near the 1 Squadron dispersal, well away from prying eyes. To my amazement, he turned up with another body – a fighter colleague of his also keen for a week-end away from Cyprus. In the middle of the taxyway, I couldn't seem to get the message across that we only had oxygen outlets for five people and, since we obviously couldn't spend all day arguing the matter, Derek and his mate were duly hauled aboard and we tried to get ourselves sorted out for the flight. The first leg to Malta was only a two and a half hour trip and I hoped that our sixth man could survive on odd doses of oxygen from somebody else's supply.

As it happened, we got through to Gibraltar without too much panic. Every so often, our luckless 'sixth man' would go blue in the face and start gasping for air, at which point someone would unhook their own oxygen mask and give him a few blasts to keep him going. I wouldn't go so far as to say that he actually enjoyed the flight, but he did make it through to Gibraltar apparently none the worse for his experience.

After a hectic forty-eight hours in Gibraltar, we all piled aboard again for the return trip to Nicosia. Because there were so many of us in the aircraft, we had found ourselves very cramped for space on the way through, so, this time, we dumped all of our bone domes, Mae Wests, pressure breathing waistcoats and other bulky items into the bomb-bay pannier, in which was already stored our uniforms, personal kit, money and presents for home – Gibraltar had provided a good opportunity to get our Christmas shopping done before we returned to UK.

As we taxied-out to the take-off point, Gibraltar Air Traffic came up to advise me that stopping at the end of the runway was not permitted and that I was to keep moving until take off. This meant that I had no opportunity to complete my pre-take off Vital Actions 'at the halt', as was our invariable practice, but had to do them as best I could on the move on the way out, while I was concentrating on taxying the aircraft safely.

Shortly after we got airborne and settled into the climb, I noticed a fairly pronounced airframe vibration which I couldn't identify at all. I checked the wheels and flaps for proper retraction, ensured that the air-brakes were closed and examined the engines minutely for any sign of malfunction. Everything appeared to be perfectly in order, but still the vibration persisted. I was in the process of checking the systems for about the third or fourth time, when Ken, who was sitting beside me on the rumble seat, remarked casually, "What's that red light on your left-hand console panel, Harry." I nearly died on the spot. The offending red light was the bomb-bay doors indicator. Somehow or other, in going through my Vital Actions on the move at Gibraltar, I had contrived to overlook closing the bomb bay doors before we took off. For the one and only time in my flying career, I had managed to get airborne with the bomb-bay doors wide open. In ninety nine cases out of a hundred, this would have been only a minor professional embarrassment. On this occasion, as I and the rest of the crew were only too well aware, the bomb bay contained, not fresh air or practice bombs, but an open pannier stuffed with our personal kit and a fair proportion of our flying clothing. Since the pannier had been exposed to the full force of the slipstream from take-off, none of us had much confidence that any of our kit would still be aboard by the time we reached Malta.

Sure enough, when we finally got down at Luqa and rushed round to inspect the damage, the pannier which had contained our kit was as clean as a whistle. Not a single item had survived except, unbelievably, a handbag I had bought for my aunt, which had caught on one at the bomb shackles and was still there, mocking us for the rest of the kit that had gone. I was so disgusted that I threw the damn thing into a rubbish container on the flight line.

While it was bad enough to have lost all of our personal kit, it was of much more 'official' concern to have been responsible for the loss of all the flying equipment that went into the Bay of Algeciras. Flying kit is very expensive and, in between worrying about our 'sixth seat' man who was still collapsing periodically, I was very apprehensive of my reception back at Nicosia when I would have to own up to having inexcusably written off several hundred pounds worth of the taxpayers money.

In the event, I was saved by the fact that we were still, however unrealistically, on 'active service'. I sneaked down to the Safety Equipment section and had a long chat with the Warrant Officer in charge. He never even batted an eyelid, bless him, as he provided me, from his section rubbish bin, with an assortment of scrapped and useless items, which he then formally accepted from me as unserviceable equipment to be traded in for brand new replacement items. Thank heaven for the service senior NCOs. They are a very special breed and have kept idiotic young officers out of serious trouble on more occasions than it would be possible to record. I did arrange for a barrel of beer to go anonymously to the Safety Equipment Section, but it was little enough expression of my heartfelt thanks to that splendid man for getting me off the hook. I thought at the time that the matter had been neatly disposed of without anyone getting to hear of it, but I did wonder one day when Peter Willie – who didn't miss much – remarked slyly, "nice to see your crew keep their kit in such good condition, Harry. It almost looks brand-new." I changed the subject very hurriedly!

During our last days in Cyprus, 'Mac' McNeile of 139 Squadron accosted me to ask whether I had heard anything about my application for Test Pilots School. He had just received his formal notification of acceptance for the course and, since he had also heard of others who had been notified, I was forced to the conclusion that I wasn't going to make it to Farnborough this time around. I resolved to just get on with the job in hand and, perhaps, try again next year.

Eventually, on December 19th, we left Cyprus to return to the UK. We arrived back to weather so bad that we were diverted, first to Valley in Anglesey for customs clearance and then, because Waddington was below limits, to Binbrook, from where we completed our homeward trip to Waddington by coach. When we arrived on the base, PW was met with a very official looking signal marked 'TOP SECRET', 'MOST IMMEDIATE', 'FOR YOUR EYES ONLY' and a whole lot more. It informed him that a very serious situation had arisen in the Near East and directed that the Squadron should be placed on twelve hour standby for a move to Cyprus in accordance with Operation Alacrity!

Christmas 1956 proved to be a very real homecoming and the festive celebrations were even more lively than usual that year. Quite shatteringly, however, in the middle of all the partying, there arrived an absolute bombshell from Air Ministry. To make way for the new squadrons of V-Bombers then in course of formation, a number of Canberra units were no longer required and were scheduled for disbandment. We learned, to our intense dismay, that 27 was to be disbanded on the last day of 1956.

This latest and totally unexpected development, threw the squadron personnel into a state of considerable turmoil. While I was coming to the end of my tour of duty anyway, many others were only half-way through, or had not long arrived. New postings for all the crews had to be arranged, either to the surviving Canberra squadrons, or to the V-Force Operational Conversion Units. With Farnborough apparently out of the reckoning, I was very conscious of the fact that I was now very much overdue for a ground tour and that the present circumstances would make such an appointment that much harder to avoid.

When Peter Willie had me in to chat about my future assignment, he brightened up my day no end by telling me that he was going to command 139 Squadron and would be happy if I would come along and join him on that unit. It was a very generous offer on his part and I wouldn't have hesitated for a second to accept gratefully, had I heard from Farnborough officially – one way or the other – on my application for ETPS. When I told PW that I still had not heard anything about Test Pilots School, he said, "Hang on. I know Sammy Wroath at Farnborough. I'll give him a call now and get an answer one way or the other." Sammy Wroath was the Group Captain Commandant of the Empire Test Pilots School and, after he and PW had chatted for a bit, PW put his hand over the mouthpiece of the telephone and whispered to me, "He's got 27 of the 28 places on the course already filled. You are one of the candidates for the 28th place." Waving me out of the office, he hissed, "leave me to have a chat with him." I left the office with my fingers crossed and, two days later, received official notification that I had been selected for Number 16 Course at Empire Test Pilots School and was to report to Farnborough on the 4th of February following.

I will always owe to Peter Willie Helmore the fact that I got the one posting in the Air Force that I desperately wanted to get. In this, as in so many instances, PW demonstrated his unswerving loyalty and commitment to his squadron members. On any occasion when his backing was needed, it was available – unreservedly and whole-heartedly. In later years, I always regretted that I never had the opportunity to thank him properly for all of his many kindnesses to me personally. Only a few years later, sailing his own boat out to take up a NATO appointment in Turkey, he was lost at sea in the Mediterranean. He was a real loss to the service – they don't seem to come in that mould any more. A character in every sense, he was, above all else, a leader who commanded the respect and loyalty of all who served with him. With PW up front, we would have gone to the gates of Hell and back and counted ourselves lucky to have been in his company.

CHAPTER 25

IN 1957, THE EMPIRE TEST PILOTS SCHOOL had its home at Farnborough, as a sort of a lodger unit on the base occupied by the Royal Aircraft Establishment. It was a relatively small organisation, situated at the Aldershot end of the RAE complex and comprising a mess – just about big enough to cope with the few permanent staff officers and the twenty or thirty students on each course – and a prefabricated headquarters building, which contained the administrative offices and the lecture and demonstration facilities. The flying facilities and the school aircraft, were sited on the far side of the airfield, on the other side of the main runway from Farnborough proper.

The ETPS Mess was something of a legend in the flying business. The staff seemed to have been there forever and the standards were of the highest. The place was run more like a very comfortable club, than as a service Mess and the atmosphere was invariably relaxed and informal. So much so, in fact, that ETPS was often referred to as 'the Farnborough high speed flying club'. Apart from the occasions when the school hosted visiting lecturers, or high ranking service officers, uniforms were seldom much in evidence and students were free to wear civilian clothes most of the time. I can remember, once, reading a notice on the Mess Board announcing the forthcoming visit of the Air Officer Commanding on his Annual Inspection and adding, almost as an afterthought, "Officers are requested to wear service dress during the visit."

It was to this delightful environment that number 16 course was introduced when we assembled formally on 4th February to begin our eleven month course. Twenty nine strong, we came from a wide variety of nationalities and flying backgrounds. The RAF contingent comprised six from Fighter Command, two from Bomber Command, one from helicopters and one from Training Command. The Royal Navy provided a contingent of five 'Dark Blues'. Bob Cockburn, Lorne Pollock and Alec Bowman represented the Royal Canadian Air Force and Dave Tate, the Royal Canadian Navy. The Royal Australian Air Force provided us with Russ Law and Doug Cameron and the Indian Air Force with 'Bobby' Dey and 'Jimmy' Chopra. From the United States, John McCormick represented the United States Air Force and Taylor Brown and Al O'Neal the United States Navy. Jean Cannac came from the French Air Force and Pete Brey – the only civilian on the course – arrived from Holland, where he worked for Fokker Aircraft.

The school was commanded by group captain 'Sammy' Wroath, backed up by Chief Test Flying Instructor, Wing Commander I N M Macdonald and five flying tutors, who would be responsible for monitoring our progress in our air exercises. It would have been hard to assemble a better, or more capable, group of instructors for the job. All of them – Johnny Johnson, Bill Morrison, Bill Sheehan, Peter Baker and Mike Crossley – had completed at least one tour of duty as a practising test pilot 'in the field' and the sort of expertise which they were able to bring to the job of helping us along was the sort that you don't get out of books. I always felt that this was one of the strengths of ETPS, as compared with some other test flying schools, at which outstanding students could be 'creamed-off' to become tutors straight away. I have no doubt that they were most capable individuals but, to me, there is no substitute for the experience of actually having done the job 'for real'. When you got a comment from any one of the ETPS tutors on how to go about a particular programme, you knew it was coming from someone who had been there himself.

The thankless task of looking after our academic instruction fell to the lot of Chief Technical Instructor 'Jimmy' Lang and his assistant, Bill Wilkinson. I always felt it was a tribute to their ability and never-ending patience, that anybody ever actually graduated from the school. They were the ones who had to take us through all the Calculus, Physics and Aerodynamics of the course syllabus and it must, at times have seemed to them a very uphill task to try to force some of the finer points of stability equations into our heads, when we would all, quite clearly, have much rather been off somewhere doing the job in the air.

The actual routine of the course was very similar to what I had been used to in Rhodesia. Once we had settled down and got through the preliminary academic instruction sessions, we had a lecture period most mornings. Thereafter, we either flew in the morning and did self-study in the afternoons, or reversed the procedure to study in the morning and fly in the afternoon. The programme was deliberately designed to be very flexible to allow for variations in the rate of progress of individual students ether in classwork or airwork and also to allow for the inevitable disruption to the flying programme brought about by periods of bad weather. It didn't take us long to discover that weather is a critical factor in arranging any sort of test flying programme. With the aids at our disposal, we could get airborne in most weather conditions but, to get good test results, it is important to get the airwork done in reasonably smooth conditions. Any sort of turbulence at your exercise altitude and you are going to find it very difficult indeed to fly sufficiently accurately to produce worthwhile results.

For our airwork, we would be using the various aircraft of the school fleet – fifteen different types of in-service aircraft, plus three different types of glider. All of the aircraft had been fully tested prior to their acceptance into service and the test results were available to the school staff as a sort of examination standard against which our attempts at the same sort of tests could be assessed. In the early days, we did our testing using the age-old test pilots standby equipment – a knee pad and a stop watch with a split second hand. With the higher performance aircraft, automatic recording equipment was fitted – Hussenot recorders which, when selected, registered a wide variety of flight data parameters on wire recordings. These recorders ultimately produced yards and yards of data strips, which had to be laboriously 'read-off' and logged in the data reduction forms appropriate to the particular test.

Right from the start of the course, it was stressed that the objective was not to turn us into test flying aces overnight – or even in eleven months. To become a capable test pilot requires years of practical experience actually doing the job on new and previously untested, aircraft. What the course aimed to do was to short-cut the learning process and provide us, in eleven months, with the sort of experience it would normally have taken a couple of years 'on the job' to acquire. Our academic studies were aimed at familiarising us with the basic physical and aerodynamic laws which affect aircraft design, performance and handling and, at the same time, at giving us sufficient familiarity with the technical side of the business to enable us to converse half-way intelligently with the designers and scientists, who tend to express themselves in the language of aerodynamic derivatives rather than in plain pilots English. Thus, stalling speed becomes $V \, sub \, s$ and the secondary effect of rudder becomes $Cn \, beta$ instead of sideslip. Without a reasonable knowledge of this scientific sub-language, communication between pilot and scientist could present considerable difficulty.

On the flying side, the school fleet provided us with the opportunity to cover virtually the entire range of test flying programmes on a variety of well-tried aircraft types. Hence, we could get used to the testing routines without having to learn the job the hard way on some new and previously untested, piece of kit. Moreover, in a small way, the school fleet gave us the opportunity to widen our experience of different types of aircraft and to access, in the air, different solutions to some of the perennial problems of aircraft design. With something like eighteen different types to work on – plus occasional experiences of other types, ether from the services or the manufacturers – ETPS provided us with the means of at least starting to put together some sort of yardstick of comparison that we could take from one cockpit to another.

Very early on in the course, I was given an enlightening demonstration of the value of multi-type experience to any aspiring test pilot. I was given an exercise to complete on the Varsity – an exercise which included an assessment of the ground handling of the aircraft. At the time, I had never before flown an aircraft fitted with nose-wheel steering – all of my previous experience had been on aircraft which were steered on the ground by differential use of the wheel brakes. With this sort of background experience, it is perhaps not surprising that I was very taken with the Varsity's steerable nose-wheel system, by which operation of a small wheel – rather like a miniature car steering wheel – enabled you to drive the aircraft very accurately when taxying. I thought it was the best invention since sliced bread and commented on it enthusiastically in my report.

During subsequent discussion of my findings, Bill Morrison asked me how many of the aircraft which I had previously flown had been equipped with a nose-wheel steering system. When I replied, 'none', he arranged for me to spend a couple of days at Boscombe Down, flying in a variety of aircraft with different nose-wheel steering systems. By the time I had tried the Vulcan, Victor, Beverley, Mk3 Shackleton and one or two others, I had got his point. I came back to Farnborough with sufficient experience of alternative systems to re-write a rather more balanced version of the ground handling section of my report.

The work which we had to undertake at Farnborough was aimed giving us familiarity with and competence in, the three basic varieties of test flying programmes: calibration testing; performance testing and handling testing.

Calibration testing is a sort of essential pre-requisite to any evaluation programme, since its sets out to determine the errors inherent in the aircraft flight instrumentation. All other programmes are going to be concerned with measuring either what the aircraft is doing, or how it is doing it, so that is essential to ensure, right at the outset, that any errors in the flight instruments, which are the aircraft measuring systems, are identified and accurately quantified.

Most of the basic instruments in an aircraft – like the air speed indicator, machmeter, altimeter and rate of climb and descent indicator, are operated by air pressure- either still air (static) pressure, pressure generated by movement (dynamic pressure), or by a cunning blend of both within the instrument. It is well know that air pressure falls off with increasing height. Hence, by using an aneroid barometer to measure the pressure at the level at which an aircraft is flying, it is possible to calculate the aircraft height. That, basically, is what an altimeter does. In much the same way, an air speed indicator feeds static plus dynamic pressure to one side of an aneroid and static pressure to the other. The difference between the two is presented as airspeed.

The problem with this sort of system is that it is very difficult to get accurate measurements of the pressures you want to use. The aircraft itself is a whacking great lump of metal, ploughing through the air at some speed, creating all sorts of disturbances to the air round about it. Its very ability to stay in the air at all is dependent on its creating pressure patterns, which can be used to generate a lift which keeps it up. These induced pressure patterns vary widely with the speed of the aircraft and, hence, its inclination to the induced airflow. As a result, it can be very difficult indeed to get accurate, undisturbed pressure readings to feed to the flight instrument. During the design of any aircraft, considerable care is taken to locate the pressure sensing points at positions on the airframe which, it is calculated, will be reasonably free from air-flow disturbances and, hence, induced pressure variations. Nevertheless, even with the best of designs, some measure of pressure error is inescapable.

This is where calibration testing comes into its own. All aircraft are put through a number of flights over an instrumented calibration range, during which the reading of each individual pressure-driven instrument is recorded for later comparison against measurements of the aircrafts exact flight parameters on each run, derived from kine-theodilite, radar, or high-speed photographic ground facilities. By the time the aircraft speed range has been covered, the differences between the two sets of readings will have defined the errors of each instrument very accurately. Later, the errors are collated for the pilot in the form of a cockpit correction card, which informs him of the pressure error allowance to be made in order to achieve any desired flight datum with absolute accuracy.

Calibration flying is typical of much of the work which goes into a flight test programme. It can be very dull, in that repeated runs over the same range are required to collect the test data. At the same time, it demands absolute and unrelenting, flying accuracy if the results are to be of any practical value. There is not much point in logging the readings for a hundred feet if you happen to be flying at some other height at the time. As they used to say at CFS, close enough simply isn't good enough. Either you get it right, or you might just as well have stayed on the ground.

The second basic variety of evaluation flying is performance testing, in which the objective of the exercise is to provide the purely quantitative data by which the performance of the aircraft may be expressed. Broadly speaking, performance testing provides the answers to the questions, 'How far will it fly?'; 'How fast?'; 'How high?'; 'What's the best climbing speed?'; 'How quickly can it turn?'. All of these and many other, aspects of aircraft performance can be expressed in strictly numerical terms – so many miles per hour, so many feet, so many miles and so many degrees per second. Performance testing is the phase of flight evaluation which provides these sorts of numbers.

Performance test flying can be and often is, a thoroughly undramatic and tedious business. Getting the raw data can be bad enough, but the real pain comes with reduction on the raw data to the form in which the results become meaningful. Unhappily, you can't just climb an aircraft up and up until it will simply climb no more and then come down content that you have established the flight ceiling. Go out tomorrow in the same aircraft and repeat the testing exactly the same way and you will find that your 'ceiling' is reached at some different height. Repeat the process over the next few days and you will find that you come down with a different result every time. Not much use when you come to write your report.

The reason for the variation in results is that the atmosphere in which aircraft operates changes from day to day. In particular, air density and temperature change, so that, on two successive days, an aircraft might be operating in quite different atmospheric environments. This doesn't make for easy performance testing. There really isn't much point in saying to a potential customer that his aircraft will do six hundred miles per hour at five thousand feet – and then adding, offhandedly, "by the way, that's always provided the temperature and density at five thousand feet is the same as it was last Thursday."

As a result of this unfortunate tendency of the atmosphere to vary from day to day, it becomes necessary to calculate, from an aircraft's performance data on any given day, what its performance would have been on a standard day – a day when every atmospheric parameter confirmed to the figures universally agreed in the international standard atmosphere. This is where the calculus comes in. If, on the day of your test, the temperature at your test altitude is a bit below standard – a negative delta t – you can work out that you are getting a bit more engine power than you have any right to expect- a positive delta p. This additional power is, in turn giving you a bit more speed (positive delta v) than you would have got on a standard day. When you get down from your sortie, you can look forward to the mind-numbing business of laboriously converting every single data point you have accumulated to the result you would have got on a standard day. To be fair, 'real' test pilots don't usually do this job themselves. They are normally off at high speed to the post-landing gin and tonic, while some poor flight-test engineer gets on with the donkey work. At ETPS, however we had to do it all ourselves – probably just to make us realise how lucky we would be later on when we could pass the job on to someone else. Boring or not, however, performance reduction is the only system which produces results that are of any practical use to a flight-test programme.

The actual methods of collecting the raw flight test data are fairly straightforward. If, for example, you want to determine the best climbing speed of an aircraft to its ceiling, you start off by measuring the time it takes to climb through one altitude band at relatively low level – say two thousand to seven thousand feet. At something like fifteen hundred feet, you note your starting weight and set the aircraft up at climbing power, trimmed-out at your first test airspeed. Holding the speed rock-steady, you start your stopwatch as you pass two thousand feet and stop it as you pass seven thousand. You then note the elapsed time to provide you with your first data point.

By repeating the process at a number of different speeds, a set of results will become available giving the different times taken to climb through the selected height band at the different air speeds used. When all the results have been reduced to ISA conditions and adjustments made to take account of the different weights at the start of each climb, it will be possible to define the speed to be flown to give the maximum rate of climb through the height band selected – it will be the speed at which least time was taken to traverse the height band. Having got this far, the next step is to work your way through a number of height bands all the way up to the ceiling of the aircraft. By repeating the test procedure at each of the bands selected, it will eventually be possible to define, for any height, the optimum speed to be flown to give maximum rate of climb at that altitude.

The procedure described is the basic text-book technique for this sort of test exercise and it works very well for non-high-performance aircraft. In a modern fighter, however, the rates of climb are so high and the time taken to go through a given height band so low, that the poor test pilot would barely have started his watch before he had rocketed far, far above his upper flight datum. The Lightning Mk6, for example, is by no means a modern aircraft – the last one came off the production line in 1967 – but its initial rate of climb has been assessed at something over fifty thousand feet a minute. Such an aircraft would go through a five thousand foot height band in about six seconds. That really doesn't leave you a lot of time for note taking on the way up!

In fact, for the high performance aircraft, different techniques, such as accelerated levels or energy climb are used to cover this part of the test programme and the test data is logged on automatic recorders. Regardless, however, of the actual test technique employed, or the equipment used to record the data, the fundamentals of the system remain the same. Accurate flying to provide the test data points and timings and subsequent reduction of the data to ISA conditions.

For most of the major flight parameters, the flight test technique used is simply to go out and measure them. To determine the altitude ceiling, you climb the aircraft until the rate of climb has fallen to a negligible value: to determine maximum air speed or Mach number, you up the speed slowly, in small increments, until you can't get the aircraft to go any faster – or, more specifically, until its acceleration has fallen to a negligible level. To determine maximum range, you fly the aircraft in a cruse climb profile, continuously adjusting speed and height as fuel is consumed, until you get down to a very low fuel state. No point in overdoing things and running the tanks bone dry. Back on the ground, you can always calculate how far you would have gone with the fuel left in the tanks at the point when you call the test off. To determine turning performance, you measure the time it takes to roll-in to any particular bank angle and then measure the number of degrees of heading the aircraft turns through in unit time.

Quite obviously, it could take a very long time indeed to go right through the performance envelope of a modern high-performance aircraft, in order to provide test data at every possible flight condition. Fortunately, much test data can be provided by flying 'stabilised levels'. Using this technique, the aircraft is trimmed-out to fly hands and feet off the controls, in level un-accelerated flight at the test altitude. The engine power required to maintain this stable flight condition is then recorded. From the engine performance graphs, the maximum power available at the test height can be determined. Any excess power available in the engine at the test condition is, in theory at least, available to be used for climbing, for acceleration, or for manoeuvre, and, by doing some very clever sums, the flight engineers can calculate precisely how much of each you could have got out of the spare power available at the time. This technique markedly reduces the time and number of flights, required to get through a flight-test performance programme – very important when you consider the cost of putting a modern aircraft into the air. The technique also enables you to restrict text-book measurement testing almost exclusively to the aircraft performance limit conditions.

The third major category of flight testing is handling testing, when you are primarily concerned, not so much with what the aircraft does, but rather with how it does it. This test phase is concerned less with measurement and more with feel of the machine in every manoeuvre of which it is capable. In many ways, it is the most demanding and most interesting, part of the test programme. The end objective is to ensure that the aircraft is safe to fly throughout its entire performance spectrum, that it does not make undue demands on the pilot to achieve accurate flight and that it gives a clear and timely warning of its entry into any hazardous flight condition. As a careful re-reading of the last sentence will make clear, the test objectives are rather intangible: 'safe', 'undue', 'accurate', 'clear' and 'timely' are all subjective values, for which the assessment of acceptable levels may well vary from one pilot to another. We used to say blithely that the objective was to produce handling qualities such that the aircraft could be flown safely and effectively by the 'average squadron pilot'. But, again, how do you define 'average'?

For some of the parameters involved, experience has provided working levels of acceptability. To cite just one example, when a pilot pulls back on the control column to initiate some manoeuvre, he exerts two distinct forces on the stick. First, he exerts 'break-out' force – the force required to complete the initial move of the control from its trimmed, 'at-rest' condition. Thereafter, to sustain the condition he has initiated, he exerts a force on the stick proportional to the 'g' generated by the manoeuvre – the 'stick force per g'. Over the years, a fairly clear picture has been built up of the limits within which these forces must fall for the aircraft to be 'comfortable' to fly. You don't want to have to push or pull like mad to break-out the control initially – but neither do you want the force to be so light that the slightest pressure on the control will start the aircraft moving away from its trimmed condition. Equally, with stick force per g, you don't want the value to be so high that manoeuvring requires the muscles of a blacksmith, or so low that you could risk overstressing the aircraft every time you move the control.

Even when you get one control nicely weighted, you have to ensure that the other two don't provide marked contrasts in the force required to operate them. In particular, you want the elevator and aileron controls to be nicely blended or 'harmonised' as they say in the trade. ETPS provided an object lesson in poor harmonisation in the Sea Hawk, one of the first aircraft to be fitted with hydraulically powered ailerons. In any turn, it required only the merest whisper on the stick sideways to stand the thing on its wing-tip, after which you had to haul back like a navvy on the manually powered elevator control to hold yourself in the turn. Some of the early Jet Provosts were quite the reverse – over-sensitive on the elevators compared with the ailerons.

With the attainment of 'good flying qualities' firmly in mind, you work your way through a handling programme by investigating every aspect of aircraft handling in every condition of flight it is possible to attain. You probe the static and dynamic stability characteristics, check the handling at high and low airspeeds and at the high Mach numbers, take it through all types of stalls and spins and fly into – and, hopefully, out of – every sort of manoeuvre the aircraft might ever get into. This is very demanding flying indeed. It takes a special breed of pilot to deliberately put a new aircraft into an inverted spin and sit there, dispassionately noting its behaviour, the rate of rotation, the degree of pitching and the forces on the controls, before he starts to think about how he is going to get the damn thing to recover. I think that it would be true to say that most test pilots earn most of their salary during the handling phases of the test programmes they undertake.

At ETPS, we worked our way steadily through the course syllabus, starting off with fairly simple test exercises and progressing, week by week, to more advanced and demanding flight evaluations. No doubt about it, it was a hard course – even in the air. There was little or no time available for 'flying for fun' – only about a hundred and forty hours of flying time were available to each student and there was an awful lot of productive exercise work to be packed into that total.

The ground school side was a nightmare for most of us. As we got deeper and deeper into the physics and aerodynamics that constituted our academic staple diet, many of us were reduced to putting in longer hours of private study at home, simply to try to keep up with the syllabus. The lecture notes we were given to help us along seemed to be comprised of a few words of English per page supplemented by reams of equations in Greek symbology – known to one and all as 'flute' music. It was – at least to me – a fairly major intellectual effort just to read the wretched notes – much less come to any understanding of their contents. I can remember one afternoon at the Blue Pool at Camberley, noting that all of the ETPS students there, ostensibly on an afternoon out with their wives and children, were engrossed in their course notes, poring over the flute music to the virtual exclusion of everything else. The wives and children were simply being left to get on with enjoying themselves as best as they could – strictly on their own.

During the first month or two, our test exercises were fairly simple ones in order to give us a chance to familiarise ourselves on the school aircraft fleet. This was type conversion very different from the carefully monitored system of extensive ground school and dual instruction most of us had been used to previously. At Farnborough, you were given the Pilots Notes and expected to get on with it. I got thirty five minutes dual in the Varsity and fifteen minutes in the Pembroke and – apart from helicopter flying – that was the sum total of my dual flying for the entire course. On my second trip in the Hunter, I went supersonic for the first time in my life and I took my instrument rating test for piston-engine aircraft on my first ever flight in a Devon.

In retrospect, this method of throwing us in 'off the deep end' was not really the best way to introduce us to type flying. At that stage, we were not test pilots – not by a long way. Most of us were straight off front line squadrons, well used to one type of aircraft and it was pushing things unnecessarily to have us flung off in totally different types of aircrafts, for which our only preparation was a quick read through the Pilot's Notes. Some of the fighter contingent had come straight off Hunters without ever having flown a piston engine aircraft in their lives, until they found themselves strapped to a Varsity and launched off. I was relatively lucky in having at least flown a few trips in aircraft other than Meteors and Canberras, but I had never flown with powered flying controls before I took a Hunter up. Had any emergency arisen during the first flight, I might well have been hard pushed to cope effectively.

At the time, we all loved the system as it was. We simply couldn't wait to get off in something we hadn't flown before – and, to be fair – the system worked. Nobody got into any sort of serious trouble. With the advantage of hindsight, however, I now feel that the system was a bit too unnecessarily 'Gung-Ho' and that we all took risks that were quite needless. Subsequently, the introductory phase was changed to limit students to holding currency on only a limited number of types, until they accumulated a bit more experience as the course progressed.

If it was all a bit dashing at Farnborough, it was sometimes even more so during our visits to the aircraft manufactures, when the companies would quite happily roll out some of their prized possessions for us to have a go at. I remember that Fairey had a Tiger Moth and two little Tipsy aircraft – the Tipsy B and the Tipsy Junior. They were powered by Czech Micron motorcycle engines and were so small that you could almost touch the ground while sitting in the cockpits. In the air, you could turn them simply by sticking your arm out into the slipstream. Hawkers had a Hurricane and a Tomtit and Blackburn had the B2 biplane. Most of these aircraft were genuine antiques – quite priceless – but we were allowed to whip them up and down, after the most cursory run round the cockpit to have the more important tits and knobs pointed out to us.

One of the highlights of the course was the periodic importation of 'specialist' types of aircraft which were provided to enhance further our growing experience of different types. Sometimes they were selected as being representative of a particular class of aircraft – the Lincoln, for example, was a fairly representative four-engine type; sometimes they were chosen for their performance; and sometimes they were chosen to give us experience of some particular design feature – the Avro 707 and Javelin delta-wing aircraft were examples of the latter category. Flying these aircraft was always stimulating and created many a pitfall for the unwary. A student on a long-past course had reached down from his seat in a Lancaster to operate the bomb-doors selector lever and had inadvertently got hold of the fuel jettison selector. He was less than popular when the flight line went ankle-deep in high octane petrol. Next day, at his second attempt to get going in the aircraft, he was very careful to ensure he had the correct lever in his grip when he selected bomb doors shut, but less careful in checking that the fuel jettison selector had been reset. It hadn't! As soon as electrical power was applied, the fuel jettison system activated again and the flight line was deluged once more. Eventually, I believe, they gave him something else to get his four-engine experience on.

In the case of the 1957 course, the specialist aircraft that gave most of us problems was the turbo-prop powered Gannet – the Royal Navy's carrier borne anti-submarine aircraft. It was actually a very good aeroplane once you got the engines started – it was getting them started in the first place that gave most of us fits. I should perhaps explain that the Gannet was powered by an extremely cleverly designed engine – the Armstrong-Siddeley Double Mamba. This was really two engines designed into one so that, although the Gannet looked just like any other single-engine, machine, it was, in fact, a true 'twin' – each engine drove one of the two in-line propeller's. Most of the 'on-station' flying was done on one engine to conserve fuel.

The starting problems stemmed, we were told, from the design of the original starting system which utilised high pressure compressed air to wind the engines up. This system was totally unacceptable to the Navy who, quite reasonably, were flatly opposed to having their carrier decks littered with air compressors and hoses. At their insistence, the system had to be redesigned to make provision for internal cartridge-powered starters. It was at this point, that things started to go wrong. When the engine starter manufacturers had a look at the Mamba engine, they assessed it to be very nearly the same size as the in-service Ghost engine. Accordingly, a double-shot starter was designed based on the Ghost installation. Unhappily, at this stage, no one drew their attention to the fact that the Mamba – while a perfectly straightforward jet engine – was being used in a turbo-prop aircraft and that, in service, it would have a very large and very heavy propeller fixed on to the end of the turbine shaft. The result was entirely predictable – the production model starter would start the engine without any trouble – provided there was no propeller attached to it. Since the Gannet very definitely needed its propellers, the solution to the starting problem was something less than wholly successful.

As a result of this situation, the technique which was eventually adopted to get the Gannet engines fired-up was, quite definitely a non-standard procedure. We were given a half-day lecture on the subject by a Naval expert – a lecture which, for me at any rate, served only to make confusion worse confounded. I had to get Cliff Evans, one of my naval friends on the course to take me through the drill in a cockpit 'dummy-run' before I had much idea of what I was trying to do.

As I remember the technique, you started off by setting one of the engines up for starting much as with any other jet. You then pressed the starter button and, at the revs built up, opened the fuel high pressure cock to get 'light-up'. As the high pressure cock was opened fully, the revs built up very rapidly to something around ninety per cent – at which point, you very rapidly reversed everything and shut the engine down again. As soon as the high pressure cock was closed, alarm bells rang, alarm lights flashed and the whole affair appeared to have got completely out of hand. Ignoring all of these distractions, you watched, eagle-eyed, until the revs dropped off to something like thirty per cent, when you hurriedly selected the second starter shot, pushed the button again, shoved on the fuel cock and hoped like mad that the thing would 'self-sustain' this time. By now, every alarm system in the aircraft was ringing, flashing and blaring at full intensity but, if you were lucky, the running start on the second go would build the revs up to the point at which the wretched engine would actually keep running.

After all of this high drama, starting the second engine was a piece of cake. You simply let the propeller free-wheel in the induced slipstream from the live engine and then used the slipstream to turn the second engine over for a routine 'air-start'. If, at this stage, you did not feel an overpowering compulsion to go and lie down in a darkened room, you were ready to go flying. I liked the Gannet very much, but, after the starting sequence, I always felt that getting into the air was a very definite anti-climax.

The Gloster Javelin was another 'specialist' which created moments of diversion for unsuspecting students. I remember that when the Javelin arrived, all of us had great difficulty in actually getting it out of dispersal. It seemed that, every time the pilot touched the toe-brakes, the nose-wheel would unlock and finish up at right angles to the desired direction of motion. The ground crew then had to rush out and straighten the wheel out manually, before the pilot could try to get un-derway again. One poor soul spent so much time jerking his way around the flight line area with the ground crew in hot pursuit that he came close to running out of fuel before he even made the taxiway.

The Gannet – which was hard enough to start – demonstrated that, on occa-sions, it could be equally hard to stop. The wheel brakes on the aircraft were small studs which projected through the flat rudder pedals. One day, one of our gallant 'dark blues' went off in the thing when he was wearing a pair of shoe with crepe soles – of the type popularly known, at the time, as 'brothel creepers'. When he tried to operate the brakes, he found that the small brake stud was simply sinking into the crepe soles of his shoes without having any effect on the brakes. Much discomfited, he had to remove his shoes very hurriedly and continue with the flight in his stockinged feet.

Yet another who was caught out by the Gannet was one of our Canadians, who had no trouble with the aircraft at all until he came in to land it. I should, perhaps mention, at this point, that this particular Canadian was built on the general lines of King Kong and had fingers like a bunch of bananas. At the time, the Gannet had a 'force' stop on the throttles at the 'flight idle' position on the quadrant – designed to prevent even the most ham-fisted from inadvertently putting the engines into ground idle while still in the air. On this particular occasion, making his first approach in the aircraft to Farnborough's short runway, out Canadian colleague never even noticed the force stop. It would have taken a really hefty effort on my part to have pulled the throttles through, but for him, the force stop might just as well not have existed. At about twenty feet off the ground, he got both throttles into ground idle, with the result that the two whacking great pro-peller's up front 'fined-off' to the point at which they were practically a flat plate stuck on the nose. Fairly predictably, the aircraft very rapidly ceased to be a flyable proposition and descended almost instantaneously to an arrival at something of the order of force six on the Richter scale. Only the fact that it was a naval aircraft, designed to cope with carrier landings, prevented a total write-off on the spot. Some years later, I noticed that the Gannet force stop had been replaced by a rather more foolproof system – perhaps, with backwoods Canadians in mind!

The part of the course flying syllabus which I liked least was the glider flying. Others on the course loved it, but I had got too used to the idea of having an en-gine along with me to take kindly to relying exclusively on gravity and air thermals. We had to fly three different types of glider – a Sedbergh trainer and two sailplanes, the Sky and the Olympia. These latter two were very high performance gliders, in which it was possible to carry out flights of extraordinary duration and range – Bob Cockburn took the Olympia down well south of Paris one day. I'm afraid that I never flew any one of them more than a couple of miles – as soon as I cast off from the Chipmunk tug which provided the air launch, I used to simply go round in circles over Lasham airfield until I ran out of height and could put the thing back on the ground again. Once the tutors grasped the idea that gliders were not my most popular aircraft type, they generally let me volunteer to fly the Chipmunk tug – which nobody else wanted to do anyway. I think that the whole course was happy with this arrangement- it let the 'no-power' addicts get on with their gliding and soaring without having to take their turn driving the tug and it let me go on, as I preferred, with a good healthy roar from the engine to sustain my morale.

Perhaps the most exciting part of the course came when we got around to learning how to fly helicopters. It was at this stage that I found good cause to be grateful for the one and only motor-cycle ride I ever had, when I had been at Moreton-in-Marsh. Since that time, I had studiously avoided having anything to do with them. This turned out to be quite an advantage when we started on helicopters, in that a helicopter throttle is a twist-grip control almost identical to that of a motor-cycle – except that it works in the reverse sense. In a helicopter, you twist FORWARD to increase power. I had no trouble adapting to this technique, but it created absolute havoc with those course members who had driven motor-cycles. Time and again, just as they were coming into the flare and power was needed to hold the machine in the hover prior to landing, back would come the twist grip, to the accompaniment of a much reduced noise level and an undignified collapse on to the ground. While I had plenty of other problems with helicopters, at least I never found any trouble with throttle manipulation.

While we were in the helicopter phase, we were regaled with endless horror stories about the perils of ground resonance – a condition in which, if I understand it aright, a slight bump on landing can cause the machine to bounce up and down uncontrollably, until the power is taken off and it settles down to earth. On one never to be forgotten occasion, we were treated to a full-scale demonstration of the phenomenon from a pilot who was delivering a Dragonfly to the school. From the hover over the landing pad, the touchdown appeared to be on one of the main wheels only and the aircraft seemed to bounce back onto the other wheel. It then commenced to bounce fairly rapidly from one wheel to the other – neither fully flying nor fully landed. Why the pilot didn't just throttle right back and slam it down I will never know, but he didn't, so that, very quickly, the bouncing from wheel to wheel became increasingly more violent. Eventually the tip of the main rotor was tilted so far over that it struck the ground. At this point, the rotor stopped turning altogether and the rest of the aircraft began to rotate very rapidly about the stationary rotor blades, with bits and pieces of the structure falling off and being scattered in all directions. In a matter of seconds, the machine literally shook itself to pieces and, when the dust had cleared, the pilot was observed to be sitting in the middle of a pile of wreckage, still strapped to his seat, which was the only part of the airframe still intact. After this spectacular incident, we all became very positive in our helicopter landings. From the hover, we either went very firmly up, or very firmly down – we certainly didn't hang about in between.

As the end of the course approached, we were required to put in our primary and secondary preferences for our next postings. I opted for 'B' squadron – the bomber and transport test squadron – at Boscombe Down, with a secondary preference for any sort of testing involving multi-engine heavies. When the postings arrived, I found that there were only two vacancies on 'B' at Boscombe – one was allocated as a RAAF exchange slot and went to Russ Law and the other, allocated to the top RAF bomber man on the course, went to Ray Morgan. I found myself assigned to 'D' squadron at Boscombe. At the time, I didn't even know what they did there.

CHAPTER 26

THE TABLOIDS CALLED IT 'Britain's Hush-Hush Airbase' or 'The Secret Test Airfield'. The more up-market dailies called it 'A Secret Test Establishment in the South of England'. Official circles know it as 'The Aeroplane and Armament Experimental Establishment'. Industry recognises it as 'A&AEE'. To those whose place of work it is, it is simply 'Boscombe' or, occasionally, 'Amesbury Air Patch'. It is one of a number of governments owned and operated research establishments and its function is to test all RAF and RN aircraft prior to their formal acceptance into service. From the standpoint of the quality of the aircraft in the RAF and the RN, it was, unquestionably, the most important airfield in Britain.

Boscombe Down is located just off the A345 between Amesbury and Salisbury, a matter of a mile or so south of Amesbury. This is a particularly attractive part of the English countryside, where the towns retain some sort of individuality and character and many of the villages seem to have stayed relatively unchanged over the past couple of hundred years. At first sight, there seems to be some element of incongruity in the siting of an ultra-modern test establishment right in the heart of rural England. One might have expected such a base to be sited in a rather more remote and less easily accessible, part of the country.

The existence of a surprising number of airfields in this particular part of England stems, at least in part, from the proximity of nearby Salisbury Plain, where so much of the pioneering activity of British military aviation took place. Although early test flying was carried out largely on an ad hoc basis and at a variety of locations, the evaluation of RAF aircraft gradually evolved, over the years, into a formal organizational structure, which finally found a permanent base at Martlesham Heath, near Ipswich. When the threat of war became significant in the late 1930s, it was felt that the location of an important test facility so close to the East Coast – and, hence, close to the potential threat – was rather less than prudent and the whole operation was moved well west to Boscombe Down, in the heart of Wiltshire.

In the 1950s, the Establishment was organized into four major trials squadrons: 'A' Squadron was responsible for the service testing of all fighter and trainer aircraft, 'B' Squadron for all bomber, maritime and transport aircraft and 'C' Squadron for all naval aircraft. 'D' Squadron – officially titled "The Airborne Forces and Helicopter Test Squadron" – was split into two separate flights. 'A' Flight was responsible for the testing of everything, other than weapons, that could be tied on to, or thrown out of, military aircraft – activities such as parachuting, supply dropping, survival-gear dropping and target towing. 'B' Flight was responsible for all helicopter testing. In addition to the trials squadrons, Boscombe hosted the Royal Air Force Handling Squadron, responsible for the compilation and updating of Pilots Notes for all in-service aircraft and a small Civil Aircraft Test Section, responsible for certain specialized aspects of the testing of civil aircraft in service use. The Commandant of the Establishment was an Air Commodore who, in practically every case, had himself been a practicing test pilot. In 1957, the

Commandant was Air Commodore A E Clouston, a pilot famous for very many pre-war record flights and who had been much occupied in the wartime testing of barrage balloon wire-cutting equipment, which he evaluated by the simple, but somewhat hair-raising, method of deliberately flying his test aircraft into balloon cables.

When I arrived at 'D' Squadron, it was to find that, apart from the Flight Commander, I was the only graduate test pilot on the strength of 'A' Flight. Lest it should hastily be concluded that this fact put me in something of a 'one-up' position on the flight, I should make it abundantly clear that it did nothing of the sort. The other three 'working level' pilots – Jimmy Culverwell, Ian Maclaren and Norman Penny – had behind them a quite extraordinarily varied and extensive flying experience and were all pilots of very high capability indeed. While they had not been accorded the somewhat doubtful privilege of having been exposed to eleven months of 'flute music', there was very little that anyone could have taught them about what to do with a stick and rudder.

The aircraft which were then currently being put through their paces in the flight included the Beverley – for heavy platform drop clearances; the Shackelton 3 – for Lindholme Survival Gear drop clearance; and the Meteor TT20 and the Hunter 5 for target towing clearances. Additionally, the flight had a Valetta for occasional parachuting and supply drop sorties, a Harvard for low speed photography of load extraction during Beverley heavy drop sorties and a Meteor 7 which we used for instrument flying practice and for instrument ratings and also for high-speed photography of ejection seat and crew escape trials on the V-bombers. From time to time, other aircraft came in for a range of test programmes – types like the Pioneer, Twin Pioneer, Scimitar, Hastings, Gannet and Canberra – so that there was always plenty of variety to 'spice-up' our staple flying diet,

The organization of the Squadron into two separate flights meant that we, in 'A' flight, were not formally concerned with the helicopter activities of 'B' flight. Nevertheless, I took every chance that was available to keep my hand in on the 'infuriated palm trees'. I found that most of the 'B' flight pilots were keen to maintain their jet Instrument Ratings and, since I was squadron Instrument Rating Examiner and had control of the Meteor 7, I was in a fairly strong bargaining position. By the judicious employment of this bargaining lever, I was able to get in a fairly regular number of trips in the Skeeter, Dragonfly and Sycamore. Maybe not the most modern helicopters around at the time, but it was all experience.

One of the big thrills of my early flying at Boscombe was getting my hands on the Beverley. At the time of its entry into service in the mid-1950s, the Beverley was not only the largest aircraft in the RAF, but also the first British aircraft specifically designed for the dropping of heavy Army equipment through rear loading doors. It could carry a payload of twenty-two tons, had a freight hold of nearly six thousand cubic feet, carried umpteen passengers, troops, or paratroops in an upper tail boom and could take-off and land in the remarkable distances of 310 yards and 350 yards respectively. In spite of its size – and it was a very big aeroplane indeed – the overwhelming impression of the Beverley was not so much its dimensions, as its bulk – close up, it looked somewhat like a small hanger with wings on. Even getting into the driving seat involved something of a climb – once you had mounted the steps into the aircraft itself, you still had to face another fairly lengthy ladder to get up to the flight deck. When settled down and ready to go, the pilot's eye level was something like thirty feet above the ground. Unkind critics alleged that it was possible to be in cloud before you had even got the engines started. 'Timber' Wood, the Blackburn test pilot who did all of the early development testing, used to say that flying the Beverley was like flying a three-bedroom council house from the upstairs front bedroom window.

With its enormous bulk, fixed undercarriage and virtual – if not total – lack of streamlining, the Beverley was not the most beautiful thing ever to take to the skies, but it was, nonetheless, a very effective machine in the role for which it was designed. Its nose wheel steering system was quite unique and occasioned much hilarity among pilots more used to a conventional system. The Beverley featured a retractable steering 'tiller' – exactly the same as one would find on a small boat – and this always introduced a distinctly 'nautical' element to ground manoeuvering. You were always slightly tempted to call for 'all ahead together' when starting off. Since the propeller system also featured reverse pitch, allowing the aircraft to be taxied in reverse, there was an even stronger temptation to call for 'all astern together' when driving the thing backwards. I remember once landing at the Company's airfield at Brough and being unable to get the propellers out of reverse pitch after landing. Every time I started off towards the buildings, the aeroplane would trundle off backwards, heading inexorably towards the Humber. After two or three tries, I had to give up and leave it to the company engineers to sort out the problem. I recall that they were not much amused: they seemed to think that it was all my fault.

I always enjoyed flying the Harvard on photographic coverage of heavy drops from the Beverley. The loads were stowed on heavy drop platforms in the freight hold and, when the drop was initiated, one would see the extractor parachute stream out from the hold to drag out the cluster of main parachutes which would support the load. Then, quite slowly it seemed, the massive heavy platform would appear, rumbling down to the tailgate before it was dragged clear of the aircraft. From the Harvard, close in, the Beverley hold looked big enough to land in. On these sorties, you had to be careful not to get yourself into the slipstream from the Beverley's Centaurus engines, or the poor little Harvard would be tossed about uncontrollably like a leaf in a tornado. Incidentally, mention of the Harvard reminds me of a trick Ian Maclaren showed me one day which I thought was very advanced stuff. Taxying back into dispersal and heading directly for his parking slot, Ian suddenly stamped hard on one brake to unlock the tail wheel. As the aircraft swung round rapidly, he then stamped equally hard again on the other brake to stop the swing and re-lock the tail wheel. The aircraft was now running backwards slowly and, with a sudden burst of throttle, he brought it to a neat halt, precisely in position and facing the right way out for the next flight. I never had the courage to try it myself. Ian was full of these little tricks: I saw him once land a Pioneer BACKWARDS into his dispersal slot. Admittedly, the Pioneer landed very slowly and there was a stiff wind blowing, but I wouldn't have liked to try the manoeuvre in such a confined space.

It is always a pleasure to watch an experienced pilot extricate himself from a potentially hazardous situation. One such occasion arose when Norman Penny went off in a Scimitar towing a supersonic target. The target was a fearsome looking piece of kit, very much like an oversized dart, about twenty feet long and with a solid steel spike, about six or eight feet long, at the nose. Quite clearly, you couldn't jettison a thing like that on the airfield at the end of the sortie, so it was arranged that he would unload it at the Everleigh dropping range before he landed back at Boscombe. I went over to Everleigh by car to act as Range Safety Officer. About fifteen minutes before Norman was due to arrive on the scene, the sky over the range suddenly filled with aircraft and parachutists started leaping out in hordes. As I watched in mounting horror, supply containers, guns, ammunition and still more paratroops started to rain down and light observation aircraft and helicopters arrived in some force to add to the general impression of World War 3. We later learned that Everleigh had been selected for a major no notice Army Airborne Forces exercise and they had picked a day when we had our own operations going on at the same range.

Right in the middle of all this bedlam, Norman Penny arrived with his fearsome dart in short trail astern and was somewhat put out to discover his jettison area swarming with everyone and everything in the airborne forces inventory. His fuel state did not permit a diversion to another range location, so that he was pretty well stuck with making his drop on to an already overcrowded range. We discussed the situation quickly on the radio and I was able to point out a small area, right on the edge of the range, which seemed to be reasonably clear of either men or equipment. Norman took it all in very calmly and then threaded his way through all the other activity to deliver his lethal load – by eyeball judgment – precisely into the one small area of the range where it was safe to do so. Any darts player would have raised a spontaneous cheer. At the sight of the dart quivering menacingly in the ground, an army major rushed over to me and demanded to know what we were playing at, hazarding life and limb with our 'light blue' toys. I had to point out that it was our range, that we had no knowledge of his plans to use it that day and, anyway – the final all-purpose service clincher – if he didn't have a sense of humour, he shouldn't have joined-up in the first place.

Around the middle of my first year in 'D' Squadron, I was given the job of evaluating the Percival EP9, a small crop-dusting aircraft that the Army were considering buying to replace their Air Observation Austers. The bulk of the trials programme was to be conducted at the Tropical Experimental Unit, which was then located at RAF Idris, just outside Tripoli in Libya. I suppose that I could truthfully say that my real test flying education began in earnest with my assignment to that programme.

The aircraft itself was quite a pleasant little flying machine – a high wing, fixed undercarriage design of an appearance that was once described as "rather what one would expect to get if the Beverley ever had pups." After a couple of introductory trips at Boscombe, the small trials team launched off to Idris, myself and the project engineer in the EP9, the rest in an Anson, which, since we had a strictly limited set of cockpit instruments, was supposed to help us out with the navigation – particularly, on the sea crossings. Almost needless to say, the only legs when we lost close contact with the Anson turned out to be the three sea crossing legs. Murphy's Law!

The trip out to Idris turned out to be something of a Cecil B de Mille production. At our cruising speed of little better than ninety odd knots, it took us seven days to complete the Boscombe – Orleans – Dijon – Orange – Nice – Pisa – Rome – Naples – Catania – Luqa – Tripoli marathon. We could almost have driven there faster. In fact, going down the Rhone Valley against a strong headwind, we were frequently overtaken by cars on the auto routes below. By the time we actually got to Idris, I felt that I had just about completed a full tour of duty on the aircraft.

For the test programme, we moved from Idris to an extremely uncomfortable and primitive location at a desert landing strip near El Azizia. Here, after a couple of days to sort ourselves out, we finally got the trials underway. The performance and handling phases of the programme went off without any significant difficulty – pretty much as I had been taught to do at Farnborough. Some of the other aspects of the trials programme – notably the operational suitability phases – did, however, provide moments of diversion and, incidentally, very valuable experience of where to draw the line in what to try in an aircraft and, perhaps more important, what not to try.

In my own defence, I might say that I was still relatively inexperienced in actual test flying, but I shudder to think of some of the daft things I was led into trying out. A good example was the asymmetric stores configuration take-off. The aircraft carried stores containers under each wing and, for some reason which, at the time, must have sounded reasonably plausible, I was induced to try a take-off one day with a full load of stores containers under one wing and nothing under the other. Why, Heaven only knows! Common sense should have told me that, in service, even if one wanted to put all of the full containers on one wing – which, itself, is highly questionable – the sensible thing to do would be to put containers filled with bricks on the other wing to balance the weight. Fairly predictably, when I launched off in the lopsided configuration I was given, one wing got airborne quite happily while the other didn't. The little aircraft turned smartly over on its back, leaving me sitting upside-down in the cockpit with petrol dripping all over the place and me fervently wishing that I had put just a bit more thought into that particular test.

When we had got the thing right way up again and straightened out the propeller – the only significant damage to the machine – we pushed on with the programme, somewhat wiser, but no whit deterred. The next drama point came when I had concluded the assessment of minimum safe flying speed, which I established at something around the forty-knot mark. When I reported my findings to the project engineer, he seemed quite happy with the numbers, until he added, almost offhandedly, "Well, we'll just try it a couple of knots lower tomorrow."

I was somewhat taken aback at this response. After all, the objective of the test was to determine the slowest speed at which the aircraft could safely be flown and that I had done. Now, it was being proposed that we try it slower still. When I expressed reservations on this idea, I was told, "but you see, Harry, we need a solid data point to anchor the bottom of the curve. If we don't establish it in the air, the results will always be regarded as speculative."

In later years, I would have very bluntly made the point that some test numbers are best left as rather speculative but, at the time, the idea of precisely fixing the data point did seem to have some merit. Anyway, next day I went out to try it. Give the project engineer his due; he was sitting beside me at the time. Inevitably, when I got down below the speed I had already established as the safe minimum, the aeroplane simply lost all interest in flying at all and threw itself down on to the landing strip – hard enough to drive the main wheels straight up into the cabin. That gave us a couple of days for reflection, while the poor mechanics fitted a new undercarriage. It is, perhaps, not much consolation to take out of this sorry episode, but, at the very least, I always could claim afterwards that I did establish the minimum safe flying speed on the EP9 to a degree of accuracy unmatched in test flying experience. Anyone who ever tries it any slower is going to crash – guaranteed!

Towards the end of my first year at Boscombe, the Royal Navy Target Towing squadron at Hal Far in Malta reported considerable difficulty in deploying their drogue targets successfully from their Meteor TT20 aircraft. In an attempt to resolve their problems, Boscombe dispatched myself and Flight Sergeant Betts, a very experienced man with target sleeves, to Malta by the first available BEA Viscount. When we arrived at Hal Far, to a very warm welcome from the Squadron, Flight Sergeant Betts got down to his examination of the target sleeves, while I tried a target 'stream' from one of their aircraft. Sure enough, it didn't work. When I landed, Betts drew me aside and, looking off somewhere into the far distance, enquired innocuously how long it would be convenient for me to stay in Malta. Somewhat taken aback, I asked if he had come to any conclusions as to the cause of the failures.

"Oh yes," he remarked casually, pointing to a mass of numbers stencilled on to the drogue containers, "these things should be streamed within, at most, six months of packing. These ones have been in the containers for up to a couple of years or more." He was, I noted, still gazing off innocently into the far distance.

Well, I don't have to be hit over the head with a hammer to get a simple point. Malta is a very pleasant spot, particularly so in late November and a few days in the sun never did anybody any harm at all.

"Now looks here, Flight Sergeant," I replied, myself fixing my attention on the far horizons, "we want to be absolutely certain of our findings before we come to any conclusions. We must be absolutely meticulous in exploring all possibilities before we commit ourselves. We certainly don't want to jump to any hasty or premature answers before we've done a thorough job, do we now?"

"Absolutely not, Sir," rejoined the excellent Flight Sergeant. "I'll just get on, then, with a thorough check of these targets and leave you to check the aircraft systems." On this suitably professional note and still avoiding looking at each other directly, we parted in high good spirits. After all, if the job is worth doing, then it's worth doing thoroughly.

I put in a couple of weeks delightful flying from Hal Far including a detachment to Sicily to participate in a target-towing exercise for the Italian Fleet – an exercise which led to the sending of a classic signal from the Squadron Commander to the Italian Fleet Headquarters. The signal read, "REFERENCE TARGET-TOWING PROCEDURES. PLEASE NOTE THAT I AM PULLING THE B..... THING, NOT PUSHING IT." Away from the flying side, I was entertained right royally by the dark blues and enjoyed what seemed like a non-stop succession of parties with them all over the Island. I remember that I got my first introduction to 'Horses Necks' – brandy and ginger ale – during one of the Squadrons 'blasts'. I liked it better than pink gin. Eventually, after due time had elapsed for us to check all that there was to be checked, Flight Sergeant Betts and I duly announced our finding that the drogue failures were due to their having been packed in the containers for too long a time. A supply of new targets was procured and the squadrons problems were solved. Much credit devolved on A&AEE for having provided two such expert advisors and Flight Sergeant Betts and I returned to UK, fully refreshed from the break and secure in the knowledge that our thorough and professional efforts had not been in vain. I could have taken a programme like that every month of the year.

Within a matter of days after my return to Boscombe, I learned that a vacancy had arisen on 'B' Squadron and that, in response to my many requests, I was to be transferred there as from the 1st of January. Needless to say, I was absolutely delighted to have the chance to get into the bomber testing field but, at the same time, I was genuinely sorry to be leaving 'D' Squadron. I had enjoyed my year there very much indeed – a year which put four hundred and ten hours and thirty types of aircraft into my log-book. It was an experience I was very lucky to have had.

CHAPTER 27

AT THE TIME WHEN I MOVED across the airfield at Boscombe, 'B' Squadron was in something of a lull in so far as major testing activity was concerned. The Mark 1 variants of the three V-bombers, which had provided the bulk of the squadrons work for the past couple of years, were very rapidly approaching the end of their test programmes and there was really only the last few bits of 'tidying-up' to be done as far as these aircraft were concerned. The same general situation applied to the Beverley, the Mark 3 Shackelton and the Comet. The Britannia was very much an on-going programme, but a lot of the test sorties were being flown from Bristol's airfield at Filton, so that there was not a lot of flying to be done on that aircraft at Boscombe. The much improved Mark 2 versions of the Valiant, Vulcan and Victor were already flying at the Manufacturer's airfields, but they were not ready yet to be transferred to A&AEE for service clearance.

In some ways, this situation was advantageous to me, in that I got the opportunity to convert on to the V-Bombers without having to try to 'horn-in' on a busy programme operating to a tight time schedule. There was still quite a lot of relatively dull routine work to be completed – clearances for some stores configurations, anti-icing trials, auto-pilot clearances and various calibration runs – and the project pilots were not averse to having someone offer a helping hand for this sort of flying. Purely because of availability, I did most of my early 'V' flying in the Vulcan, rather less in the Valiant and least of all in the Victor. Perhaps predictably, I came to like the Vulcan very much indeed. It was a lovely aircraft, unusual in that it had a 'fighter' type, single-grip control column, as opposed to the more conventional bomber 'spectacle-grip' control and it handled, in many ways, very much like a fighter aircraft. There is an old adage in aviation that "if it looks right, it will generally fly right." This was certainly true as far as the Vulcan was concerned. It looked good and it flew as well as it looked.

Because of my experience in the Beverley, I got in on the tail-end of the Rocket Assisted Take-off Trials – a test programme, I might say, which never came to fruition in service. The Beverley already had a quite impressive short take-off ground roll but, once airborne, its climb-out was a long way short of dramatic. At heavy all- up weights, its initial rate of climb was low enough to pose problems when operating out of any confined area – and the Beverley was doing a lot of precisely this type of flying in the Radfan, when operating from Aden. I had done quite a lot of short take-off and landing work in both the Beverley and the Twin Pioneer while in 'D' Squadron and I had often been struck by the fact that STOL aircraft seldom seemed to have the sort of steep climb-out and approach capability which would have enabled them to utilise fully their very short ground roll. There was a view at the time that, for some aircraft of this type, you could get off the ground, or stop in a couple of hundred yards – provided that you had a ten mile unobstructed climb-out or approach path. In real life, you very seldom do.

The rocket installation on the Beverley – eight Scarab rocket motors fitted into each side of the rear fuselage – was supposed to provide a considerable enhancement to the initial rate of climb. The idea was that you fired up the rocket engines when you were just about approaching unstick speed and then hauled back – hard! On my first live run, Ray Bray, who was project pilot for the trial, was flying the aircraft. Right on cue, just as we were about ten knots below our unstuck speed, Ray hit the firing button. The effect was instantaneous and highly spectacular, to say the least. The poor old Beverley, trundling sedately along the runway as befits a massive transport aircraft, suddenly got the most tremendous boot up the rear and almost leapt into the air, literally like a scalded cat. I was never able to rid myself of the impression that it behaved rather as a portly and dignified archbishop in procession, who suddenly experienced a firework going off down the back of his ecclesiastical trousers.

The aircraft's acceleration from the point of rocket ignition was so marked that Ray had the control column hard back against his chest to avoid exceeding the flap limiting speed. At this point, the Beverley was going up at a climb angle which the designers certainly never had in mind when it was on the drawing board. At about fifteen hundred feet, the rockets burned out – very abruptly – and the Beverley was left hanging in the air at an angle that appeared to far exceed its normal stalling angle. This somewhat extreme attitude necessitated a very forceful shove forward on the control column, to try to ensure that we didn't go back down equally as rapidly as we had come up. When the virtual stall recovery had been completed, the rocket cages jettisoned and the aircraft cleaned up, the pilots could unclench their teeth, wipe away the sweat from their brow and carry on with the rest of the flight. Who says the only thrills come in high-performance aircraft?

As I remarked earlier, the Beverley rocket system never made it into service – not, I hasten to add, because of any deficiency in the system itself. In fact, it worked very well and certainly did it job of providing dramatic improvement to the initial rate of climb. It did, however, put the aircraft into a somewhat dangerous attitude shortly after take-off and this was felt to be unacceptable. Moreover, the rocket engines of the day were not as reliable as later models and one had always to bear in mind the possible consequences of rocket failure during take-off from a really restricted area.

Another early 'B' Squadron experience taught me that the aspiring test pilot should always ensure that he is in possession of all the facts relating to a particular trial before he takes it on – and I do mean ALL the facts. One day, the Boss came in and enquired whether anyone was still current on the Shackelton, to take part on a trial involving, if I remember correctly, heat-soaking some of the new radio equipment. The trial was to be run at Aden in order to be sure of getting the high ambient temperatures which would be necessary to check the equipment's capability to operate in tropical conditions. I had done a fair bit of Shackelton flying in 'D' Squadron on the Lindholme Gear drop trials and was still reasonably current. I got the job.

The trials aircraft was due to be flown into Boscombe from the manufacturers, where the new radio installation had been undertaken and was scheduled to arrive on the Saturday morning of our departure to Aden. In the meantime, I was to get on with the route planning and preparation of the trials schedule.

When the Saturday morning arrived and I made my way down to the flight line, I was somewhat discomfited to discover that the only Shackelton in sight was a Mark 2, the later variant of the original conventional tail-wheel design. All of my Shackelton flying had been in the Mark 3, which was a tricycle landing gear design and I had never flown in, much less landed one of the earlier marks. When I telephoned the Boss to advise him of the situation, Wing Commander Saxibly cheerfully responded that the Mark 2 was, "an absolute piece of cake, Harry. Just stick the bottom of the front gun turret on the horizon and you're in the perfect landing attitude. Nothing to it."

Somewhat less than fully convinced that this massive lump of metal would prove to be quite such a 'piece of cake', I got it fired up and headed off for our first ten hour leg to El Adem. By the time we arrived there, as might have been expected, it was pitch dark and I couldn't even see the front gun turret, much less the horizon. I do not recommend a strange airfield in the middle of the night as the ideal stage for one's first landing in a new type of aircraft, but I got it down alright before retiring, somewhat shattered, for what was left of the hours of darkness.

After a day off to recover, we continued with a six and a half hour leg down to Khartoum where, because of the prevailing political situation, we were limited to something like a maximum of three hours on the ground for refuelling, before getting out again. On landing at Khartoum – yes, the gun turret idea worked fine – I was given a signal to the effect that Aden was too busy with active operations to accept us, that the trial was postponed and we should pack everything up and return to Boscombe. A little disappointed, we finished refuelling and headed off again back towards El Adem.

On the way back north, it occurred to us that there might be a better way than night stopping at El Adem. With all due respect to El Adem, it wasn't exactly one of the fun spots of the North African coast – although, to be fair, I did see my first genuine belly dancer in a bar in nearby Tobruk. Malta was altogether a brighter spot, so we obtained clearance to overfly El Adem and carry on to Luqa. The weather forecast for Malta was good and we had plenty of fuel on board – even though we were now facing something of a longish flight to get to Luqa.

When we were still a couple of hours distant from Malta the weather reports started to indicate an unexpected and significant, deterioration in the conditions at Luqa. There was quite a lot of cloud forming and light rain was being experienced. As we closed the island, the weather seemed to get progressively worse as we got progressively closer. By the time we had got to within a hundred miles or so, the cloud base had come down below limits, it was raining heavily and there was a strong cross-wind blowing right across the main runway. In this situation we had to start looking for someplace to which we could divert. We had now been airborne for something like seventeen hours in total that day and were looking forward, more than just a little, to getting down on the ground again. A weather diversion was really not the most popular option just at that time.

Eventually, we were advised that Idris was reasonably clear, so we headed off again towards Tripoli – hoping earnestly to get there before we all fell asleep. Inevitably, it was dark by the time we got into the Idris circuit: equally inevitably there was a howling cross-wind straight across the runway. Perhaps even more inevitably, I didn't pull off one of my thousand great landings. The Idris runway was about two thousand yards long and I used pretty well every inch of it. But we walked away from our arrival, so it goes down in the book as a safe return to earth. In the circumstances, I might, perhaps, reasonably classify it as 'fair'. When we got into dispersal and fell out of the aeroplane, we found to our unspeakable delight, that the Wing Commander OC Flying had arranged to open the bar for our benefit. It must have been about three in the morning, but that lovely man – may God grant him many sons – had reckoned that we might be able to do with a drink when we finally got down. Hand on heart, I can testify that he was absolutely right.

Back at Boscombe, I carried on with the routine of 'backing-up' on other peoples projects and participating in various small programmes on those aircraft on which I had most experience. An odd feature of that first year in 'B' Squadron was that I shared an office with Ray Morgan and Russ Law, both of whom had, like myself, been studying for the law before they joined the service – Ray Morgan at Manchester and Russ Law in Sydney. Our humble abode was referred to, occasionally, as 'Temple Bar'.

It is funny, sometimes, how initial reactions to people can be utterly misleading. One of the pilots in B Squadron at the time was Peter Bardon, who was heavily tied up with the Britannia programme and often away at the manufacturer's works at Filton. He was a tall, dark and handsome fellow, very reserved, very English and, I thought, a little lacking in any sort of sense of humour. From our first few meetings, I got the impression that he and I had very little in common and that it would be a case of just learning to 'rub-along' together and avoiding outright friction.

One night, Jean and I threw a party at our house to which all of the squadron pilots were invited. That's when I learned how misleading first impressions can be. Behind Peter Bardon's typically English, unemotional and somewhat dry exterior, there lived an absolute life and soul of any party. Not too long previously, his wife had come out of hospital with a week-old baby, to be immediately pressed into service as crew on a sailing boat that Peter had acquired. He had never sailed before, but had prudently provided himself with a textbook on the subject – entitled something like 'How to Sail Around the World in a Hundred Lessons'. His account of the trip they undertook to Brittany – with his wife feeding the baby, while she read to him the next lesson from his textbook – was little short of hysterical. It just goes to show that you can never tell about people. Peter became a close – and valued – friend.

Sometime later, Peter and I flew a short landing programme on the Twin Pioneer. The normal technique employed to get a steep approach into the landing area was to get on plenty of power so that you could get the nose well up and then sort of 'walk' the aeroplane down the final approach, teetering continuously on the edge of the stall. Peter's technique was something else entirely. He would maintain height at a thousand feet until he was practically right over his intended touchdown point, when he would throttle off completely, drop full flap and stuff the nose down until he was heading earthwards at a thoroughly alarming angle. At what seemed to me to be virtually the last instant before we drove straight into the ground, he would haul back sharply on the control column, so that he practically rotated right through to the stalling angle on the spot. This sudden flare killed off the excess speed to a nicety and the aircraft settled down instantly and ran practically no distance at all. I was very impressed with his technique, but doubted my ability to judge the initiation of the flare quite as precisely as he had. You daren't start it too late, or you would have already arrived; too early and you could be left twenty feet in the air, virtually fully stalled and with almost no hope of recovery. When I asked how he judged it so neatly, he replied, quite seriously, "Its easy. You just keep looking at the ground on the way down till you suddenly think JESUS CHRIST! Then you haul back like mad." I believed him, but I never had the nerve to try it myself.

After a time I was allocated a programme of my own on the Squadron. This was a relatively small trial on a new piece of low-level navigation equipment which it was proposed to fit to the Canberra Bl(8), then in service with RAF Germany. It didn't involve testing any new aircraft, but it was a start to being responsible for a programme of my own. Even better, the trials were to be undertaken from RAF Laarbruch in order to allow the trial navigator to evaluate the equipment over the operational area where it would ultimately be used in service. I remember that I was given a 'no restrictions' low-level clearance from Headquarters RAF Germany to let me get right down to the deck, as and when required. This made for quite a lot of very exciting – and demanding – low-level, high-speed sorties over a variety of terrains in North Germany. I very quickly learned why the squadron crews in Germany were so meticulous in plotting every known electrical power line on their maps. Most of their flying was at low-level and, from low down, the cables are almost invisible until you are very close to them. Only the supporting pylons provide any idea of where the cables are. That is why it is so important to keep a really accurate record of all power lines in your flying area. A high-speed encounter with a set of high tension power cables can absolutely ruin the whole day for the average aircrew.

Back again at Boscombe, I was assigned to the trial programme to evaluate an avionics refit in the Shackleton and, from then onwards, took my turn, like every other pilot on the Squadron in picking up various trial programmes on a variety of aircraft, as and when they came up. The fact is often overlooked that, in addition to major programmes on brand-new aircraft – which came up relatively infrequently – Boscombe Down handled a continuous stream of programmes involving modifications and improvements to aircraft already in service. Very few, if any, aircraft go through their service life completely unchanged – most are continually upgraded to take advantage of new developments in technology, or to eliminate problems that have become evident in squadron service. Some of these modification programmes involve relatively minor changes to the aircraft – an up-rated engine, a new piece of avionics, or an alteration to the aircraft structure. Others can involve virtually a complete redesign of the whole machine – the Canberra PR9 was still a Canberra, but it was almost completely different from any other Mark of Canberra, even from its direct linear predecessors, the PR3 and the PR7. Whatever the nature or extent of the modification programme, its effects on the aircrafts performance and handling have to be systematically evaluated before the altered aircraft can be released into Service.

There is a latent hazard in any modification programme, in that the pilot re-sponsible for the clearance is normally fairly experienced on the type before he starts and it is sometimes quite difficult to remember that, familiar as the aircraft is, the one you are now strapped to is, to a greater or lesser degree, quite different from any other type you may have flown previously. It may look much the same; it may even feel much the same; but it isn't the sane – and you ignore that fact at your peril. When I was given the Canberra PR9 programme, I had something like twelve hundred hours experience in Canberras and had flown almost every vari-ant of the aircraft ever produced – B2, PR3, T4, B6, PR7, B(I)8 and TT18. I had at least as much Canberra time as any other pilot at Boscombe – probably rather more in fact – but I still had a sharp lesson to learn about how to set about testing a relatively familiar type.

One day, I set off to establish the safety speeds of the aircraft. This is a trial to determine the lowest speed at which control can be maintained in the event of engine failure on take-off. The technique employed is to set the aircraft up in the take-off configuration, with the wheels down and flaps set as appropriate and all control trimmers selected to the take-off settings. The aircraft is then slowed right down and full take-off power applied to both engines. At the first test speed – normally safely on the high side to begin with – one engine is throttled back ab-ruptly to simulate an engine failure. The aircraft then goes into the classic engine failure sequence of yawing, rolling and side-slipping towards the dead engine. The pilot just sits there, hands and feet off the controls, for, as I recall, five sec-onds, to observe and measure the aircraft response, before he initiates recovery action without re-trimming and without throttling back on the live engine. As-suming that he can recover successfully, he then runs through the same sequence again, failing the same engine at a slightly lower speed. As the engine failure speed gets lower and lower, the reaction of the aircraft becomes quicker and more pronounced – at times, it can become downright violent – and recovery becomes progressively more difficult. Eventually, the speed is reached at which the engine failure can only just be counteracted and below which the aircraft becomes un-controllable. That is the safety speed for the engine in use. At this point, the pilot goes back to square one and repeats the whole procedure for the other engine.

On most piston-engined aircraft, there are some differences between the safety speeds established for the two engines. This is because the propeller, which actu-ally delivers the thrust, slightly displaces the thrust-line away from the centre-line of the engine. Hence, unless the propellers rotate in opposite directions, the thrust-line of one engine is normally further from the aircraft centre-line than the other. As a result, the turning force exerted by that engine is slightly greater than that exerted by its partner. With jet engines, on the other hand, the thrust line normally runs right through the engine centre line, so that there is little discerni-ble difference in the effects of failing either engine. Certainly, this was the case as far as the Canberra was concerned – and I had sat through an awful lot of simu-lated engine failures in that aircraft.

On the occasion in question, I went through the routine on one of the engines at about three thousand feet – you have to do this test fairly low down in order to develop engine thrust outputs as close as you can get to the powers available at ground level during real take-offs. Everything went absolutely swimmingly, with the trials navigator making notes for me at his position down in the nose of the aircraft. Eventually, I had the safety speed well and truly established – all runs on the same engine, but then the speeds were always the same for both engines on the Canberra. Everybody knew that. As a last check, I took the aircraft down to a thousand feet to make sure that my final result was valid at a height as close as I could reasonably get to take-off height. This first run – on the engine I had used throughout the trial – went off like clockwork. Then, just to dot the 'i's' and cross the 't's', I tried failing the other engine at the same speed. That was my first – and, I might say, very nearly my last – big mistake of the day.

I had barely got the throttle closed, when the aircraft whipped violently on its back, yawing like mad and apparently set on performing a series of flick rolls, given half a chance. With wheels down and very much out of trim, I wasn't really set up for a low-level aerobatics exercise at the time and the situation became somewhat confused for a second or two. I had never envisaged trying to recover from an engine failure from the upside-down position and seemingly juddering on the verge of an inverted spin. While I was desperately trying to retract the wheels, bring up the power on the dead engine, stop the yaw and get myself right way up again, the navigator suddenly appeared, floating about the cockpit without any connection to any part of the aeroplane. I learned later that he had thought we were all through for the day and had unfastened his straps to stow his equipment away. In the negative 'g' condition we were in, he was now virtually weightless – he and all his bits of kit 'free-floating' about the place completely uncontrollably. When I had got his flying boot out of my face and managed to turn right way up again, he came down on to the cockpit floor with the most frightful crash and seemed to take little active interest in the subsequent proceedings. At the time, I was too busy to pay much attention to his misfortunes, but we eventually got ourselves sorted out again and crept back to Boscombe considerably more shaken than we ever need have been.

When I got down, I checked back through every Canberra report ever written to try to find out what had gone wrong. In due course, in the report on the BI(8), I found what I was looking for – different safety speeds for the two engines. The reason according to the project pilot – who was clearly a lot smarter than me – was that the BI(8) canopy was a non-standard Canberra fit – a fighter type hood, offset to one side of the fuselage and, therefore, effectively displacing the fuselage centre-line slightly to one side. The PR9 had the same type of offset canopy and it was overlooking that little item that very nearly cost me my neck – and the poor navigator as well.

Next day, I took the aircraft back up and did the safety speed trial again – properly, this time – and I never again took anything for granted in any aeroplane I ever flew. Even if they had just changed the light bulbs, I treated it with all the respect due to a totally different machine. I might add that I was a long time before I could persuade Flight Lieutenant Jim Newberry to fly with me again.

CHAPTER 28

ONE OF THE GREAT PLEASURES of being at Boscombe Down was that it was possible to fly just about any of the aircraft which came onto the base. Obviously, in the early stages of a major programme on a new aircraft, only the project pilot or his deputy had much of a chance of doing any of the available flying but, on a modification programme, it was often possible to worm your way into the driver's seat – particularly if you volunteered to do some of the duller, less stimulating phases of the programme. Very few people can resist an approach from someone who offers to take some of the 'donkey work' off their back.

At the time, even if it were not spelled out formally as the official policy of the Establishment, it was at least tacitly understood that the trials pilots were encouraged to broaden their experience by flying in as many different types of aircraft as they could reasonably get their hands on. It was clearly recognised – and quite correctly – that a good test pilot's greatest asset is his background experience of a wide diversity of cockpit layouts, flight systems and handling characteristics. At the design stage of an aircraft's life and during the early flight trials, the inputs from an experienced test pilot can be invaluable to the aircraft designers and engineers. While these highly qualified personnel have a wide theoretical knowledge of the range of alternative aerodynamics and system options which may be applied to a particular design feature, only the test pilot is likely to have any practical experience of and familiarity with, the various alternatives where it counts – in the air. The wider the test pilots flying background, the greater the diversity of practical experience which he is able to bring to bear and the more valuable is his input.

Quite apart from the diversity of experience to be obtained from 'type' flying, there is another considerable advantage to be gained in what is generally referred to as 'rate response adaptability'. This factor may be defined as the capability of a pilot to adapt quickly and effectively from one type, or class of aircraft to another. I have known many pilots who were excellent performers in the type of aircraft with which they were familiar, but who found it very difficult – and, in some cases, downright impossible – to transfer their skills into another cockpit. They simply did not have the capability to adapt effectively to the new environment and to the changed event 'rate'. In the test flying business, the inability to adapt to different 'rate responses' would be quite unacceptable, in that the very nature of the job – particularly at an establishment like A&AEE – necessarily involves a fair amount of 'cockpit-jumping'. It was by no means unusual for pilots at the Establishment to fly in two, three or even four different classes of aircraft in one day – and, by that, I don't just mean different types of fighters, bombers or whatever but four distinctly different CLASSES of aircraft. Even in 'D' Squadron, it was nothing out of the ordinary to do, perhaps, a heavy drop sortie in the Beverley first thing in the morning, followed by a target-towing trip in a Hunter or Meteor. In the afternoon, you might get a quick helicopter ride and wind the day up with some drop photography from a Harvard or Gannet. When you are doing this sort of flying day and daily, you have to be very well adapted to 'rate responses'. You have to feel completely at home in the aeroplane of the moment from the instant your behind hits the seat.

In 'B' Squadron, we always looked forward to our flights with the fighter or naval squadrons. Being well used to fairly lengthy sorties, we generally regarded the short endurance, up and down flights they provided as something of a welcome relief. We used to rile our hosts by enquiring innocently whether it was worthwhile putting on a flying suit for one of their sorties. For anything less than an hour, we used to say, it was hardly worth the bother of changing out of uniform. The pilots on the other two squadrons, on the other hand, used to look forward to trips with us with a degree of trepidation. Used to going up and down like yo-yo's, they regarded anything over an hour in the air as something of an endurance test. We did try to fit our guests in on some of the shorter sorties but, unhappily for them, this wasn't always possible. Give then credit, though; they still kept coming back. I remember flying Alan Merriman, one of my friends in 'A' Squadron, up to Edinburgh in an Anson so that he could attend a meeting at Ferranti. When we were somewhere in the vicinity of York he enquired earnestly if we would be landing soon. My response that we were then at about the half-way mark in the flight almost reduced him to tears. "Honest to God, Harry," he wailed, "I've never been airborne this long in my life." At the end of his meeting in Edinburgh, he returned to Boscombe by train claiming that it would probably be quicker and that, anyway, he was completely unsuited, constitutionally, for endurance flying.

Many years later, I took a fighter pilot friend of mine, from a Lightning Squadron, to fly with me in a Nimrod. Even by heavy aircraft standards, the pre-start check list for the Nimrod was extremely lengthy, in that the aircraft was packed with electronic, radio and radar gear, all of which had to be functionally checked before you got underway. When the first cup of coffee arrived in the flight deck, my friend was absolutely flabbergasted. Not only was it, he remarked in an awed voice, the first time he had ever had coffee served to him in an operational aircraft, but he certainly had not expected it to arrive while we were still in dispersal and before we had even got the engines started.

With Boscombe's tacit encouragement of 'type flying' we happily flew just about everything that was available on the base at the time. The 'A' Squadron stock included the Hunter T7, the Gnat, the Jet Provost, the Javelin – including the re-heated version and, latterly, the Lightning. I remember being much taken with the re-heated Javelin: when you engaged the afterburners below 8000 feet, the noise level and fuel consumption went up and the speed went down. 'C' Squadron had the Sea Vixen, the Sea Hawk, the Scimitar and the Buccaneer – which I didn't manage to get into. 'C' Squadron was very good to me. They let me fly one of the very few remaining Fireflys and, on another 'one-off' I got a quick forty minutes or so in a Wyvern, the Navy's turboprop strike fighter. This latter was a remarkable aeroplane. For a single seat fighter/strike aircraft, it seemed enormous. From the cockpit, the engine cowling seemed to stretch almost to the far horizon. In the air, its performance was unremarkable – at least until it came time to put it down on the ground again. At this point, the pilot quickly discovered something of a reversal of normal flying principles. As power increased, the aircraft slowed down; as power was reduced it accelerated. All this was due to their being no direct link between the throttle and the propeller constant speed unit. As the throttle was closed, the propeller sensed the reduction in engine power and 'fined-off' to compensate; similarly with the throttles opening, it sensed an engine overspeed and 'coarsened-off' to compensate. I discovered this feature the hard way on my first attempt to put the thing down, when I floated half way across Wiltshire before I got the hang of it.

It was a tremendous experience at Boscombe to have the opportunity to mix with pilots from a wide range of flying backgrounds. Boscombe was not a bomber base, not a transport base, not a helicopter base, not a fighter base and not a naval base, but all these types were operated there and the pilots in various squadrons brought with them to the place, something of the attitudes and the approach to the job, in-bred in them from their earlier operational backgrounds.

Not that I have ever believed in type-casting. I have known far too many fighter pilots who didn't fit into the 'kick the tyres, light the fires, last one airborne is a sissy' mould. Equally, I have known too many bomber pilots far removed from the 'quiet, withdrawn, pipe-smoking, pint in the corner' prototype. Quite apart from the fact that I never felt that I fitted into that particular mould myself, I have known too many bomber men who could be genuine, flat-out 'ravers', given half the chance.

'A' Squadron, the Boscombe fighter brigade, were a very lively lot indeed. Generally slightly younger than the pilots in the other squadrons, their parties were legendary – all-out, no-holds-barred affairs which directly reflected their infectiously enthusiastic approach to their work and their play. They provided a certain air of dash and élan to the Establishment. I have a theory that these qualities are developed in a pilot in a directly inverse ratio to the length of his average flight. At forty minutes a time, you have a bit of capacity for a somewhat dashing approach to your flying. When you are looking at three, six, nine or even more hours strapped to the seat, you tend to develop something more akin to stoical resignation. There is an old Air Force maxim which runs;

> *"You can tell a bomber pilot by the spread around his rear;*
> *You can tell a wireless op by the rings around his ear;*
> *You can tell a navigator by his maps and charts and such;*
> *And you can tell a fighter pilot – but you can't tell him much!"*

There might just be something in it!

'C' Squadron were another fairly animated bunch – a small detachment of 'dark blues' pitched into the middle of an establishment where the majority of the flying personnel came from the RAF. In the middle of their crew room, they had a pair of RAF pilot wings hanging on a string from the ceiling. When they were incensed by some piece of 'light blue' bureaucracy, they would stride purposefully into the crew room, give the pair of wings a tremendous whack and bellow, "BLOODY, BLOODY RAF." This always seemed to make them feel better. Between themselves, they alluded to us 'light blues' as 'crabfats', in much the same way as we referred to them generically as 'fishheads'. Perhaps remarkably, we all got along very well together.

I think that it was taking up golf again that just about put the gilt on the gingerbread for me as far as Boscombe Down was concerned. The work was varied, fascinating and important. The airfield was delightfully situated in a very attractive part of the country. The people on the base were the best in the business, as convivial on the ground as they were good in the air. There was golf right on the doorstep to provide the perfect relaxation. What more, in all conscience, could anyone reasonably have asked for?

CHAPTER 29

IN MANY WAYS, Boscombe Down was one of the most rewarding postings that any RAF pilot could have hoped for. Quite apart from the flying side of things – which was unequalled anywhere else in the Country – it was a very pleasant place indeed at which to serve. It was nicely located, with very good access to the delightful countryside all about and, at the same time, it was far enough from London – and, accordingly, from the Headquarters of the Ministry of Supply or Ministry of Aviation – to keep the top brass from breathing down your neck all the time. The Establishment Married Quarter area was pretty well scaled to the number of married personnel on the base, so that most people could find some place to live right there on the station. When Jean and I first arrived, there was a bit of a population 'bulge' at the place and we spent most of our first year in a hiring in Salisbury, before we moved on to the station. Even at that, there was very little inconvenience involved, in that the house itself was quite nice and it was only a matter of a few miles to commute to the airfield.

The social life at Boscombe was full and varied. As we had been used to elsewhere, the Mess was the focal point of station social activities and there was a continuous programme of events of all sorts to attract you for a night out. I always felt that the Ladies Dining-In nights were among the best social occasions it was possible to imagine – the Mess dining tables decorated with flowers and all the Mess silver, the guests resplendent in full Mess Dress with, here and there, a splash of different colour supplied by either civilian guests, or by the uniforms of officers from different services, the ladies in their evening dresses, the band playing softly at the end of the room, the odd mixture of extreme formality until the Loyal Toast and easy, relaxed, informality thereafter.

In some ways, such occasions were a little like something left over from an earlier and more gracious, time, but they were a real treat to be savoured. I often used to wonder – in fact, I still do – whether occasions like those still took place in the world outside. Sometimes, in order to boost Mess Funds, a Ladies Dining-In would be combined with a Casino Night, when the Mess Ante-Room would be transformed into a sort of gambling den, featuring roulette, blackjack, horse racing, slot machines and various other attractions. Volunteers would fill the role of croupiers in relays and, almost invariably, the wagering would be fast and furious. I don't think I can ever recall an occasion when the Mess lost money on a Casino Night. Usually, they made a considerable surplus – a much more popular way of raising money than putting up Mess Subscriptions. On many of these nights, the dancing and general merrymaking went on throughout the night and the Mess would normally provide early breakfast next morning for those hardy souls who had the stamina to see the festivities through. Nobody seemed to find it at all odd when the breakfasting revellers were joined at table by those aircrew scheduled for the first flights of the day.

The high spot of the Mess social year was the Summer Ball. This was the stations major annual Mess Function and one that provided Mess Members with the opportunity to bring in guests from other units or from the civilian community in recognition of the hospitality extended to them throughout the year. A very considerable amount of work went into preparing the Mess for the event. Every public room was completely transformed in accordance with a pre-selected 'theme' and some of the transformations were quite staggering in their imagination and ingenuity. I can remember the Ante-Room, one year, being changed into the lounge deck of a luxury liner. False walls, painted skilfully to represent a distant shore, were pitted with thousands of almost invisible pin-prick holes, through which a cleverly 'stepped' back-lighting system created a very realistic impression of the lights on shore passing slowly by.

Other transformations which I readily recall include the Ladies Room as a sort of Jacques Cousteau type of underwater world, the realism of which was heightened by floor to ceiling tanks of fish; the billiard Room as a world War 1 front-line canteen, complete with cane furniture, an original 1916-vintage NAAFI van and ultra-violet lit aircraft and zeppelins in the searchlight-crossed night sky overhead; and the main entrance hall as a Roman Temple, that looked as though it would not have been out of place in any of D.W. Griffith's epics.

All of the work on the Mess was carried out by the Mess members themselves in their spare time during the month or so prior to the event. Every year, we used to swear, "Never again -next year we'll just stick a few flowers about the place." But, next year, when June rolled round, we would be back at exactly the same sort of frenzied activity to get the place in shape. The results 'on the night' always made the effort more than worthwhile.

I really cannot resist the story of one year, when some part of the Mess was to be transformed into a sort of Arcadian garden. At ETPS, Lionel Taylor, one of 'A' Squadron's dashing young bachelors, had made the acquaintance of June Thorburn, the film actress, and, through her, had some sort of entree to the Pinewood film Studios. From the Property Department there, he borrowed a number of vaguely 'Arcadian-looking' artefacts, which were distributed about the place to lend 'atmosphere'. Among these pieces and, as it turned out, surplus to requirements, was a statue of a cherub in much the same sort of playful pose as that adopted by Eros in Piccadilly. To get this particular piece out of the way, it was deposited, somewhat carelessly, in the Ladies Powder Room – and immediately forgotten. But not, I regret to say, by all. Before the night of the Ball, some wretched individual cut a fig-leaf out of aluminium sheet and affixed it strategically to the statue. Very proper you may well observe – but surely not when the thing is wired to a very loud bell in the Entrance Hall. It is, perhaps, a testimony to the unquenchable curiosity of man – using the term in a purely generic context – that the bell rang virtually non-stop all through the night.

There was never any flying on the day after a Summer Ball. Generally, they were held on a Friday night so that you had the whole weekend to recover. And you needed it, believe me. The food supply on the night was on the grand scale, buffets of varied types in practically every room, to say nothing of the main meal of the evening. The champagne bill must have gone a long way to keeping the French growers in business and there was every type of other drink available that even the most selective guest might have opted for. There was even a very large bowl of a desperate mixture – introduced to us by the Americans at ETPS – which contained dry ice, so that it foamed and smoked continuously. I don't think that anyone ever knew the precise ingredients, but it had to be treated with considerable caution. A full glass would just about have felled a bullock.

After one of these glorious nights, I remember going out to Stonehenge in the very early hours of the morning to watch the Druids celebrate the Summer Solstice. With Jean and I, on that occasion were our guests, Tony Lawrence from 27 Squadron and his fiancée, Ray Morgan and his wife with their guests and a few others. It was odd to watch the Druids, completely oblivious of our presence, going through the rites that had been enacted at Stonehenge almost from the beginning of time. Afterwards, I always regretted that it had been a rather cloudy morning, so that we didn't actually see the sun come up to lay its first rays on the circle of forbidding-looking stones. But it was quite an experience, nonetheless. When the ceremonies were over, we all drove back to the Mess to join the survivors of the Ball for eggs and bacon, before heading home, in broad daylight, for a good days sleep.

During my time at Boscombe, I experienced one very peculiar incident, that I have never since been able to explain satisfactorily – even to myself. It arose out of some trials that Peter Twiss was doing in Norway in the supersonic Fairey Delta 2. Peter was then the Fairey Chief Test Pilot and had been inhibited from doing much in the way of exploring the aircrafts performance supersonically in the UK, because of the crowded airspace and environmental restrictions. Accordingly, the Company arranged with the Norwegian government for him to take the machine to Norway, where the airspace was much less busy and where he could make sonic booms to his heart's content up and down the coastline.

From time to time, various spare parts and items of test equipment, would be flown out to the trials detachment at Stavanger. I flew a couple of these support trips in whatever aircraft happened to be available at the time – very pleasant they were too, with accommodation provided at Stavanger Golf Club and plenty of opportunity to visit the old town itself. On the occasion in question, I set off from Boscombe in a Valetta, with Lionel Taylor of 'A' Squadron sharing the flying with me. Lionel, an incorrigible bachelor, was keen to see for himself whether the girls of Stavanger really were, as the legend goes, the prettiest in all of Norway. We had arranged between us that I would do the landing at Stavanger and he would bring us back to Boscombe.

On the outward trip, Lionel actually did most of the flying, while I handled the radio communications on the airways and through the control areas. When we finally made contact with Stavanger Approach, I took over control of the aircraft and got us set up for a standard circuit join and landing. It was an absolutely beautiful day and we could see the airfield from quite a long way off. I should mention at this point that, since the occasion when I had dumped all the crew's kit into the water on take-off from Gibraltar, I had become something of a check-list addict. If the checklist is followed conscientiously, there should be no possible chance of ever overlooking any of the Vital Actions. Accordingly, on this occasion, we were following the standard practice by having Lionel read the checks, while I actioned them and confirmed completion.

As we entered the downwind leg, Lionel started his recital of the pre-landing check-list. "Altimeter set to QNH." I checked that I had airfield pressure set on the instrument pressure setting indicator and responded, "Set." "Engine revs 2400" continued Lionel. I pushed the propeller pitch levers fully forward and responded "max revs set." "Flaps to 20 degrees," went on Lionel. I heard his check quite distinctly, so that there was no question of any sort of misunderstanding but, at that point and without the slightest hesitation, I reached forward and selected wheels down. I was absolutely clear in my mind that it was the wrong action – wheels down was the NEXT item on the check-list – but I went ahead and lowered the undercarriage regardless.

Needless to say, Lionel gave me some stick on the spot. "Lord love us," he complained, "all you bomber drivers are the same. Half-blind, half-deaf, no wonder they give you a crew to look after you. I said flaps, you dozy b...., not wheels."

While he was just getting into his stride about how we ought to include a nanny in the crew, I reached forward and selected the flap lever to the required setting. Nothing happened! The lever went down, but the indicator needle remained stubbornly stuck against the 'UP' mark. Moreover, I could feel, from the trim of the aircraft, that the flaps hadn't moved.

At this point, I advised Air Traffic Control that we were having a slight problem and was cleared out of the circuit to investigate the situation further, safely out of everybody else's way. What we discovered, when we had a chance to check out the systems, was that we had lost all the hydraulically powered services. We couldn't even get the flaps to move by using the manual reversion hand-pump. There was no particular danger involved – it was simply a case that we were going to have to make a flapless landing, which was a fairly straightforward procedure. Fortunately, the wheel brakes on the Valetta were pneumatically operated, so that, even though we would be touching down slightly faster than usual, we would be able to stop without any difficulty.

Eventually, having exhausted all the checks and fall-back actions available to us, we re-joined the circuit and went in for an uneventful landing – accompanied all the way down the runway by a posse of ambulances, fire tenders and rescue vehicles. When we got into our parking slot and shut the aircraft down, the flight engineer started to burrow into the innards of the machine to try to find out what had gone wrong. What he finally discovered was that a hydraulic pipeline had broken sometime during the flight, allowing all of the fluid in the system to escape. When we arrived in the circuit at Stavanger, the only hydraulic fluid in the aircraft was the contents of the small hydraulic reservoir – containing only enough fluid to permit the operation of just one service, before the whole system went completely dead. If I had selected flaps down in accordance with Lionel's instruction, we would not have been able, subsequently, to lower the wheels and would have been committed to a belly landing. While this is not necessarily a particularly dangerous proposition, it doesn't normally do the aircraft a lot of good and most pilots are quite happy to avoid ever having to demonstrate how well they could carry it out.

A flapless landing is a whole lot easier on both aircraft and crew. Since that day, I have often wondered what it was that compelled me to change the order of the Vital Actions, even when I was perfectly well aware that I was executing them the wrong way round. It is still almost inconceivable to me that any professional pilot, thoroughly well used to working with a check-list, could have acted as I did. But, no doubt about it, it worked out well in the end and saved me from having to clutter up the airfield at Stavanger with a damaged aeroplane. Maybe there really are guardian angels. Incidentally, the broken hydraulic pipe was brazed back together in about thirty minutes and Lionel's Vital Actions prior to landing back at Boscombe were carried out strictly in the order prescribed in the check-list.

I remember this time at Boscombe particularly well, because we were then experiencing a series of accidents which cost us the lives of a number of crews on the unit and which cast the most chilling atmosphere of depression and loss over the whole Establishment. This was the other side of test flying – the bitter price that sometimes has to be paid for pushing new aircraft to their limits. 'A' Squadron lost 'Red' Roberts in a Gnat – he actually got out of the aircraft, but too low for his parachute to deploy fully and Dickie Mays, when his Javelin ejection seat fired accidentally. 'C Squadron had a Sea Vixen hit by a buzzard on a high-speed run at low level during tropical trials at Kano in Nigeria. The crew ejected but, in the process, John Neilson damaged his back very seriously. In 'B' Squadron, our turn came when the first Mk 2 Victor broke up while doing high Mach runs somewhere over the Irish Sea. Ray Morgan and Jerry Stockman and their crew lost their lives. Ray was one of the best friends I had in the Service. We had known each other in Bomber Command, had done ETPS together and had shared an office for nearly two years. I was his executor and I can honestly say that I never did a job in my life that gave me a greater sense of loss. In Jerry Stockman's case, his death was, if such a thing is possible, even more poignant: he was Dickie May's brother-in-law.

That was a ghastly time at Boscombe. In addition to our own pilots, we lost a company pilot from Saunders Roe, attached to the unit to test a prototype mixed power plant fighter. The aircraft rocket engine blew up on take-off. For too long a time, it seemed, every week brought some new tragedy to add to the sense of shock and terrible loss. In all, I suppose, there were only something like twenty-five service test pilots on the unit and to lose four of our number killed and one seriously injured, was a devastating experience in such a close-knit group. As if all of this tragedy wasn't enough, I learned that Tony Lawrence and his pilot, Barry Heywood – both old friends from 27 Squadron – had been killed in a Canberra crash off Flamborough Head. Not long afterwards, Des Russell, my old Driffield Squadron Commander, was killed landing on a new aircraft carrier. One of the arrestor wires broke and his aircraft rolled off the deck into the sea. He didn't get out and was drowned. This dreadful accident was featured on the news programmes of the television networks. News they called it – an armchair front seat to watch a fine man die. That wasn't news reporting; it was plain and simple ghoulish sensationalism.

All aircrew go through their working lives with the level-headed awareness that violent death is a very real possibility. This is not fear in any sense – there is no place in any aeroplane for a frightened pilot – but simply a practical acceptance of the fact that flying does involve a measure of hazard somewhat greater than is present in most other occupations. In test flying, realistically, that element of hazard is even greater, since much of a test pilots work involves either new aircraft or extreme situations – and, often enough, both. Most of the time, the realisation of the risk involved is simply accepted and then pushed firmly to the back of the mind. Most of the time, that is where it stays, an ugly but inescapable part of the background to everyday existence.

At the times when accidents do occur – particularly accidents which involve people who are close to you it is difficult to avoid a heightened awareness of the risks of the job. In spite of yourself and in spite of disciplining yourself to keep your mind strictly on what you are doing and on nothing else, the dark visualisations of your unvoiced fears can creep insidiously into your consciousness. You can't help re-enacting the most recent disaster in your mind, with yourself in the driver's seat. I suppose this is what fear really is – not the occurrence itself, but simply the dread of it ever happening to you.

In common with most other pilots, I have often been asked about fear. Many people not involved in the business seem to have the impression that the average pilot is a sort of a steely-eyed, square-jawed hero figure, daily 'dicing with death' in the skies and manfully putting lesser mortals to shame with his dauntless disregard of all danger. What nonsense! 'Biggles' exists only in the pages of fiction. Pilots are like anybody else – people doing a job. Their training, skill and professional approach, enables them to cope with most of the perils of their trade, but even the very best recognise that situations can arise from which they would have to be very lucky to survive. Given a structural failure, or a total loss of control, there is very little that any pilot can do to restore the situation. That's where the real fear comes from – the cold-blooded recognition that you might one day find yourself in a situation that you simply can't do anything about, no matter how good you might be.

You never get this sort of fear in the air; even in a full-blooded emergency, you are so busy and the adrenalin is pumping so hard, that you have neither the time nor the capacity to feel physically afraid. It is only much later, when the close calls and near-misses come back to mind, mostly in the dark hours of the night, that you go through the sweat and torment of recognising how close you have been, or might someday come, to the edge of nothingness.

I think that practically everyone who has ever flown to any extent has been through this sort of experience. You would have to be pretty dull-witted or unimaginative not to. But you go on doing the job because it is what you are good at, because it is what you want to do and because you have come to accept the hazards involved simply as part of your trade. This is neither heroism nor stupidity – simply realism. To be honest, there are very few real heroes in the flying business. It just isn't that kind of occupation. Certainly, it can be exciting and even hazardous – particularly, when viewed from the outside. When you are on the inside, however, doing the job yourself, you recognise it – if you have any common sense at all – for exactly what it is. A difficult and demanding occupation in which things can and do, go wrong. And when they do go wrong, they can go terribly wrong and with stunning and terrifying suddenness. Only very young or very inexperienced pilots can get by with the comforting delusion that 'it couldn't happen to me'. The more flying you do, the more you have to accept the hard fact that it could. It probably has already happened to pilots a whole lot better than you, so that, at the end of the day, you just have to accept the situation as a fact of life, keep your mind exclusively in the present and simply get on with the job.

Maybe that's one of the reasons why we had as many parties as we did. Sometimes, you really need them.

Towards the end of my time at Boscombe Down, I was involved in an incident that drove home to me the fact that the really frightening situation is the one over which you have little or no control. At the time, I was working with John Cruse on the Mark 2 Vulcan and we had recently participated in a discussion with the Company about the results of some 'wheels-up' crash landing tests they had conducted with models of the aircraft. Like most delta winged aircraft, the Vulcan landed in a very pronounced nose high attitude and, in any 'no-wheels' landing, the back end of the aircraft was going to make contact with the ground while the nose was still quite a long way up in the air. The Company's model tests indicated that, in such a situation, the initial impact would bring the nose down on to the ground with sufficient force to cause the fuselage to fracture just aft of the crew compartment. The rest of the aircraft, including all the fuel on board, would then probably continue on – right over the nose section which housed the crew. Very comforting!

One day, with John doing the driving, we got airborne on an auto-pilot assessment sortie and, right after take-off, found ourselves in a situation even worse than the one which the Company had considered during their model test programme. When we selected wheels up, we achieved retraction of the two main undercarriage bogies, but couldn't get the nose-wheel to lock in the up position. Nor, when we recycled the selection to try again, could we get the nose-wheel to lock down. Although we had no way of knowing it at the time, the problem had been caused by a fracture failure in the nose-wheel hydraulic jack. The initial undercarriage selection had unlatched the mechanical 'down' lock, but the leak of hydraulic fluid through the jack fracture was preventing the system from developing sufficient push on the leg to move the nose-wheel assembly into either locked position. It was simply dangling there, oscillating gently in the slipstream and incapable of being locked either up or down.

Unaware of the nature of the problem, we made repeated attempts to try to get the thing to lock in either position, but all of our efforts proved to be quite unavailing. Throughout, the nose-wheel indicator light remained obstinately red. By this time, we were only too uncomfortably aware that we were in a serious situation. With only the main wheels lockable in the down position, a normal landing was not a feasible proposition, since the nose-wheel assembly would almost certainly collapse on contact with the runway. The resulting impact shock on the nose section of the aircraft would probably be even greater than in the 'no-wheels' case, since the nose would have further to drop before contact. On the other hand, a belly-landing with the nose-wheel swinging about unpredictably, wasn't much of a prospect either.

After we had exhausted the checklist emergency procedures and tried out one or two suggestions from the engineers on the ground, we requested a chase plane to get airborne to come up and have a look at us. His report confirmed what we had already established. The main wheels were going up and down normally but, regardless of the selection, the nose-wheel was just swinging freely, neither locked up nor locked down. In practically any other type of emergency situation, we would have had the option of abandoning the aircraft. Nobody ever wants to get themselves to this last extremity – and certainly not in a test aircraft, the loss of which is certain to put the whole programme back by many months, at the very least. Nevertheless, as a last resort, John and I would normally have been able to use our ejection seats to 'bang-out' and the three rear crewmembers – who had no ejection seats – would have made their escape through a floor hatch in the rear compartment. Unhappily for all concerned, this escape hatch opened directly in front of the nose-wheel. With the wheel down, a parachute escape from the rear compartment egress hatch was out of the question – the escapee would have been jumping straight into the massive metal assembly. For the crew members in the rear compartment, there was no other way out.

With this unpalatable fact very much in our minds, we spent the better part of the next two or three hours yanking the aircraft all over the sky in an attempt to 'jerk' the nose-wheel into a locked down position. We pulled 'g', we racked it into tight turns, we yawed it violently, we pulled it sharply out of dives. In near desperation, we did everything we could think of to get that wheel locked down – and all to absolutely no avail. In spite of all our efforts, the cockpit indicator light continued to glare at us – unblinking and, it seemed, irrevocably red.

We still had one trick up our sleeve which John was not at all keen to commit us to. The Vulcan had an emergency pneumatic undercarriage lowering system which operated completely independently of the normal hydraulic system. This was a 'one-shot', last gasp, option which utilised high pressure compressed air to literally 'blow' the wheels down. The snag was that, once you pulled the plug, the hydraulic fluid from the normal undercarriage system was vented to atmosphere, in order to remove any back pressure from fighting against the emergency system. Once you committed yourself to the emergency system, you were completely stuck with the result – you had no power of any sort left to try to change things thereafter. In the absence of any knowledge of what was causing our problem, John was, quite properly, loth to initiate a system, which would leave us in a situation in which all options were irrecoverably closed off. If he pulled the plug and the nose-wheel didn't lock down, we could well wind up with the main wheels locked down and the nose-wheel not – absolutely the worst possible combination to be left with.

After we had been airborne for about four hours, we simply ran out of options. The choice had narrowed down to either going in to land as we were, or staking everything on the emergency system. John took a deep breath, leaned forward and pulled the plug. With every eye in the aeroplane riveted on the undercarriage position indicator lights, we saw the main wheel lights go red – indicating that the wheels were unlocked and in-transit – and then go green as the downlocks engaged. The nose-wheel light stayed red throughout. Sickeningly, we all realised that the gamble had failed – we were now irrevocably stuck in the worst of all possible situations – and with no way out.

As we headed back to the field for the landing, John and I discussed the technique he would use to try to get us down. He decided to go for a touchdown a good bit faster than normal, in order to give himself plenty of elevator power to try to lower the nose on to the runway positively, but firmly, while he still had enough elevator control available to try to cushion the impact. I knew John to be a capable, competent and experienced pilot, with a fine sense of touch and a natural feel for handling a big aircraft. I couldn't have asked for a better man to be in the left-hand seat but, at the same time, I was only too well aware that he was taking on a real piece of trick flying, when the odds were heavily stacked against him. As we swung away from the overhead to position for the approach, I noticed all of the ground emergency and rescue vehicles getting themselves into position for the touch-down. Very necessary and very comforting in a way, but hardly calculated to raise your spirits in the circumstances.

When John got us settled down in a long straight-in approach, I subconsciously noted the distance to run on the Instrument Landing System marker beacon lights. As the Inner Marker light started to flash, at about two hundred feet and less than a mile to go, the aircraft gave a very slight tremor as we passed through some mild turbulence and, to my utter stupefaction, I noticed the nose-wheel indicator light go green. Everybody else in the aeroplane noticed it too. The yell of, "Its locked!" just about lifted the canopy. Seconds later, we were safely down and rolling smoothly along the runway – the most relieved crew in the entire RAF, as we almost unbelievably savoured our uneventful return to Mother Earth.

Later, we discovered that the fracture in the nose-wheel jack had effectively disabled both undercarriage lowering systems. The emergency high-pressure air had been lost through exactly the same break as the hydraulic fluid from the normal system. There had been absolutely nothing that we could have done in the air to have got that wheel to lock down. What we found most astonishing was that we had spent nearly four hours wrenching the aeroplane all over the sky to try to 'jar' the nose-wheel into the locked position – and, all without the slightest hint of success. Yet, at the very last gasp, a mild patch of turbulence had been enough to get it to lock down. As I think I may have remarked before, in the flying business it is sometimes better to be lucky than good. On that day, all of us in the Vulcan used up a fair bit of the luck in our accounts.

When I got out of the aeroplane after this incident, I was extremely uncomfortable. Nothing to do with the flight – this was a very personal discomfort. For the last hour or two in the air, my face and head had been extremely itchy and, in the middle of all our other problems, I had been continuously forced to drag off my 'bone-dome' and oxygen mask to give myself a good scratching. When, eventually, I was driven to consult the Unit Medical Officer, he diagnosed chickenpox and consigned me to quarantine at home for the next couple of weeks. I had to wear gloves most of the time to try to stop scratching myself. Moreover, the affliction seemed to be concentrated on my face and head, so that I couldn't shave or comb my hair. Even washing was a fairly major problem. In very short order, I began to look like the original 'wild man of the hills', unkempt, unshaven, my face and head pitted with spots. I could only get out of the house at nights to get some fresh air, so that I skulked about the place like some sort of latter-day Phantom of the Opera. If any young or impressionable person had encountered me during these midnight outings, they might well have been driven to rush off, screaming, into the night. Until that time, I had always thought of chickenpox as a childhood malady. I'll never know why I had to wait till I was nearly thirty two to try it out. A late developer, obviously. I suppose that I've still got mumps, measles and tonsillitis to look forward to!

As I approached the end of my tour at Boscombe Down, the prospect of having to come off flying altogether began to look more and more likely. I was now so long overdue for a ground tour that it had become something of a joke. Almost uniquely among my contemporaries, I had done thirteen years non-stop in one sort of cockpit or another, putting in three full flying tours in the process – to say nothing of the courses at CFS and ETPS. I had accumulated over three thousand hours in more than eighty different types of aircraft and had flown just about every type of aircraft in service – and a few others besides. I was a graduate test pilot, an A category flying instructor and a Master Green Instrument Rating Examiner. I was a cast-iron, racing certainty for a 'mahogany bomber' somewhere.

But, then, you never know the minute till the minute after. During the last couple of months of my tour, the Boss came into the crewroom one day with the news that the United States Air Force had decided to open up a slot for an exchange test pilot from the RAF at their Flight Test Center at Edwards Air Force Base in California. When I looked at the qualification specification which the Americans had provided, I found that I seemed to be able to meet the requirements, so I immediately put in an application to be considered for the post. So also, I might say, did a whole lot of others – many of them with at least as much experience as I had, if not more. We all knew of Edwards by reputation. A long succession of very advanced research aircraft had been flown from there since Captain Charles Yeager had first gone through the 'sound barrier' in the Bell X-l. It was the site for all of the performance and handling testing of every aircraft destined for service in the USAF. At the time, it was probably the most well-known and potentially exciting, test establishment anywhere in the world. For any test pilot, the chance of a posting there represented an opportunity in a million.

Almost unbelievably, I got the job. Much later, I found out that this was due more to the way the Americans had worded their qualification specification, than to any particular merit on my part. The vacancy was in the Bomber/Cargo Section of Flight Test Operations and the 'spec' reflected the sort of flying which went on in the Section. What the USAF asked for was a pilot who was a graduate of a recognised Test Pilots School, with a minimum of three years practical test flying experience at a research Establishment. Additionally, the candidate had to have completed a tour of duty in a jet bomber squadron, had to have test experience in both bomber and transport aircraft and had to be, desirably, helicopter qualified. There were probably a number of pilots who could have outdone my claims to the post on any single one of these requirements – but, as it turned out, I was probably about the only individual qualified to apply who could meet every one of the requirements. The helicopter qualification was the major stumbling-block for practically every other candidate who applied. Of the people with bomber and transport backgrounds, I was the only one who had had the chance, during my time in 'D' Squadron, to do anything more than just gain time as second pilots.

When I finally got the official intimation that I had been selected for the appointment, Jean and I were pitched headlong into a flurry of preparation for our move to the United States. I remember that I had to be fitted for a special issue of Number 1 tropical uniform – incredibly, produced by Woolwich Arsenal and thoughtfully supplied fully lined, so that the wearer would be reasonably safe from any chills in the average hundred and ten degrees summer heat of the Mojave Desert. I think that I wore it once. The Flight Test Centre very thoughtfully provided an information pack to give us some idea of what to expect on arrival and this proved to be a very useful guide to our pre-departure preparations.

In due course, we got ourselves to Southampton in early November and there, on a miserably wet night, embarked on board the unaccustomed luxury of the Queen Mary. Next morning, with hearts high in spite of having just watched 'The Last Voyage' – a most harrowing shipwreck film – on television, we set sail for the New world.

CHAPTER 30

THE DAYS OF THE GREAT transatlantic luxury liners have long since passed into history. The 'Queen Mary', the 'Normandie', the 'Queen Elizabeth' and the 'Bremen' are no more and only dated, flickering, newsreels recall the bustling ports, the atmosphere of high anticipation, the decks thronged with passengers, the bands, the blaring of sirens and hooters, the streamers cascading from every deck, the broadcast calls for "All visitors ashore please." It was all so different then. When the massive hawsers were finally pulled aboard and the fussing tugs had gently eased the great vessels away from the quayside, the passengers could settle down to something like four or five days of the most civilised form of transport ever devised, cosseted and pampered all of the way, blissfully assured of the best of attention and service, the best of food and drink, the best of entertainment and the most elegant and sumptuous of appointments. A relaxing and enjoyable holiday in itself and an opportunity to adapt gently and imperceptibly from the way of life in one world, to the new environment of another. Nowadays, transatlantic travellers are herded into their inadequate space in a flimsy aluminium tube possessed of all of the elegance of a municipal bus, stuffed with processed, prepackaged meals, bored to distraction by packaged 'muzak' and third-rate, small-screen movies and pushed out at their destination eight or nine hours later, hot, tired, scruffy and bemused to the degree that it takes them something like forty eight hours to recover from the experience. And we call this progress!

Jean and Carol Anne and I did rather better than average on our voyage on the 'Queen Mary', in that we enjoyed no less than seven days on board. On the first night out, while picking up the passengers embarking at Cherbourg, the ships propellers fouled a harbour wire to force a twenty four hour delay before we could get underway again. This delay resulted in our arriving at New York on the afternoon of our sixth day out from Southampton. As we made our way slowly up the Hudson river, the promenade decks were thronged with passengers taking in the sights of the Manhattan skyline so familiar from hundreds of Hollywood films. The Empire State Building, Ellis Island, the Statue of Liberty and the Staten Island Ferries were probably as well known to the newcomers as they were to the homecoming Americans on board.

Our arrival at New York coincided with the American Presidential elections. By law, no passengers were permitted to disembark on that day – much to the irritation of the American passengers on board, for whom the delay at Cherbourg had meant that they would have no opportunity to cast their votes. All passengers were restricted to the ship until the polling booths had closed, so that we spent the night in our luxury floating hotel, safely moored at Pier 48 in the heart of the city. Throughout the night, continuous television and radio broadcasts reported the progress of the election which resulted in John F Kennedy being appointed President-elect of the United States. There were a lot of impromptu parties on board to mark the developing political picture – celebrations or wakes depending on the views of the participants. At one stage during the long night, I remember us exchanging a few words with a young singer, on her way to try to break into the American entertainment world. Jean had heard her perform at home and had formed the very firm opinion that she possessed real 'star' quality. Her name was Shirley Bassey.

Next morning, when we disembarked, we were exposed, for the first time, to the new and somewhat shattering, experience of New York City. The towering buildings, the seemingly enormous cars, the bustle of the teeming crowds, the constant noise and the chaotic traffic, created an initial impression that was, at once, overwhelming and slightly frightening. The whole place seemed garish, strident and utterly alien. Millions of people hemmed into a small patch of real estate, hustling and bustling about their business – feverish, colourful, noisy and impatient. I must be honest and say that I didn't like it at all. Recalling a quotation from, I think, Walt Whitman, that 'after New York, it (the United States) is all Connecticut', I was rather looking forward to Connecticut.

I was very impressed, though, with Grand Central Station, from where we were due to travel by train to Washington. It seemed almost miraculous that such a huge structure could be centrally heated to such a comfortable level in spite of the very cold November weather outside. The trains, too, were equally impressive – spotlessly clean, very comfortable and staffed by massively dignified coloured attendants whose gentle courtesy was quite delightful. Carol Anne was most impressed when one of the attendants insisted on cleaning her shoes, so that she would arrive in Washington looking her best. His quiet, "My pleasure, Missy" quite made her day.

In Washington, we were booked into a hotel for a few days, while I attended the Embassy for a succession of briefings on the responsibilities and duties of my exchange post. During this time, we had some chance to become familiar with a few of the new ways to which we would have to adapt. Oddly enough, we found most difficulty in adapting to American eating habits. For a start, the meals seemed enormous – even the smallest steaks on offer in the restaurants overlapped the sizeable dishes on which they were served by a generous margin. Dutifully, we ate our way to near-stupefaction – generally arrived at by the time we had got about a third of the way through the portion served – only to be asked, anxiously, "wasn't it to your liking, then?" The habit of serving a salad first – and on its own – also caused us initial puzzlement. I remember sitting for quite a long time in a restaurant, waiting for the main course to arrive so that we could get started. When the waitress finally enquired if there was any problem and we explained that we were waiting for our meal, she bustled off to get the main dish, muttering to herself and clearly of the view that we came into the 'crazy foreigners' category.

After a couple of days, we left Washington to travel by rail to Chicago, from where we were booked to catch the Super Chief trans-continental express to Los Angeles. We all liked Chicago very much. It was a very beautiful city indeed, very friendly and boasting some of the best jazz clubs in the United States. I would have liked to have spent more time there. While New York had been very much as we had expected, Chicago was altogether different. Although we had certainly not anticipated the place to be swarming with 1930s style gangsters in the Al Capone tradition, I think that we had expected a much more obviously industrialised and less attractive, place than the elegant city it actually turned out to be.

The Super Chief journey from Chicago to Los Angeles was an experience in itself and an excellent introduction to the sheer scale of the United States. It took two nights and three days to complete the journey – very comfortable, very punctual and offering a splendid observation car from which one could take in the passing panorama in air-conditioned comfort. Many of the places through which we passed were already familiar – at least by name – and there was a continuous sense of seeing something that one had only heard about, or read about, come to life before one's eyes. I remember thinking, as we rumbled slowly through Dodge City in the early hours of the morning, that the town and the surrounding countryside, was almost exactly as I would have expected from a hundred westerns. On another occasion, running through the desert, one half expected to see Geronimo and a host of Indians appear on the crest of the escarpments on either side of the line. It was an odd experience to be in a totally strange country for the first time, with every experience new and different and yet, at the same time, to have the feeling of being thoroughly familiar with it all.

In due course, the Super Chief pulled into the Station at Los Angeles and we were practically there. Only about another ninety miles to go, out into the wasteland of the Mojave Desert and the Air Force Flight Test Center. As we collected ourselves and our luggage on the platform of the Spanish-style Los Angeles station, slightly dazed still from the long journey and dazzled by the brightness and colour of a Californian morning, I noticed a powerfully built man, in the uniform of the United States Air Force, making his way purposefully through the crowd in our direction. As he came towards us, a broad grin on his face and hand outstretched, we turned to meet, for the first time, the man I unreservedly rate as the most unforgettable character I have ever met in my life. Captain John E 'Jack' Allavie, USAF, was a native of Council Bluffs, Iowa. Flying mad since childhood, he had tried to enlist in the Royal Canadian Air Force while he was about sixteen, so that he could get into the war before it was all over. Eventually accepted into the United States Army Air Corps at barely eighteen, he came to England with the 8th Air Force and spent his war years flying B-17s on the mass daylight raids over Germany. Seventeen years later, he still approached every day in life with the same sort of flat-out, full-throttle approach bred in those days. I don't believe that Jack ever did anything half-heartedly in his life. Whether it was flying or fun, he was in it up to the neck and with total commitment. His stamina and energy were awesome – I used to get exhausted just watching him, let alone trying to keep up with him. He saw everything in blacks and whites – never in any sort of shade of grey. If he didn't like you, you were never in any doubt of the fact: if he liked you, his shirt was your shirt. He was fervently patriotic, very pro-British, argumentative, cheerful, loyal, kind, opinionated and one hundred and ten per cent professional. A genuine 'one off' character and the best friend I have ever had.

With Jack at the wheel of the Air Force staff car, we threaded our way through the freeway maze of Los Angeles, passed through the San Fernando Valley and the San Gabriel Range and headed out into the bleak scrubland of the Mojave Desert. It was our first opportunity to see the cactus, the thorny greasewood bushes and the grotesquely shaped Joshua trees, so characteristic of the Southern California desert landscape. After about an hour and a half on the road and not long after passing through the little town of Lancaster, we arrived at a turnoff from the main road. At the entrance to the turnoff, was a very large sign emblazoned 'United States Air Force Flight Test Center' and bearing the Center crest with its evocative motto 'Ad Inexplorata' – 'Into the Unknown'. I couldn't help feeling, at the time, that it was peculiarly appropriate for us.

As we turned off the main road past the sign, there was not a sign of a building anywhere in sight. I asked Jack, "Are we here, then?" He grinned and replied, airily, in the phrase that was to become so familiar to me, "Close enough for government work." What I didn't realise, on that first occasion, was that Edwards Air Force Base was probably the biggest military installation in the United States, in terms of ground area. From the turnoff from the main road, it was another eighteen miles to the housing area and something like another four or five beyond that to the Flight Line.

At that time, it would probably be fair to say that Edwards Air Force Base had evolved a little like Topsy – it just 'growed'. During World War 2, there had been a weapons training unit stationed on the edge of Muroc Dry Lake, where a replica of a Japanese warship had been constructed to provide a target for bombing practice. The replica was known locally as the Muroc-Maru and was reconstructed every time some eagle-eyed bombardier knocked it down. Later, when the first high speed research aircraft were produced in the 'X' series, the Air Force high speed test unit was moved from Wright-Patterson Air Force Base, near Dayton, Ohio, to capitalise on two features of the Muroc Area. One was the weather factor – almost three hundred and fifty days of near-perfect flying weather in any average year. At Edwards, the joke ran that you got one weather forecast issued in mid-January for the rest of the calendar year – 'CAVU' -clear skies and visibility unlimited. The joke wasn't far from the plain truth.

The other feature of the area which made it so ideal for test flying – and particularly for test flying high performance aircraft – was the dry lake – or, more correctly, dry lakes. There are literally thousands of these dry lakes scattered throughout the desert regions of Southern California, Nevada and Utah. They have been dry since prehistoric times and are really very large expanses of dry silt and clay, baked rock-hard by the sun. Once a year, the January rains pool on the surfaces, which are simply too hard to absorb much of the moisture. As the water moves back and forth over the surface in response to the action of the wind, it acts like a gigantic plane, smoothing and levelling the surface until it is almost as flat as a billiard table and with a surface harder and stronger than concrete. By the time the rains have evaporated, all of these immense natural landing areas have been completely and perfectly resurfaced. I have taxied a B-52, at something over two hundred and fifty tons, over the Muroc lake bed and been unable to pick up even a tyre print to mark the aircrafts passage.

Muroc Lake itself is something like twelve miles long and five and a bit miles wide – a vast, sixty five square miles of natural landing strip – perfectly flat, completely barren, no rocks, no vegetation, no hills, no obstacles. And Muroc is only one of literally thousands of such lakes in the area. I would judge it to be almost impossible to experience an engine failure in that part of the world and not have a choice of dry lakes to set down on. No doubt about it: God must have had test pilots in mind when he laid out that part of the world! Sometime in the 1950s, it was calculated that the availability of Muroc Lake had saved something over eight hundred million dollars in aircraft damage which would have occurred had it not been there – not to mention the lives which had been spared.

When the first test organisation moved to Muroc Lake – it only became Edwards Air Force Base much later – it was very much a hardship posting. There were no proper facilities available on-site, either for the aircraft or the personnel. For those who couldn't get any accommodation in the local area – and there wasn't much available in the middle of the desert – caravans, mobile homes and even tents, were very much the order of the day. Even when the first base housing was hastily thrown up, it was very much sub-standard for an area like the Mojave Desert, which can be blisteringly hot by day and bitterly cold at night. Much of the original housing area – locally known as either 'Kerosene Flats' or 'Tarpaulin Flats' – was little more than a collection of what looked like large packing cases, dumped down on the bare earth. No doubt about it, the pioneer testers at Muroc and their families, were a really hardy breed. Virtually out on their own, ninety miles from anywhere, in a desert 'hell-hole' with only the rattlesnakes for company and left to get on with some of the most demanding and dangerous research flying ever undertaken by any test establishment anywhere. Any success they had – and they had plenty – they earned the hard way!

As the Muroc Lake detachment grew over the years into Edwards Air Force Base – named after Captain Glen W Edwards who was killed testing the Northrop YB-49 'Flying Wing' in 1948 – so the facilities and appointments of the Base were systematically improved to keep pace with the growing importance of the installation. When Jack swung the staff car into the housing area, Jean and I were very much impressed with the attractive bungalow ranch style homes, spaciously laid out in what was virtually a reasonably sized and typically American suburb. The type of house had been determined by a Committee headed by a Senator Capehart and was known throughout the Service as Capehart Housing. Each home was fitted with all modern kitchen and domestic appliances – freezer, refrigerator, washing machine and drier, sink-fitted garbage disposal unit – and was fully centrally heated and air conditioned. The lawns, front and back, had water sprinkler systems installed, so that the whole area could be watered automatically simply by turning on the master cock. It was a very high standard of base housing indeed. As far as Jean and Carol and I were concerned, however, there was one drawback – and a very major drawback indeed. In the RAF, all Married Quarters come fully equipped with everything – furniture, carpets, curtains, dishes, crockery, cutlery – the lot! About all you need when you move in, is a towel, a tube of toothpaste and a couple of nails to hang up the pictures. The USAF did it all quite differently. Under their system, all houses were supplied totally empty and reasonable allowances were paid to families to cover the costs of them having to move ALL of their household effects from place to place. We had been allocated a house – 6857 Lindbergh Avenue – but all it contained, apart from the fixtures, was lots of fresh Californian air.

Almost needless to say, Jack Allavie had anticipated this problem and had arranged for us to spend the first couple of days at 'Desert Villas', the accommodation facility which the Base provided for transient personnel. It wasn't

Capehart, but at least it put a roof over our heads. In the meantime, Jack put together a collection of essential pieces of furniture from Base Social Services which then enabled us to move into our new home with someplace to sleep, someplace to sit down and someplace to eat. That gave us a little breathing space before we had to launch ourselves on the local economy to furnish the place properly. Jack also provided us with a car – his second family car, a Pontiac, which I came to love dearly. It had a stick shift, no power steering and no power brakes, so that I could at least drive it without wandering all over the road or going through the windscreen every time I touched the brakes. Even when we bought ourselves our own transportation, I didn't want to give Jack his one back. It was a lovely vehicle.

In due course, Jean and I went down to Lancaster and furnished the whole house, virtually completely, from Sears Roebuck. I remember being very impressed with the store; it was absolutely enormous by the UK standards of those days and the parking lot was bigger than any I had ever seen. Nowadays, in the UK, we are thoroughly accustomed to large superstores, shopping centres and bulk buying. In those days, we found it to be a real culture shock. You could get lost quite easily in the supermarkets until you became familiar with the layout. Equally, when you were used to shopping every second day or so for relatively small quantities of consumables, it took some time to get used to buying household commodities in amounts such as seemed likely to last us through our entire tour. Jean and I had about a week in which to organise our respective bits of settling-in before I started work in earnest – about a week to get a new home set up absolutely from scratch, to learn new shopping techniques, to organise a car, licences and insurance, to settle Carol Anne into the Base school and to try to find our way about a base so huge that we were apt to get completely lost every time we drove out of our driveway. I had to get myself through the administrative arrival procedures, organise security clearances, draw flying kit – including an eye-popping orange flying suit – and familiarise myself with a mass of information on USAF flying procedures, the local flying area, danger zones, airways, control zones, local Flying Orders and Base Regulations. We didn't have a lot of time to sit and wonder what to do next.

At that early stage, it was very difficult to cope with the deluge of hospitality which was extended to us. All of our neighbours seemed to go out of their way to drop in, either just to say "Hello" and "Welcome," or to invite us to drop by for a meal, a drink, a cup of coffee, or a chat. We were the only 'Brits' on the base, apart from a couple of English girls who had been GI brides and everyone seemed keen to make us feel at home and welcome in their country. Very early on, I formed the impression that the Americans were a friendly, relaxed and genuinely hospitable people and I retain that view to this day.

Two impressions from that very early time at Edwards stick in my recollection. The first was the first Thanksgiving dinner we ever attended. Bob Heaton, who was to be one of my colleagues in Bomber Test and his wife, Martha, asked us round to share Thanksgiving with them. I don't think that I have ever been part of a nicer family occasion. The Heaton's house was furnished in American Colonial style, which provided the perfect setting for this uniquely American occasion. Their three little girls were dressed in very pretty gingham dresses and made a picture almost exactly like one of Norman Rockwell's prints from the Saturday

Evening Post. At table, the family joined hands as Bob very simply thanked God for the blessings the family had enjoyed throughout the year. I really felt rather privileged to have been able to share the occasion with them. Ever since then, I have always thought of Thanksgiving as the very nicest American festival and I still cherish the memory of the first one I enjoyed.

The second impression which has stayed with me is of the real friendship extended to us at that time by Jack Allavie and his charming wife Rosemary. They were absolute towers of strength while we were trying to find our feet. Nothing was too much trouble for them. If we needed something, they supplied it; if we didn't know how to do something, they had the answer – or, more often, came right round and did it for us themselves. We must have been an endless trial to both of them, but you would never have known it. They virtually carried us on their backs, until we knew enough to take our first faltering steps on our own. I could never thank them adequately for their friendship and unstinted help. We owe both of them a debt of gratitude that we will never be able to come close to repaying.

The Tartan Baron - Rhodesia 1951.

B-52 / X-15 take off.

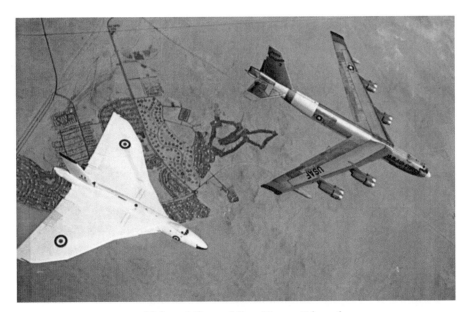

Vulcan Mk2 and B-52H over Edwards.

Jean, Carol and I ~ Edwards AFB, 1962.

Formation of T-38s.

Jack and I, ready to go.

In the chair - St Mawgan.

Award of the 'Blue Max'.

Graham's Wings Day.

CHAPTER 31

WHEN I HAD COMPLETED all of the administration necessary to 'arrive' formally on to Edwards, I found that I was assigned to the 6512th Test Group (Aircraft) – the official designation of what was known locally as 'Flight Test Operations' or, more simply, 'Flight Test'. At the time, there were two major research organisations on the Base – the 6512th Test Group, which was responsible for all of the aircraft testing, and, far away on the other side of the Dry Lake, the Rocket Research Facility. This latter facility was involved in the development and ground testing of rocket fuels – and, in particular, some of the exotic, unstable and highly volatile fuels then being developed for late generation vehicles in the rocket inventory.

In many ways, the command structure of the Base was very similar to what I had been used to at Boscombe Down. General John W Carpenter, the Commanding General, occupied a position directly analogous to the Commandant, A&AEE, exercising overall command of all Base activities. In the flight test field, the command 'chain' ran from the General's office, through the Director of Flight Test, Colonel Clay Tice, to the Flight Line Office of the Director of Flight Test Operations, Lieutenant Colonel Clarence E Anderson, the man in charge of the overall, day-to-day running of the various test programmes.

The 'Flight Line' at Edwards parallels the main runway along the western edge of Muroc Lake. It is the location for the huge concrete ramp which provides the aircraft parking area and the various hangers, crewrooms and servicing facilities are strung out along this area. In addition to providing all of the services associated with Flight Test – including a cafeteria to save one having to drive the five miles to the housing area for meals – the Flight Line also provided a home for the newly entitled Aerospace Research Pilots School, which not only trained all of the USAF test pilots, but had recently been charged with the initial training of all candidates for the various astronaut programmes.

Branching off from the main Flight Line was 'Contractors Row' – a long line of hangers and test facilities leased from the Air Force by the various major American aircraft companies. The signs along the Row spelled out a list of the 'who's who' in American aviation – North American, Convair, McDonnell-Douglas, Boeing and many others. When a new aircraft was under test at Edwards, the contractor generally saw to it that there was a flock of company experts available on-site at their facility, to ensure that specialist advice and assistance was right there, on the spot, if required.

At the end of Contractors Row was the Headquarters and support facilities of the NASA High Speed Station – a small, but highly important, element of the vast National Aviation and Space Administration organisation. The NASA Edwards Station had participated in the flying of the 'X' series of research aircraft almost from the time that the programmes started and their pilots, Joe Walker, Jack McKay and a relative newcomer named Neil Armstrong, were probably unrivalled, as a group, in their combined experience of pure research flying.

Flight Test Operations was housed in one building on the Flight Line which accommodated all four of the operational test sections – Fighter, Bomber/Cargo, Helicopters and Special Projects. The sections shared the services of a small clerical staff of civilian secretaries who looked after the typing of test reports and provided general administrative support. The building also housed its own radio terminal, to permit monitoring of all R/T traffic on the frequency used for all test flights and its own flying clothing locker room. One additional feature which absolutely staggered me the first time I saw it was a room full of cages of snakes – mostly western diamondback rattlesnakes and sidewinders, but with a few other equally unpleasant varieties thrown in for good measure. This particular room belonged to the Survival Section who had the responsibility of teaching us how to survive, in the event that we ever had to crash land or bale-out in the inhospitable terrain all around the Base. Later on, I came to appreciate the value of the Survival Section but, at first, I used to shudder every time I had to go through that damned room to pick up my flight gear.

During the first week or so, I met most of the other pilots in Flight Test, at least to say "hello" to. They were a very experienced group indeed. I came to Edwards with something over three thousand flying hours to my credit – only to discover that such a total was relatively insignificant as far as Flight Test was concerned. In the Bomber/Cargo Section, the average number of hours flown by the section pilots was over nine thousand: even in the Fighter Section, the average topped the five thousand mark. Most of the pilots had impressive operational backgrounds from either World War 2 or the Korean war – and quite a few had flown in both conflicts. Many had spent a long time in the Research and Development business, either at Edwards, or at one of the other testing facilities operated by Air Research and Development Command. In sum, they represented about as experienced and capable a group of pilots as it would have been possible to assemble anywhere. To me, they seemed not only awesomely experienced, but also extremely colourful. America does seem to produce a fair number of characters who are somewhat larger than life and most of the pilots at Edwards would have readily stood out in any crowd. I suppose that this situation was almost inevitable, in that their whole background marked them out as strong personalities possessed of a high degree of individuality. At first, I found them a bit overpowering.

The 'Boss', Lieutenant Colonel Clarence E Anderson – known variously and according to ones degree of familiarity, as either 'Colonel Andy' or 'Bud' – was a dyed-in-the-wool fighter pilot who had flown Mustangs from England during the war when he had shot down enough enemy aircraft to qualify as a triple ace – with something to spare. He was a long-time friend and squadron colleague of Chuck Yeager. Colonel Andy had been in the Research and Development business at Wright Patterson AFB, flying some very odd and extremely hazardous programmes, such as a wing-tip-to-wing-tip coupling programme when he 'hooked up' an F-84 to the wing tip of a B-29. He also flew the FICON programme, which required him to fly a F-84 fighter virtually into the bomb bay of a B-36 bomber to 'latch on' as a sort of 'on-board' fighter escort. He was a hard-bitten fighter 'pro' and would not have been my first choice of opposition in any dogfight. He was very quiet, except possibly during some of the more rambunctious Friday night 'Beer Calls'. He looked to be about sixteen years old – a genuine 'baby-face' – and his wife, Ellie, used to tell of going into a bar with him on leave somewhere, when the bartender was a little dubious about serving him with strong drink. The bartender asked Ellie, in all seriousness, whether "the kid was old enough to be in here." Andy was so mad that he rushed back to the hotel, changed into uniform and reappeared, some twenty minutes later, with his service and combat decorations extending from his chest to somewhere in the vicinity of his knees. He got his drink. When I had my initial interview with him, he asked me what I liked to do. When I said that I liked to fly aeroplanes – any aeroplanes – he leaned across his desk and said, "fly right here and I'll see to it that you fly every aeroplane on the Base." He was as good as his word, too.

In Bomber/Cargo Test, we seemed to have two chiefs – either 'Fitz' Fulton, or Ken Lewis. They seemed to take it in turns to be Section Chief for a while then, when they got tired of it, or got busy on a project, they would hand over command to the other. Fitzhugh LeRoy Fulton must be one of the most experienced pilots in the world. A tall, lanky, Georgian, he had something like eleven thousand hours in more than a hundred and eighty military types – he didn't count civilian aircraft – when I joined the section. He seemed to have been at Edwards forever and had been launch pilot for nearly all of the early 'X' aircraft launches. He had done every test in the book many times over and was the man to talk to if you ever wanted advice on how to set about any particular project. When Fitz finally retired from the Service, he moved right along Contractors Row to join the NASA High Speed Station. I last heard of him flying the Boeing 747 which launched the first Space Shuttle test flights at Edwards. By now, he must have logged more hours in the air than any ten pilots selected at random and he must have flown just about everything that ever had wings fitted to it.

Ken Lewis, from Aspen, Colorado, could have served as a stand-in for Gary Cooper. He had much the same tall, rangy, build and much the same sort of deliberate, unhurried, manner. I could always picture Ken easing himself into the saddle to ride out against the 'baddies' – he was tailor-made for the part. Softly-spoken and even-tempered, Ken seemed to me to represent the archetypal Westerner. I honestly don't know if he had ever been on a horse in his life – skiing and golf were his off-duty interests – but he really did look the part. He had been much involved in the testing of the Mach 2+ B-58 Hustler bomber and had walked away from a couple of very bad accidents in that aircraft.

The Operations Officer slot in the Section was filled by Major Frank Cole, a West Point graduate and a most delightful individual. Witty, sophisticated and charming, Frank had done an exchange tour with the RAF in a Bomber Command Canberra squadron – a tour which, I always felt, had done him little good in a career sense. In the RAF, high annual assessments are very hard indeed to come by. A rating of 6 or 7 denotes an officer of well above average performance and capability; an 8 puts you in the truly exceptional category; and if you get a 9, you are normally first in line for canonisation. The USAF assessment system seemed to expect everybody to be superman in a blue suit. Consistent 9s were the order of the day in their assessments – the vast majority of them criminally over-inflated and making it next to impossible to distinguish the truly outstanding man from the average 'Joe'. When Frank came back from the RAF with genuine 7s and 8s on his record, well merited by his thoroughly professional performance and outstanding capability, it seemed as if the USAF wanted to know where he'd gone wrong. That's what happens when you devalue an assessment system by bad and stupid reporting.

The rest of the Bomber/Cargo section included Jack Allavie, with vast bomber experience going back to the B-17 and inordinately proud of being one of the few American test pilots to have been trained at ETPS Farnborough – he was a graduate of number 14 Course; Bob Heaton, ex-Strategic Air Command B-47 man, very quiet and very professional; Charlie Kuyk, also ex-SAC, a former US Marine who had transferred to the Army to attend West Point and then later on, transferred again to the Air Force. He subsequently attended the US Navy Staff College to complete a 'full house' of experience in all of the US armed forces. Charlie had captained the West Point ice hockey and football teams and had shoulders on him like a barn door. During a visit by some RAF pilots, he was prevailed upon to demonstrate the function of a defensive lineman. In the course of his demonstration, he asked three of us simply to try to push our way past him. It was like running full-tilt into a brick wall. When I asked him afterwards if he had never considered professional football, he replied, quite seriously, "Oh no, Harry, I'm much too small and light for that sort of game." When I took a good look at him – all six foot four, thirteen or fourteen stone and magnificently built – it made me wonder what sort of monsters the pros were looking for.

Also on the bomber strength, were John Campbell, from Chattanooga, Tennessee, fresh from representing United States interest in the P1127 Kestrel joint test programme in the UK; Carl Cross, who paired up with his friend, John Blackwell from Base Headquarters, in all golf events, to form a 'proprietary' partnership; Texan Doug Benefield, later to be test pilot on the B-1 bomber; and Ted Sturmthal – invariably referred to by Jack Allavie and to his intense annoyance, as Emil Von Sturmthal. Ted was a bit of a walking piloting miracle. He was extremely short sighted – so much so, that he would have failed any aviation eye test hands down.

When the Korean War was on and a great many people were finding good reasons to be doing something else, Ted camped out in the office of the Chief of Staff of the United States Air Force until the great man had him in for an interview. Ted explained that he needed to get the eyesight regulations waived to allow him into pilot training and that the Chief of Staff was the only man in the Service who could order the Surgeon General to grant such a waiver. Much impressed, the Chief of Staff responded by making the necessary order and Ted was on his way. I first flew with him in a B-52 before I had learned of his background and when he asked me – on the final approach – if I could see the runway, I thought he was having me on. At the time, we were about four miles out!

Across the corridor from the Bomber/Cargo Section was the Helicopter Section under Lieutenant Colonel Walt Hodgson. Just after I arrived, Walt took a new and untested, helicopter high into the Sierras to rescue a hunter who had broken his leg during a winter trip into the mountain wilderness above Bishop. It was a particularly dangerous sortie, involving flying the new machine to an altitude very close to the existing helicopter world record, over very difficult mountain terrain and in foul weather conditions. When Walt had finally managed to pick him up, the hunter complained bitterly that it had taken so long to get him out of the mountains. Walt used to say, "I felt like taking him straight back, kicking him out and telling him to make his own way down"

Along the corridor a little was the Fighter Section with Major Walter Daniels in charge. Walter was a hard little Oklahoman, a World War 2 P-47 Thunderbolt pilot and a fanatical golfer. Oddly enough, when I first met him, I went through much the same experience as I had with Peter Bardon at Boscombe Down. I thought that he was going to be hard to get on with, but I found that his seeming abruptness was just native Oklahoma reserve. Later, we became close friends and played a lot of golf together. Also in the Fighter Section were Bob White, a native New Yorker, another P-51 combat veteran, recently appointed as the Air Force No 1 pilot on the X-15 project; Bob Rushworth, from Maine, an ex-transport pilot who had spent his war flying supply missions over the infamous 'Hump' and now back-up to Bob White for the X-15. Henry Gordon and Russ Rogers – where would any self-respecting fighter unit be without Flash Gordon and Buck Rogers – and Pete Knight – the latter three nominated as project pilots for Dyna Soar, the or-bital vehicle research project scheduled to follow the X-15. The last two in the Fighter Section were the pair whose programme I shared to 'get my feet wet' at Edwards. Jim MacDivitt was a young captain who very soon moved on to the as-tronaut programme. I met him in Paris some five years later, by which time he was a young general. Now, that IS promotion! His partner in the T-38 programme was another genuine 'character'. Swart H Nelson was a native of Arizona, having been brought up on an Apache reservation. Built like a grizzly bear, he knew more about survival than anyone else I have ever met. At Edwards, we had to do three periods of survival training each year – sea survival off Catalina Island; winter survival up in the High Sierras; and desert survival anywhere out in the Mojave. I used to move heaven and earth to arrange my annual survival stints to coincide with 'Nelly's. Give him a knife and he could be dropped down anywhere – and live like a king. In the Sierras, he would trap rabbits and other game, fish trout out of the icy streams, shoot 'chuckers' – a breed of wildfowl – with bow and arrow and cook the days fare in a warm, waterproof, lean-to he would rig up in about thirty minutes. In the desert, he could almost smell water – in the bends of old rivers, or in parched-looking cacti and he would catch, kill, skin and serve up rattlesnake steaks as easily as I would have opened a tin of beans. Incidentally, rattlesnake isn't half bad – it tastes a lot like veal. His wife told me that, when they were post-ed to Alaska, she bought a couple of pounds of meat at the BX on the night of their arrival. Thereafter, for the rest of their tour, Nelly provided all their fish and game from his hunting trips.

Nelly lived off-base, just outside Palmdale – almost inevitably, in a house he had built himself. One evening, when we were his guests at dinner, his wife hit the wrong pedal on their car and drove it straight through the back of the garage. At this point, the far end of the living room collapsed, along with the garage, in a heap of rubble. Nelly was completely unconcerned – "have to build it up again tomorrow" was his laconic comment. Years later, after three tours of duty in Vi-etnam, he left the Service to go cattle ranching in Peru or Ecuador or Paraguay – I forget which. When he sold out his interests, he was left a very wealthy man in-deed. He then bought a house close to an Air Force Base in Virginia, travelled 'space available' all over the world and enjoyed himself up to the hilt. He arrived on my doorstep one evening when I was living in London, with a couple of crates of the vilest wine I have ever tasted – Corsican, I think it was. You could have run your car on the stuff. We drank martinis during his visit and I think that Jean used the wine later to flush out the drains.

At the far end of the Flight Test building was the Special Projects Section – a very 'hush-hush' outfit, flying the Lockheed U-2, the infamous 'spy in the sky'. At the time, they were doing a lot of the test work associated with development of systems and equipment packages for various space satellites. The Section Chief was Major Harry Andonian – another ETPS graduate and a genuine 'one-off' character. Small and dapper, outsize cigar at a jaunty angle, Harry always gave me the impression of being a more subtle, commissioned version of Sergeant Bilko. He was an inveterate 'wheeler-dealer', who always had some scheme hatching to improve the quality of his life-style. Someone once said to me, "Harry has never really grasped the fact that he's supposed to be working for the Government: he figures it's the other way around."

Some of his ploys were breathtaking. We used to do a B-47 run to Hawaii where we lived at Hickam AFB and used public transportation to get into Honolulu. Not Harry! He thought Hickam was too noisy and public transport too inhibiting. By some means known only to himself, he always wangled special orders for this trip, so that HIS crew drew accommodation in the Surfrider Motel, on Princess Ala-moana Boulevard in downtown Honolulu and HIS crew got the use of hire cars at Government expense – not one hire car for the crew, but one EACH! Probably his crowning achievement came with him persuading – I nearly wrote 'conning' – Ken Lewis to let him swap one of the Bomber Sections B-47s for a spare C-135 at Wright Patterson. We could certainly have used the C-135 so that, somewhat doubtfully, Ken let him go ahead. When the swap was duly effected – guess what? Who was the only C-135 qualified pilot at Edwards? Right first time! Very suspi-ciously, every time one of the Bomber Section was due to check out in the thing, it developed inexplicable mechanical problems and had to go back into the hanger. While this was going on, Harry contacted the Rome Air Development Center with the news that Edwards had a C-135 just hanging about looking for a good pro-gramme. They came up with a project to measure the earth's gravity at various locations and left it to Harry to 'flesh-out' the programme details. I came across him in his office one day, surrounded by maps and travel guides. He was industri-ously scribbling down a draft test itinerary; Rio de Janeiro, Buenos Aires, Sydney, Bali, Tokyo, London, Paris... Compared to Harry, Bilko was a bumbling amateur!

Further down the flight-line, surveying the world he knew so well from the office of Commandant, United States Air Force Aerospace Research Pilots School, lived Colonel Charles E 'Chuck' Yeager It would be a complete waste of time for me to write much about him: everything that could possibly be written about his exploits has already been written. War time fighter 'ace', escapee from a German POW camp, first man to go through the 'sound barrier', first man to Mach 3.5, pilot of every research aircraft in the US inventory – the man was a living legend in the aviation world. I must be honest and say that, when I first came to Ed-wards, I regarded this sort of 'superman' reputation with rather more than a grain of salt. Obviously, the man had to be good, but I was reasonably sure that his reputation had been more than a touch inflated by what I regarded, at the time, as American 'ballyhoo'. I couldn't possibly have been more wrong.

As I knew him, Chuck Yeager was one of the quietest, most modest individuals I have ever met. He had a dry west Virginia sense of humour. One day he commented to me on the fact that the School, of which he was Commandant, required candidates to hold a Masters or Doctors degree before they would even be considered for interview for a place on the course. "If it had been like this in my day," he remarked, wryly, "I'd never have been allowed past the front door." I flew with him quite a few times and it was doing so that showed me something of the real quality of the man. When I landed after our first trip together, I felt like hanging up my wings and looking for another line of business. This had nothing to do with his record. In my time, I have known many pilots with distinguished combat records, quite a few escaped POWs, lots of very capable test pilots and plenty who had undertaken difficult and hazardous programmes. Yeager was all this – and much more. He had a feel for an aeroplane more sensitive than I have ever come across in anyone else. He wasn't just a natural pilot – in the air, he became part of the aeroplane itself. It spoke to him through his feel of the controls – a feel that allowed him to coax it and gentle it to performances and standards of accuracy not granted to the rest of us mere mortals. Quite simply, he was the best I have ever seen – or could even imagine. What Fred Astaire was to a dance floor, Chuck Yeager was to an aeroplane – any aeroplane. In the aviation world, he was THE MAN! To me, at least, he always will be.

CHAPTER 32

JEAN AND I WERE CHATTING idly over an early evening meal – taken somewhat earlier than was our usual routine, since I was scheduled to fly that night. Outside, the light was fading very quickly and the first dim stars were starting to appear in the clear evening sky. Jean asked if I was going to be late back and I shook my head, "I shouldn't think so, we're due off at eight, should be down by nine thirty at the latest, probably be home by ten." I sat back and lit up a cigarette, before I added, "Nelly is pulling my leg for tonight. He's got us down for some night formation." When Jean asked, "What do you mean, pulling your leg?" I laughed and replied, "Dear, you can do a lot of things with an aeroplane at night – but formation flying isn't one of them. He's just having me on."

I was still smiling quietly to myself as I turned the car out of the driveway and headed towards the flight line. During the past month, I had been working with Nelly and Jim MacDivitt as the AFFTC representatives on the T-38 joint test programme – a programme also involving a number of pilots from Air Training Command and designed to confirm the operational suitability of the aircraft for the advanced training role. In some ways, it was an odd programme to start with at Edwards. I was basically a 'bomber' man – but, at least, my experience as an Instructor had come in very handy. Moreover, I loved the aeroplane – I still feel that the T-38 was one of the best American aircraft I ever flew. Developed from the Northrop N-156 lightweight fighter, the T-38 Talon was a very high performance aeroplane and it handled beautifully. Powered by two small, but very efficient General Electric turbojets with afterburners – as the Americans termed re-heat – it was easily capable of Mach 1.4 and its rate of climb was electrifying – of the order of thirty five thousand feet a minute. In fact, Walt Daniels took one to a time-to-height world record which lasted for all of forty eight hours. When the Navy got wind of another Air Force entry in the record books, they rushed an F-4 Phantom on to the runway at Patuxent River and immediately took the record back. Hardly surprising – the Phantom had enough raw power to push a hanger supersonic!

The T-38 programme was an ideal opportunity for me to ease myself into the routine of flying at Edwards. It gave me plenty of experience of the local flying area and USAF flying procedures and – perhaps, most importantly – familiarity with American R/T procedures. All voices tend to sound a little garbled over aircraft radios and when you are relatively unused to both the accents and the terminology, it can be quite difficult to follow what is actually being said. Even when you do follow things quite clearly, it is still possible to arrive at misunderstandings, simply as a result of not being used to the national idiom. During one of my early formation flights, Jim MacDivitt called me to "select A/B." I popped the air brakes. As Jim disappeared over the horizon, he yelled, "I meant AFTERBURNER, Goddammit!" Embarrassed, I yelled back, "If you meant reheat, why didn't you say so?" It took me some time to live that one down.

When I got to the office that night, I found that Nelly had everything set up for a formation briefing. According to the blackboard, he was going to lead, with Jim MacDivitt flying the 'box' slot. I was down for the number 2 position, with Colonel Peterson, the newly-arrived Director of Flight Test, scheduled as number 3. My immediate reaction was that they were all in on it, so I determined to go along with the 'gag' and say nothing until Nelly got round to telling us what we were really going to be doing.

As the briefing progressed, with routine coverage of frequencies, manoeuvres and emergency procedures, it did cross my mind that everybody seemed to be taking it all quite seriously. I started to wonder uneasily whether I might not have misjudged the situation somewhat. I sincerely hoped that I hadn't – I hadn't flown any serious formation for the better part of six or seven years and I had never flown formation at all at night – not ever! Still hoping that the briefing was all part of an elaborate 'send-up', I began to pay close attention to what Nelly was saying.

When we got ourselves lined up on the runway in 'finger-four' formation, I realised, with a sinking feeling of apprehension, that the joke was on me. At that stage, it was a bit late in the day to come up with the admission that I had never flown night formation before. I riveted my attention onto the little 'station-keeping' lights on Nelly's machine and resolved to do my best to 'hang in there'. As the only RAF pilot on the place, I was damned if I was going to back off now. When Nelly drawled, "Rolling now," I shoved the throttles forward, switched in the afterburners and launched hopefully into the dark.

The first few minutes airborne were sheer purgatory. For most of the time, I couldn't see Nelly's aircraft clearly enough to position myself accurately in the vertical plane. Fore-and-aft wasn't too difficult since I could use the glow from his tail-pipes to keep myself from getting too far ahead or behind, but not being able to position myself by observing both top and bottom surfaces of his wing made it very difficult to judge whether I was high or low. I spent too much time wandering up and down like a drunken sailor before I latched on to the idea of using the 'station-keeping' lights effectively. I cursed myself silently for not having paid enough attention during the briefing – I'd thought that Nelly's homilies on station-keeping had all been part of the joke.

Eventually, after ten or so minutes of popping up and down like a cork, I managed to settle into a reasonable position and started to relax somewhat. Even at that, I was soaked in sweat and still pretty tense. Trying to hold station on those tiny pin-pricks of light was as difficult as anything I had ever tried and I was having to work as hard as I knew how to avoid falling away out of the formation. Fortunately, Nelly was taking it very gently. I learned later that this was supposed to be for Colonel Pete's benefit – although a very experienced fighter pilot, he didn't have a lot of time in the T-38. Anyway, Nelly kept everything smooth and easy as we progressed in a series of slow climbing turns to about twenty thousand feet and headed westward towards the sprawl of lights that marked Los Angeles, some ninety miles distant.

when we crossed the coast, Nelly put us through a few very mild manoeuvres to tighten the formation up – gentle turns, dives and climbs. White knuckled, I hung on grimly – mentally blessing Alan Brindle for the hours of formation flying he had put me through. After a few minutes of this, Nelly came up on the radio, "OK, that's enough for one night. We'll just shoot a couple of aeros, then we'll go on home." I didn't want to believe that I'd understood him properly. "A couple of aeros"! I was having enough trouble as it was, just staying in position, without trying any trick stuff like formation aerobatics. I knew that I should really have pulled out – formation aerobatics is demanding enough by day – but I had got it into my head that I was flying for the RAF that night and there was no way that I was going to cry off. If Nelly was prepared to lead, then I was stubbornly prepared to try my level best to follow.

Dripping sweat from every pore and verging on a state of advanced lockjaw, I hung on desperately through the first few wing-overs, loops and barrel rolls. It didn't get any easier as one manoeuvre followed another, with me praying fervently that Nelly would call it a night. Eventually, he pulled up again into a straight loop just ever so slightly slow on the entry speed. As we came over the top, I could feel the aircraft getting away from me – I was 'jazzing' the throttles like mad and waving the stick all over the place to try to stay in place, but I was fighting a losing battle. We were just too slow to have any room left for position adjustment. I felt the controls go all 'mushy' and the first juddering of the incipient stall. I simply couldn't hold it any longer. As I was on the point of pressing the microphone button to say that I was parting company from the formation, Colonel Pete came up on the radio cheerfully, "I don't know about you Harry, but I'm planning to spin left. You can make your own arrangements." At that instant, we both fell away into the blackness.

Breaking away sharply right to keep out of Colonel Pete's way, I brought the aircraft back under control and eventually picked up Nelly and Jim, by now out of their loop and heading back inland. Colonel Pete and I struggled back into formation in time to join them for the run back to Edwards where, mercifully, we broke formation for individual stream landings. I don't think I could have coped with a formation landing at that stage.

When we got back in for de-briefing, everyone seemed to regard the sortie as just another routine trip. I forced a 'nothing to it' sickly grin and didn't say a word. When I got home I must have been seven pounds lighter and I was still shaking. Just a little old night formation trip – USAF style! It put years on me.

In retrospect, I suppose that my nightmare baptism to night formation was a small price to pay for all of the value- and fun – I got out of the T-38 programme. Because the Headquarters of Air Training Command was located at Randolph AFB we made frequent visits to San Antonio in Texas. And yes, Texas is big -very big indeed. On the flight from Edwards, the halfway point is inside Texas – and San Antonio is only halfway across Texas. I liked the place – it still had a somewhat rambunctious atmosphere about it. At the time, so I was informed, Texas was a 'dry' state – a fact which didn't seem to inhibit the Texans from hoisting a glass or two when the occasion demanded. When you are in San Antonio, you have to visit the Alamo. So I did. On the way back into town, the cab driver chatted with me about various aspects of the site. He concluded, in all seriousness, by informing me, "Did you know that it cost John Wayne more to make the movie, than it cost the United States to have the Goddam war with Mexico?"

While I was involved with the T-38 programme, I was also checking out in most of the Bomber/Cargo section aircraft. The B-57 – the USAF version of the Canberra – was reasonably familiar, although it felt a lot heavier than the RAF versions I had flown. The T-29, T-39, C-130 and T-37 were fairly straightforward conversions: the B-47 and B-52 rather less so. The B-47 was still in widespread service with Strategic Air Command and was very different from anything I had flown before. It was a deceptively big aircraft with a wingspan in excess of a hundred feet and an all-up weight of more than two hundred thousand pounds. Its sharply swept wings and very clean design, conferred a very high performance for such a big bomber. It was very adaptable and very manoeuvrable in the air – Charlie Kuyk took me through a LABS (Low Altitude Bombing System) attack profile once and it seemed the oddest thing do be doing low-level 'rolls off the top' in such a massive six -engined bomber.

In the air, it was a delight to fly: the problems arose when it came time to get back on the ground. Being so 'clean', aerodynamically, it lost speed very slowly and it had no real airbrakes fitted – the front undercarriage was partially lowered to provide a bit of extra drag. This problem of losing speed was compounded by the early model jet engines, which could be thoroughly temperamental at low throttle settings. It wasn't a good idea to throttle them back below about sixty per cent power on the approach, otherwise, if you suddenly had to go round again, you couldn't always rely on getting a good response from them. They were just a bit too prone to compressor stalling at low power settings. As a result, we normally carried at least sixty per cent power on all six engines until we were absolutely certain of 'making it'. With this sort of power, it was even more difficult to hold the speed down – if the nose dipped just a fraction, the speed would increase very rapidly indeed and it would be almost impossible to get rid of it again while still descending.

Unfortunately, really precise speed control was absolutely crucial when landing the brute. It was fitted with a 'bicycle' landing gear – the front and aft sets of main wheels retracted into the fuselage and the wings carried only flimsy wing-tip outriggers. With this configuration, it was critical to contact the runway at the correct fuselage angle – and the fuselage angle is determined by the speed. At the right angle – and speed – you touched down with the rear landing gear making contact a fraction before the front gear. A hair slow and the rear gear contact 'threw'" the nose gear down with an impact like a ton of bricks. Even worse was a slightly fast contact which touched the front gear first: this set up a sort of 'porpoising' action, from one set of main wheels to the other, which jarred the aircraft violently every time either set made contact. As aileron control was lost with reducing speed, there was a very real danger of 'writing-off' the outriggers – and the outboard engines which were mounted on underslung pods quite close to the wing-tips. You really had to hit your approach and touchdown speeds right 'on the money' to get a good landing out of a '47'. An error of as little as a knot or two either way and you could be in trouble. With an approach chute deployed for extra drag, landings were a bit easier – you had to carry extra power anyway – but they were never REALLY easy.

I was taken through my check out by Jack Allavie and Charlie Kuyk. Charlie even demonstrated for me all the grief you could find on landing by deliberately touching down at incorrect speeds. He was so experienced on the aircraft that he thought nothing of it, but I was very, very, impressed. After his demonstration, I ALWAYS treated the '47' with the very greatest respect when it came to putting it back on the ground. It was totally unforgiving – you either put it down right, or you were in for a whole lot of trouble.

Oddly enough, the B-52, although a much bigger aeroplane and fitted with the same sort of landing gear configuration, was a lot easier to land. Not exactly easy – but easier. It really was an enormous machine – one hundred and eighty five feet wingspan, one hundred and sixty feet long, weight up to two hundred and fifty tons. On the pre-flight check, you could get tired just walking round it. It was fitted with the first cross-wind landing gear I ever flew with – a system which allowed touchdown to be made with the aircraft pointing across the runway into wind, while the wheels were aligned directly down the runway. Initially, I found the stick forces very heavy, after the RAF bombers I had been used to. I have quite small hands and so, on the final turn across wind before landing, I often used to take my right hand off the eight throttles to get a bit more leverage on the stick. Every time I did, Jack Allavie would rap me across the knuckles with a ruler and yell, "Get back on the throttles." Eventually, I learned to do so, but it was always a real struggle to fly that big aircraft accurately with only one hand on the yoke. I used to complain to him bitterly that any self-respecting co-pilot would have worked the throttles for me, but I got precious little sympathy out of him. Jack was a good friend but, in the air, he was all professional – also he had fingers like a bunch of bananas.

During one take-off when Jack was in the left-hand seat, we were pounding down the runway with all eight engines at full bore, water-methanol on and just approaching unstick, when there was suddenly the most unearthly screech from somewhere down in the nose. I thought instantly that one of the front wheels had seized. At this point, an object flew at us from between Jack's rudder pedals, shot up his leg and over his shoulder and disappeared into the back of the aeroplane. When we got down and had a good look around the rear crew compartment, we discovered a terrified stray cat which had somehow got into the aircraft overnight. It was absolutely petrified with fear, its hair sticking straight out. It took quite a long time to coax it out from under the rear equipment panels, so that the ground crew could get on with their servicing. Like a lot of wines, cats don't travel well – not in aeroplanes, anyway.

The B-52s were very important to the Bomber/Cargo Section. Not only was Charlie Kuyk about to start the Operational Reliability Trials of the 'H' model, but two venerable 'A' models were used as launch vehicles for the X-15, the latest of the 'X' research series to fly at Edwards. With rocket-powered research aircraft, the on-board propellant fuel capacity is limited and every drop has to be used to attain the performance goals in terms of speed and altitude. If the aircraft had to take-off normally and then climb to the high altitudes at which their work is conducted, they would use so much propellant simply getting up there that their burning time at altitude would be too short to give the performance they were designed to produce. In these circumstances, nearly all of the 'performance' research aircraft have been air-launched – carried up to altitude by a 'mother-ship', which has operated very much as the first stage does in a multi-stage rocket. It gets the research aircraft up to altitude with a full load of propellants – in fact, the propellants are continually 'topped-up' from the mother-ship almost up to the second of launch. With the earlier X-1, X-1A, X-1B, X-1E:, X-2 and D-558, either the B-29 or B-50 bombers had been able to cope with the mother-ship role. For the X-15, with performance goals that went far, far, beyond anything that had been attained before, a bigger and more powerful, 'parent' was required and two early production B-52As were converted to undertake the role.

It might just be worthwhile, for a moment, to discuss these 'pure research' aircraft which feature so large in Edwards history. The breed was really born out of World War 2 and the invention of the jet engine, both of which events remorselessly pushed aircraft speeds closer and closer to the speed of sound – the sound barrier. In those days, many respected aviation authorities believed that aircraft would never get past the barrier of Mach 1 because, so they reasoned, the air 'compressibility' would build up layer upon layer of air on the forward surfaces, through which no aircraft would be able to batter its way. In Britain, the Chief Scientific Adviser to the Air Ministry had advised that manned supersonic flight was 'impracticable' and that flying too close to the barrier could be too dangerous. Largely on the basis of this advice, a Miles Aircraft supersonic project was cancelled.

In the United States, the view was taken that it would be worthwhile – even essential – to build a research aircraft to probe the flight regime in the vicinity of Mach 1. No flight test aerodynamic data existed for this regime, because nobody had ever flown fast enough to gather it and wind-tunnel tests were inhibited by the effects of compressibility 'choking' the tunnel. So it was that the Bell Aircraft Corporation produced the X-1 – a tiny rocket-powered aircraft, the basic shape of which had been adapted from that of a .50 calibre bullet. Its' tiny, razor edge wings supported the pilot and five hundred pounds of instrumentation, designed to record the pressures, temperatures, strains and stresses of flight up to the barrier. For a time, the aircraft was 'hawked' around the Industry test pilots who were offered very large sums to undertake the first flights. That got the machine tested up to Mach 0.8 – just enough to convince the US Government that it would fly. Beyond that, no amount of money seemed to be able to persuade anyone to start probing much further. The death of Jeffrey de Havilland in the Swallow was still fresh in everybody's mind.

Eventually, the Air Force solved the problem by assigning a young Captain – an experienced and capable fighter test pilot – to take on the project and fly the thing as fast as it would go. The young Captains name was Charles E Yeager. On October 14th, 1947, nursing a couple of cracked ribs in his side, he crawled down the ladder in the bomb bay of the B-29 mother ship, squeezed into the tiny cockpit of 'Glamorous Glennis' – named for his wife – and prepared for a speed run to take him to Mach 0.98. As the little aircraft dropped away from the mother ship, he hit four switches to fire up the four-chamber rocket motor and pulled into a steep climb to forty two thousand feet. Coming over the top, he rode his way through the severe jolting and buffeting until, quite suddenly, the Machmeter needle, which had been oscillating around 0.98, jumped off the scale entirely. The first ever sonic 'boom' reverberated across the empty Mojave Desert and young Captain Yeager had flown his way into immortality. The era of supersonic flight had arrived.

The implications of Yeager's flight opened a whole new age in aviation. As the myth of the impenetrable 'sound barrier' vanished for ever, designers all around the world began feverishly to produce new concepts for supersonic aircraft. The famous 'Century Series' of US fighter aircraft was born during this period. For all of the designers, engineers and scientists, now absorbed in the new challenges of supersonic design, the only real, full-scale, aerodynamic data available was that which was being brought back from each test flight by the five hundred pounds of instrumentation and recording equipment on-board the X-1. As the aircraft was flown faster and faster, eventually reaching about 1000 mph, so the data available to the experts accumulated – not estimates, not wind-tunnel tests, not guesses, but hard aerodynamic FACTS brought back by pilots who, day by day, pushed the frontiers of knowledge further and further into the supersonic flight regime.

Following Yeager's milestone flight, a whole string of pure research aircraft began to appear. The X-2 – designed for at least 2000 mph – was beset by difficulties, so that Bell pushed on, in tandem, with modifications to the original X-1 design. This latter initiative led to the X-1A, the X-1B and the X-1E. Douglas produced the jet-powered Skystreak and the mixed jet and rocket powered D-558-II Skyrocket – later converted to pure rocket power. Northrop produced the X-4, an experimental, jet-powered, 'flying wing'. Bell produced the X-5, the world's first variable wing-sweep jet. Convair produced the XF-92 delta-wing jet – the experimental parent of the later F-102 and F-106. Douglas produced the jet-powered X-3 the 'Flying Stiletto' – 66 Feet long, but with a wingspan of only 22 feet. The X-13 was an early design for vertical take-off – a conventional aircraft mounted on its tail on a specially constructed tower. The X-i4 was an early true Vertical Take Off and Landing design, incorporating both propulsive and lifting jets.

With these tools, the small group of research test pilots pushed the aerodynamic frontiers ever faster and higher. Douglas test pilot Bill Bridgeman took the D-55B-II to Mach 1.89 and 79,000 Feet. Marine Colonel Marion Carl took it to 83,000 feet and NASA pilot Scott Crossfield to Mach 2.0. Days later, Yeager flew the X-1A to Mach 2.5. Kit Murray took the same aircraft to 90,000 Feet. Pete Everest took the X-2 to Mach 2.93 and Kincheloe raised the altitude mark to 126,000 feet. In none of these flights was 'record-breaking' much of a serious consideration to the pilots concerned. For publicity purposes, it may have been important to the manufacturer, or to the services concerned – they, after all, have to fight for the money to fund their programmes – but, to the pilots, record breaking is a somewhat stupid concept. If you have an aeroplane which is faster than anything else in the sky, it doesn't take a lot of effort to capture the world speed record – given the ability to fly the thing, anybody could do it. The primary concern of the research pilot is to bring back data from new and previously unexplored, regimes of flight. If, along the way, you break a few records and get some publicity, that's nice – but it isn't the object of the exercise. It is worth remembering that while Yeager, Everest, Murray, Apt and Kincheloe were flying these exotic programmes, they were also doing a normal days work at Edwards as ordinary service test pilots – no different from any of their colleagues working on any other, less glamorous, project.

It might also be borne in mind that the data that was brought back wasn't always palatable, or easily won. When Bridgeman flew the Skyrocket to Mach 1.87, he ran into extreme directional oscillations – at times, the nose was swinging as much as 75 degrees off centre-line. That is really the hard way to find out about directional stability at high supersonic speeds. During Yeager's Mach 2.5 run in the X-1A, the aircraft yawed and rolled violently as the rockets burned out. In the thin air at 76,000 feet, he simply didn't have enough control power to correct the situation and the aircraft literally 'swapped ends', tumbling crazily out of control through 50,000 feet. Almost unconscious, Yeager was thrown about the cockpit so violently that he broke the cockpit canopy in a number of places – with his head. Recovering consciousness in an inverted spin over Tehachapi, some miles north of the Base, Yeager still had enough left to recover and 'dead-stick' the aircraft back on to the lake-bed. He brought back the data that led to the problems of high-speed oscillations and inertia roll-coupling being recognised and resolved. I have seen the records of that particular flight and I doubt whether any other pilot in the world would have survived it.

Some of the pilots didn't survive. They flew 'into the unknown' and they didn't make it back. Ziegler in the X-2E, Popson in the X-5, Apt in the X-2, Kincheloe in the F-104 – all lost their lives in the research programmes. They knew and accepted the risks and when the time came, they paid the final, grim, price.

CHAPTER 33

IN EARLY 1954, IT WAS becoming clear that some of the new aircraft coming into service were capable of performances that would rival those of the stable of research aircraft. If further advances were to be made in aviation, some new tool was going to be needed to open up the way into hypersonic flight – flight at around Mach 5 – and to altitudes at the very fringes of space. This requirement was heavily reinforced by the need to gather data to support the burgeoning space-flight programmes, then in-train. Sooner or later, pilots were going to have to 'fly' back from space, rather than be dumped into the ocean on the end of a cluster of parachutes. Reliable data was desperately needed on thermodynamics, control systems, life support, re-entry manoeuvres and a thousand other critical parameters. To gather this essential data, a new research craft was going to be required.

In October 1954, the NASA Committee on Aeronautics endorsed a proposal "For the immediate initiation of a project to design and construct a research airplane capable of achieving speeds of the order of Mach number 7 and altitudes of several hundred thousand feet, for the exploration of the problems of stability and control of manned aircraft and aerodynamic heating in the severe form associated with flight at extreme speeds and altitudes." At the time, the boldness of the proposal was breathtaking. No aircraft had flown beyond Mach 3.5 and about 90,000 feet. No power plant existed, or was in prospect, capable of driving an aircraft even remotely near to Mach 7. No material existed capable of withstanding the searing friction heat generated at that sort of speed. No aerodynamic data existed on which the design of such an aircraft could be soundly based. The whole proposal represented a truly colossal leap into the unknown. It might even prove to be totally unachievable.

In May 1955, Bell, Douglas, North American and Republic submitted design study bids in response to the NASA proposal. In December, the contract was awarded to North American and Scott Crossfield, the long-time Chief Pilot of the NASA Edwards high-speed station – and a pilot with unrivalled experience of rocket-powered aircraft – left NASA to join North American as design consultant on the new project. The project for the new aircraft was entitled Project X-15.

Three and a half years – and more than two million man-hours of engineering effort – later, the hanger doors of the North American Los Angeles Division were cranked open and X-15 number one was officially 'rolled-out' for its launching ceremony. Vice-President Richard Nixon, Senators, Congressmen, most of the Company 'brass', invited VIPs and a plane load of aviation reporters were on hand for the event. As the aircraft came slowly into view, the reaction of the invited audience was perhaps most honestly summed up by one reporter who remarked to a colleague, "What in the hell kind of airplane is that?" Long and slim, with a massive cruciform tail assembly and painted dead black, the machine resembled nothing so much as a huge black dart. Its first impact on the outside world was more of awed wonder than anything else.

In appearance, the X-15 wasn't all that far removed from some of the early 'Buck Rogers' concepts of rocket ships. Its stubby, 22 foot span wings were set rather more than halfway back along its 50 foot length, almost directly in front of the massive, four-section tail assembly. The tail carried all of the aerodynamic flight controls – the wings carried only the landing flaps. The 'all-moving' horizontal fins served as both ailerons and elevators. Moved in the same direction, they acted as elevators: moved in opposite directions, as ailerons. The upper half of the upper vertical fin and the lower half of the lower vertical fin, served as rudders. The lower half of the upper fin housed the air-brakes. Because the lower half of the vertical fin extended below the landing gear, it was jettisoned before touchdown and recovered by parachute. If it had ever failed to jettison, the X-15 would have become the world's highest speed plough.

Basically, the fuselage contained a nose section, housing the pilot and about 1300 pounds of instrumentation; two large propellant tanks, containing about nine tons of anhydrous ammonia and liquid oxygen; and the XLR-99 rocket engine. Most of the 'plumbing' of the aircraft was carried in two streamlined fairings along the sides of the fuselage – a design solution that gave the fuselage a curiously 'squashed' appearance. Because the rocket engine only ran for ninety seconds at full power, engine-driven auxiliary systems were not practicable: instead, the hydraulic and electrical systems were run from two auxiliary power units (APUs) which operated by passing hydrogen peroxide over a catalyst bed. The superheated steam thus generated drove the APU turbines. Fuel pressure was maintained by helium. For cooling and cockpit pressurisation, nitrogen was used. By the time the X-15 was filled up with all its gases and chemicals, it smelled rather like a science laboratory.

In the first aircraft, the pilot had three control 'sticks' – a conventional centre stick, a right-hand high 'g' sidearm controller and a left-hand sidearm controller for the ballistic reaction control system. This latter system squirted bursts of superheated steam from six nozzles – four in the nose and two at the wing tips – to permit attitude control in the 'near-space' environment, where the air density was too low for conventional aerodynamic controls to be of any effect. Strictly speaking, the X-15 couldn't be 'flown' on the reaction controls – in the sense that it couldn't change direction. Once launched into near-space, the aircraft was on a ballistic trajectory, just like a bullet. The function of the ballistic control system was simply to allow the pilot to change the aircraft attitude within its pre-ordained flight path – a capability crucial to flying controlled re-entry manoeuvres. The landing gear of the X-15 was very odd indeed – only two wheels and both of them on the nose-wheel assembly. At the back, instead of wheels, were two steel skids to absorb the shock of the 200 mph landing. Obviously, there were no brakes. To cope with the anticipated airframe skin temperature range of from about 1200 degrees down to 300 degrees below zero, North American used a new metal, Iconel-X – a nickel and steel alloy developed by the International Nickel Company – for the aircraft 'skin'. To save weight, much of the aircraft surfaces had to be ground to watchmakers' tolerances. Underneath the Iconel-X, much of the sub-structure was constructed of titanium and stainless steel – aluminium was only used in areas far removed from the predicted airframe 'hot-spots'.

Because of problems with the new rocket engine, the first flights by Scott Crossfield and by the Air Force/NASA team of pilots assigned to the project, were made with two of the old XLR-1 engines installed as a temporary measure. Even with this grossly underpowered 'lash-up', the craft had, by late 1960, been flown to 2196 mph by Joe Walker and to 136,500 feet by Bob White. Moreover, these flights were made on just over a quarter of the power that would be available from the XLR-99 engine when it finally arrived. With the new engine, the X-15 would have a thrust to weight ratio of almost exactly two to one at launch: at the instant of burn-out, the ratio would be a staggering four to one. Oddly enough, the XLR-99 engine had just been fitted to the X-15 and completed successful ground runs, at the time that I finished my check-out as one of the B-52 launch pilots. In a sense, the new engine and I started work on the project together.

CHAPTER 34

AT FIVE FORTY FIVE in the morning, the Mojave Desert is dark and sharply cold. As I pulled into the driveway of Jack Allavie's house, I was glad of the quilted USAF flight jacket I was wearing over my flying overalls. The car engine hadn't had time to warm up enough to make the heater effective. As Jack appeared and got into the right hand seat, he too was wearing his heavy flight jacket, making his solid frame seem even bulkier than usual. As we headed down the long straight road past Base Headquarters towards the distant flight line, we didn't have a lot to say to each other. Nobody feels much like chatting in the very early hours of the morning. We drew up the collars of our flight jackets and tried to coax some heat into the body of the car.

We were scheduled to fly an X-15 drop mission – one we had been trying, without success, to get off for a couple of weeks. Bob White was due to take the research aircraft on an altitude run, aiming to fly out to something like fifty-three miles above the earth. If all went well, this would be the first time a piloted aircraft would fly into space and back again – 'space' having been somewhat arbitrarily defined by NASA as fifty miles altitude. During eight previous attempts to complete this particular flight, we had been dogged by a series of maddening minor malfunctions, which had resulted in the launch having to be aborted – on the last sortie, we had got to within a few seconds of the launch point before a last-minute component failure had forced yet another cancellation.

With this flight being something of a milestone in the programme, everyone was becoming just a little edgy about the run of forced aborts. I couldn't help feeling sympathy for Bob White who, time and again, had geared himself up for the launch, only to have to call it off and drag back to Edwards, still locked under the wing of the B-52. During his re-entry manoeuvre, Bob was going to have to fly the X-15 at an angle of attack of about twenty-six degrees to keep within the structural and heating limitations of the aircraft; at just over twenty-seven degrees, the controllability of the aircraft was judged 'questionable'. That didn't leave him much of a margin to play with, in a completely new and previously unexplored, regime of flight. Oddly enough, Bob appeared to be the calmest of all concerned – he simply took each abort as a fact of life and got on with planning the next attempt. In his place, I think that I would have been a bundle of nerves but, if he was feeling any strain, it certainly wasn't evident to anybody else.

As we neared the flight line, most of the buildings were still closed and dark, but Jack and I could make out the familiar splashes of lights that marked the areas of early morning activity on a 'launch' day. The cargo/helicopter and fighter hangers were well lit up, as the ground crews worked to prepare the transport aircraft, helicopters and fighter 'chase' planes that would fly the various support missions. At the far end of Flight Test Operations, the bomber section lights were already on – some thoughtful soul getting the coffee pot on!

Along Contractors Row, only the windows of the North American facility were showing any lights – their specialist support team worked 'round-the-clock' prior to every launch.

At the far end of the ramp, there was an absolute blaze of arc-lights around the 'mating area', where the X-15 had already been loaded on to its mounting below the wing of the B-52. This area was the focal point of all of the pre-launch activity, as the final systems checks were carried out on both aircraft, last-minute snags rectified and a veritable army of technicians and specialists assured themselves that every piece of equipment that could be checked on the ground had been meticulously checked. And then re-checked! And then re-checked again! This area always reminded me of the pit-stop area before a major motor race. One got the impression of chaotic and frenzied activity but, in fact, every single operation by each of the individuals involved was planned down to the last detail and slot-ted into its proper place in the three-day preparation sequence.

As Jack and I parked the car and stamped, still stiff and cold, into Flight Test, we found Doug Benefield and John Campbell just about ready to leave. They were due to fly the C-130 support aircraft that would take the fire tender and medical and emergency personnel, up to Delamar Lake – the dry lake nearest to the launch point – which would serve as an emergency landing ground for the X-15 in the event of any malfunction in the launch area. They would stay on the ground at Delamar, listening out on their radio, until the B-52 got airborne from Edwards. Then they would get airborne again with a team of paramedics whose job it would be to parachute directly to the aid of the X-15 pilot in the event of a crash landing, or bale-out, away from one of the nominated emergency lake landing sites.

Across the hall, two of the helicopter section pilots were also on their way out – one to Delamar and one to Hidden Hills Lake, almost half-way between Delamar and Edwards. They were trained to get rescue personnel to the scene of an emer-gency in double-quick time and also to use the rotor downwash to blow any smoke or flames away from the emergency crews operating in a crash situation. The third helicopter – to cover the take-off and landing at Edwards – wouldn't be required until later, when the B-52 taxied out. The lucky pilot who had drawn the Edwards slot could plan to arrive on the scene at a rather more gentlemanly hour than the 'early birds', who had to be in position at their distant locations by the time the B-52 was ready to take-off.

While Jack got on with the weather briefing and flight authorisation, I made us both a mug of coffee and phoned down to the mating area to confirm that the pre-launch sequence was running to time. While we drank our coffee, Jack re-viewed – as he did for every launch flight we made together in the B-52 – the normal and emergency procedures we would use during the forthcoming flight. We had been over these same procedures countless times before, but Jack Allavie, under a boisterous, extrovert exterior, was a professional test pilot to his finger-tips. Nothing – absolutely nothing – was left to chance on any X-15 launch he flew. Accordingly and even though we both knew the procedures by heart, we worked our way through each phase of the flight and each possible emergency situation, reviewing the normal, back-up and emergency techniques that we might have to use. On this particular flight, Jack would be in the left-hand seat and would fly the take-off and climb to altitude. He would then turn the aircraft over to me to fly the actual launch, so that he could give his undivided attention to monitoring the vital launch indicator panel and the manual back-up launch system, which would be used in the event that the three electrically operated shackles which held the X-15 in place failed to function normally.

As we picked up our parachutes and flight gear and headed off down the ramp towards the mating area, we crossed with Jim MacDivitt and Jack McKay arriving at the Fighter Section to prepare for their 'chase' missions. They would stay with the X-15 from take-off until launch, to monitor the control and system checks in the air and to provide visual back-up during the pre-launch engine prime and start sequences. Each would have a photographer in the back seat of their aircraft to record every stage of the operation. Later, when the X-15 had re-entered the atmosphere and descended to something like 50,000 feet in the Edwards area, it would be picked up by another two chase planes, piloted by Bill Dana and Milt Thompson of NASA and shepherded back for its landing on the north lake bed.

At the mating area, the whole scene was dominated by the enormous 200-plus ton bulk of the B-52, its huge vertical tail towering forty feet in the air. Under the right wing, amid an apparent jumble of access ladders, hoses and electrical connections, hung the squat, black, dart-like shape of the X-15, cocooned in clouds of vapour from its various fuel and chemicals vent pipes and with its fuselage already coated in a thick covering of frost in the vicinity of the liquid oxygen tank. The liquid oxygen, or LOX, was cooled to something like minus 300 degrees Fahrenheit and 'boiled off' continuously right up to the instant of launch. To keep the tank fully topped up, it would be replenished continuously from a huge supply tank in the bomb-bay of the B-52. The characteristic pungent stink of ammonia hung heavily in the air and Jack and I were provided with small breathing masks to wear during our pre-flight inspection of the mother-ship. Without them, you could really clear your head in a hurry by taking in a few sniffs of the ammonia vapour.

There was always a degree of tension in and around the mating area. Liquid oxygen and anhydrous ammonia are extremely sensitive and volatile propellants. Brought together, they ignite spontaneously with explosive effect. Everyone in the mating area was warily conscious that the X-15 was loaded with nine tons of the stuff, the B-52 carried the replenishment tanks and there were plenty of re-supply vehicles within the area – all the ingredients for a major disaster if the propellants were brought into contact prematurely. At this stage in the proceedings, the X-15 was literally a very large – and very powerful – bomb. Little wonder that everyone involved was doubly and triply careful and that the faces, under the harsh arc-lights, looked drawn and strained.

When Jack and I had finished our external inspection of the B-52, the sun was already up over the rim of the desert and it was becoming comfortably warmer. After a check of the documentation, Jack signed for the aircraft and we donned our parachutes and made our way into the aircraft and up to the flight deck. Once settled in, we worked our way steadily through the aircraft checklist up to the engine start checks. At the same time, Stan Butchart, the rear crew X-15 panel operator, ran through his checks on the B-52/X-15 umbilical system, which would provide the X-15 with propellant top-up, radio links and oxygen supply up to the moment of launch.

During the check sequence, we saw Bob White emerge from the physiological caravan in which he had been 'suiting-up' and make has way, awkward in his full pressure suit and helmet, across the ramp to the access ladder to the X-15 cockpit. When he was settled in and connected up to the umbilical oxygen and radio links, we were able to say "Good Morning," and listen in as he went through his own set of checks – monitored by the launch controller in his van at the edge of the mating area.

Eventually, with all checks completed on both aircraft, Jack obtained clearance to start the engines on the B-52. As, one by one, the eight engines thundered into life, the mass of equipment, vehicles and personnel withdrew rapidly from the mating area until, with the last starter trolley wheeled away, we were on our own and almost ready to move out. A number of vehicles containing emergency and control personnel, hoisted orange and white chequered flags on small poles attached to their rear bumpers and formed themselves into a loose line, prepared to follow us out to the runway. This was the 'caravan' that attended every X-15 launch. If anything were to go wrong up to the take-off point, these essential personnel wanted to be as close as possible to the event, so that they could render assistance with the absolute minimum of delay.

After about another half an hour of post-start checks, further checks of the umbilical system and X-15 system checks, we were ready to taxi out.

"Eddy Tower, this is zero-zero-three. Taxi."

"Roger, zero-zero-three. Cleared taxi to runway four. Winds are light and variable, less than five knots. Surface temperature is sixty three degrees and rising. Altimeter is three-zero-zero-six."

Jack and I leaned forward to set our altimeter sub-scales to the airfield pressure setting, before Jack keyed his microphone again to Bob White, "Ready to roll, buddy?" When Bob came back quietly with his standard, "ready when you are," Jack released the parking brake and slowly brought up the throttles to get us moving. As soon as the aircraft began to inch its way forward, he throttled back for a gentle check of the wheel brakes, before bringing the power up again to roll us out onto the main taxiway. Settled down on the long stretch of taxiway leading out to the end of the main runway, we could see the starters and ladders being pulled away from a two-seat F-104 and a T-38 on the ramp in front of the Fighter Section – Jim MacDivitt and Jack McKay ready to follow us out to the take-off point. To our left, we could see assorted fire tenders and crash rescue vehicles in position off the sides of the main runway and the Base rescue helicopter, already airborne, hovering lazily in a position half-way down and to the side of, the runway.

As we proceeded slowly down the taxiway, Jack keyed his microphone again, "Say, Bob, the temperature's up a bit. It's going to be a long run to unstick today." Right on cue, Bob came right back with the good-humoured needle that always exists between fighter and bomber pilots. "Sure you and Harry can manage, Jack? I'll be happy to crawl over and give you a hand, if you have any little problems." Kicking himself for giving the opening, Jack snapped back, "Dammit, Bob, you know we never let beginners into this thing. You just stick to your toy airplanes and leave the real flying to the pros."

I knew what was in Jacks mind. In his usual relaxed manner, he was alerting Bob to the fact that the ground air temperature was high enough to lengthen our take-off roll quite considerably. Because the X-15 was hung under the wing of the B-52, the mother-ship inboard flaps had been cut away on the starboard side to accommodate the X-15 tail. Accordingly, it had been necessary to de-activate the inboard flap sections on both sides of the aircraft. As a safety measure, both outboard flap sections had been de-activated as well. Consequently, the B-52 took-off and landed without any flap at all. This meant an unstick speed and touchdown speed anything up to forty knots faster than on a standard B-52 – and a much longer run to unstick. Moreover, the hotter the day, the longer the run. The Edwards runway was about 15,000 feet long – a good three miles – and we would be using most of it in getting up to our unstick speed.

As we approached the end of the taxiway, Edwards Tower cleared us directly on to the active runway and Jack swung the huge bomber gently around to point straight down the centreline. All around us were the black tyre marks of a thousand previous landings and the far end of the runway shimmered in the fast rising heat. Jack applied the parking brake and spoke on the intercom system, "All OK in here?" Glancing around to confirm that everyone was giving him a thumbs-up, he called Bob White again with a last minute check. "You all set, Bob?" When Bob came back, "Ready when you are," Jack keyed his microphone again, "Eddy Tower, zero-zero-three. Ready to roll." As the Tower came back with take-off clearance, Jack took a firm grip of the throttles with his right hand and slowly eased all eight forward. With the whine of the engines rising higher and higher, I backed him up on the throttles with my left hand. The aircraft nosed gently down as the power increased, until Jack leaned forward to release the parking brake. Shuddering slightly, the great aircraft lurched forward as Jack brought the throttles fully open and switched in the water-methanol power boost. Slowly at first, then with rapidly increasing speed, we started off down the runway.

As we picked up speed, I called out the passage of the runway markers, "Five thousand feet... seven thousand... nine thousand." At ten thousand feet, we stormed past the gaggle of control vehicles off to the right of the runway, deafening the occupants with the thunder of our passage. Eleven thousand feet and, with one eye on the airspeed indicator, I called, "unstick now." Immediately, Jack pulled back firmly on the control column and we felt the forward landing gear leave the runway as the nose rose steeply into the climbing attitude. Seconds later, we felt the rear landing gear unstick and we were airborne, the ground falling away rapidly below us, as the eight engines of the B-52 bore us effortlessly aloft towards the cloudless blue above.

As we cleaned the aircraft up, retracting the wheels, switching off the water-methanol and settling down at normal climbing power, the tension in the cockpit was still high. From our standpoint, this was the most dangerous phase of the entire flight. Until we passed 26,000 feet, the X-15 couldn't be released to make a piloted recovery in the event of any emergency. It was designed to be landed empty of all fuel and the pilot needed a minimum of 26,000 feet to jettison his propellants. On two occasions earlier in the programme, pilots had tried to save the aircraft by landing with residual propellants in the tanks and, both times, the landing gear had collapsed – not a pleasant prospect at a touchdown speed of over two hundred miles an hour. Above 26,000 feet, Jack could jettison the X-15 immediately in the event of an emergency and leave Bob to either bale-out or attempt to land as he saw fit. Below 26,000 feet, none of the mother-ship pilots would have jettisoned the X-15 until the pilot had ejected. Until he did, there were only about thirty feet of air and some few hundredths of an inch of aluminium, separating us in the B-52 from a nine-ton bomb. Even a relatively minor explosion would have blown the starboard wing clear off the B-52.

As we passed through 26,000 feet in the climb, there was a perceptible relaxing of tension in the cockpit of the B-52 and we settled down to the familiar routine of the slow climb up to 45,000 feet. We were heading out almost due North-East and could already pick out the outline of Hidden Hills dry lake just off the nose and far below to the left. Further off to the left stretched the sterile expanse of Death Valley and, rapidly coming into view just off to the right, the glittering sprawl of Las Vegas and the blue waters of Lake Mead beyond.

As we levelled out at 45,000 feet, I tuned our navigation direction-finding indicator to the VOR/TACAN facility at Mormon Mesa, which lay directly ahead on our track. By checking our radial bearing from the facility, I was able to confirm that we were holding a good outbound track. This was important on all X-15 launches, because the actual drop was made almost as soon as the turn back towards Edwards had been completed. Since so many of the X-15 flights were made on a ballistic trajectory, it was crucial to make the launch as close as possible to the planned launch point – and on the right heading. Otherwise, on re-entry, the X-15 pilot could find himself considerably displaced from his planned recovery position – and with not a lot of scope for recovering the situation in his high-speed glider. Today, with Bob planned to go ballistic almost immediately after the drop, it would be doubly important to get him off to an accurate start.

Throughout the outbound leg, the radio was alive almost continuously with the long litany of the X-15 pre-launch checklist. As Bob worked his way steadily through the list strapped to his knee, he reported on the temperatures and pressures showing on his system indicators, on the operation of his various controls, on the operation of his telemetry equipment and on the engine status during the warm-up and prime operations. Every item on the long list was confirmed either by Launch Control back at Edwards, by the telemetry range station at Beatty, or by the chase planes, which had been flying close formation since take-off. The function of the chase plane pilots was particularly crucial to the operation, in that they were all intimately familiar with the X-15 and its systems and, most importantly, they were actually on the spot – a matter of a few feet away from the aircraft and observing every operation as it happened. This was one of the lessons that the Americans learned the hard way during their research programmes – you can have all of the telemetry and radio links in the world, but there is just no substitute for a pair of expert eyes watching what is going on as it happens.

On the left hand side of the B-52 cockpit was a small panel with five green bulbs on it – the launch panel. Three of the bulbs indicated the status of the three bomb shackles that held the X-15 in place under the mother-ships wing. The fourth bulb was the 'ready-to-launch' indicator, actuated by the X-15 pilot when he was ready to be dropped. The fifth bulb was the 'launch' light, which came on when the 'drop' switch was actuated. In the early days of the programme, the X-15 was actually dropped by the pilot of the B-52 – the same procedure as had been used in all of the previous air-launch programmes. Experience had indicated that this wasn't the best – or safest – technique. Bill Bridgeman was launched once in the Douglas Skyrocket with an on-board fire in the rocket engine, because he couldn't break-in on the mother-ship pilots' countdown. Today, Bob White would actually initiate the drop himself on Jacks countdown – if he wasn't happy about the launch, he simply wouldn't press the button.

Just beside the launch panel were two back-up launch switches. One was a duplicate electrical switch to enable Jack to make the drop in the event that Bob's cockpit switch failed to operate. The other was a hydraulic actuator to operate the release shackles mechanically, in the event that the electrical release system became totally inoperative. Because the positioning of the aircraft at launch was so critical, the left-hand seat pilot of the B-52 concentrated exclusively on the launch panel and the back-up switches during the final stages of the launch sequence, so that he could react instantly to any malfunction in the release mechanisms.

As the VORTAC indicator needle swung drunkenly around the dial to mark our passage directly over the Mormon Mesa station, Jack waved me to take control of the aircraft for the ten minutes or so up to the launch point. I held the control column gently as the VORTAC needle steadied down to point directly behind us on 217 degrees – putting us dead on our track of 037 degrees outbound. I caressed the throttles gently to hold our Mach number on 0.8 and fiddled with the trimmers. All pilots do this when they take over control of an aircraft. From long experience, I knew that Jack would never hand over control with the aircraft even slightly off speed or out of trim, but it was a way of getting the feel of the machine as quickly as possible. After my first few seconds of fiddling with the controls, I knew that the aircraft would be exactly as it was when Jack handed over.

As we continued the run outbound, Jack picked up the countdown at the 12-minute mark. Bob immediately responded with his 12-minute checks, confirmed either by the panel operator, or by one of the chase pilots. At the 11-minute mark, he initiated engine pre-cool and confirmed his inertial velocity and attitude gauge indications. At 10 minutes, I called a check on the B-52 magnetic heading and eased the control column gently to the left to start us into a slow, wide, ten-degree bank turn As the left wing started to dip, I eased the throttles forward to hold our speed steady on Mach 0.8. At 6 minutes to go, Jack called "Six minute mark, Bob. Please confirm all remaining time checks ." Calmly, Bob responded, "Roger, six minutes, auxiliary cabin pressure ON." At 5 minutes, the propellant top-off was completed and the X-15 disconnected from all B-52 umbilical systems except the radio link. As the last few time checks were called and the appropriate checks actioned, I eased off the left bank and steadied the B-52 down on the launch heading of 222 degrees. I left the throttles where they were and eased in a little nose-down trim to let the speed build up to launch speed of Mach 0.82. From now on, my only concern was to hold height, speed and heading absolutely rock steady up to the instant of release.

At one minute to go, Jack selected the Launch Master Switch ON and Bob initiated his engine prime sequence – immediately confirmed by Chase 1. In these last seconds before launch, the thoughts of every single person involved in the project go out to the man in the cockpit of the X-15. This is the time when he is truly and absolutely alone. Part of his mind attends methodically to the last few items on the check-list, but he must already be gearing himself up for the sudden, lurching drop into the emptiness below him and the awesome, raging burst to heights and speeds which no one has ever experienced before.

Jack's level monotone continued steadily. "Ten...Nine...Eight... Seven... Six... Five..." – the green "ready-to-launch" light winked from the panel – "Four... Three... Two... One... LAUNCH."

As the X-15 dropped away, the B-52 tried to nose-up sharply and roll off quickly to the left. The second that I felt the drop, I was already moving the control column forward and to the right and easing the trimmers to get us back into balanced flight. The actions were routine, almost automatic from dozens of other launch flights. Jack and I were both straining forward to pick up our first sight of the X-15, by now well below us, but with its engine already lit-up and coming up to full power. In a matter of seconds, we could make it out, rising dead ahead of us, climbing on a trail of fire from the rocket exhaust. The angle of climb was staggering – we knew that Bob was programmed to go up at an attitude of more than forty degrees but, from the cockpit of the B-52, he looked to be going almost straight up. In seconds, the aircraft itself was out of sight, but we could still follow the trail of flame and vapour up to the instant of burn-out – which seemed to take place almost directly above us.

On the radio, we could follow Bob's progress. Just seconds after he settled into his climb, we heard his awed, "Jesus, this is really going up," then later, "I can see all the way from North of San Francisco to well into Mexico." Then the calls faded. We were too far away to pick up his re-entry and landing back at Edwards, where he touched down successfully almost exactly ten minutes after leaving the shackles on the B-52. We still had something over an hour to go to get home!

When we eventually got back to Edwards, we could make out the X-15 on the North lake bed, surrounded by an army of servicing personnel already preparing to start getting it ready for the next flight in the programme. A week from now, it would be another flight, another performance target, another launch.

We acknowledged Edwards Tower's notification of the post-flight debriefing time, as Jack took over control of the B-52 again for his 'successful launch' party piece. Bringing the giant bomber low in over the lake bed at better than three hundred knots, he hauled it up directly over the X-15 in a very fair 'fighter' break. From that point, as he throttled back to idle in a steep climbing turn to a thousand feet, I knew that he wouldn't touch the throttles again until he was turning off the runway. That's quite a trick – not for beginners even in a light and responsive fighter; with about a hundred and fifty tons of massive bomber strapped on to you, it takes real flying skill to pull it off. I had a fair bit of experience on the aircraft, but I wouldn't have tried it – I always reckoned that I was good; but I never felt that I was quite THAT good!

At the debriefing, as Bob sipped his dry martini – the Physiological Sections prize for every successful launch – the initial data came in 'hot-off-the press' from the telemetry stations. Bob's maximum speed during the flight was confirmed at 3,784 mph and his peak altitude at just under 315,000 feet – less than half a mile short of sixty miles STRAIGHT UP! He had become the first man in history to 'fly' an aircraft into space and back again – the first winged astronaut and only the fifth American to qualify for astronauts 'wings'. The previous four had all earned their wings in the Mercury programme.

I am still proud of my small part in the X-15 programme. Very few pilots indeed get the chance to work on a programme that is so far ahead of its time and which is continually breaking new ground in so many aspects of aerospace research. In all, I suppose I flew something like twenty successful launch missions and I flew every type of support mission associated with the programme. If I never did anything else in the flying business, I could reasonably claim to have earned my pay with the X-15 project. Moreover, I must make the point that I have always been grateful to the United States Air Force for permitting me to participate. I was at Edwards at the right time and, foreigner or not, they treated me exactly as they would have treated any American pilot filling my 'slot' in Bomber Test

In the interests of completeness, I should add that I did formally request Colonel Anderson to let me fly the X-15 itself. He just about fell about the place laughing. "Sure thing, Harry," he responded, "right after me and about a couple of hundred others who'd all give their eye teeth for a crack at it. Tell you what I'll do," he went on, "you can go break a couple of records in the simulator. That's about as close as either of us is going to get to the real thing." Anyway, I tried. And I did go to the simulator. And I did fly to unimaginable heights and speeds – safely on the ground! If the experience did nothing else, it confirmed my admiration and respect for the pilots who were flying the real thing – they really earned their flying pay the hard way.

Shortly after Bob White's flight, it was announced that the X-15 team had been awarded the NASA Outstanding Achievement Award and the Pilot Team had been awarded the Collier Trophy for Achievement in Astronautics. We all flew through to Washington for the various presentations, which marked a sort of 'grand slam' for Bob White. He was promoted, awarded the Distinguished Service Cross and awarded his Astronauts wings – pinned on by President Kennedy at a ceremony at the White House. Following this latter ceremony, President Kennedy slyly insisted on pointing out to me some damage to the fabric of the building, which, so he told me absolutely straight-faced, was a relic from "the last time the Brits were here in force." Fortunately, he didn't ask me to pay up for the repairs.

One small incident sticks in my mind from that visit to Washington. In the middle of all of the ballyhoo and publicity, a few of us sneaked into a restaurant bar on our own for a quiet drink. While we were there, we were engaged in conversation by a middle-aged gentleman and his wife who were on vacation in Washington from their home somewhere in the Middle West. The gentleman seemed to know all about the X-15 – the papers had been pretty well full of it – and he asked Bob White and Joe Walker if they were the ones who had been doing all of this exotic sort of flying. When Bob modestly responded that we were all test pilots from Edwards, the gentleman seemed little impressed. After asking one or two questions – clearly, more out of politeness than anything else – he leaned forward confidentially and put what was obviously the question uppermost in his mind. "But have any of you ever looped the loop?" I could see all of my companions struggling hard to keep a straight face, as Bob replied quietly that, "Yes, I think that we've all done the occasional loop or two." Satisfied, our friend leaned back, quite content now that we were the genuine article – real 'hot' pilots who had actually looped the loop. That's your real conservative Middle America for you. You can fly faster than a speeding bullet, or out into space but to qualify as a regular 'hotshot' you have to be able to claim that you've actually looped the loop. If it did nothing else, that encounter certainly left us all with an enhanced sense of perspective.

CHAPTER 35

WHEN YOU GO TO LIVE in another country, many of the ways of doing things are so different and the experiences are so novel, that you tend to remember the first year or two, not so much as an orderly sequence of events, but rather as a set of random and highly coloured, 'snapshot' impressions. Certainly, that was my experience of the early time we spent in the United States, when so much of our day-to day life seemed to be so very different from what we had been used to in the UK. Even today, it is the association of events with particular individuals, or with places, which calls them to mind most vividly and most readily.

Pasadena, for example, always recalls for me the New Year's Day collegiate football game at the Rose Bowl, to which we are taken by Charlie Kuyk and his wife. The pre-game spectacle is dazzling – hours of show-biz razzmatazz. Through the streets of the city, flower-bedecked floats bearing a succession of local 'Queens'; marching bands; mounted parades of local celebrities, politicians and movie stars, most of them picturesquely attired in western or Spanish costumes; coffee and 'hot-dog' vendors; and a crowd of spectators so large that it seemed as if all of California has come to take part. Then the game itself, in a stadium so well appointed, clean and comfortable as to make the average UK football ground seem like something out of Dickens. On the field, an encounter that gives the initial impression of being just slightly short of all-out war – bone-crunching clashes, spectacular running and bullet-like passing of the ball, all to the accompaniment of frenzied cavorting by troupes of pretty 'cheer leaders' and uninhibited 'short-burst' renditions by the marching bands of the two universities involved. During the half-time 'entertainment', I form the impression that one of the colourfully costumed bands has about as much manpower available as the British Army.

Las Vegas – a four hour drive through some of the most inhospitable, sun-scorched wilderness on earth – skirting around the southern edge of Death Valley – and then the city, literally, right out in the middle of nowhere. Like coming across Monte Carlo in the middle of the Sahara. Garish, noisy, seemingly going full blast twenty-four hours a day. No clocks to be seen anywhere – by order of the City Council. Relatively inexpensive hotels, food, drink and entertainment – enjoy a Dean Martin performance in one of the bar lounges for only the price of a drink. Slot machines everywhere – even on the inside doors of the toilet cubicles. In the Desert Inn, a continuous dull, throbbing, roaring noise. At first, I thought it was an artificial waterfall. It turns out to be the sound of hundreds – if not thousands – of slot machines operating non-stop around the clock. Western breakfasts – steak, eggs, ham, sausages, waffles, hash browns, toast, coffee ~ all you can eat for a dollar. Four or five golf courses – greener and lusher than seems believable in such a location. The Casino security guards – all very large, hard-eyed citizens, with a massive Colt revolver worn casually on the hip and the general appearance of being perfectly willing to unholster their cannon and start blasting away, given the slightest of provocation. Disneyland for adults and unique – no other place like it on earth.

Carmel, just south of San Francisco – an absolute haven to go to for weekends away from the blazing desert. Cool, misty mornings – for which the locals apologised incessantly. We love it. Delightful golf courses at Pebble Beach and Cypress Point. The drive back South along the Coastal Highway past Big Sur – some of the most beautiful scenery in all of California.

Barbecue parties in the cool desert evenings on someone's patio. I particularly like John and Bette Campbell's barbecues – he used to bring back fresh water bass from his hunting trips up into the Sierras. With a freshly tossed salad and some French bread, they make a prime meal. When they come off the fire, you can tap them smartly with the flat of a knife and the flesh just falls away from the bone. Absolutely delicious! To enjoy them fully, you have to be prudent with John's pre-dinner drinks. He mixes martinis that would crack concrete.

The Stars and Stripes – and the beginnings of an understanding of how strongly the Americans feel about their national flag. Driving home one early evening with Jack Allavie, an abrupt order to stop the car. The flag outside Base Headquarters has become detached from the bottom halyard and is flapping furiously in the very strong wind. Jack calls out the Air Police, who look up the sixty-odd foot flagpole whipping in the wind and decide that they will get it fixed tomorrow. Home with Jack for an after-work martini or two, to be joined by John Campbell bearing a large bottle of Jack Daniels. Sitting chatting amiably and watching Jack get darker and more brooding, by the minute. Suddenly, he boils over. "If those sons of b.....s won't fix the flag, we'll do it ourselves." Back to Base Headquarters. It is now pitch dark and the wind is really howling. I'm British and therefore neutral; Jack is about fourteen stone and not built for climbing flagpoles; that leaves John Campbell – by now, just about light-headed enough to try anything for a bit of peace and quiet. Up he goes – to about thirty feet, by which time the wind, the cold and the whipping of the pole sobers him up right rapidly. He hangs on for grim death – he won't go up and he can't seem to come down. Jack is leaping about in a fury. "Get up there, Goddammit and fix the flag." Eventually, we have to call the Air Police, who call the engineers, who get a 'cherry-picker' out of a hanger to pick John off the flagpole. While they're about it, they fix the flag. We pour some more Jack Daniels into John to revive him and then we all go home satisfied. At Edwards, at least, when the flag flies, the flag flies right.

Christmas 1961 and I buy Jean a set of golf clubs – the best seventy dollar investment I ever made. She becomes about as addicted to the game as I am. Since that time, she has NEVER – and I do mean NEVER – complained about the time I spend on the course, because she now understands for herself the magnetism of the game. Moral to all golfers: never let your wife become a golfing widow. Buy her a set of her own and turn her into a golfing wife.

American TV advertising – generally pretty dreadful, with car salesmen going berserk trying to put over the sale of the century. One advertisement I remember with pleasure depicted a sporting locker room where a young player is applying a thick hairdressing. Enter a well-known 'name' sportsman with, "You're not still using that greasy kids' stuff? You should use Vitalis." Cut to the two of them being met by two gorgeous wives/girlfriends, both drooling over the now manly, nongreasy kids' stuff, hair-dos. Capitalising on the use of many famous sportsmen in this advertisement, an enterprising company quickly produced its own hairdressing called, believe it or not, 'Greasy Kids Stuff'. It sold like hot cakes. Say what you like, the Americans do have a sense of humour.

Blissful, men-only, weekends every couple of months in San Diego. Fly down to Lindbergh Field in a T-29 with Steve Cameron, Hugh Dingus and Ed Clark. Pick up the car left by Steve's brother and drive out to the Torrey Pines Motel. Then, forty-eight hours of golf at Torrey Pines, poker in the motel and meals out along the San Diego waterfront, finishing up at Mickey Finns, which sold more beer, so I was told, than any other establishment West of the Mississippi River. It had a fire engine on the roof and the best jazz band I've ever heard. I still have my membership card, although I believe that the club is now no more.

Hawaii – so beautiful that even the travel agents can't overstate its attraction. Weekends at Fort DeRussy – owned by the US Army and located right slap-bang in the middle of Waikiki Beach. Five dollars a night to stay on a piece of real estate that must be worth millions a square foot. No wonder all the major hotel chains would love to get the Army out and themselves in. Dinners at the Cannon Club, the Officers Club almost at the top of Diamond Head: at eight in the evening, they pull back the curtains in the dining room and you are looking out over the most breathtaking view of Honolulu and Waikiki Beach. Eat your heart out, Mr Hilton!

Jack Allavie in the B-52 on an X-15 launch when we have to abort and come home with the X-15 still under the wing. The left rear set of wheels won't come down, so Jack takes off his parachute and squeezes through a tiny access hatch on to the bomb-bay catwalk. He edges along to the rear wheel assembly and prods the offending micro-switch with a navigation ruler. Hanging on to a strut with one hand and with nothing but fresh air between him and the desert, he prods away until the wheels unlock and swing down. Then he crawls back to the cockpit. He doesn't even mention it at debriefing – just tells the ground crew quietly to check the micro-switch before the next flight.

The South – slow, courteous, relaxed. Time to get to know people, to sit and talk to them. The invariable invitation to, "make yourself to home and set a spell." Hominy grits with your breakfast – tried once and then abandoned as an acquired taste. Warm, sultry, nights and sweaty hot days. Trying to putt on a golf course at Macon, Georgia, with the perspiration running down my nose and on to the ball in a steady, distracting, drip. A revival meeting in Atlanta – thousands of people caught up in a fever of religious awareness. Bands, gospel singers, yells of "Hallelujah," "I see the light," and "Praise the Lawd." Unbelievable! The obvious pleasure of the coloured caddies when Hugh Dingus takes me to his home course. They are genuinely pleased to see him – and him a true Southerner. Visiting the sad battlefields of the War Between the States – the tangible evocation of a world and a way of life, literally 'Gone with the Wind'. The sense of awful waste.

Movie stars visiting Edwards. Danny Kaye – up to put on a Base Christmas show – singing, dancing, clowning, in Flight Test Operations. Jimmy Stewart, Brigadier General USAF Reserve – more handsome than seemed real – tall, tanned, with piercing blue eyes and a very quiet personality. A modest and delightful man. He was happy to learn that his bar was still going strong at Bassingbourn. Betty Grable and Harry James at a craps table at Las Vegas where my friend Chuck Ludwig wins me about six hundred dollars and himself walks away with wads of bills stuffed into every pocket about his person. Gloria Swanson at a party at Robbs in Los Angeles – impossible to believe her age. Beautiful, vivacious and charming.

Jack Elam, screen actors golf champion, in a fourball at Riviera. Nobody remembers his name, but everyone has seen him. He made a career out of being the 'bad guy' in countless westerns. If you ever see someone callously shooting down the old rancher and his wife, or tearing the daughters blouse off, it's odds-on to be Jack Elam. A shy, gentle man and an excellent golfer.

Walt Daniels and a demonstration of authority. He arrives in Flight Test Operations one day to find the place jammed with every senior officer on the Base and the radio red hot. Bob Rushworth is airborne in an F-104 and has a serious control malfunction. He is getting advice on what to do from the world and his wife. Walt asks me "what in the H... is going on?" When I tell him, he pushes through the throng and picks up the microphone. "Bob, have you tried this?" "Yes." "Have you tried that?" "Yes." "OK, get yourself over to the bombing range and punch out." Bob Rushworth comes back by parachute and Walt goes back to his office. He's Chief of Fighters and he doesn't need any help in sorting out any emergency on any aircraft that he's responsible for.

Bob Hoover – an ex-Edwards test pilot now in charge of military liaison with North American. One of the all-time great aerobatic display pilots. At a Palmdale Open Day, flying his own P-51 Mustang, he starts his display with a flick roll straight from take-off – a manoeuvre bordering on the suicidal to most pilots. When he lands, a young USAF pilot congratulates him on his performance and adds, "But, of course, you can only pull that sort of stunt in something like a P-51." Without a word, Bob picks up his helmet and makes his way out to an F-100 standing on the ramp. Seconds later, as he gets airborne, afterburner blazing, he pulls the heavy fighter into an immaculate flick roll, comes round for a touch-and-go landing and, as he gets off again, repeats the performance. When he strolls back in from his final landing, there is no comment at all. All that could be said, he said in the air.

Flying with Bob White in an F-104 while he practises for his X-15 landings. With the engine throttled back, wheels and flaps down and air-brakes extended, the F-104 glides pretty much like the X-15. Also pretty much like a brick. We always have a bet on whether he can touchdown exactly opposite one of the lake bed runway marker indicators. If he makes it within ten yards, I am due him a martini. From 40,000 feet, he hits it time after time. I get sick of buying him martinis.

Flying with Chuck Yeager in a T-39 trying to get a set of speed/power points. I reckon that a good pilot can get one about every ten minutes if he's lucky. Charlie reels them off so easily that I'm hard pushed simply to record the data. Every time he says "now" the cockpit indicator needles clang into position and hold there as if they are riveted onto the dial. I feel like crying; he makes it look so easy.

Flying with Charlie Kuyk on the B-52H Operational Reliability Trial -twenty-six hour sorties twice a week with a standard five-man crew and no autopilot. Nearly two thousand hours of flying in just six months. Like most of the other B-52 pilots, I did a few of these back-breaker sorties. Charlie flew nearly all of them. And

at weekends, he flew all over the country picking up spare parts to keep the programme moving. He must have packed several years flying time into that six
months.

Tonopah, Nevada – near Mud Lake, one of the lakes over which we launch the
X-15. I have flown up in the C-130 support aircraft. When the launch is delayed,
we go into Tonopah, an old silver mining town that looks like the set of a Western
movie. Hitching rails all along Main Street; strings of donkeys being led by the
few remaining prospectors; a saloon with genuine swing doors and sawdust on
the floor. The airport manager is an old USAF fighter pilot: I fly him once or twice
in the C-130 and he lets me fly his own P-38. I win out on the deal – there are a lot
of C-130s in the world; very few P-38s.

Innumerable talks to various civic groups on the work of the Flight Test Center.
The USAF is very conscious of its responsibility to promote good public relations.
Following my talk to the Chamber of Commerce at Bakersfield, the Mayor asks
me what I do in my spare time. When I tell him that I golf, he says, "OK, Harry,
you are now an honorary member of Bakersfield Country Club." The course is
delightful and the Clubhouse about on a par with the Taj Mahal. God only knows
what it costs the members who actually pay the subscriptions but, every time I'm
in Bakersfield, I play free. When you come in off the course, you just drop off all
your golfing clothes in a heap in the locker-room. They are then dry cleaned on
the spot and ready for you to pick up by the time you've had a sandwich and a
beer.

Sergeant Gomez, crew chief on a T-39 programme I ran. He's Mexican and he
introduces me to little yellow peppers so hot that you can't bite them or else the
juice burns your lips. I get to like them as much as I like all other varieties of hot,
spicy Mexican dishes. Gomez likes his hot peppers with ice cream.

Disneyland – and a cable-car ride up to Heidi's Cottage on the top of a mountain. Carol Anne wants to see it and a cable-car is the only way to get there. I'm
terrified of heights, but I go up with her – with my eyes closed all the way. Coming
down, the wretched thing stops and we sit there, swinging helplessly, sixty feet
above the ground. Carol Anne holds my hand and tells me, "Don't worry, Daddy,
we'll be down soon." And I'm supposed to be the big, brave, test pilot.

Playing golf with Chuck Ludwig one Saturday in an Edwards medal competition. Coming up to the 18th hole, he has it in his pocket. His drive, right down the
middle of the 18th fairway, comes to rest about an inch behind a small Joshua tree
– also right in the middle of the 18th Fairway. Chuck goes white with rage and
takes six. He loses the competition by one shot. Next morning, the Joshua tree is
gone – neatly sawn off at ground level. The Club Committee get very upset about
vandalism on the course, but the culprit is never discovered.

Flying a C-130B back From Hawaii, when a seal on the cargo doors fails and we
lose pressurisation. At the lower altitude we have to fly to keep the passengers
breathing, we haven't enough fuel to reach the West Coast. Steve Cameron, the
flight engineer, could take a C-130 to pieces with a nail file. He cracks the cargo
doors a fraction and stuffs the space with paper towels. Then he gets the passengers to pee on the paper towels and re-locks the doors. When we go back to
altitude, the sodden paper towels freeze into a solid seal and the pressurisation

holds all the way back to Edwards. You won't find that one in any servicing manual.

The desert – cruel, hard, merciless. A small child wanders away from home one afternoon and becomes lost. We search all night without success. Next day, the child is found, frozen to death. Weeks later, the desert blooms – a 'once in a blue moon' phenomenon. As far as the eye can see, a carpet of flowers and plants of every imaginable colour, waving gently in the soft breeze. Like paradise.

Friday night in the Club and everyone discussing an appeal from USAF for volunteers for the US bobsled team for the next Olympics. Jack is giving the fighter pilots Hell for not volunteering. They say, "Jack, we're all tied up. Why don't you go in for it yourself?" Next day, he phones Russ Sleigh, another old Edwards man, now Director of Safety, 13th Air Force and the pair of them volunteer. Rosemary Allavie goes white when she finds out, but she knows Jack too well to waste time arguing. I fly the pair of them up to Lake Placid and watch them check out in a sled from the half-mile mark. The one ahead of them leaves the run at the first bend and slow rolls over the countryside before he is carried off to hospital. Jack and Russ both qualify and get their licence. They try to persuade me to have a go, but I tell them, in their own vernacular, "Mrs Archer didn't raise no idiot sons." Russ Sleigh had driven at Indianapolis and was a former speedboat racing champion of America, but even he admitted that the bobsled run was "hair-raising."

Over Mud Lake in a C-130 for an X-15 launch with Jack McKay flying. On launch, the X-15 engine won't light up. Jack tries one relight too many. By the time he gives up, he hasn't enough time left to jettison all of his propellants Inevitably – Murphy's Law – he gets another malfunction – the flaps don't extend fully. He touches down hot and heavy and one of the rear landing skids collapses. At about 230 mph, the aircraft turns onto its back as it screeches over the lake bed – the only bits touching the ground, the vertical tail, the wing tip and Jack's bonedome. The aeroplane goes into the hanger; Jack goes into hospital. Both return at about the same time – the aeroplane is as good as new, but Jack is about half an inch shorter, the result of compressed vertebrae. It doesn't seem to bother him.

Puerto Rico – and a couple of days with Doug Benefield hauling heavy fuel from Florida to Ramey for the U-2s. Then a week off before hauling the remaining fuel back to Florida. Doug's brother is tennis pro at the Caribe Hilton. When he finds out that I play golf, he fixes me up with a game with one of the assistant pros at Dorado Beach. The pro is small and wiry. He has the biggest wind-up I've ever seen and he hits the ball over the horizon. His length is unbelievable. His name is Rodriguez: his nickname 'Chi-Chi'. Later, he makes a fortune on the American 'tour'. On his day, he hits the ball past anybody.

Flying a C-130 back from Eglin in Florida with a cargo of snakes and a small alligator for the 'Farm' at Edwards, In the early hours of the morning, Steve Cameron comes up to report that the alligator is loose in the hold. I only relax when he assures me it can't get up the ladder to the flight deck. Down the back, a sleeping Harry Andonian wakes up to find himself 'eyeball~to-eyeball' with the alligator which is lying on his chest. It's only about four feet long, but it has jaws like a tractor shovel. Harry rockets up to the flight deck and refuses to go back 'downstairs' again. As always, Steve Cameron copes with it all. When we land, Harry and I refuse to leave the cockpit till Steve swears that he's got the alligator all wrapped up – and safely tied up – again. He carries it out of the aeroplane, muttering, "Pilots!" darkly, under his breath.

'Snapshot' impressions: random recollections. Odd incidents that spring to mind whenever I think of Edwards. People, places and events that haven't been forgotten. Sometimes I have to look through the photograph album to convince myself that it all really did happen – that it wasn't just some sort of Technicolor waking dream. I sometimes wonder to myself how I get to be so lucky as to be a part of it all.

CHAPTER 36

FOR A PROFESSIONAL PILOT, a tour of duty at Edwards Air Force Base was very much like being a greedy child turned loose in a sweet shop. The opportunities for flying a very wide variety of aircraft types existed right there on the Base and there were practically no restrictions to inhibit anyone who was keen to have a go at them. It was normal practice for the flying hours allocated to any particular programme to be very tightly controlled – test flying, after all, is a very expensive business. Nevertheless, in much the same way as at Boscombe Down, there was nearly always an opportunity to get to fly a new aircraft if one was prepared to take on some of the less attractive parts of the programme. Moreover, by doing so, one provided the project pilot with a 'breather' to do a bit of forward planning and gave him a chance to discuss the aircraft handling and performance with someone else who had, at least, flown the thing.

During the whole time I was at Edwards, I think that I missed out on flying only one of the aircraft that went through the Center – the F-105, which came back to the Base for a modification programme so short that I don't think that anyone other than the project pilot actually got it into the air. Since I got my hands on practically everything else – fighters, bombers, transports and helicopters – I really can't complain about the one that got away.

Quite apart from the opportunities that were available on the Base, there were many other chances to broaden ones flying experience through contacts at other Air Bases, in Industry, or in the other Services. Courtesy of Russ Sleigh, I flew a KC-97 refuelling sortie and got my first experience flying off water in a Grumman amphibian. Through North American, I got the P-51 Mustang. Through the United States Forestry Service, I got the B-17 Flying Fortress and the PBY-5A Catalina. Through the US Army, I got the B-25 Mitchell and also a much appreciated trip in a Ryan Monoplane – a sister ship to the one Lindbergh flew in his first solo flight across the Atlantic. Through the US Navy, I got the Buckeye and the F-4 Phantom. I still had a very long way to go to get anywhere near Fitz Fulton's total of types flown, but I was getting the chance to fly a lot of aircraft which had, in one way or another, become aviation 'classics' and which very few other pilots would ever get the chance to try their hand in.

One particular type I remember very clearly was the Piaggio 166 – a high wing, twin 'pusher' engined, light transport. My opportunity to fly this one came about in very bizarre circumstances, which, even today, seem to me to have been totally half-baked. It all began with the opening of Chavez Ravine as the new home of the Los Angeles Dodgers baseball team. North American wanted to have Jack Allavie, Walt Daniels and myself as their guests for the occasion and they hired the Piaggio and a pilot from a charter firm to transport us back and forth from Edwards to a small airport near Los Angeles. I must be honest and admit that I've never been much of a baseball fan – I think it's a game you have to grow up with. I never really understood either the rules or the tactics. This latter point was made abundantly clear to me during the game when one of the 'star' hitters on the team was 'walked' to first base by the pitcher throwing him balls that he couldn't even reach, much less hit. It was explained to me that this tactic was to remove the threat of this big hitter: the hitter who followed him was alleged to be so bad that he would have had difficulty hitting his grandmother with a shovel. Almost inevitably, this latter individual stepped on to the plate and proceeded to clout the first ball he received clear out of the stadium for a winning home run. So much for tactics!

After the game, the whole group of us – including, I should add, the charter pilot – repaired to Robbs for a fairly lively party. During the festivities, I recall, a reveller at an adjoining table got into a fit of laughing so violent that he fell off his chair. Everyone though that this was hilarious, until Jack Allavie realised that the poor man was actually having a choking fit and was just about on the point of departing from the scene permanently. Jack immediately hoisted him over the table and pounded him heartily until he recovered.

When the party finally ended, in the early hours of the morning, a company car took Jack, Walt and I – together with the charter pilot – back to the airfield for the trip back to Edwards. During this car ride, it became clear that the charter pilot had enjoyed the party even more than we had: not to put too fine a point on it, he was plain 'stoned' – slumped senseless in the back seat, snoring heavily and clearly in no condition to stand up unaided, much less fly. I suppose that what we should have done at that point was simply get the car driver to take the three of us back to Edwards. But no, we were all pilots and pilots don't drive when they can fly. If the damned charter pilot couldn't fly the thing, then one of us would do it for him. After all, it was just another aeroplane.

When we all piled out in front of the Piaggio, Walt Daniels immediately became difficult. The thing had two engines, which, he observed, clearly put it beyond the pale as far as any self-respecting fighter pilot was concerned. Announcing firmly that he didn't even like to live in the same street as people who flew aeroplanes with more than one engine, he crawled into the back of the machine and immediately fell fast asleep. That left it squarely up to Jack and me, as the multi-engine masterminds. We couldn't find anything remotely resembling a Flight Manual in the cockpit, but we did, at least, find a Battery Master Switch so that we could get some light into the cockpit to help us find our way around. When we felt that we had identified the more important looking knobs and levers, we gingerly cranked up one engine. When it didn't burst into flames on the spot, we were sufficiently encouraged to get the other one going, get the navigation lights and radio on and steel ourselves to try to get the thing into the air. All credit to Piaggio ~ they built a nice, easy to fly, aeroplane. We got it off without any bother and had a nice uneventful thirty minutes back to Edwards. On the way, Jack and I prudently tried out a few approaches to the stall with wheels and flaps down, so that we would have some idea of what speeds to use for approach and touchdown. Then we went ahead and landed it without any problems. We parked it outside Flight Test and left the charter pilot still sleeping soundly in the back when we went home. Next morning, it was gone. I often wondered how he explained away his overnight stop away from his home base. I put the Piaggio P166 in my logbook and felt that I was quite entitled to consider myself 'qualified on type'.

Towards the end of my tour at Edwards, I was running a performance programme on a heavily instrumented T-39 Sabreliner, when North American asked the Commanding General if they could borrow the aircraft for a certification programme to clear the civil version of the aircraft. I had only a few range runs to do to finish off my programme and I could get the data just as easily on a non-instrumented aircraft, so I agreed readily. North American then asked if I could be released to them to fly the civil certification programme, on the grounds that I was already thoroughly familiar with the test aircraft. They would put a company pilot in the right hand seat and he would sign all of the reports for the civil authorities. Accordingly, I spent a couple of weeks down in Los Angeles flying off the civil clearance programme, after which the test aircraft went back into the hanger for an overhaul.

About six weeks later, I got a call from North American to ask me whether I had flown off the last few range flights to wrap up my own programme on the T-39. When I said that I hadn't managed to find another aircraft yet, they told me that they had a couple of overseas delivery flights coming up and that, if I liked, I could pick up my range data on any one of them I cared to fly. One of the delivery flights was to Wiesbaden in Germany and the other to Fukuoka in Japan. Since I had been to Germany before, but never to Japan, I elected to go for the delivery flight to Fukuoka.

The flight out to Japan provided me with one of the best trips I have ever made – from both the flying and general interest, standpoints. Because of the weather, it took eight days to get to Fukuoka, but every day of that time was full of interest in one way or another.

On the first day out, I went from Los Angeles to Tacoma, Washington and then on to Anchorage in Alaska. My next scheduled stop was at Adak, in the Aleutian Islands, but I had to spend a few days at Anchorage because of gale force winds, blizzards and fog all along the Aleutian Chain.

One day, in the airport building, I ran across a small group of entertainers who, so I was told, had been performing at the Base. I didn't see the performance, but I noticed a few of them tinkering around a piano in the lounge while they were waiting for their flight back south to be called. One heavily built fellow was humming a tune and singing short snatches, to the pianist's accompaniment. Somebody said to me that the singer had been asked to make a recording of the melody, but couldn't make up his mind whether or not it was his sort of song. His name, I was informed, was Tony Bennett and the tune, which was being played quietly in the corner, was 'I Left my Heart in San Francisco'.

When the weather finally cleared in the Aleutians, I got under way again to Adak, then on, southward and westward across the Pacific Ocean, through Midway Island, Wake Island and Guam Island, to Manila, in the Philippines. From Manila, northward to Okinawa and then on again, on the final leg, to Fukuoka, on Japan's southernmost island of Kyushu and not all that far away From Nagasaki. I had planned to take a few days off after the trip, so I immediately cadged a lift in a C-47 and headed off to Tokyo. When I finally dumped my bags in the Sanno Hotel, I was ready to relax for a bit and all set to see what I could of Japan in the time I had available.

Right from the off, I had a tremendous advantage at my disposal. Before I had left Edwards, Colonel Peterson had given me a letter of introduction to one of his friends in the Military Administration Office in Tokyo. From the time I called on Colonel Pete's friend to deliver my letter, everything became gold-plated. I liked playing golf? A car would arrive at the hotel to take me out to Kasumigaseki, where one of the Tokyo staff, a young, 3 handicap, Major, would be delighted to provide a game any time I felt like one. I'd like a couple of days at a traditional Japanese Inn? Here is a booking for a delightful establishment on the slopes of Mount Fuji. I should admit that I only stayed 'Japanese Style' for a couple of days, before sleeping on the floor with a wooden pillow and breakfasts of raw eggs and very weak tea, led me to relapse back to 'European Style', which provided conventional beds and conventional feeding. I found Japan to be fascinating – completely different from anything I had ever experienced before. Although I didn't get out of Tokyo very much, I did book on to a number of guided tours around the places of interest within the City – and there are enough places of interest in Tokyo to keep the visitor busy for a very long time indeed. I liked the Japanese I met – invariably polite and, as I discovered, formidable drinkers of whisky. I should never admit it as a Scot, but I did come to develop quite a taste for Suntory. It's quite a pleasant drop of what's good for you. One other brand which I saw in a bar lounge – in a bottle smothered in Union Jacks, thistles and highland cattle ~ bore the legend 'guaranteed brewed in the grounds of Buckingham Palace'. I left that one very severely alone.

One of the things about Tokyo that really fascinated me was the train system. The punctuality of the services was awesome: if you got there ten seconds after the train was due to leave you'd missed it. The crowds who fought their way into the carriages could have given a few lessons to London commuters: if you didn't have a black belt in one or two of the martial arts, it was wise to avoid the initial rush when the doors opened. I always expected to hear the odd 'Banzai' as the mob fought to get on board. For the weak, the aged and the non-combative, there were official 'pushers-on' who forced you bodily into the carriages to make sure that the train pulled out on time. And there was no subtlety about their efforts either. It was all straightforward brute force and damn the consequences. On one of my train trips, I was astounded to see one chap, neatly attired in a conventional business suit, calmly undressing down to his drawers, before donning a much more comfortable kimono for the rest of his journey. Nobody paid him the slightest attention.

On a number of evenings, my golfing partner and his wife took me to ChinZan-so, a most delightful restaurant in what had once been the town 'pleasure house' of a nobleman. The furnishings of the main building were exquisite and the gardens an absolute picture. I know that some people like a measure of disorder in a garden but, at ChinZan-so, every stone, every bush and every blade of grass, seemed to be perfectly sited and meticulously groomed. It was exactly like some of the Japanese prints one sees.

In the restaurant, each table had a flat metal plate in the centre, heated from below by a small spirit lamp. When the waitress arrived, she provided, for each person, a bowl of rice, flavoured with a delicate soy sauce. She also carried, in much the same way as a violinist sets his instrument – between chin and hand – a wooden platter on which were strips of meat, fish and vegetables. These morsels were transferred by chopsticks on to the cooking plate and then, almost instantly it seemed, into the diner's bowl. By judicious timing, the waitress ensured that each mouthful of food came to the diner absolutely freshly cooked. The platters were replaced throughout the meal until the diner reached saturation point – at which stage, I noted, there was no unconsumed, but already cooked, items to be thrown away. The food was delicious and was washed down by lots of Japanese beer, tea or sake. I was informed that belching was considered *de rigeur* in Japan and certainly there were some satisfied eruptions going on all around. Altogether, with the colourfully kimonoed waitresses fluttering about like so many butter-flies, ChinZan-so was a delightful and very different, experience and I enjoyed it very much.

One culture difference I observed at ChinZan-so occurred on an evening when I was hosting the party. I had left on the table a sum sufficient to pay for the meal and to provide a gratuity for the waitress who had attended to us. When we were almost out of the building, the major-domo came running after us, apparently very worried that I had left more money on the table than was required to pay for our meal. When I said that the excess was for the waitress, he became very upset. In halting English, he made it clear that if money were left for the girl, she would lose much respect among her colleagues, who would assume that her services had been so poorly executed that her customers were being forced to leave bribes in an attempt to ensure better service next time. Pressing the excess sum back upon me, he advised that, on our next visit, we should ask for the same girl by name. In this way, her colleagues would learn that her services had given pleasure to the guests and she would, accordingly, gain face in their eyes.

While on the general subject of eating in Japan, I really ought to risk the wrath of my American friends – and particularly those from Texas – by averring that the Japanese produce steaks that are, unquestionably, without equal anywhere else in the world. Readers of Ian Fleming's James Bond books will be familiar with the preparation of 'Kobe' beef for the markets. As I understand it, the cattle are fed on oats and maize soaked in beer and have their hides constantly massaged with raw gin. By the time they are led off to the abattoir, they are probably too drunk to care much. I have certainly seen steers tottering about the place, clearly having a real problem in even standing upright. At all events, the beef they produce is incomparable. At the time I was in Japan, the American authorities considered the preparation of Kobe beef to be unhygienic and there was half-hearted advice that it should be avoided. Perhaps inevitably, practically every American I saw was wolfing into the stuff with gusto – Americans, as a whole, don't really take kindly to directives from above, half-hearted or otherwise. I must admit that I tackled Kobe steaks at every possible opportunity myself – they were so tender that you could cut them with a fork.

When I had run out of time in Japan, I hitched a ride on a US Navy C-118 back to San Francisco, by way of Wake Island and Hawaii – where, by sheer good for-tune, an engine oil leak kept us on the ground for two days. That's one of the odd things about flying – one finds that perfectly serviceable aeroplanes tend to de-velop inexplicable minor malfunctions whenever one touches down at some desirable location – and they always take about a couple of days to rectify. That's where the Services beat civil air transport hands down. The airlines only ever strand you in some hell-hole at three o'clock in the morning, with all the bars and restaurants closed and no hotel accommodation within fifty miles. As I relaxed on the patio of the Marine Officers Club at Kaneohe, with a tall, cool drink firmly in hand, I couldn't help reflecting that the US Navy orders it better. Moreover, I mused happily, I was being paid for this!

Not long after I returned from this trip, I received intimation that I was to be posted home. During my time in the United States, I had sat and passed, the 'Q' qualifying examination to make myself eligible for the RAF Staff College and I now found that I was to attend the next course, due to start at Bracknell in January of 1964. At long last, I had finally run out of flying appointments. Oddly enough, I rather welcomed the chance to try something different. I had enjoyed a good run of 'cockpit' assignments – unbroken since I first climbed into a Tiger Moth – so I really had no grounds for complaint. Moreover, the past seven years of test flying had given me more pleasure and fulfilment than any pilot has a reasonable right to expect. I really couldn't just go on doing it forever – there are always new pilots coming up who deserve their chance at the 'goodies' in life – and I couldn't think of any flying posting that wouldn't have seemed like something of an anti-climax.

It may be that another reason for my being willing to hang up my wings for a spell was that many of my colleagues at Edwards had also moved on from the Base. There had been many new faces in to replace them – excellent replacements in every way – but they weren't the ones I had lived and flown with. It was time for me to move on. Jean and I had hoped to recoup some of our outlay on furnishing our house by selling the contents off to my replacement and his family. Air Ministry firmly hit that idea on the head by replacing me with a bachelor, who would be living in the Bachelor Officers Quarters and whose taste in motor cars was likely to run to something a bit sportier than our Fairlane family sedan. We couldn't bring much of our acquisitions back with us, so we had to unload most of our possessions on to the second-hand market – which, in the United States, comes pretty close to giving things away. That return to the UK was a very expensive move for us. The financial pain was, however, more than offset by the warmth of feeling we experienced from all of our friends at Edwards during the month or so prior to our departure. We had so many parties thrown to wish us farewell that we barely had time to get the packing done.

Eventually, we flew back to New York where, from the top of the Empire State Building, we watched the Queen Mary nosing up the Hudson River to take us home. It was a very odd feeling. In one way, we were very glad to be going home to our friends and relatives yet, at the same time, we were all genuinely sorry to be taking our leave of so many other friends in a country that had made us feel so welcome and treated us so generously. After three eventful years, we had come to regard the United States as somewhere pretty close to what we could call home. Now, twenty odd years later, I often look back and think how lucky I was to get that posting to Edwards. It was an experience I wouldn't have missed for the world. I regard that tour of duty as one of the genuine high spots of my flying career and I am still inordinately proud of my service with the United States Air Force. In every sense, it was a pleasure and a privilege to serve with them.

CHAPTER 37

THE ROYAL AIR FORCE Staff College, sited at Bracknell in Berkshire, was the first Service 'Institute of Higher Learning' normally encountered by the promising young officer on his upward passage through the ranks. Given that the officer had rendered himself eligible for staff training by passing the appropriate qualifying examination, it was usually encountered not long after the officer had made Squadron Leader rank. In a very real sense, the course marked the transition from junior to senior rank; from aircrew specialist to all-round military officer; from shop-floor to management.

The basic objective of the course was to provide the specialist training necessary to prepare a relatively junior 'senior' officer for an appointment on the Staff of the Ministry of Defence, or of a Command or Group Headquarters. It provided the opportunity for the student to dramatically expand his knowledge and understanding of the purpose and organisation of the military services overall and to become familiar with the function and structure of higher command at Ministry and Headquarters level. It introduced the beginner to the complex and delicate inter-relationship between the military and the political worlds. Perhaps most importantly, it provided the prospective staff officer with his first really detailed consideration of the influence of financial management and budgetary control, on operational planning and capability.

A very important aspect of the course was the teaching of prospective staff officers to think logically and to write and to express themselves, economically. The objective of this training is, again, quite straightforward. Staff officers generally work for high ranking – and very busy – senior officers – it is sometimes quite depressing to the ambitious young officer to realise quite how hard the 'top brass' do work. Such senior officers tend to have little patience with factually unsound, or poorly reasoned, submissions and they certainly have neither the time nor the inclination to wade through thirty pages of purple prose, no matter how elegantly constructed. They want the facts right, the argument logical and the presentation concise – and, preferably, on half a sheet of paper. If you don't give them what they want, you tend to have a very limited career in a staff appointment.

Initially, at least, this part of the course syllabus was generally regarded by the course members as a bit of a joke. Some wag could always be relied on to trot out the hoary old policeman's report of, "On the night of the 37th, I was proceeding in an easterly direction..." Later, the matter was not treated so lightly, when the students started to appreciate that the aim of the game was to train them to do something which they had probably never had to do before – to reason their way systematically, logically and dispassionately, through complex situations and then to express their arguments and conclusions concisely and unambiguously. The techniques aren't really a lot of use if you just want to knock out a few chatty lines to Aunt Agatha, but they are the essential groundwork for tackling some of the 'real life' staff problems you are going to come up against later.

The 'military thinking' part of the course was much occupied with 'appreciations' – or, more correctly, with learning how to 'appreciate the situation'. This was really nothing more than a technique for analysing a particular situation or problem by identifying and weighing the factors which bear on the subject matter, by assessing the known or likely effect of the factors which have been identified and by logically deducing an answer, or optimum course of action, from the results. The technique doesn't work for every kind of problem – subjective problems, such as why one person likes oysters while another doesn't, can't be tackled sensibly by the appreciation process. For problems based on matters of fact, however, the technique works quite well and constitutes a very useful tool for the staff officer in tackling problems when a lot of conflicting factors bear on the subject matter – a situation, I might say, which occurs practically all the time in real life. On my favourite television programme, I have always felt that Mr Spock had a fair grasp of the principles involved: Dr McCoy, on the other hand, has obviously never been within miles of a Staff College in his life.

On the 'writing' side, the aim was to get the student to strip away from his work anything that was not essential to the flow of the argument. Keep it short; keep it clear; keep it simple. The instructional staff were absolutely ruthless with students' submissions. In the early stages, your exercise papers generally came back with about three quarters of the text struck out and with every page covered with red ink annotations of 'not relevant', 'prolix', 'waffle', 'ambiguous', 'padding' and 'redundant'. One felt bitterly that the Staff would have probably carped at Julius Caesar for his classic "Veni, Vidi, Vici" on the grounds that the "vidi" was, from a military standpoint, superfluous to his report.

To familiarise the students with this new way of thinking and expressing themselves, the course provided a series of exercise problems of the sort that are the day-to-day, bread and butter work of many staff officers. You are to organise the move of X number of reinforcement personnel and equipment from A to B. Quite a straightforward exercise in logistics. Except that the railways are on strike, the weather is marginal for air transport, the support equipment won't fit into the available helicopters and there isn't enough accommodation at the en-route refuelling stop. Destination airfields don't have full bad-weather landing aids, sea transport can only be commandeered by invoking an Act-in-Council, the country between A and B won't permit overflight, the destination runway is too short to accommodate heavy transports, half the nominated personnel are on leave and can't be contacted and there is a conflicting urgent demand for the same reinforcement personnel to go to the aid of an ally in a minor war on the other side of the globe. By the way, the operation is due to start at six o'clock tomorrow morning and your master wants your detailed recommendations and plan of action, sometime in the next thirty minutes. One of the lessons that the student staff officer learns – and learns very quickly – is that, for most problems, there is no one, unique, right answer and a whole lot of other solutions clearly definable as wrong. Practically any solution to practically any problem can be made to work, given only that money, time and resources, are available to make it work. The trick is to be able to identify the solution that is practicable, affordable and timely. In this respect, instructional staff at the College were very fair. Their solution to the various exercise problems – the 'pink' solution, as it was known – was never put forward as 'THE' solution – it was simply provided as one 'POSSIBLE' solution which, at the very least, took account of all of the factors involved.

I liked Staff College. The work was new and interesting and, although a lot of hard effort went into the various exercises, the pace of the course overall was very civilised. Someone once said that Staff College was "a six month course feverishly crammed into a year," and there was a fair bit of truth in the remark. Some years later, it did become a six-month course and I don't doubt that the students on later courses had to work a good deal harder than we did.

Early on in the course, there occurred a classic example of Royal Navy 'one-upmanship'. We were having a lecture from one of the Housemasters at Eton on aspects of the English language. In the course of his address, the lecturer touched on the subject of slang – and, in particular, on the manner in which some words and expressions, originally used as slang, had been rendered 'respectable' by re-peated and widespread, usage. In this context, he instanced the word 'gen', originally a purely RAF slang synonym for information, but one now generally accepted as a reasonably proper term in its own right. At this point, he remarked that he was quite sure that this was the case, at least as far as the RAF was con-cerned. Turning to one of the Army students on the course, he confirmed that this was also the case among the 'brown jobs'. Looking around for one of our Royal Navy students, he went on to enquire whether the case was also true for the 'dark blues'. After a moments silence, Commander Julian St Aubyn Sayer rose languidly to his full six foot plus and responded acidly, "Sir, in the Royal Navy, the expres-sion is recognised...........but, of course, never used." It brought the house down.

One of the great perks of the year at Bracknell was that the College had an ar-rangement with the famous Wentworth Golf Club, by which students could enjoy a year's temporary membership for something like five pounds. I made very good use of this arrangement. While in the United States, I had brought my handicap down to four and I was very keen to make sure that it didn't go back up again. Hence, I played Wentworth a lot – often with either Adrian Saddler or Gavin Christie who were Tom Halliburton's two young assistants in those days. I re-member once calculating that my rounds of golf at Wentworth cost me something less than eight pence a round over the year. I remember, too, getting one of the best lessons I have ever had from Adrian Saddler. He had just beaten me for the umpteenth time and I was so frustrated that I complained bitterly, "I don't know how you beat me, Adrian. You don't hit the ball any better than I do." He looked at me steadily for a long minute. "No," he agreed, quietly, "I don't hit the ball any better than you do, Harry. But I don't hit it as badly as you do either." While I tried to work that out, he pointed out that, when he missed a shot, he missed it safely: when I missed a shot, I was either comprehensively lost, knee-deep in gorse bushes, buried in the face of a bunker, or on the wrong side of the green. He left me with a parting shot that I have never forgotten. "You have to learn, Harry, that you don't win golf matches with good shots: you lose them with bad shots." I learned a very valuable lesson that day – one that I have tried very hard to keep firmly in mind ever since. I still hit my fair share of bad shots – every amateur does: but I try like mad never to hit a 'destructive' bad shot. Nowadays, I have a good, hard, look at the potential trouble before I start blazing away.

In May of my Staff College year, Graham Michael Archer arrived upon the scene. During our return trip from the United States, Jean had complained of morning sickness, which she construed as indicative of a forthcoming 'happy event'. I thought that it was probably seasickness. I was wrong. Graham was born at the Aldershot Hospital, which may, in some way, account for him later developing into a supporter of Arsenal. I can think of no other reason to explain this aberration.

At the end of the Course, I was posted to the staff of the Assistant Chief Of Air Staff (Operational Requirements) – ACAS(OR) for short – at the Ministry of Defence in Whitehall. Domestically, we were originally planned to take over a Married Quarter at one of the RAF Stations in the London area, but this arrangement fell through when the outgoing occupant failed to drain off the water during a cold spell and the ceiling collapsed from the resultant flooding. Ultimately, we wound up moving into a hiring in Ruislip and I settled down to the extremely dreary life of a London commuter. I never did get to accept commuting as a way of life. The travel – however you tackle it – is miserable and depressing. I hated every minute of it. Originally, too, the job I had was a bit of a non-event. I found that I was half of the two-man Ministry of Defence 'space' cell, the other half of which was a young engineer Squadron Leader named Andy Kedar. Andy was a very bright colleague indeed. An engineer by trade, he was a university graduate, who had later completed a space technology course at one of the Californian Universities. He had also done a pilots course up to 'wings' standard. A very capable and knowledgeable individual indeed and a very good working partner. He was one of the very few individuals I have ever met who had the knack of being able to explain the most complex technologies in terms that any layman could understand. If you could grasp the concept of water running through a pipe, then Andy could make you understand electronics, fluidics, radar, or anything else.

Our function in the Ministry was to serve the Air Staff, as required, as advisors on space vehicles and space technology – myself on piloting aspects and flight systems, Andy on propulsion systems and technology generally. The only problem with the job was that there really wasn't any job to do. At the time, the Ministry expenditure on space systems was precisely zero – notwithstanding that there were something like forty or more committees of one sort or another formally constituted to advise the Government generally on space matters. Apart from monitoring what these committees were up to – which was, generally, precious little – and reading Aviation Week, to keep abreast of American and Russian projects, Andy and I had little enough to do to justify our existence.

After a couple of months of this pointless sort of existence, I became thoroughly fed up with the whole situation. In desperation, I drafted a note to ACAS(OR) pointing out that we were not really being usefully employed and that we could, conceivably, be of a lot more use to his Department if we were redirected into doing something like trying to identify likely future operational requirements. Oddly enough, there was, at the time, no formal machinery in the Ministry for doing this sort of work. Forward requirements seemed to fall somewhat uneasily between the Policy and Operational Requirements Staffs and tended to result in a late requirement for a Mark 2 version of whatever piece of kit was doing the job at the moment. Rightly or wrongly, I felt that there was some scope for a small cell to try to look into the future, taking into account likely future threats, possible technological developments and various political scenarios and try to distil out – even in very broad terms – a feel for the sorts of aircraft and equipment we might need, or have the capability to produce, in the future.

Very fortunately, Air Marshal Empson, himself a former test pilot, was sufficiently receptive to the proposition to authorise us to go ahead. Andy and I were formally reconstituted to become the 'Forward Looking Cell' and were turned loose on our study of the future, with a very generally worded directive to consider the tactical strike/reconnaissance role some twenty to twenty five years ahead.

Almost overnight, our situation was transformed. We had a directive to tackle one of the most fascinating and interesting jobs open to any staff officer – trying to come up with soundly based arguments and specific recommendations, on where the service ought to be thinking of going in the future. We were accorded access to the Intelligence organisations, to the Technical Establishments and to Industry and we were then left to get on with the job in our own way and in our own time. If the work did nothing else for me, it did convince me – beyond any argument – that there is an imperative requirement for this sort of work to be conducted continuously by the Service Departments. A lot of it may be based on hypotheses, which may or may not prove to be correct in the event, but, at the very least, there is a systematic attempt to identify and analyse all of the factors which have to be taken into account and to assess their probable influence on events. Such a methodology will not come up with finalised blueprints for the future. What it can do, however, is produce a relatively narrow range of potentially practicable options which are worthy of further, serious consideration.

When we had finished the first draft of our study, Andy and I were somewhat discountenanced to discover that it was immediately accorded a limited circulation security grading – so limited, in fact, that we weren't on it. Although we had written the study, we were not now allowed to see it – or even refer to it. It took quite a while before we were able to get ourselves on 'the list' and permitted to get on with redrafting and updating our work. When we had finalised our efforts, we were turned loose on another study on almost identical lines. After I had been in the job for about fourteen months, Andy and I had a visit from Frank McClory, from the Air Secretary's Department. He was trying to understand why, in the Ministry Staff Directory, I was listed as the technology specialist and Andy as the pilot aspects specialist. Obviously, in the printing, the job descriptions had become swapped. While Frank was with us, I took the opportunity to try to find out a little about the Service promotion system, in which, up until that time, I hadn't been all that much interested. Frank couldn't have been more helpful. Patiently, he went over the whole promotion process, pointing out that the Promotion Boards, who did the actual selection, liked to be able to assess a General Duties candidate in his professional aircrew capacity, in his performance as a staff officer and in his performance in a command appointment. Noting dryly that I was probably interested in my own prospects, he went on to point out that I had done practically nothing but sit in a cockpit for most of my career to date. He went on, "Obviously, I haven't even seen your annual reports, Harry, but it seems reasonable to expect that you have had fairly good assessments as far as your flying ability is concerned. But you've never held a command appointment, so there will be nothing to guide a Board on that aspect. Moreover, you've only been in this staff job for just over a year, so there will only be one report of your staff performance on file. Overall, I'd say that you need at least another couple of reports in this job before you can expect to come up for serious consideration."

I was very grateful to Frank for his comments. It is quite impossible ever to gauge your own promotion prospects and the official Air Secretary's Department response to any tentative query is always along the lines of "you're doing fine – keep working hard and your promotion will come along in due course." Encouraging – but not exactly definitive. Of course, they can't be definitive – they never know, in advance, how many promotion vacancies are going to be available at any given time, or how formidable is going to be the strength of the candidates in contention. Frank's unofficial homily had, at least, given me a better understanding of the system than I had ever had before. I put promotion out of my mind – until the end of my tour, at least – and just got on with the job.

I had really become interested in promotion primarily as a result of dissatisfaction with the house we were living in. If I was likely to be posted in the near future, it was probably as well to just stay on: if not, it was worth looking around for a rather better alternative. At the time, some new houses were being built not too far away and Jean and I had begun to consider seriously the prospect of going into the private housing market ourselves. Now that it seemed to be a reasonable bet that I was going to be in London for the best part of the next couple of years, we started to look a lot harder at house buying. Almost two weeks to the day after I had my chat with Frank, I walked into my office to find on my desk a posting notice from Air Secretary's Department. I was to go to RAF Manby for refresher flying, prior to assuming command of number 100 Squadron, Bomber Command, at RAF Wittering, with the acting rank of Wing Commander. So much for forward planning! As I may have remarked before, it just goes to show that you never know the minute until the minute after.

CHAPTER 38

I ALWAYS HAD A very high regard for the School of Refresher Flying. It existed primarily to deal with people who, for one reason or another, had been away from flying for some time and had to be brought 'back up to speed' again, prior to their return to a flying appointment. What impressed me about the organisation was that it made absolutely no concessions to previous experience. You might have been one of the great 'aces' in your previous flying post but, at the school, you started all over again from square one. You had a couple of weeks ground school on the Jet Provost aircraft systems and then about three weeks of stalling, spinning, general handling, aerobatics, instrument flying, night flying, formation and navigation exercises. Just like the basic and advanced flying syllabuses all over again although much compressed in time. Throughout all of the air exercises, the instructors – who were frequently heavily outranked by their students – stuck firmly to the course schedule. It was their responsibility to ensure that the student could cope with all aspects of the syllabus and they discharged their responsibility to the letter. Occasionally, a student bound for fighters might find the course slightly shaded to aerobatics and formation flying, while one bound for heavier aircraft might find himself doing a bit more instrument flying than average. Overall, though, every student had to meet the required standard in all parts of the course, or he simply didn't get through. The job of the young instructors was anything but easy. It is one thing to take a 'real' student pilot through a course of flying instruction. It is quite a different proposition to do the same thing with a 'student' who is senior in rank and, quite probably, a very experienced pilot to boot. When I started at Manby, I had a lot of flying hours under my belt, I had flown something like a hundred and fifty different types of aircraft and I held a number of specialist flying qualifications. All of which counted for precisely nothing – and quite rightly so. Before my young instructor was prepared to turn me out again into the front line, he wanted to be convinced that I could demonstrate my capability in the only place where it matters – in the cockpit. I have always thought that the School approach to the job they had to do was exactly right. They took nothing for granted.

I had only been off flying for about two and a half years, so that I didn't experience any difficulty in getting back into the swing again. In a way, it's a bit like swimming, or riding a bicycle. Once you are back into a flying suit and get your hands and feet on the controls again, the old skills come flooding back and it only takes a couple of trips before you start to feel that you have never been away from it. Except that, suddenly and overwhelmingly, you realise how much you have missed it all and you thank heaven that you are, once again, back where you really belong.

After my statutory thirty hours at Manby, I reported in to the Victor Training Flight at RAF Wittering to start my conversion on to the Victor Mark 2. This involved a very intensive six weeks of ground school which covered not only the usual aircraft systems and operating procedures, but also the technical and operating details of the aircrafts offensive warload – the Blue Steel nuclear stand-off weapon, which could be launched against a target from a considerable distance away. That appealed to me no end. Most targets of any significance tend to be heavily defended and I have never hankered for the heroic 'bombs-down-the throat' approach, if I could have the option of getting the weapon away from a safe stand-off distance.

The ground school phase also gave me a chance to get to know the other four members of the crew with whom I would be operating – three young Pilot Officers straight out of training and an equally young Flying Officer from a Canberra squadron in Germany. When I met them for the first time, I felt like the original 'Ancient Aviator' – they all looked so young. For the first time in my career, I started to be uncomfortably aware that, at thirty-nine years old, I was just about old enough to be father to any one of them. Maybe not quite – but close. With these youngsters as a crew, I'd have to stay on my toes. I should say that it couldn't have been easy for them either. They were used to operating with people in their own age group and at about their own level of rank and experience. Suddenly, they had wound up crewed with a very experienced Wing Commander pilot, who was also going to be their squadron commander. I couldn't avoid the feeling that there was a certain amount of nervous trepidation on both sides.

For me, at least, any concern I might have felt was very quickly dismissed, as it became clear that, once again, I had struck lucky with a crew. Relatively inexperienced they may have been, but, as far as keenness and compatibility was concerned, no pilot could have done better. Co-pilot Ian Aubrey-Rees was virtually straight out of Cranwell, a sound, steady, pilot, who very quickly impressed me with one of the cardinal virtues in the flying business – reliability. When Ian was asked to undertake any job, you could then forget about it, secure in the knowledge that he would get it done quickly, effectively and without any fuss. Very early on, I marked him down as a potential future aircraft captain. Cranwell had given him the basics. Now, all he needed was the opportunity to get a bit of experience in the air under his belt. Colin Hunt, who filled the Navigator/Radar slot, was fresh from Navigation School. A serious and responsible young man, Colin was another with a strong streak of reliability in him. He had a very mature approach to his work, which, somehow, always made me think of him as rather older than he actually was. In many ways, he reminded me of Ken Mason, with whom I had flown years before in the Canberra force. He had the same sort of methodical, painstaking way of tackling his work. Jim Brazier was our Air Electronics Officer, responsible for the operation of all of our electronic countermeasure equipment. A former Halton apprentice and ground tradesmen, Jim was a natural-born wit and a mimic of almost professional quality. When he handled the radios on cross-country sorties, he used to drive the Air Traffic Control Centres wild by running through his repertoire of 'voices' on his successive transmissions. He could handle them all to perfection – Scots, Welsh, Irish, Australian, American, Indian, German, French... you name it, Jim could produce it. The Centres used to come back at us continually to ask us to confirm our callsign. They must have thought that there were dozens of us taking it in turns to handle the radio.

The important Navigator/Plotter slot was filled by Chris Meakin, married and with a young baby and a very cool and collected operator indeed. Chris had come to Victors from one of the RAF Germany Canberra squadrons, so that he had quite a bit of useful experience behind him. Although he was only about twenty-two, as I recall, he had an unmistakable air of authority about him. In a very real sense, the Nav/Plotter was the 'heart' of a V Force bomber crew. In the Victor, not only did he have responsibility for all of the navigation aspects, but he also had to monitor and ultimately launch, the Blue Steel missile. The workload was extremely high and the responsibility considerable. Chris took to it all like a duck takes to water. Calm, unflappable and always in control, he was exactly the type of rear crew colleague any pilot would have given his eye teeth to fly with.

With this happy little band about me, I launched into the flying phase of the Victor conversion course. The programme aimed to convert the new crew on to the aircraft and to provide a measure of initial familiarisation with the V Force Standard Operating Procedures. As it happened, it was a very interesting time to enter the force, in that the whole concept of operations was in the process of being drastically changed. For years, the force had operated at very high altitudes, relying on speed and height to provide immunity from the prospective defences. Quite recently, the threat to high flying aircraft from Surface-to-Air guided missiles had been demonstrated in the most dramatic fashion when Gary Powers U-2 had, so it was reported, been knocked down by a Russian SAM from a height in excess of 60,000 feet. Recognition of the current capability of defensive weapons of this sort led the V Force to revise completely its whole concept of operations and to concentrate its future activities on operations conducted exclusively at very low altitude – operating under the radar screen and in a regime where Surface-to-Air missiles were markedly less effective. This change to the low-level role introduced the force to many new problems, in that neither the aircraft nor the equipment had been designed with low altitude flying in mind. The much increased dynamic loads encountered at low levels dramatically affected the predicted fatigue life of the aircraft; the mapping radar picture was very different at 600 feet than that which was produced at high altitude; and – and, perhaps, most importantly – the aircraft carried no terrain avoidance radar to look ahead along the aircrafts flight path and register any obstructions en-route. Without such equipment, low-level flying at night was a really sporty proposition – with only the plotter's running commentary of track features to advise you of the obstructions ahead. No wonder the plotter was such a key crew member. If he got his navigation wrong, or wasn't right on the ball with his commentary, the crew's low-flying career could very easily come to an abrupt and very unpleasant, end.

One of the real pleasures of the flying conversion phase was that our instructor turned out to be my old friend and colleague, Barry Gould, with whom I had gone through flying training in Rhodesia. It was a delight to meet up with him again and it certainly made the conversion to the Victor that much easier for me. Although I had flown the Mark 1 version of the aircraft at Boscombe Down, I had never before flown the Mark 2 which was a very different piece of kit indeed. Barry shepherded us through the course without any particular problems, and, en-route, gave us the benefit of his own, very considerable, experience of the aircraft and its operating techniques.

I must say that, although I still had a very soft spot for the Vulcan, I very quickly came to have a real affection for the Victor. It was a very easy aeroplane to fly, practically viceless and as comfortable as one could reasonably expect. It was a big machine, with a distinctive 'crescent' wing shape and a very high performance for a bomber aircraft ~ the Sapphire engines of the Mark 1 variant had been replaced by Rolls Royce Conway by-pass turbofans giving almost twice the thrust of the earlier power plants. The all-up weight was around the 175,000 pounds mark – just short of ninety tons. Not as big as the B-52s I had flown with the USAF – in fact, the B-52 carried a fuel load heavier than the all-up weight of a fully laden Victor – but big enough, nevertheless. One feature that was very impressive indeed was the aircraft's weapon carrying capability. Although the primary offensive armament was the Blue Steel missile, it was possible to carry an internal warload of up to thirty-five 1000-pound bombs for non-nuclear operations – a very potent load of conventional ordnance by anybody's standards.

When we had flown off the fifteen or so conversion sorties of the Victor Training Flight syllabus, we were certified competent to operate the aircraft as a flying machine – but we were not yet ready to operate the aircraft in a front line squadron. Before we could take our place in the front line, we had to undergo a very intensive and very highly classified, course on the Blue Steel missile, covering both the aerodynamic vehicle – Blue Steel, in essence, was simply a small rocket powered aircraft ~ and the nuclear weapon which it carried. The course certainly drove home to the students the frightful responsibilities involved in the carriage of a nuclear weapon – responsibilities exemplified by the seemingly endless list of 'fail-safe' mechanisms and procedures which were entailed in operating with one on board.

Over the years, I have listened to countless impassioned arguments on the question of nuclear weapons – some of them so ill-informed as to be totally absurd. For the crews who actually had to operate with them, the arguments were, perhaps, rather more clear-cut. The political decision had been made to arm us with these weapons and it was our job to be able to operate with them to maximum effectiveness. Nobody I ever knew in the business took the responsibilities of the job other than deadly seriously. Young the majority of them may have been, but they – better than practically anybody else – knew the effects of the weapons that they carried. Such knowledge bred in them a hard, realistic, professionalism, which was unmatched in any other force within the RAF up to that time.

With the Blue Steel course successfully behind us – AND the aero medical course, AND the survival course – we finally arrived at 100 Squadron to join the V Force officially as fully-fledged Victor aircrew. For me, there was the added sweetener that I was to assume command of the Squadron. My first time in command and an experience I could hardly contain myself to wait for. In all of the Air Force, command of a front line squadron is probably the appointment more highly prized than any other. Of course, many other appointments carry higher rank, more status and greater responsibility but, to aircrew, flying is what the Air Force is all about, to be part of an operational squadron is heaven and to have the opportunity to command one is like being offered a seat on the celestial board. Quite simply, there is no other job like it.

I was particularly proud to be given the opportunity to take over 100 Squadron, the first squadron in the history of the British Forces to be formed specifically for night bombing. The official history of its early days of operations on the Western Front makes fascinating and occasionally amusing, reading. During the battles for Vimy Ridge and Arras, the pilot and crew of a FE2 were returning from a night raid on a railway junction through which German reinforcements were being channelled. Flying through heavy rain and snow showers, they became thoroughly lost, at which point they decided to land to check their bearings and to warm themselves up with a cup of coffee before proceeding further. After they had shut down their engine, they were about to ask for directions from a group of people hurrying to the scene, when they suddenly realised, to their horror, that the individuals concerned were German soldiers. They had, in fact, landed behind the German lines. Fortunately, their desperate attempts to get the engine going again were successful and, at the last minute, they got airborne in pitch darkness, directly over their potential captors and through some very close-range small arms fire. They made it back to base successfully. It was the crew's second operational sortie.

After World War 1 – in which the Squadron claimed with pride that the last RAF aircraft to return from a raid on the night before the Armistice belonged to No 100 – the squadron operated from a variety of bases before converting, in 1931, to the torpedo-bomber role. When Japan entered World War 2, the Squadron was based at Singapore, flying the obsolete 100 mph Vickers Vildebeeste biplane. Operating this antiquated aircraft, the Squadron made many raids on enemy held airfields before being almost totally wiped out during an attack against Japanese landing forces at Endau. Following the fall of Singapore, the remnants of the Squadron withdrew to Java, where they operated as a composite unit together with what was left of 36 Squadron. Again, in attacks on enemy convoys invading the island, very severe losses were sustained and both 100 Squadron and 36 Squadron virtually ceased to exist.

In 1942, the Squadron re-formed at Waltham, Grimsby and, by March of 1943, was operating Lancasters as part of the main force of Bomber Command. In 1946, it re-equipped with the Avro Lincoln, with which aircraft it operated against the Malayan terrorists in 1950 and against the Mau-Mau in Kenya in 1954. On its return from Kenya, the squadron re-equipped with the Canberra B2, which it operated until its disbandment in 1959. In May 1962, the Squadron re-formed again at RAF Wittering as a Victor B2 unit of the Medium Bomber Force – once more, back in the main Force of Bomber Command.

The Squadron crest – reputedly 'borrowed' from the 12th/17th Lancers during World War 1 – comprised a 'death-head' skull and crossbones. The Squadron motto, symbolising the long association with Malaya, was 'Sarang Tebuan Jangan Dijolok' – which was generally rendered in English as "don't put your hand into the hornets' nest." Occasionally, Squadron personnel fell back on the less well authenticated translation of 'don't stick your thumb in the tigers bum'. Less elegant, perhaps, but unquestionably pithier!

When you are in the situation of being about to take over command of a squadron, it is understandably natural, although undeniably un-Christian, to harbour a sneaking hope that your predecessor will have proved himself to be a bit of a deadbeat. In this way, you can comfort yourself that your unworthiness for the appointment will be overlooked, at least initially, in the flood of relief that will flow through the ranks on your arrival. It took me about ten seconds of my first meeting with my predecessor in command of 100 Squadron to realise that such a comforting situation was certainly not about to come my way. Wing Commander John Herrington was representative of the very best type of ex-Cranwell cadet, a first class pilot, a natural leader and a commander who had welded his squadron into an efficient, high-morale unit. Right from the off, I recognised that he was going to be a hard act to follow – a fact which was somewhat forcibly rammed home to me in the mess very early on, when one of the Squadron navigators 'in his cups' informed me gloomily that "we've got a bloody good squadron here and don't want it messed up." I formed the perhaps not entirely unwarranted impression that the squadron was looking forward to my arrival in much the same frame of mind as the citizens of Rome awaited the attentions of Attila the Hun.

Mercifully, command hand-overs in the services tend to be brief. The new man arrives; the formalities are briskly discharged; and the old man departs. Two days of administration at the most and then you are in the chair, responsible for umpteen million pounds worth of aircraft, about sixty highly trained aircrew and the administrative services necessary to look after the paperwork. You are in command.

On the face of it, the job of the commander of a frontline squadron is relatively straightforward – to supervise and plan the training of his squadron aircrew in such a way that they are all capable of carrying out the potential wartime mission of the squadron effectively and to administer and discipline, the unit as required. Nowadays, in the service and elsewhere, this is called 'man management' – a term that I abhor for its implicit connotations of personnel manipulation. Certainly, the job involves management, but its paramount requirement is what used to be and should still be, called 'leadership'. That's what a commander is there to do – to lead and to lead strongly and effectively. If he simply wants to do management, he ought to join the Administrative Branch. It is simply not possible to 'manage' an operational unit: it has to be led – and, for it to be effective, it has to be well led. On a front-line Squadron, you had best be ready, willing and able to do the leading, or you should be looking for another line of work.

In the practical world, the job is complicated by the fact that every squadron commander operates in an environment of two-way loyalties and responsibilities – upwards, through his Station Commander and Group Commander to his Commander-in-Chief and downwards to his squadron members. Most of the time, these two sets of loyalties and responsibilities coincide, in which case life is a relative bed of roses. On occasions, however, the two sets of loyalties and responsibilities do not even come close, in which ease it is the squadron commander who has to tackle the job of conciliation – fighting as hard and as persuasively as he can to get higher authority to give due weight to the views of the crews who are actually doing the job while, at the same time, bending every effort to ensure that his squadron members understand and willingly accept the orders and directives of the higher levels of command. In either case, the buck – as they say – stops on the squadron commander's desk.

In my time, I have served with many squadron commanders, no two of whom approached the job in the same way. In practically every ease, the way in which an individual responds to a command appointment reflects his individual personality. Some make a lot of noise; some are quiet and unobtrusive. Some bully; others persuade. Some give overmuch weight to the views of higher authority; some are prone to set too much store on the squadron-level attitudes. There are no 'golden rules' on how to get the job done. Each man has to get on with it in his own way and using his own personal set of guidelines to solve his daily problems.

In such a situation, it is perhaps inevitable that there are as many different approaches to command, as there are commanders. At the end of the day, it is the basic character of the individual that determines how he goes about his task and which sets the tone of his time in the post. For good or ill, the squadron reflects the commander. Judge it and he is judged.

In my own case, I was extremely lucky in that, very shortly after I had assumed command, a new senior Flight Commander was posted on to the Squadron – Squadron Leader Bob Hall, a very experienced navigator/plotter, who had served on many bomber squadrons including, latterly, Number 617 Squadron – the famous 'Dambusters'. In the course of his long experience in the Command, Bob had probably forgotten more about the routine, day-to-day organisation and running of a front line squadron than I was ever likely to learn. As an individual, he was direct, honest and considerate. Not one to have the wool pulled easily ever his eyes but, at the same time, very sensitive to the everyday issues which were important to squadron members. For the business of running an operational unit, no squadron commander could have asked for a better colleague.

After we had felt each other out, it became clear – at least to me – that Bob and I could work well together. He took on the wearisome job of looking after the details of squadron administration and left me free, for the most part, to concentrate on the two aspects of the job that I felt to be of paramount importance – providing old-fashioned leadership and concentrating on operational capability. On the basis of this arrangement we eventually fashioned a squadron which virtually ran itself – much of the responsibility for organising the day-to-day life of the squadron was delegated to junior squadron members. Flying and ground training programmes, leave rosters, duty alert crew rosters, detachment rosters, 'Ranger' rosters, sporting and social events – all of these activities were scheduled and organised by members of the squadron themselves, a system which gave a lot of experience and responsibility to relatively junior officers and which, at the same time, left Bob and I reasonably clear to concentrate our attention on the major issues.

In the middle 1960s, the V Force operated in two distinct roles: it was part of the overall Western nuclear deterrent force and, at the same time, was the British independent deterrent. In terms of its training, equipment, leadership and motivation, it was probably the most professionally capable force the RAF had ever deployed. In every sense, it was a 'corps d'elite' and the Commander-in-Chief, Sir Kenneth Cross, ensured that, wherever possible, it was treated as such. There was, I remember, quite a considerable amount of resentful muttering from the other arms of the service when the V Force got priority treatment in all of their activities, but it was great when you were one of those on the receiving end of the 'gold star' treatment. Overall, while quite a few noses were unquestionably put out of joint at the time, the force deserved everything it got. The job was very demanding, the responsibilities awesome and the pressures unrelenting. The award of a few 'perks' was a small price to pay for the very high standards which were consistently maintained.

One of the ways in which you paid for the 'perks' was by QRA – Quick Reaction Alert. This was a Command-wide procedure designed to prevent the force being caught on the ground by a surprise attack. It aimed to ensure that at least two fully-armed aircraft from each bomber station could be launched against their targets, even in the event of a completely unexpected, 'out-of-the-blue', Pearl Harbour type of surprise attack. Crews did three or four days at a time on 'alert' status and, with perhaps ten fully operational crews on each squadron, the duty came round quite frequently. At the alert dispersal, the aircraft were maintained in a fully primed, combat ready, condition throughout twenty-four hours a day, three hundred and sixty five days a year and the crews on alert had to be capable of being airborne within minutes of a callout. The crews never separated on QRA because they had to carry their 'war-bag' with them at all times. Where one went, all five went – yes, even there too! They were restricted to the Mess, the Squadron Offices or the QRA huts where they slept. They had their own car, complete with klaxon, flashing lights and a sump heater to ensure that the engine would always start first time. The call-out was triggered by an alarm bell, which was sounded over the station Tannoy system and exercise call-outs were frequently activated by Bomber Command Headquarters to test the effectiveness of the force.

The problem was that you never knew whether a call-out was an exercise or the real thing. Although the odds were against a surprise attack against the UK, it was, nevertheless, a time of considerable political tension in the world as a whole. Accordingly, EVERY call-out had to be taken seriously. When the bell went, the QRA crews responded like Pavlov's dogs. Day or night, wherever you were, whatever you were doing, you dropped everything on the spot, piled into the car and tore off, lights blazing and klaxon blaring for the QRA dispersal. At the aircraft, there was no leisurely preparation for flight: you rocketed up to the flight deck and, as your backside hit the seat, you were already pressing the engine start buttons, the co-pilot was getting his headset on to work the radios, the chocks were being pulled away, and, as the last engine fired, you were ready to roll. In the years I did QRA, I think that the longest time it ever took us to be ready to roll was six minutes – and that was from being in bed in the QRA hut when the bell went. A by-product of this sort of life was that, when the average V Force aircrew left the force, it took about a year to get back to responding normally when a telephone bell rang. In the early stages, you were already half-way through the door after the first ring.

In addition to QRA which guarded against the 'no warning' surprise attack, the force as a whole was trained to get off the ground extremely quickly during a time of tension. The Ballistic Missile Early Warning System (BMEWS) gave warning of the launch of hostile missiles and it was essential to get the whole force airborne in the very short warning time available before the arrival of the incoming warheads. During a time of heightened political tension, elements of the nuclear-armed bomber force were dispersed to other airfields throughout the country in order to avoid the possibility of the whole force being caught at the main bomber bases. This dispersal tactic was frequently exercised by Command Headquarters and the whole bomber force could be launched in a matter of a very few minutes – certainly, well within the warning time available. For a sizeable force of heavy bombers, this represented a very high standard of professional competence indeed and it took a lot of training effort and dedicated hard work to ensure that the system worked – and worked every time. Years later, I watched a Fighter Alert Force intercept 'scramble' and was not much impressed. The situations were not entirely identical, since the fighter aircraft was parked in a Hardened Aircraft Shelter, while we used to park on the Operational Readiness Platforms at the end of the runway. On the other hand, their crew was in the shelter right next to the aircraft, while we might have been anywhere on the airfield when the alarm went. Even allowing for these factors, I still reckon that we could have got the entire V Force airborne by the time that fighter had got itself out to the take-off point.

With QRA and Force exercises to cope with, on top of the Crew Classification System, life in the V Force was no bed of roses. The crews were under non-stop pressure of work and the incessant demand for perfection imposed considerable domestic strains. Leave was taken, not when it suited you, but when the squadron could spare you. You had to be available at all times for very short-notice recall, you were working very odd hours – what would nowadays be called 'unsocial' hours – and you did a lot of detachments away from home on dispersal exercises, Lone Rangers, overseas training and major Command exercises. Many of the young wives found it difficult to cope with the continual and unpredictable turmoil of the life and domestic strains were common. I believe that the V Force had the highest incidence of divorce and separation cases in the history of the RAF. Even the flying was hard work – the first part of most sorties was at high altitude to get the maximum possible fuel economy, but the 'business' part of the flight was always carried out at low-level. A heavy bomber isn't the best sort of vehicle for low-altitude operations, because it doesn't ride the 'bumps' of air turbulence as well as a smaller aircraft. Bird strikes are a constant worry, as are high-tension cables, tall buildings, hills and so on. When you are trying to cope with all of this at night, in poor weather conditions and with no terrain avoidance radar to warn you of obstructions on track, you pretty soon lose the image of 'dancing the skies on laughter-silvered wings'. A hard, demanding, business that leaves little or no margin for mistakes. Try going from Swansea to Rhyl, through the Welsh mountains, at low-level on a dark and dirty night just to get a feel for it. Stimulating, yes; challenging, yes; professionally satisfying, yes; but not, by any stretch of the imagination, what you would describe as a whole lot of fun.

Looking back on it now, I suppose that the time I spent in 100 Squadron effectively constituted my last tour of duty in the Air Force as a front-line operational squadron pilot. Not, I hasten to add, because either the RAF or I felt that I was getting past it all. It was simply a question of rank. Wing Commander is the highest rank that can be held by a front line pilot – and then only in the post of Commanding Officer. Any more rank and you take yourself out of the front line as an aircrew member. At the next rank level, Group Captain, you may be lucky enough to get command of a flying station and you may, in fact, do quite a bit of time in the air, but you will never again fly as a member of an operational squadron. When you have done your flying tour as a Wing Commander, that's it as far as your operational flying days are concerned. Effectively, you hang up your flying boots – at least, your squadron ones.

In these circumstances, it would be superfluous for me to say that I enjoyed every minute of my time on 100 Squadron. To me, the operational front-line of the RAF is where the service is seen and experienced, at its best. The squadron is like a regiment to the Army or a ship to the Navy. It is the fighting unit of the service, within which you and your fellow-members are bound together in a way that is experienced nowhere else. You – and they – feel yourselves to be part of a tradition that goes back a long way and part of a living piece of service history to which countless others of your predecessors have contributed. In your day, you make your own small contribution to that piece of history and you become a part of it and it becomes a part of you. Years later, I was talking to a friend – a Colonel in the United States Marine Corps – about a mutual acquaintance to whom I referred as an 'ex-Marine'. Very quickly, my friend cut in to advise me that there was, "no such thing as an ex-Marine."

"Once a Marine," he told me severely, "always a Marine. He can be serving or retired but, either way, he's still a Marine."

I know what he meant. Even today, when memory is not as sharp as it may have been once, I can still remember practically every individual with whom I served on a front line squadron. They were, and, to me, still are, 'the squadron'.

CHAPTER 39

AFTER I HAD BEEN in the post for a few months, 100 Squadron added fresh lustre to its laurels when it practically swept the board in the annual Bomber Command Bombing and Navigation Competition. Among the prizes lifted was the Laurence Minot Trophy, the premier award for all-round professional capability in all of the events in the competition. It was a once-in-a-lifetime experience to mount the rostrum at the presentation ceremony to receive, from the Commander-in-Chief, the Trophy that represented recognition of 100 Squadron as the best in the Command. I only wished that John Herrington could have shared it with me – so much of the preparatory work that went into winning the competition was initiated during his time in command. It seemed a pity that he missed out on the rewards.

One odd feature which surfaced just after the competition and at the time when we were starting to make preliminary arrangements for the next year's event, concerned one of our 'star' navigators who could always be relied on to turn in results – particularly, in astro navigation – which were better than anyone else's. This wasn't just an occasional phenomenon – he did it time after time. Since 'astro' was such a crucial element in 'limited aids' navigation, I resolved to find out how he achieved these outstanding results, in order that the rest of us could get ourselves up to his standard.

The thing about this particular individual was that, not only were his results consistently exceptional, but they were actually better than was theoretically possible with the equipment he was using. During astro-navigation legs, the radar operator takes star 'shots' with a navigational octant mounted in the roof of the aircraft. The readings are then computed to produce a position line, which is plotted on the navigators chart. Astro shots on three stars – the normal procedure - produce a 'cocked hat' plot on the chart at the point where the position lines intersect. In theory at least, the aircraft is somewhere within the cocked hat. The inbuilt manufacturing and optical errors in the octant were such that the best result which could possibly be achieved under absolutely perfect conditions was of the order of seven to ten miles. With that equipment, under perfect conditions, it simply wasn't possible to do better. And yet, time after time, this particular navigator would fix himself to an accuracy of five miles or better. And, what's more, he was getting these results under anything but perfect conditions – in a heavy aircraft, wallowing about at 45,000 feet. A bit like the magicians final trick, "not only difficult, Ladies and Gentlemen, but downright impossible."

When I discussed his technique with him, I found that he didn't seem to be doing anything different from anyone else and he quite honestly couldn't account for the results he achieved. He just did his job and there they were – inside five miles practically every time. We must have gone over his technique many times but, at the end of the day, neither of us could offer any rational explanation of why he was so much better than everyone else.

Finally, in desperation, I had him pass me his navigation log and chart after every astro trip he did and then Chris Meakin and I would laboriously backtrack over every calculation he had made and every position line he had plotted. After a couple of weeks of this we began to notice odd, inexplicable shifts of his position lines. It seemed that he would plot his three position lines straight from the octant readings and then, for no reason that either of us could ascertain, he would shift one, or possibly even two of the position lines a mile or two to either side of its original plotted position. Quite clearly, he was applying some sort of correction factor to his original plots, but neither Chris nor I could work out how or why.

Eventually, when we had him in to explain these unfathomable shifts of his position lines, he was unable to account for them in any sort of logical way. The best he could do was say that the position line as plotted "hadn't felt right," and that something – he couldn't explain what – had moved him to shift it a bit until it did "feel right." He could no more explain why it hadn't felt night than he could explain why he had moved it a particular distance so that it did. I must admit that I was driven to the point of distraction by being quite unable to get from him any sort of reasonable rationalisation for his individualistic plot correction technique. It wasn't that he didn't want to be helpful. He simply didn't know himself how he did it. When he plotted a line, he just KNEW whether it felt right on not. If it didn't feel night, he moved it around a bit till it did. Needless to say, this wasn't a great deal of help to the rest of us. In the end, we just gave up trying to work out how he did it. We went on working like slaves to get our ten mile errors, while he went on happily 'feeling' his way to five miles on better. To this day, I still can't understand how he did it.

Another extraordinary individual on the squadron was one of the pilots who would have fitted very closely to any Commanding Officer's concept of the ideal squadron member. Reserved, careful, utterly dependable, he could have served as the archetypal phlegmatic Englishman, – seemingly unemotional, practical, stolid, at first sight maybe even slightly dull. Certainly not a man ever to display much of his feelings, or act impulsively. Yet the same individual, invited to make up numbers at a party, had stood quietly in a corner with his drink until a particular girl arrived on the scene. They had never met and had not even been introduced when he made his way across the room to her and said quite simply, "Hello, I'm glad we met tonight because you're the girl I'm going to marry." At this point, neither of them even knew the other's name. The girl was so completely flabbergasted by this somewhat unorthodox approach that she simply didn't know what to say in reply. A few months later, however, she had recovered sufficiently to reply "I do" at the end of her walk down the aisle. I don't think that I would have believed the story, except that it was told to me by the girl concerned. I think that she could hardly believe that it had happened herself.

Another of the characters I remember with pleasure was Flight Lieutenant Stevenson – 'Wee Steevie' to all who knew him. We had known each other for years, during which time we had kicked each other over countless soccer pitches. Steevie was a real Glasgow hard case. On the field, he was just like Billy Bremner who used to play for Leeds. Put him on one side of a brick wall and the ball on the other and he'd go through the wall without a seconds hesitation. A really outstanding navigator, Steevie was the sort of catalyst every squadron needs. Noisy, argumentative, dedicated, up to his neck in any and every squadron activity, a terror at any party, he was the sort of person around whom things always seemed to be happening. One day, playing in the garden with his small son, aged about five or so, Steevie went for a fifty-fifty ball with the boy. At the last gasp, he thought, "I can't go in like this. He's only a youngster." for probably the only time in his life, he drew back in the tackle. Unfortunately, his son – obviously a real chip off the old block – didn't and Steevie wound up with a broken leg. Next day, with his leg in plaster up to the waist, he turned up at the squadron to fly on a Command exercise. If he had been obliged to bale out, he would undoubtedly have done himself serious damage, but he wasn't going to leave his crew with a replacement navigator just for a little thing like a broken leg. I hope they still make them like that.

Mention of football reminds me that, around this time, I was entering, if not already well into, the twilight of my not very illustrious soccer career. This painful fact was brutally highlighted during my rather ill-judged participation in an inter-squadron match. Although I was really past playing competitive football, I felt that I could still 'poach' in the penalty area, provided that someone else did the running about. The fact that I was a long way out of playing condition was evident after about five minutes when the small amount of running about I had done had produced very little other than near exhaustion and spots before my eyes. To-wards the end of the game, going for a through ball into the penalty area, I was unceremoniously flattened by the opposing centre half who was clearly of the 'take no prisoners' persuasion. As the game raged about me, I was left prone in the mud, lungs bursting, legs like lead, more spots before the eyes and feeling like death. At this point, amid a storm of abuse from the spectators, I made out Jim Brazier's voice, "Don't just lay there, Boss. Do some push-ups". I could have stran-gled him on the spot, but at least, it got me back on my feet.

From time to time, odd crazes erupt in the Service. Often enough there is no rational reason for them: they just happen. At one time, for example, there was the 'Fandango' craze, which was an inescapable ingredient of every dining-in night. After the loyal toast, when the festivities were getting well under way, someone was sure to yell, "Anyone who can't dance a Fandango is a queer." At this point, everyone in the Mess would leap to their feet, strike a pose which they fondly imagined represented a Spanish dancer and bellow "Olé!" I know that it sounds ridiculous. Damn it, it was ridiculous! But I have seen grown men reduced to tears of laughter by this sort of idiocy. At Wittering, a similar sort of craze be-gan when someone at a dining-in yelled to the assembly, "Sing us a World War 1 song then." Like a shot, everyone was up and off into 'There's a Long Long Trail A-winding', 'Take Me Back To Dear Old Blighty' or 'Mademoiselle From Armen-tieres'. Over a period, when this nonsense became popular, 100 Squadron somehow or other came to be associated with 'It's a Long Way To Tipperary'. Night after night, as soon as the ploy was called, we were off and running, fortis-simo and with feeling. Wherever we went, we contrived to have that song played – at Mess functions, on parades, at parties, at sports events, everywhere. We even got it played on some radio request programmes. And when we couldn't get it played, we sang it ourselves, unaccompanied and with gusto. It became a part of our squadron life. During the thrash that followed every major exercise, 100 Squadron could be relied on for an en-masse performance. Often enough, it would break out for no reason at all – I remember one particularly stirring rendition in the Mess dining room – at breakfast. The whole thing was absolutely mad, but the tradition stuck. Even today, I just have to hear the first few bars and I'm right back at Wittering with 100 Squadron in full voice.

In August of 1967, 100 Squadron was lucky enough to be selected to send two aircraft to Toronto to participate in the Canadian International Air Show, which was being held as part of the Canadian Centenary celebrations. It wasn't my turn for an overseas flight but, because of the obvious tie-up between 100 Squadron and Canada celebrating one hundred years of federation, the Air Officer Commanding ordered me to accompany the detachment. To be honest, I would rather have gone with my own crew, or sent someone else to command the small detachment, but 'orders is orders' – and, anyway, it was a very pleasant order to have to carry out.

Just how pleasant it was all to be was made strikingly clear from the moment we touched down at Toronto. The organisers of the Air Show and the people of Toronto, seemed to go out of their way to make the occasion a really memorable one for all of the participants. We were accommodated in a hotel right next to the airfield, cars were made available – I had a choice of two – and the hospitality was genuine and overwhelming. I had flown in quite a few Air Shows previously and my general experience had been that, once you had done your bit, the organisers couldn't get you out of the place fast enough. That certainly wasn't the case in Toronto – after the last day of the Show, they laid on a party for all the participants, which turned out to be a truly memorable thrash. The organising Committee and the representatives of the Civic Council, stuck it out gamely and seemed to enjoy themselves as much as the aircrew did. During the party, two very large and purposeful-looking Texans came up to inform me that one of our two Victors had been requisitioned for the Confederate Air Force by the authority of Colonel Jethro E Culpepper. In return, I was enlisted into the Confederate Air Force in the rank of sergeant, with strict orders to learn the correct procedure for giving the rebel 'yell'. My efforts at producing this blood-curdling whoop met with some disdain as being much too inhibited and I was bluntly advised that I would have to work hard on this aspect of my performance if I ever wished to progress in my career with the 'rebs'. I should add that Colonel Culpepper graciously permitted 'his' Victor to continue in the service of Her Majesty on condition that the CAF emblem was conspicuously displayed on the airframe. It was, too, until rain and wind wore it off.

The participation of our two Victors in the Air Show was in a format which is fairly standard for heavy bombers in displays: one slow pass, with wheels and flaps down, airbrakes extended and bomb doors open, followed by a full power turning climb-out into a tight circuit of the airfield and a second pass along the display line, low and fast. I hadn't planned to do any of the flying myself, since I was only there as detachment commander and the two squadron crews were perfectly capable of doing the display without any help from me. When I saw the first rehearsal, however, I very quickly realised that the visual impact of having two aircraft in the display was being completely lost by the very wide separation between the aircraft as they made their display runs. One aircraft on its own might have been fine but, in the widely separated 'line astern' formation that was being flown, the display looked ridiculous. Moreover, it was very difficult for the pilot of the second aircraft to hold his spacing accurately. As I have remarked before, accurate station keeping is a lot easier in a tight formation than in a loose one.

The problem in tightening up the formation was that neither of the two squadron display pilots had flown close formation since they had completed their training. Bomber pilots don't normally fly formation at all in their squadron careers, except on the very rare occasions when they participate in a fly-past. Fortunately, I did have a fair bit of experience in formating in heavy aircraft – from a lot of in-flight refuelling sorties during my test flying days. Accordingly, most of our subsequent rehearsals were spent well away from the airfield with me bringing the number two man very rapidly up to speed in how to get in close – and how to stay there.

We had to feel our way around a bit at first to find the position where we were least affected by the slipstream and downwash from the lead aircraft, but once we had found the right 'slot', there were no problems at all. Admittedly, the aircraft in front did look VERY close, but after a bit you just got used to it.

On the day, the display went off like clockwork. I watched it from the stands along the lakefront and it was really quite impressive to watch the two heavy aircraft going through their paces almost as if they were tied close together. When it was all over, we were all gratified to learn from the organisers that they hadn't expected to see our two 'heavies' cavorting about like a pair of fighters. I know that the pilot of our second aircraft was absolutely wringing with perspiration when he landed but in the air, you would have thought that he'd been flying close formation every day of his life.

CHAPTER 40

DURING THE RETURN FLIGHT from Toronto, we were about half way across the Atlantic when we experienced a sudden and inexplicable malfunction in the fuel supply system. Quite abruptly and with no forewarning of any trouble, we found ourselves unable to feed the engines from the main fuselage group of fuel tanks. There was no possibility of reaching the UK on the fuel remaining in the other fuel tanks, nor could we make it back to the North American mainland. In such a situation, only one practical option remains open – head for the nearest diversion airfield and get down on the ground before you start to develop any other problems. In our case, the option was extremely simple, in that the only airfield we could reach with the fuel we had left was the US Base at Keflavik in Iceland.

The diversion to Keflavik went off without a hitch and we made the airfield with a small reserve of fuel to spare. The weather was quite reasonable – cold, with scattered light snow showers, but with excellent visibility and quite a high cloud ceiling. The only problem was that Keflavik Air Traffic advised us that there had been recent rain, that the runway surface was icy in patches and that there was a fairly strong cross-wind blowing. These factors virtually committed us to deploying the braking parachute on landing – something we generally preferred to avoid if possible when landing away from V Force main airfields.

I should explain that the Victor, like many other high-performance aircraft, was fitted with a braking parachute, installed in a rear fuselage compartment behind the fin and rudder. On landing, the parachute was 'streamed' as soon as possible after touchdown to provide a very powerful retardation to the aircraft and to take the strain off the wheel brakes. After the aircraft had cleared the active runway, the parachute was jettisoned on the taxiway, to be collected by the ground servicing personnel for later repacking back into the aircraft. This arrangement was fine at airfields where Victor experienced ground personnel were available to do the repacking. When they were not, as was the case at most non-V Force airfields, the poor aircrew had to do the repacking themselves. We had all been trained to do the job, but it was a very tedious chore indeed. Repacking a personal parachute is bad enough – there is an awful lot of material in a parachute ~ but an aircraft parachute is enormous by comparison. When you get it all straightened out prior to refolding and repacking, it seems that it will never possibly fit back into its storage compartment. And what's more, repacking is a job that has to be done right, otherwise the parachute will either not fit back into the compartment or, more importantly, it will probably not deploy properly next time it is streamed.

At Keflavik, we had no choice. It was better to face up to the back-breaking chore of repacking the parachute, than to risk going off the end of an icy runway and then having to think up some good answers for the subsequent Board of Inquiry. We weren't happy about it, but we streamed the thing anyway. When we got out of the aircraft at the flight line, it was numbingly cold. We had been flying in lightweight flight suits worn over a singlet and a pair of shorts and the minute we stepped out on to the ramp, the icy wind went through us like a knife. In about ten seconds flat, I was as cold as I have ever been in my life. Even when the Americans very kindly provided us with fur-lined parkas, it was still freezing.

It was at this point that we realised that we would have to tackle the re-packing of the braking parachute right away, or we would never get the job done at all. In that cold, the material would have gone as stiff as a board in no time at all. Dolefully, we all trooped out to the end of the runway where, for the next hour or so, we smoothed, folded and re-folded what seemed like acres of nylon, until we had the thing re-packed. This was a bare hands job and, in that cold, it was nobody's idea of a fun way to spend an afternoon. When we finally had it safely stowed back into the aircraft again, we rushed off to the Officers Quarter's showers where we stood under floods of scalding water, with a bottle of whisky circulating around the stalls, until we started to feel semi-human again. If I had ever had to face the same situation again, I think I would have been strongly tempted to go ahead and land without using the chute and take my chances on the Board of Inquiry.

In the V Force, we all saw quite a bit of Canada – or, to be more strictly accurate, we all saw quite a bit of Goose Hay, Labrador, which, so a lot of Canadians would tell you, isn't really the same thing at all. Maybe that's a bit unfair, but even the local inhabitants wouldn't claim that Goose Bay comes into the tourists 'must visit' category. The climate can be extreme and the place gives the impression of being stuck out in the middle of a million miles of nowhere. Oddly enough, it was the remoteness, the emptiness and the climate, which made the place so important to Bomber Command. When the Canadian Government offered the use of the facilities of the base to the RAF for training flying, one of the most difficult of the V Force problems – realistic operational training ~ was solved virtually overnight.

Quite simply, operational training involves flying the aircraft as if you were actually going to war. For a variety of reasons, it is difficult to get realistic operational training within the confines of the relatively densely populated UK. In particular, it is almost impossible to get low flying done at operational speeds and altitudes. Certainly, there are low flying areas in the UK, but they are relatively small and there is always the problem of aircraft noise to be considered. In addition, since so many aircraft use the UK low-flying areas, you can seldom get down to operational low flying because of the necessity to conform to stringent safety regulations. At the same time, it is crucial that aircrews are trained to operate under the conditions that will apply for them in real operations. Close simply isn't good enough. If you are going to have to fly low to survive, then you had better be able to fly really low. And it's a whole new world the lower you get. When you start off, 300 feet seems pretty low. By the time you have worked your way down to 100 feet or lower, 300 feet seems like high altitude: you go up there occasionally for a breather.

In these circumstances, Goose Bay was an absolute godsend to the force. The base was relatively isolated, the surrounding area was vast and empty, there was very little air traffic and there were very few centres of population. I remember flying a six-hour sortie from Goose Bay once, north up into the tundra, then along to Hudson Bay, down the Bay Shore and then back to Goose. In the entire flight, we saw not one sign of human habitation. We could have had our bomb doors skimming the ground and no one would have been bothered.

Quite apart From the obvious advantages of Goose in making it possible to carry out really effective operational low flying, there was the added consideration that much of the terrain had a lot in common with the sort of country over which we might one day have had to operate for real. This meant that the radar operators could get invaluable experience in matching the ground features which occur in that type of terrain with the picture displayed on their screen. Radar picture interpretation is difficult enough at any time – particularly so at low altitudes – and it is a lot easier for the operator when he has had the opportunity to become thoroughly familiar with typical returns beforehand and to accumulate practical experience of the ways in which the different ground features show up. Our radar operators simply couldn't get that sort of familiarity and experience in the UK, where the nature of the terrain was so markedly different.

All in all, Goose Hay was an extremely important asset to Bomber Command, in that it provided the opportunity to achieve the one aspect of our training that was difficult to get in the UK – operational realism. The availability of the base made a very important contribution to the overall capability of the RAF bomber force.

CHAPTER 41

WHILE NOBODY QUESTIONED the value of the availability of the facilities at Goose Bay from the operational point of view, it was generally recognised, nevertheless, that the place did have one or two minor drawbacks domestically. For a start, it was located right out in the middle of nowhere and it enjoyed – if that is the word – a climate of considerable extremes: in winter, chillingly cold and under umpteen feet of snow; in summer, sweaty hot and miserable from the existence of swarms of gnats. The nearest centre of habitation, Happy Valley, was a very small place indeed and there was little there for off-base recreation or amusement. As a result, most of the activities with which we diverted ourselves during our non-flying time at Goose Bay were definitely in the 'home made' category. Many of us took the opportunity to go out into the local area with the instructors from the Survival Section on the main RCAF part of the base. For the most part, the instructors were locally employed civilians – genuine 'backwoodsmen', rough, tough, independent and resourceful. What they didn't know about survival and living off the land, wasn't worth knowing. We were lucky – and duly grateful – to have the opportunity of learning from them. If you ever have to go down in the wilderness of Labrador, you really want to know how to keep yourself alive. It might be quite a while before anyone gets along to lift you out.

On one of these expeditions, I remember camping by the shore of a frozen lake in a raging blizzard. One of the instructors shrugged himself into his parka and snowshoes to announce tersely that he was "going fishing." Curious, I got into my outdoor gear and stumbled after him. Outside the tent, the driving snow had reduced visibility to almost zero, so he made me tie myself to his belt with a piece of cord. He seemed to know where he was going, but I noticed that he stopped every couple of yards to break a twig or small branch on a tree, presumably, marking a trail for the return journey. Once down at the lakeshore, he proceeded to knock a hole in the surface ice with a small hatchet. Then, he produced his fishing tackle – a piece of thread and a bent pin. Dropping the pin into the hole, he proceeded to haul out fish nineteen to the dozen. I have never seen anything like it – the fish must have been practically queuing up to take the hook. When he passed the line over to me, I found that I could do just as well – when I peered down into the clear water in the hole, I could see literally dozens of fish jostling each other to get at the line. "Dumb fish," he yelled at me above the wind, "place has probably never been fished before. They're just curious." Well, dumb or not, the fish certainly couldn't wait to be hooked. Anyone with the patience to do it single-handed could have supplied Billingsgate – and all with a piece of thread and a bent pin.

Another interesting Goose Hay diversion arose out of a scratch soccer match, which we played against a team of the RCAF personnel on the base. At the end of the game, we were challenged to a return fixture – at ice hockey. Since very few of our side could skate, let alone contemplate ice hockey against a team of Canadians, the proposition was very quickly recognised as a non-starter. "OK," the

Canadians agreed, "maybe we'd have too much of an edge at hockey. So we'll take you on at Broomball." At this point, I don't think that any member of the RAF party had even heard of Broomball, much less played it, but a challenge is a challenge and we arranged to meet them next afternoon at the Base Ice Rink to find out what the game was all about.

I suppose that we should have suspected the worst when we turned up next afternoon to find the Canadians unpacking crates and crates of beer. "It's an energetic game," they told us, "you can get pretty damn thirsty." When the crates were unpacked and we had all had a beer or two to 'break the ice', they explained how the game was to be played. As I understood the explanation, it sounded to be like ice hockey for raving loonies. It was played on the rink, but there all similarity ended. Instead of ice skates, you wore plimsolls; instead of a stick, you had a sort of yard broom – the kind of thing that witches fly around on – lots of twigs tied together on the end of a pole. Instead of a puck, you had a football. The objective of the exercise was to put the football into the opponent's goal. If there were any other rules, I never heard about them, although it seemed to be tacitly understood – at least by the Canadians – that direct physical assault was frowned on and that any player was free to leave the ice at any time for a drink. On that basis, we launched off on one of the most crazily hilarious afternoons I can ever remember.

The fun of the game comes from the fact that, once you get yourself moving in any given direction, it is well-nigh impossible to slow down, stop, or change direction, unless you hit something. After the first minute or so, the soles of your plimsolls are so slippery that you have quite a job just staying upright. When you start chasing a ball, it becomes even more of a job. After a bit, you tend to adopt a flat-footed, scuttling, sort of motion, using the broom as an aid to balance, rather than as an implement for the game. The entire playing time seems to develop into a virtually non-stop succession of unavoidable, crunching, collisions – with your teammates, with the opposition, with the goalposts and with the barricades. I know that it sounds sheer idiocy – and it is! At the same time, it is hilarious to play and even more hilarious to watch. In addition, like they said, it is hot, hard, work and you need to drink a lot – and the more you drink, the more hilarious it gets. What made it even funnier – particularly when you were watching – was that the Canadians had a well-practised technique for slipping any tackle. When you made contact with one, he would give a little twist of the hips – nothing violent, but just enough to send you rocketing towards a shattering impact with another player, or with the barricades. Exactly like the ball in a pinball machine. To give credit to the RAF, we saw the game through to the final whistle, by which time the Canadians were leading by what could only be described as a commanding margin. I don't think that we ever had the ball into their half, much less anywhere near their goal. Not that the result seemed to matter to anybody. We had spent most of the afternoon on our backsides, we were black and blue all over, we were absolutely exhausted and we were all pretty drunk. We had had a marvellous time. I have never seen Broomball played anywhere other than at Goose Bay, but I have never been able to understand why it has not been taken up by television. It's a natural for the 'box' and would make genuinely compulsive viewing – as a comedy feature rather than as a sports event.

CHAPTER 42

IN THE LOW FLYING which we did from Goose Bay, one of the recurring problems was in knowing where to draw the line when you started to go low. From the operational standpoint, you certainly want to be low enough to minimise the chances of radar detection, fighter interception and engagement by SAMs. In theory, the lower the better. In practice, however, one has to use a bit of discretion – if you are not careful, it is only too easy to slip down and down, until you eventually reach an altitude at which you are more of a danger to yourself than are the potential enemy defences. Many bombers have survived engagements with enemy defences. Very few, if any, have got away with a high-speed contact with Mother Earth. Of course, there were regulations in abundance to spell out unequivocally just how low you were supposed to go. But, although the regulations were undoubtedly entirely sensible, they were, as they always are in peacetime, quite properly shaded towards flight safety. The flying crews were thoroughly familiar with the official limits but, at Goose Bay, they were a long way from Higher Authority and their flying was being carried out over a wilderness where there were no prying eyes to report back if they got a bit lower than the limits. Moreover, after a bit of time at low level, most pilots start to get quite comfortable and to slip, almost unconsciously, a bit closer to the ground.

On one sortie, we flew From Goose, we had just about completed the low-level section of the flight, when we received a radio call from a small airstrip not too far off our track – one of a number that we used as radio relay stations to pass our position reports back to Goose. The operator was complaining that, in all the time he had been relaying messages from the V bombers passing by, he had never actually seen one. "Why don't you," he invited, "come on over and give us a fly-by?" Well, we were all for keeping up good relations with our friends and allies and the place was only a matter of ten miles or so off our track, so we tuned in his radio beacon and swung off to go over and let him see what a Victor looked like close up.

I should make the point that, at the time, we had been down on the deck for the better part of an hour or so and had become thoroughly comfortable and relaxed in our low-level condition. When the little strip came in sight, I eased the aircraft round in a fairly wide turn to line up for a run across the field on a line between the grass landing strip and the airfield buildings. At this point, Jim Brazier crawled forward into the bomb aimers compartment down in the nose to give them a wave as we went by. As I straightened out from the turn, we were perfectly positioned for our fly-by. The air was as smooth as could be and I was absolutely at ease. I edged the throttles forward to let the speed build up and gently settled the aircraft lower and lower and lower. As we howled across the field, we must have been really low, because Jim's awed voice came back from the nose compartment with, "for God's sake, Boss, don't put the wheels down, or we're going to go up"

Once past the boundary of the airstrip, I pulled up a bit and swung the aircraft round to get back to our original track. As a parting shot, the airfield radio operator called us with, "thanks a lot. Come on back sometime and show us what the damned thing looks like from underneath." He was in a fairly small two-storey control tower, so I suppose we must have been pretty low to have him looking down on us as we went by. Maybe, that was one of the times when I overdid it just a bit.

CHAPTER 43

THE YEAR 1966 WAS the fiftieth anniversary of the formation of the Royal Air Force. As part of the celebrations to mark the Golden Jubilee, it was planned to carry out a major fly-past, comprised of representative elements of all of the flying Commands of the Service in review formation, before Her Majesty the Queen at RAF Abingdon. In accordance with service tradition, the formation was to be led by the representative elements of Bomber Command and, as one of the then current bomber Squadron Commanders, I was lucky enough to draw the honour of leading the review.

A Royal Review is an event of major importance for any service. Constitutionally, the reigning monarch is the ultimate commander of every man and woman wearing the uniform of any one of the UK military services. The Oath of Allegiance is sworn to the Queen and to nobody else. Hence, it is a signal honour for any service to be reviewed by Her Majesty at any time. On this particular occasion, marking fifty years of history of the Royal Air Force as an independent service, the event would be something even more special.

Quite obviously, I was both delighted and honoured to be in the position of 'leading the parade', as it were. At the same time, I had no illusions that the job was going to be an easy one. Leading any large formation is never a particularly simple exercise – particularly on an occasion like a Royal Review, when you have to hit your timing in front of the reviewing stand absolutely exactly. When Her Majesty, the Secretary of State and most of the Air Council are waiting expectantly on the reviewing platform, you had best get your formation there on the second – otherwise, you might spend the next few years in some extremely dispiriting appointment, brooding darkly over where you went wrong. At the very best, you are going to face some very unpleasant interviews with your Station Commander, your Group Commander, your Commander-in-Chief and so on up the line. Possibly worst of all, you will carry with you, for the rest of your career, the 'tag' of the man who messed up a Royal Review. No wonder potential formation leaders lie awake at night in a cold sweat.

Once we had sorted out the general plan of the Review formation and decided on routes and timings, we got down to the serious business of getting in some practice in the air. This initial practice was carried out at station level and was largely undertaken for the benefit of the 'heavy' element. For the fighter pilots involved, close formation flying was a regular 'bread and butter' part of their daily flying routine and they could be expected to be able to perform to a very high standard more or less at the drop of a hat. For the bombers, transports, maritime patrollers and other representatives of the BUFFS (Big Ugly Flying Fings), formation flying of any sort was something they were rarely called on to do. I don't want to overstate this point, in that any 'heavy' pilot can, of course, fly his aircraft in formation it he has to. However, that is just formation flying – not close formation of the standard expected for a Royal Review. To achieve the precision necessary for that sort of exercise, any pilot who isn't doing formation fairly regularly is going to need some hard practice in order to become good enough.

I don't know how the other 'heavies' got on with their practices, but it took a few hard-working sorties to get the bombers welded together – even as a station formation. Compared to the light, fast, '"nippy' fighters, the aircraft were big, relatively slow to accelerate or decelerate and quite heavy on the controls. Moreover, big aircraft generate quite considerable disturbances in the air about them, in the way of downwash, jet efflux and general turbulence. An hour or so of tight formation in a 'heavy' can tire you out very quickly indeed.

When we had got ourselves up to an acceptable standard with our station elements, we started practising getting the whole formation joined up as one cohesive unit. For convenience, some of the fighter elements were detached to other airfields near to the display route – we had a Hunter detachment at Wittering – but the heavier aircraft were all to be launched from their home bases. You can't bring the Air Force to a complete standstill just because of a display flight – no matter how important it is. In terms of our actual assembly technique, I was fairly well clear in my mind as to how NOT to set about it. Some time previously, I had taken part in a fly-past where all of the individual elements were left to time themselves into their proper place in the stream. It was an absolute debacle – all the aircraft got there in the end, but hardly any of the elements were in their proper position in the sequence. This time, we arranged to have each element allocated to a 'holding' position close to the main route and situated in accordance with the element's position in the formation. In this way, all the individual elements had to do was get to their holding point, pick up the approaching formation visually and then slot themselves in at the back end.

The system worked very well and we never had the least trouble in putting the formation together in the correct order – probably because we were doing the assembly the easy way. If you start to make it complicated, you can almost guarantee that you are going to get problems. Where we did run into difficulties was in holding the formation tight enough for the display with so many aircraft ploughing their way through the sky – and particularly with a lot of the big ones up front. The turbulence down the back end was very difficult to cope with. Some of the lighter aircraft were being thrown all over the place and were finding it very hard work to stay in position. I went down the back end myself on one of the rehearsals and got some first-hand experience on just how difficult it was. Even the Victor, heavy as it was, was being tossed about like a canoe in rough water.

Very quickly, we realised that we could only hold very tight display formation for relatively short periods, during which time the pilots sweated to 'stick in' as hard and as close as they knew how. For the rest of the route, we relaxed the tightness a bit and concentrated on making our timing points exactly. In the lead aircraft, Chris Meakin was ultimately responsible for our timing, but we carried two other 'spare' navigators just in case Chris dropped dead in the middle of it all. You must always have an odd number of navigators if they are doing the same job, on the grounds that an even number of them will always disagree among themselves – on principle. You need the odd one to hold the casting vote.

So we flew off rehearsal after rehearsal, gradually working the formation tighter and tighter and concentrating all the way round the route on the all-important timing. When the great day finally arrived, we flew the route in a fairly relaxed spacing until we were about five minutes away from the sight of the spectators. Then, we tightened everything up – just as we had practised it – and made our fly-past in immaculate, precise, close review formation. I know that it looked good – just like they used to do it at Hendon pre-war – because I saw all of the films taken from the ground as we went by. And, what's more, we were timed directly in front of the Reviewing Stand within a second and a half of our scheduled time. I still believe the C-in-C's watch was out, but I would take timing to that sort of accuracy any day. Next day, when we did it all again for the public open day at Abingdon, we got it within a single second.

One of the things I never managed to live down with the rest of my crew was my inability ever to see Abingdon. During the final run-in, there were ground beacon lights every ten miles or so along track, Abingdon had all its runway and strobe lights on and they tell me that you could see the place from fifty miles away. I never saw it once. Every single time, I would get to the final run-in, peering goggle-eyed through the windscreen and yelling anxiously to Ian, "where the Hell is Abingdon?" He would raise his eyes to Heaven for strength and then murmur soothingly "right down there, Boss, for God's sake. Right in front of you." A major airfield, lights all over the place and thousands of spectators – and I never saw it once. Maybe, that's why they made me a bomber pilot.

One of the slightly amusing by-products of the Royal Review was that it threw the bomber and fighter worlds into rather closer contact than they were used to. To make the formation assembly easier, some of the fighter elements were detached to airfields close to the fly-past route and many of these airfields were main bomber bases. As I noted earlier, we had a Hunter detachment living temporarily with us at Wittering, using one of the old dispersal areas on the north side of the airfield. Almost inevitably, with representatives of two totally different operational flying worlds living cheek-by-jowl on the same base and in the same mess, the age-old 'us' and 'them' attitudes, which have existed between fighters and bombers since Pontius was a pilot, began to emerge as a factor in station life.

Personally, I have never really understood why there should be any cause for differences of view or attitude between the two worlds. It must surely be clear, to even the meanest intellect, that bomber men are God's chosen people in the flying world. They are the supreme individualists, always operating completely alone, sustained in their awesome task only by their superb professionalism, iron discipline and outstanding dedication. Unflinchingly, they face all of the hazards of long hours in the air, the darkness of the night and the fury of the weather. They are totally committed to their chosen role in war – to defy the enemy and the elements in reaching out into the very heartland of the foe, there to lay waste both his resources and his will. They are kind, loving, considerate to old ladies and animals, witty, sophisticated and invariably overpoweringly attractive to women.

Now, in stating these self-evident truths, I don't want to give the impression that I have anything other than a high regard for fighter pilots. Not a bit of it! I think it is greatly to their credit that they manage to get their itsy-bitsy little aeroplanes up and down the way they do – I have known cases where they have managed to stay airborne for a whole hour. And I think it's great the way they can tie their own shoelaces and go to the bathroom themselves and everything. Some of them can even drink two whole half pints without falling down. I know that they do lots of useful things in the air, like shooting at towed targets and I'm told that they occasionally hit one. And they do lots of other good things which I'm sure I ought to be able to remember, but can't – just at the moment. Some of my best friends are fighter pilots and splendid fellows they are – in their own way. I just wouldn't want my daughter to become too closely involved with one. Oh, yes, I remember now – they also do fighter 'breaks'.

It was over this little matter of fighter breaks that the rivalry which had been simmering at Wittering finally came to a head. After the rehearsal formation had dispersed, the Victors would get themselves organised into a long stream during the return to Wittering for their normal, 'straight-in', bomber approach to land. Not so the Hunters! With typical flamboyance, they would shift into section fours in echelon starboard and howl in very low and very fast for a spectacular upward break peeling off individually and very rapidly, into the circuit for a stream landing. All 'steely' stuff, but very noisy and quite unnecessary.

On the first few occasions, the Hunters' break was made from a position just about over the end of the runway. After a bit, however, the break point started to move closer and closer to our flight line, until the whole operation had become less of a controlled break and more of a good old-fashioned 'beat-up' of the bomber dispersal area. By the time our formation crews got back on the ground, our non-flying crews and ground personnel were generally darkly brooding and bitter and there was always the irritating tinkle of light-hearted, boyish laughter wafting over to us from the direction of the Hunter dispersal.

Clearly, it was intolerable that this situation should be allowed to continue. After all, we had our acknowledged status as the 'crème de la crème' to consider. To be upstaged by a bunch of juvenile 'jet jockeys' – and on our own base, too – was totally unacceptable. Come what may, they had to be put firmly in their place.

Eventually, after much feverish, secretive conferring in smoke-filled, darkened rooms, well away from any contact with the station authorities, the decision was duly arrived at to fight fire with fire. Low flying was, after all, a daily routine to us. If the fighters liked to play at breaks and beat-ups, we would give them a break and a beat-up to remember.

A couple of days later, when the formation rehearsal was over and we were on our way back to Wittering, my number two and I dropped back to the end of the bomber stream. When the entire stream ahead of us had landed, number two pulled in front of me and went in along the north side of the airfield for a low, noisy, pass right over the fighter dispersal. Low and noisy, but not TOO low and not TOO noisy. His run was only a decoy to bring the fighter lot out of their offices to see what was going on. As he pulled away – in a deliberately less than spectacular climb-out – they were probably thinking that if that was the best we could do, we shouldn't have bothered. Only, it wasn't the best we could do – not by a very long way.

At precisely that instant, I was right down on the deck in the field bordering the fighter dispersal. Not too fast – I didn't want to make too much noise – but fast enough to have a bit in hand to hop over the trees at the edge of the dispersal. Just as the fighter contingent was turning away, slightly disappointed at our 'display', I arrived on the scene. As I approached the very centre of the dispersal area, I stood the Victor on its tail, rammed the throttles forward to the stops and let them have something like eighty thousand pounds of thrust all to themselves in a storm of downwash, jet efflux and ear-splitting, shattering noise.

This little incident landed me with a painful interview with our Station Commander, Group Captain Paul Mallorie, who – as my bad luck would have it – had happened to be in the Air Traffic Control tower just at the wrong time. He gave me well-deserved Hell. "You're a Squadron Commander, Harry," he told me reproachfully, "You're supposed to know better than to get caught up in that kind of nonsense." To his eternal credit, he kept the incident to himself – after all, he was a bomber man too. But I was still lucky to get away with it.

On the credit side, apart from one outburst during which he alleged that his equipment was now scattered all over the airfield and that one or two of his people had been blown off their feet, the fighter squadron commander wouldn't speak to me for weeks. Fighter breaks reverted very strictly to the end of the runway and life returned to normal all round.

I now look back on this piece of idiocy as something for which I richly deserved a very severe reprimand, if not court martial. It was a flagrant breach of airmanship, flying discipline, common sense and aircrew professionalism – a bravado exercise for which I would have made any of my own squadron pilots pay dearly. I know all that. All I can say is that it seemed like a good idea at the time and I still can't bring myself to regret doing it. Like I say, fighter pilots are great but, every so often, you just have to bring them back into line.

CHAPTER 44

DURING 1968, A NUMBER OF momentous events occurred which had a profound influence on the future structure of the Royal Air Force, and, in particular,
on the front-line, operational Commands. Since the late 1930s, the service front-
line had been built around a number of operational commands, defined by the
type of function which they fulfilled. Bomber Command, Fighter Command,
Coastal Command and Transport Command were operational structures tried
and tested both in war and in peace. Even when Transport Command and some
of the Tactical Air Force units were amalgamated together into Air Support
Command, the service front line was still broadly comprised of a number of func-
tion-orientated components.

Since the Korean War in the early fifties, however, there had been a steady and
accelerating decrease in the number of front-line aircraft in the service. New
equipment had become more and more hideously expensive – to the point where
it cost almost as much, in equivalent terms, to produce a single shell for an artillery piece, as it had cost, during the war, to produce a front-line fighter aircraft
like the Spitfire. As the cost of equipment went inexorably up and up, so the
number of aircraft in the front-line of the service went, equally inexorably, down
and down. By the late sixties, for example, we had fewer fighter AIRCRAFT in the
UK than we had SQUADRONS of fighter aircraft in the early fifties. In these circumstances, it was clear that some major rationalisation of the structure of the
service was inevitable to cope with the vastly altered circumstances. In the case of
the operational commands, it came with the amalgamation of all of the front-line
units of the Service within one, newly-created operational Command – Strike
Command, which came into being on 30th April 1968. At a stroke, Bomber
Command, Fighter Command and all the others who had written so much of the
glory into the pages of the history of the RAF, were disestablished and passed into
history. Henceforward, all of the operational front-line units of the service would
operate as functional Groups of one unified command, controlled and directed by
one single Headquarters and commanded by one single Commander-in-Chief.

Shortly after the creation of Strike Command, I attended a dinner and formal
parade at probably the most famous of all bomber stations, RAF Scampton, to
mark the dissolution of Bomber Command. At dinner, the tables were crammed
with past and present luminaries of the bomber world, many of them legends
both within and outside of, the service. On taking my place at table, I found that
my immediate neighbour was Group Captain Leonard Cheshire, VC, DSO, DFC,
one of the famous wartime commanders of Number 617 Squadron – the Dambusters – and the second of only two holders of the Victoria Cross I was ever to
have the chance to meet. Next morning, after a brief ceremony on the airfield, a
single Lancaster flew low overhead to dip in salute as the Bomber Command
standard was lowered for the last time. As it did, an era came to an end.

As 1968 progressed, there were more turbulent events in store for the bomber
element of the infant Strike Command. In particular, two situations developed

which brought still more changes in their train. One was the emergence of operational assessments which indicated clearly that the V bombers – by now getting to be fairly 'long in the tooth' would be likely to sustain very severe losses in carrying out their wartime missions, in the face of ground and air defences which were increasing in effectiveness and capability all the time. The other factor was the achievement of effective operational capability by the Polaris-armed nuclear submarine force of the Royal Navy.

Inevitably, these two factors led to the decision to transfer the nuclear deterrent role from the RAF to the Royal Navy. The aircraft were now outdated by the opposition and the successor aircraft that might have kept the bomber force in existence – TSR2 – had long since been cancelled and the airframes and engines broken up for the scrapheap. Unpalatable as it was, the world of the long range strategic bomber, as so many of us had known it, was coming to an end – at least insofar as the UK and the RAF was concerned. Although the run- down of the V Force was to be carried out over a number of years, the Victor squadrons had, we discovered, already been scheduled for early disbandment to permit the aircraft to be returned to the manufacturers for conversion to the air tanker role. Hence, for Wittering, it wasn't long before the Squadron disbandments began – cheerless occasions where not even the traditional round of parties did much to offset the general gloom. 100's turn came in September and practically my last official duty as Squadron Commander was to attend the 'laying-up' of our squadron standard in the Chapel of the Royal Air Force College, at Cranwell. I spent a few weeks fighting with the Posting Staffs for acceptable re-assignments for the squadron aircrew and then it was all over. The old order had gone for ever – sadly, not with a bang, but with a whimper – and it would never come back again.

Depressing though it all was at the time, the Air Force doesn't pay you to cry in your beer, or wallow in nostalgia over the 'good old days'. One era had ended and a new one was underway. The thing to do was to turn one's back on the past and get on with whatever job one was called on to do today. In my own case, the job I was called on to do was to go back to the Ministry of Defence to the same desk I had sat at before I was posted to 100 Squadron. When I complained that I had done the job before, I was brightly informed, "ah, but this time you will be filling the Wing Commander slot." Useless to point out that, last time, there had been no Wing Commander slot, so that effectively I would be doing exactly the same as I had been doing previously. As usual, I was advised airily that it would be all good career stuff for me and I should just pick up my bowler hat and get on with it. Looking back, I seem to have been singularly unsuccessful in my clashes with the Posting Staffs all through my entire career.

Anyway, there it was – back to the mahogany bomber in Whitehall. And, to be fair, I could have thought of worse postings. At least, the work of forward studies was interesting and it was an activity that I knew something about. Like all good military officers, I gritted my teeth, squared my shoulders and got on with it.

Before long, I was back in the Ministry routine, commuting back and forth from a Married Quarter at Stanmore. The work was as stimulating and interesting as it had been before and I was lucky enough to be working directly for Air Vice Marshal Mike Giddings, who was then the incumbent of the post of Assistant Chief of Air Staff (Operational Requirements). A former test pilot himself and –

so I learned ~ a gifted musician and composer, he once gave me the best piece of advice I ever heard for anybody serving a tour of duty in a staff appointment. "In this place," he advised me, "life is a succession of panics. Every piece of paper is wanted yesterday, if not earlier. If you ever get the feeling that you're being pressured, Harry, go back to your room, lock the door and take the phone off the hook. Then take a sheet of blank paper and write on it in very large capital letters, "WHAT IS IT THAT I AM TRYING TO DO?" "If you do that," he went on, "at least you might be able to remember the objective of the exercise." I certainly found the advice to be invaluable. I have always believed that, in the Ministry, too much time and effort was expended in providing instant answers and not nearly enough time in defining the problem. Using Air Marshal Giddings's technique, you could, at least, keep the primary question in the forefront of your thinking.

I enjoyed working with Air Marshal Giddings because he was one of the few senior officers I ever met who could give you a job and then leave you alone to get on with it. Whenever we discussed a new project for study, he would ask me how long I estimated it would take to complete the work. The normal timescale was anything between four and six months, sometimes longer. When I had given him my estimate, he would mark up his diary, tell me to call him if I needed any assistance and then turn me loose. From that point, I seldom, if ever, heard from him until the due date, when he expected me in his office at ten o'clock sharp with the finished study in my hand.

With a range of varied studies to keep me out of mischief, I worked my way steadily through my first full tour in Whitehall. I liked the work and enjoyed the freedom my Boss allowed me, but I never did come close to enjoying working and living as a London commuter. To be frank, I had hated commuting during my first short spell in the Ministry. I hated it then and I hated it until the day I retired. To me, it was no kind of life at all to spend a large part of the day just getting in to the office in the morning and then back again at night. Often, in the crowded tube, or stuck in some traffic jam, I used to look around at my fellow-commuters and console myself with the thought that, at the worst, I would only have to endure three years of it. For many of them, it was a life sentence. Still, other people's misfortunes aren't really much of a consolation.

There was a certain amount of diversion in the small Married Quarter 'patch' we were living on at Stanmore. All of our neighbours were fellow-commuters to one or other of the Ministry of Defence buildings in London. One, with whom I used to share lifts down to the tube station, was Group Captain Ray Davenport. At the time, he was running a 2.4 litre Jaguar and he asked me to give him a hand one weekend to fix an irritating leak from one of the coolant hoses. The problem was that the leak was from a jubilee clip directly underneath the engine – in a very confined space, which made it very difficult to get at. After we had fiddled around for what seemed ages, Ray finally succeeded in locating the tip of an angled screwdriver into the slot of the jubilee clip. Just as he was on the very point of tightening it up, the pressure from the screwdriver pushed the jubilee clip around bodily on the hose, into a position where we simply couldn't get the screwdriver at it, no matter how much we tried.

At this point, we abandoned the exercise and retired for a beer, Ray remarking that he would get the garage at the station to fix it on Monday. In due course, we dropped the car off at the garage and proceeded into London for our days toil. At the end of the day, we met up again for the return journey. When we got back to Stanmore, Ray went into the garage to settle his bill and pick up the car, while I hung about outside, waiting for him to finish his business. In a matter of seconds, Ray staggered back through the garage door, white-faced, almost incoherent and waving in his hand the bill he had just been presented with. "TO TIGHTENING CLIP ON COOLANT HOSE... £98." Ray was just about apoplectic, but it just goes to show that garages tend to do things the easy way. When they found that the clip really was difficult to get at, they simply lifted out the whole engine.

Our immediate next-door neighbours, Wing Commander Jeremy Jones and his wife Imogen, were great animal lovers. Apart from about nine cats – if memory serves me correctly – they had two dogs, one of which was a Pyrenean Mountain dog called Babbity, of uncertain disposition and not a lot smaller, it seemed, than your average Clydesdale horse. On one occasion, when they were going up to a show in town, Imogen asked Jean if she would look after Babbity during their absence. Now, we both like dogs, but we were rather more used to animals that were smaller than we were. Somewhat uncertainly, Jean asked if Imogen wanted her to sit in their house for the evening. "Good God, no," responded Imogen, appalled, "Babbity would have your leg off. Just go to the letter-box every now and then and make a few soothing noises for her." I honestly don't know if Jean ever carried out her brief: somehow or other, I doubt it.

During the last year of my tour in London, Jean and I decided to get into the private housing sector – well, Jean did – and we bought a house in Caversham Park Village, near Reading, for what seemed, at the time, to be more money than there was in the world. That was probably the luckiest move we ever made, domestically. This was in late 1970, just right at the start of the house prices boom that continued for the next ten years or so. Within six months, we couldn't have bought our garage for what we paid for the whole place. They say that there is a providence that looks after fools and drunks. I think that the same providence must have taken a few minutes off around that time to look after us. When we made the move, we thought that it was all going to be a bit of a gamble. We had no idea what a thoroughly splendid gamble it was going to turn out to be.

One other advantage of going to Reading was that I managed to join Sonning Golf Club, which had a very nice course, a delightful clubhouse and a very friendly membership. Just after I had been accepted for membership, the secretary fixed me up with a game with a slightly built youngster who was visiting the course for the day and looking for someone to play with. So it was that my first ever game at my new Club was played in the pleasant company of a young Carl Mason, now a well-established and successful professional golfer on the tournament circuit.

In due course, my tour at the Ministry came towards its end. On every Annual Report I completed, I had requested a return to flying duties, even though I knew that it was a pretty forlorn hope. I had done my flying tour as a Wing Commander and there was little or no prospect of getting a second one. Still, if you never ask, you never get. So I asked, and, pretty much as I expected, I didn't get. But, at least, I got out of London. For my next assignment, I was appointed to the forthcoming Air Warfare Course at the College of Air Warfare at Manby, in Lincolnshire.

CHAPTER 45

AT THE TIME WHEN I attended it, the Royal Air Force College of Air Warfare existed to meet the requirement of preparing its graduates to fill more senior and responsible appointments in the operations and operations-related, staffs of the Ministry, or the various Command and Group Headquarters. Its objectives were quite different from those of the Staff College at Bracknell, where the instruction was aimed at improving our basic skills in dealing with the fundamentals and procedures of staff work – logical reasoning, concise writing, preparation and handling of paperwork. On the Air Warfare Course, the objective was to lead the student to a thorough understanding of the nature of military power and to a firm grasp of the principles that affect the application of military force towards the attainment of a defined aim.

Most of the students already possessed very considerable practical experience in one or other of the 'sharp-end' branches of the service. All of the representatives of the General Duties Branch had done their time as squadron pilots and most had served in the front-line as either senior flight commanders or squadron Commanders. In their own operational fields, they had all, as the Americans are wont to remark, "paid their dues." What they had to learn at Manby was not so much 'how to do it', but rather 'why to do it', 'when to do it', 'what to do it with' and 'the likely results of doing it'.

This sort of curriculum led the student into very detailed study of the whole range of offensive and defensive weapons systems applicable to all of the different operational roles – their costs, their capabilities, their limitations and the employment options available with them. From this detailed study of the available and prospective 'tools of the trade', the student was led into calculating damage criteria, force requirements, likely loss and unserviceability rates and all the other unglamorous, but nonetheless important, mathematical minutiae which have to be taken into account in the formulation of a practical plan of operations.

In a wider context, basic strategic and tactical options were studied and analysed. This was a particularly interesting part of the course, since it drove home very forcibly the critical inter-relationship between what you want to do and the sort of kit you have available to do it with. We studied the lesson of the pre-war Luftwaffe, the basic strategic thinking of which was largely designed around the concept of an all-powerful bombing force. The idea was admirable – and, probably, even strategically correct – but the Germans never managed to produce the right type of bomber aircraft to make the concept workable. Equally, we studied the RAF's tragic early wartime experience of daylight attacks with formations of bombers – a tactical option, which was abandoned after the first few attempts, had incurred catastrophic losses. At the time, our bombers simply didn't have the defensive firepower to make the tactic work. Later, when the US 8th Air Force got itself properly organised, it provided its aircraft with the necessary defensive firepower – and the escort fighters – to make the concept of massed daylight attacks work successfully.

I think that we all found it fascinating to analyse past campaigns to identify the different strategic and tactical concepts that had determined the way in which the battles had developed. Clearly, waging a war is not simply a matter of the numbers of active participants who are at one another's throats at any given time. If it were, the big battalions would march smartly to victory every time the bell went. In practice, so many other factors are involved – the type and quality of the equipment available, the staff work in terms of planning and preparation, the industrial and financial backing, the standard of training and, always a crucial factor, the morale, stubbornness, – bloody-mindedness if you like – of the combatants.

As well as looking back into the past, we spent a considerable amount of time looking well forward ~ to new weapons concepts which, at the time, were either just coming into service, or were being developed at the research establishments, or by the manufacturers. Would they be practical? Would they be affordable? Would they impinge on existing operational concepts? During the course, I remember seeing a film of US experience in attacking a supply bridge somewhere on the Ho Chi Minh supply trail in North Vietnam. The USAF had mounted literally hundreds of attacks on this particular target with free-fall bombs, which were not particularly accurate ballistically. Although the attacks had been pressed home with very great determination and skill, they had been completely unsuccessful. The countryside around the bridge was pockmarked with literally thousands of bomb craters, but the bridge itself remained unscathed. When the laser-guided bomb was introduced into the USAF inventory in South East Asia, yet another raid was launched against this most difficult target. Two aircraft only – one to carry the bombs and one to mark the impact points with a laser illuminator. That was all it took. All three bombs from the weapon carrier hit the bridge structure fair and square – one at each end and then, when the bridge was literally hanging in the air, the third smack in the middle. Two aircraft, three bombs and a bridge reduced to a pile of rubble. That is weapon system effectiveness with a capital E. But, of course, weapons like these don't come cheap and, like any other system, they have their own limitations.

I found the whole syllabus of the course to be fascinating and, without any question, it brought about, in all of us, a deeper and more penetrating understanding of the business we were involved in. Slowly but surely, the Air Force was transforming us from capable and enthusiastic 'throttle-benders', into knowledgeable and responsible professional military officers, well equipped, both intellectually and practically, to handle the problems of a more senior staff duty.

Away from the classrooms and the private study activities, the course was undoubtedly the best I was ever on from the standpoint of the personalities of the students. It helped a lot that we were all pretty much around the same rank level. Eric Bennett, who had returned from secondment to the Royal Jordanian Air Force, had just made Air Commodore, but the rest of us were all either fairly senior Wing Commanders or fairly junior Group Captains. There was no shortage of strong personalities in the group but, perhaps surprisingly, we all rubbed along together in a very close and friendly way. During the course exercises and discussions, the arguments might well rage fast and furious, but later, in the bar, or in the 'cuddy' – which was an all-night, help-yourself bar for the 'convenience' of the students – we all got along together famously. Some of the courses that went through Manby were notoriously 'po-faced' – all hard work, dedication and strictly no laughs along the way. Somehow or other, our course fell into a different way of doing it. We worked hard, certainly – but we made sure that we enjoyed ourselves to the full while we were about it. Some of the characters from the course remain very vividly in my memory. Paddy Hine, whom I had known in the Ministry – former member of 111 Squadron's 'Black Arrows', and, in his day, one of the best golfers the RAF ever had. He won the Brabazon Trophy, one of the premier amateur events in the UK, when we was just seventeen – the youngest ever to lift the Trophy. Peter Larrad, a Mirage fighter pilot from the RAAF – the sort of character most Britishers imagined the average 'Aussie' to be, blunt, direct and informal, but possessed of a very sharp sense of humour and a holy terror at any party. Reggie Spiers, very experienced test pilot and a wickedly droll wit. Reggie could always see the funny side of any situation – and, somehow or other, make everybody else see it too. Dennis Caldwell ex-Lightning 'ace' and one of those fighter pilots who really couldn't hold more than one half pint of anything. On one memorable occasion, he risked the second half at a party, missed his footing on exit and wound up face down in the gravel of the driveway. Next morning, he wasn't so much bitter about the cuts and bruises on his face and hands, or the ruin of his natty suit. What really burned him was the fact that he had been picked up and hauled off to Sick Quarters for repair "by a bloody bomber pilot." for Dennis, that was the ultimate indignity.

Among so many characters with whom it really was fun to serve, I remember with particular affection John and Edith Scambler. John was a tactical transport pilot and one of the relatively few course members to bring his wife with him to live locally during the course. Edith was Dutch, stunningly attractive and one of the genuinely nicest people I have ever known. For the duration of the Course, her home was 'Open House' to all of us and we were all captivated by her. To John's discomfiture, we would occasionally serenade her with "Tell me pretty maiden, are there any more at home like you." If there are, then Holland must be a delightful place indeed.

To gain first-hand experience, we made many visits to operational units and Headquarters during the course. One such visit, to a NATO sub-headquarters in Turkey was quite an eye-opener – at least as far as I was concerned. I don't really remember what I had expected Turkey to be like, but Izmir was certainly vastly different from anything I had anticipated. It was really very much like Nice, or Beirut as it used to be. Modern, smart and sophisticated, it had, at the same time, the genuine flavour of the 'mysterious east'. The souk – the open-air bazaar – seemed like something straight out of the Arabian Nights – narrow alleyways thronged with jewellers, coppersmiths, basket weavers and merchants of all kinds. Hot, dusty and noisy, teeming with traders, customers and tourists, it gave the impression of being a piece of the living past going on unchanged and unchanging, almost completely unaffected by the modern world. It was a fascinating spot.

On another visit, to the British Army of the Rhine in Germany, we were taken to the Paderborn range area to observe a large-scale tank division exercise. I remember this occasion particularly well, since the range area was very wet and muddy – not at all the sort of environment to have a lot of appeal to delicate flying types. At one stage, a very large Colonel virtually insisted that we lie down on the ground, up to the ears in mud and slush, so that we could get a realistic 'feel' for what a battle was like for the ground troops. As I lay there, very uncomfortable, cold and wet, this large soldier asked me, "What can you see of the battle, then?" When I replied, truthfully, that I really couldn't see a hell of a lot, he seemed quite satisfied and enjoined me seriously to try to remember that sensation whenever I next "flashed over the combat area." I'm not sure that the experience affected my strategic thinking a lot, but it certainly made me a lot more sympathetic to the poor infantry soldier. Give me a nice warm aeroplane any day – and back to base for a bath and a decent meal when your daily dose of operations is over.

Mind you, maybe it's not all bad on the ground. In the middle of this exercise at Paderborn, the course was hosted to lunch 'in the field' by, I think, the Blues and Royals. The occasion was a revelation – a slap-up lunch that would have done credit to any UK Mess, full service, the regimental silver on the tables and a selection of excellent wines to ease away the trauma of having been face down in the mud. All of this, unbelievably, in a tent in the middle of the battle area. When the meal was over, everything was neatly packed up and the Army then got on with the 'war'. I suspect that this sort of activity wasn't exactly an everyday occurrence, but it was very impressive, nevertheless.

When the Air warfare Course came to an end, I found a very unexpected and pleasant surprise waiting for me. I was promoted to acting Group Captain and posted to Headquarters, Strike Command, in the post of Group Captain (Offensive Operations). Domestically, this assignment was very convenient, since the Headquarters at High Wycombe was within easy commuting distance of our house at Caversham. We wouldn't have to change Carol's school for the umpteenth time and I would be able to continue my membership at Sonning Golf Club. All in all, we had every reason to be very happy with the appointment.

CHAPTER 46

AT THE TIME OF MY move to High Wycombe, Strike Command had only been in operation for a matter of a few years and was still very much in the process of resolving the many problems that had arisen from the centralisation of command of all of the operational Air Force under one Headquarters. The first Commander-in-Chief, Air Chief Marshal Sir Wallace Kyle, had only just moved on, to be replaced by a former Battle of Britain fighter pilot, Air Chief Marshal Sir Andrew Humphreys. The new C-in-C was a very remarkable officer, with a wide and diverse experience in the business of higher command and possessed of a razor-sharp intellect that came close to making all who had personal dealings with him feel that they were suffering from retarded mental development.

Very early on in my tour at the Headquarters, there arose some immensely tricky problem, which was proving to be extremely difficult to resolve. I forget now the precise nature of the problem, but it involved most of the Staff in high-pressure meetings, conferences, minute writing and briefings. All of which, as I recall, didn't get us a lot nearer to any practicable solution. Eventually, the still unresolved issue was raised at one of the C-in-C's regular Staff Meetings. After listening to all of the complicated arguments on all sides of the question, Sir Andrew sat back in his chair, peered over the top of his half-glasses and said quietly, "Now, what you seem to be saying to me is......." He then restated the problem, succinctly and exhaustively, in a couple of minutes – and in such a way that, even as he was speaking, the solution became obvious to everyone in the room. When he had finished his short resume, he went on, "It seems to me that what we ought to be thinking about doing is..." and went on to spell out, equally succinctly and exhaustively, all the actions that would be necessary to put the situation right. Later, I became quite used to this sort of 'virtuoso' staff performance from the C-in-C. Quite simply, he had the sort of mind which could unerringly strip away from an argument everything but the absolute essentials, so that the real pros and cons of any situation seemed always to be clearly defined and uncomplicated to him. And, when he had analysed a situation, he then had the ability to see the way ahead clearly and unambiguously and the experience to translate his view of what had to be done into practical courses of action. There were times when one was led to wonder why the RAF bothered to provide him with a staff at all. If he hadn't had to attend conferences, visit units and generally see what was going on around the Command, he could probably have dropped into the office once or twice a day and run the whole Headquarters single-handed.

The Senior Air Staff Officer (SASO) at the Headquarters was one of the real 'characters' of the Service. Air Commodore Phillip Lageson was South African and one of that rare breed, the natural-born leader. Flamboyant and mildly eccentric – he had been known to lash about him playfully with a rhino whip – he never allowed himself to be caught up in 'panic' situations. No matter how pressurised things became, he always managed to remain calm, good-humoured and cheerful. He was an absolute joy to work with and contributed enormously to the very happy atmosphere that existed in the Air Staff side of the Headquarters. On one occasion, during a 'paper' command and control exercise, two very important signals authorizing the subsequent 'operations' arrived in the wrong sequence. Air Commodore Lageson was acting as C-in-C and I was acting as Operations Controller. Because the signals arrived the wrong way around, I initiated a course of action which was totally incorrect, leading to the 'launch' of the nuclear force on the wrong plan and to the wrong targets. The resultant mix-up led inevitably to a complete debacle. As the whole thing degenerated into chaos, Air Commodore Lageson looked me squarely in the eye to enquire, "Harry, do you honestly believe it would have been possible for us to have made a more comprehensive foul-up than this?" When I replied dolefully that I doubted it, he cancelled the exercise on the spot, announced that we would review the situation tomorrow to learn from the mistakes which had been made and invited me to his office for a much-needed gin and tonic. Who wouldn't have felt lucky to be working for a Boss like that?

In the Headquarters, the work of the Air Staff involved the day to day running of the operational elements of the Command, liaising with the Ministry of Defence on the one hand and the Operational Groups on the other to resolve any problems that arose and to develop practical, effective operational procedures to cater for all the contingencies that might have to be faced at any time. This was staff work at its most interesting – all of the work was directly related to the activities of the operational front line and was intimately concerned with all of the current issues of unit strengths, equipment, operational training, exercises, deployments and war and contingency planning. My particular areas of responsibility were thoroughly familiar to me from previous experience and I found the work to be stimulating and rewarding. In one way, I couldn't help thinking back to my days on squadrons when everyone used to delight in blaming every single bad occurrence, from equipment malfunctions to natural disasters, on THEM – the grey amorphous mass of the staffs at headquarters whose one aim in life, so it used to be averred, was to make life impossible for the people on the stations. Now the boot was on the other foot. Now, I was, myself, one of THEM. And, conscientiously as I and everyone else at Headquarters worked, I was uncomfortably certain that the front-liners would still be moaning about the "superannuated pen-pushers in their cushy chairs at Group/Command/the Ministry" who were generally regarded as having last had experience in a cockpit sometime around the time of Bleriot.

Because the work dealt so intimately with the front-line, the sense of being cut off from the actual flying was much more intense than it ever was in the Ministry. In the Ministry, the whole atmosphere of civilian dress, commuting and a working environment right in the centre of London, made you feel as if the world of uniforms, station life and flying was something that you had been through in a previous existence and was now a million miles away. You became somewhat inured to being removed from it all. At an operational Headquarters, on the other hand, you felt that you were so close to it and yet not close enough truly to be a part of it. At times, the compulsion to get back among the front-line again became so overpowering that it became necessary to fall back on the old standby of restless staff officers – the staff visit. During these occasions, you inflicted yourself on some luckless station in the guise of "seeing things at first hand." I don't believe that the stratagem ever fooled anybody. All of the really useful staff visits were made by the Squadron Leader or Wing Commander role specialists. Still, if you didn't overdo things, an occasional judicious staff visit did, at least, get you out of the office and some sympathetic Station Commander might be sufficiently moved to offer you a trip in one of his aeroplanes. Incidentally, it was during one of these staff visits that I first encountered what I later came to recognise as the 'translation to Group Captain' syndrome. Until my promotion, I had generally been treated as just another normal individual of average health and mental capability. Somewhat to my discomfiture, I discovered that promotion changed all that quite markedly. I found that people were continually trying to carry my brief case – presumably on the grounds that I was now well past carrying it myself. Young officers with whom I engaged in conversation seemed to take inordinate pains to enunciate very slowly and clearly – somewhat in the manner in which one might address the slightly deaf, or the plainly half-witted. I almost expected them to rush across to help me to my feet when getting out of a chair. It is quite extraordinary the effect that this sort of behaviour has on one. When people start treating you as though you were tottering on the verge of senile decay, you have to resort to muttering firmly to yourself, "I am only 45. I am in full possession of all my faculties. I am only 45. I am in."

Almost invariably, any job has some type of 'perk' associated with it and it wasn't long before I discovered that one of the perks which went with mine was the position of Chairman of the Fincastle Committee. At first, I thought that this was simply another Committee that I had to chair, but further research disclosed a much more pleasant reality. In the maritime reconnaissance and anti-submarine world, there had long been a competition between squadrons of the 'old commonwealth' – the UK, Canada, Australia and New Zealand. This competition – the Fincastle Competition ~ was held periodically at a location agreed between the participants as being convenient to them all. Since at least three of the competitor nations are separated by about half the globe, it is perhaps not altogether surprising that the location agreed upon for the competition should, more often than not, turn out to be a rather pleasant spot. The adjudicators for the competition represented the four Air Forces involved. The Canadians, Australians and New Zealanders were represented by the air advisers to their respective High Commissions in London. The RAF, by tradition, supplied the Chairman of Adjudicators and, by some great good fortune, this position was discharged by the officer holding the appointment of Group Captain (Offensive Operations) at Strike Command. In other words, by me. Not bad for someone whose experience in the role was limited to reading about it and on every uncomfortable sortie in a Shackleton from Kinloss during a visit with the Air Warfare Course.

At first, I was much concerned that I might have to exhibit some penetrating knowledge of the anti-submarine world in order to get the job done, but I quickly learned that the adjudicators really had little to do other than to get their staffs to set up the initial organisation for the event, attend on-site during the flying and present the prizes at the end of it all. When I discovered that Peter Larrad ~ by now Air Adviser to the Australian High Commission – was to be one of the adjudicators, I relaxed somewhat. If an Australian fighter pilot could get himself into the act, I reckoned that I was not going to be too much out of place. I relaxed even more when I learned that the competition was to be held in Singapore ~ on the somewhat doubtful grounds that this was a location equally convenient – or, perhaps, equally inconvenient – to all the participants. In the event, I couldn't accompany the adjudication party on their flight out to Singapore, because I was tied up with some piece of work at Headquarters, which delayed my departure until they were already on-site. When I did finally totter down the aircraft steps at Changi after the long night flight out from UK, it was to find Peter Larrad and the New Zealand adjudicator waiting for me as a sort of two-man reception committee. I should say that the New Zealand representative from London had not been able to get away, so a replacement, a very lively Group Captain of the RNZAF, had been flown in from New Zealand to take his place.

On arrival, I was pretty tired and quite ready to head for the nearest bed to sleep off the effects of flight out. Not so my reception committee. They had been out on the town all night and had just about worked up enough of a head of steam to be ready for a party. They compromised sufficiently to allow time for breakfast before we roared off to do the town again – the breakfast made memorable for me by my New Zealand colleague's selection of a light meal to fortify him for the day – half a raw pineapple, a large steak and half a dozen fried eggs and a quart of beer. They breed them hardy on the other side of the world. I hastily swallowed my tea and toast, dumped my bags at the International Hotel and was swept off on a twelve-hour rampage through the fun spots of Singapore City – a day-long jaunt that passed in a daze of massive over-indulgence and plain fatigue. When I finally fell into bed that night, I had almost forgotten where I was and what I was supposed to be doing there. My colleagues, seemingly none the worse for wear, appeared to be planning another 'offensive sweep' downtown. To keep the record straight, I should make it quite clear that the Fincastle adjudication committee discharged all of its responsibilities during the event, soberly, responsibly and effectively. I wish I could say as much for the way we passed our off-duty time. Singapore is a bustling, vibrant, exciting place and it offers a full range of entertainments and diversions for those with the stamina to last the pace. Personally, I began to run out of stamina somewhere around day three, by which time, a general lack of sleep, over-exposure to the 'bright lights' and too many outings to "a little place I know" had taken a heavy toll. The relentless heat didn't help a lot either. Hangovers are bad enough in a cold climate, but in glaring sunlight and temperatures in the high eighties, they feel even worse.

After a few days of this hectic social life, I felt the need for a night off – a quiet dinner in the hotel and early to bed. I pleaded the necessity to catch up on some paper work as an excuse to duck out of another night on the town and, when the others had gone, settled down for a relaxed evening at something like a normal pace. On my way into dinner, I stopped by the hotel bar for a pre-prandial whisky and fell into conversation with three Japanese who were chatting animatedly about golf. When they discovered that I was from Scotland and had actually played St Andrews, I was made most heartily welcome in their company. We had a couple of drinks together and then they very kindly invited me to join them for dinner so that we could continue our conversation. I have a fondness for Japanese food, so I was happy to accept – a nice quiet meal, I thought, chatting about golf and then off for an early night in bed. I should have known better. I should have remembered the Japanese predilection for drinking whisky. We wound up in a Japanese restaurant on the seafront, gorging ourselves on the most delicious chillied crabs, fished barehanded out of a large galvanised metal tub and washed down with neat Johnnie Walker. Just the ticket for a quiet night in. Next morning, not only was the hangover back in full force, but there was a considerable digestive disorder to go along with it.

When the Fincastle competition came to an end, at least two of the countries involved had reason to be quite happy with the results. The RAF Nimrod crew actually won the event, but the captain of the winning crew was a young Australian Flying Officer serving on an exchange tour of duty with the RAF at Kinloss. I presented the prizes, delivered myself of a few well-chosen words to mark the occasion and headed off back to High Wycombe. Singapore is a marvellous place to visit but, next time I go there, I intend to avoid, like the plague, all contact with Australians, New Zealanders and Japanese. Then, maybe, I'll have a chance of remembering a little of what it was actually like.

CHAPTER 47

BACK IN THE FAR-OFF DAYS when, as 'green' young officers, I and my contemporaries were being introduced to secondary duties, we used to mutter darkly that it must surely be marvellous to be a senior officer, with a whole staff available to do the bulk of the work for you and no secondary duties to divert you from your primary occupation. It just goes to show exactly how green we were, that we almost believed this to be the case. When you are spending weary hours of what you regard as your spare time in counting fire extinguishers or inspecting barrack blocks for structural deficiencies, there is an understandable tendency to imagine that these and other secondary duties have been dreamed up by THEM simply in order to keep you on the go for all the hours of the day. You fall to dreaming of what it must be like to be one of THEM, light-heartedly unloading all of the really tedious jobs on to some other poor sod's back.

What you don't realise at that stage, of course, is that secondary duties are by no means limited to very junior officers. There are secondary duties and secondary duties. They come in a variety of forms and they come – unhappily, for youthful dreams – at each and every rank level in the service. When I was commanding 100 Squadron, I landed the job of President of the Mess Committee and I can honestly say that I would much rather have been counting fire extinguishers any day.

I hadn't been at Strike Command all that long when the question of secondary duties arose. There was a list of such duties considered appropriate to Group Captain Rank and involving a wide range of service, social and recreational activities throughout the Command. Selections from the list were regularly 'farmed-out' to the various Group Captains on the Headquarters Staff. It was generally pure chance which determined the nature of the duty that came one's way – a matter of which secondary duty became vacant at the time when one happened to be available. At this stage of my career, however, I was sufficiently wise in the ways of the world not to wait around to be landed with some chore that had simply come up in rotation. Instead, on discovering that the position of Chairman of Strike Command Golf was about to become vacant, I jumped in rather smartly to volunteer for the post.

Over the years, I had so much sheer fun and enjoyment out of service golf that I regarded my job as Chairman of Strike Command golf less as a chore and more as a welcome opportunity to put something back into service golf in repayment for all of the pleasure I had been afforded from it.

In my primary job, I found that, included among the operational role responsibilities of the Offensive Operations Staff at Strike Command, was the RAF's tactical strike/attack force. This was a role that had been bedevilled by difficulties for many years as a result of the cancellation, or abandonment, of a number of aircraft projects. Originally, it had been planned to replace the ageing Canberras with TSR2 which was actually being flown on its development trials when the decision to cancel the project was made. At the time of TSR2's cancellation, a number of alternative Canberra replacement options were considered: A UK variable geometry design, an Anglo-French variable-geometry design and the American F-111. All held centre-stage for brief periods before they, too, were rejected for one reason or another. And, all the time, the Canberra was becoming more and more outdated as a front line combat aircraft – by this time, it had been in service with the operational squadrons for something like twenty years. There was a project underway for a multinationally produced aircraft, which was seen as the long-term solution to the tactical strike/attack role equipment problem, but this project, at the time, was barely into the early design stages. This Multi Role Combat Aircraft (MRCA) – referred to variously as 'Mother Riley's Cardboard Aeroplane', or 'Must Redesign Canberra Again – would ultimately, in the shape of the highly successful Tornado, solve the problem. At the time, however, Tornado was a long way off in the future and something needed to be done quickly to maintain a credible capability in the role.

The solution arrived at was to take over from the Royal Navy their force of Buccaneer aircraft as an interim measure, pending the entry into service of the MRCA. Some years previously, the RAF had rejected the Buccaneer as a potential Canberra replacement on the grounds that it had been designed specifically for naval operations from aircraft carriers – and, moreover, the RAF's chosen replacement, the ill-fated TSR2, was, at the time, seemingly well on course for entry into service. Oddly enough, the 'last-resort' acceptance of the Buccaneer proved to be very much to the RAF's advantage. It turned out to be a much better aircraft than anyone had honestly anticipated and in the relatively new low-level operational environment, it had the very great advantage of having been designed, from the outset, to operate very close to the ground. It had a high wing loading and it rode the gusts and turbulence very well. It was very strongly built, had a good range, could carry its weapon load internally and had a very reasonable turn of speed. All in all, it turned out to be an effective and economic gap-filler between the Canberra and the Tornado.

With the acquisition of the Buccaneers, there was a lot of work to be done at both Command and Group Headquarters in establishing and refining the options for tactical employment, standard operating procedures, training programmes and equipment up-dating programmes. The Buccaneer's capability for in-flight refuelling brought about a requirement to integrate the strike/attack operations with the operations of the tanker force and the maritime aspects of the role involved much co-operation and co-ordination with the operations of naval forces. In this latter context – the co-ordination of strike/attack aircraft operations with the activities of naval forces – the Danish Air Force and Navy had done a lot of work in integrating the operations of attack aircraft and fast patrol boats in attacks on naval surface units, convoy shipping and amphibious assault forces. We had a number of discussions with their staffs on the subject, as a result of which I, my Buccaneer role expert Wing Commander Dickie Dawes and another Group Captain from the Headquarters, were invited to attend one of their exercises in the Kattegat to observe their tactics being put into effect. In due course, our little party flew to Copenhagen for a round of meetings and discussions, preparatory to being briefed on the exercise that we were to witness. To get to the exercise location, we were, as I recall, to be taken by helicopter to, I think, the port of Arhus and thence by fast patrol boat to the frigate that was to be the command ship for the exercise.

Now, I have long since suspected that I am something of a Jonah insofar as any form of ship is concerned. On the way out to the United States, the Queen Mary, with me on board, fouled its propellers at Cherbourg. On a 'Navy Day' outing from Staff College, the destroyer I was on collided with another vessel, and, when I was on a US aircraft carrier off San Diego, they fired the wrong catapult and flung off some poor soul who had barely got his engines started, while his 'full-throttle' companion on the adjoining catapult was left wondering why it was that he was being left behind, still firmly attached to the deck.

When the helicopter dropped us off at the harbour, I found that the crew of the fast patrol boat, which was waiting for us, looked as if they had stepped straight put at the pages of some Viking Saga. All tall, heavily bearded and weather-beaten, they gave the impression that, given a horned helmet and a double-headed axe, they were just about ready to take on all comers.

The craft we were led on to was quite sizeable – a converted German E-boat – and the harbour was quite small. As we three 'light blues' stood on the foredeck to try to keep out of the way of the crew, there was a great bellowing of orders, a shattering roar from the engines and the vessel rocketed away from the dock – straight into the side of a small Norwegian yacht which was moored nearby. Un-fortunately, at that precise instant, one of the crew of the yacht was up at the top of the mast doing something very nautical. The shock of the impact caused the mast of the yacht to whip smartly, instantly catapulting this unfortunate individ-ual straight into the harbour. For a minute or two, pure bedlam reigned, with both crews – and, apparently, a sizeable proportion of the population of the town – all yelling at one another in an apparently extremely forthright exchange of views. We three RAF types immediately resorted to typically British aloofness in a crisis situation by gazing fixedly seaward to mark our dissociation from this unseemly continental uproar.

After a bit, the furore subsided somewhat. The unfortunate mast climber was fished out of the water, there was another shattering burst of engine and our ves-sel shot off backwards – this time, straight into the harbour wall. I began to suspect that the throttles on the craft had no intermediate position between fully shut and fully open. We hung on even tighter, still gazing glassily out to sea and secretly wondering if we would ever get much further than the gap in the harbour wall before we sunk something, or were ourselves sunk. Most of the town, it now seemed, was on hand to offer vociferous comment or advice and it was becoming increasingly difficult to maintain the 'stiff upper lip' facade in the face of the in-creasing pandemonium. Eventually, after a few more ricochets off various buoys, harbour walls and other vessels, we staggered out into the open sea. The crew gave every impression of enjoying themselves enormously, but I suspect that my col-leagues, like myself, were already worrying about our transfer to the frigate when – and, possibly, if – we ever managed to make contact with it. The prospect of being dangled about in a breeches-buoy between two ships crewed by these rum-bustious characters wasn't exactly something that we were looking forward to.

In due course, when we did, in fact, make contact with the frigate, things turned out to be a whole lot worse than anything that we might have fearfully anticipated. While I was still waiting for the dreaded breeches-buoy to be produced, I observed, with undiluted horror, a scrambling net being draped along the side of the frigate's hull. Turning to the Captain of our craft, I found him gesturing towards the other ship as he announced cheerfully, in fractured English, "Ja, Ja. I get in close. Then you joomp." I didn't want to believe what I had heard. "Joomp," the man had said. He had to be off his rocker. All very well for a bunch of latter-day Vikings to go leaping about from one ship to another in the open main, but definitely not to be recommended for mature and responsible RAF staff officers, no longer quite in the first flush of impetuous youth.

Still, there didn't seem to be any practicable alternative on offer at the time. As the two vessels closed, we positioned ourselves along the side and watched the side of the frigate get closer and closer. We appeared to be going up and down like a yo-yo, so that the thought of missing the net altogether was very much in my mind. Like my companions, I suspect, I steeled myself, consigned my soul to the Lord and thought bravely of England, Home and Duty. When, at last, our Captain bellowed "JOOMP," we joomped. Believe me, we joomped! My Group Captain colleague – somewhat less sylph-like in build than myself – almost made it onto the deck in one, so galvanised was he. We all three hit the scrambling net with all available fingers hooked like talons of steel – I don't think that ten wild horses could have loosened my grip on the ropes. For a second or two, we clung on for dear life, terrified beyond imagination, until some of the crew of the frigate swarmed nonchalantly over the side to drag us aboard. With great good humour, they fed us with steaming hot coffee, generously laced with brandy, to restore us somewhat and bustled us forward into the operations centre to watch the exercise get under way.

To be absolutely honest, I don't remember a great deal of the exercise. It was very competently executed and all of the elements involved seemed to work together very smoothly. Unfortunately, I kept on breaking out in a cold sweat every five minutes or so and even the assurance that we would be taken back to harbour and landed ashore in a conventional manner did little to stop my trembling. From that day onward, I have stayed rigorously away from marine vessels of any size, shape, or form whatsoever. If I can't walk there, drive there, or fly there, I don't go. Sailing may be fine for sailors, but my very firm conviction is that it is definitely not for me.

After I had been at High Wycombe for about a year or so, I had an informal chat with Air Vice Marshal Lageson who was sounding out the members of his staff as to their ideas on where they ought to go next, when their tour of duty at the Headquarters came to an end. He had assumed that I would want to go back into the bomber world but, much as I had enjoyed every minute of my time in both the Canberra Force and the V Force, I felt that that particular era was over, or very nearly so and that it was time to think about something different.

My predecessor in post had gone from High Wycombe into the Buccaneer force and there was certainly a lot of appeal in considering following him in that direction. I had, however, done a fair bit of low-flying in my time and I felt that there might be something of doing a familiar job about the role – albeit with a new aircraft and with new weapons options. However, I suppose that, over the years, I had developed a personal affinity for big aircraft and I felt that my previous experience could probably best be deployed to advantage in the world of the multi-engined 'heavies'. Jack Allavie used to say that he liked the sort of aeroplane where, if the engineer reported that number forty-seven was running a bit rough, your immediate response ought to be "which side?" I felt much the same way myself.

It's odd how pilots come to develop a liking for one class of aircraft, or one type of flying. In many cases, personal preferences arise from the simple fact that you are posted in to a particular role at the start of your flying career and you develop competence and experience in that role to the extent that it becomes familiar and comfortable to you. Any other type of flying is, somehow, different and, because you are not so used to it, you tend to like it rather less. So, for example, you start off on fighters or ground-attack aircraft and you become used to the business of one-man, or at most two-man crew operation, high performance aircraft and relatively short endurance sorties. Start off the other way and you become attached to sizeable crews, aircraft which are large and heavy and long hours in the air.

My own case was somewhat different from the normal situation, in that, although my squadron tours had been on bomber aircraft, I had, in fact, done a lot of fighter flying – both in the instructional role and in test flying. I had flown more types of fighter aircraft than I had bombers and many of the bombers I had flown had been capable of higher performance than contemporary fighter types. In the early fifties, there wasn't a fighter in the sky that could match the Canberra for altitude and speed. And, later on, the B-58 Hustler and the R-5 Vigilante would run away from any of the front-line fighters of their day.

In the end, I suppose that the factor which, more than any other, conditioned me to 'heavies' was flying as part of a crew. I had been lucky enough to do a lot of flying which was both stimulating and rewarding, but nothing I had done ever gave quite the same unique pleasure and professional satisfaction as doing the job as part of an efficient and well-integrated crew. When you land from a sortie during which every crew member has fulfilled his individual crew function and the whole team has blended together as a single, cohesive entity to get the task accomplished smoothly and effectively, there is a feeling of satisfaction and achievement which, at least to me, is different and better than anything else in the flying world.

To be quite fair, I must admit that my personal preference, in so far as role flying was concerned, didn't weigh all that heavily with me when I was trying to come to a conclusion about where I would prefer to go after I had finished at Strike Command. After all, if I were lucky enough to be posted to a flying Station, it would be as Commanding Officer and not as a squadron aircrew member. There would be no question of being part of a crew. Any flying I managed to get would be purely on the basis of being fitted in as an extra crew member in order to accumulate experience of the standard operating procedures and operational techniques.

With all of these considerations at the back of my mind, I reviewed the field of likely available options. Lacking front-line squadron fighter experience, I was unlikely to get either a fighter station or a ground-attack station. I had already had a fair crack at the bomber and low-level strike/attack roles, and, although I had done a lot of transport flying in a variety of aircraft, I wasn't overly attracted to the role. That left only one operational area which seemed to fill the bill as far as I was concerned – the long-range maritime reconnaissance and anti- submarine world of what used to be called Coastal Command, now operating as Number 18 Group of Strike Command.

The more I thought about it, the more the idea of moving into the maritime role began to appeal to me. Although I had no previous flying experience in the role, my responsibilities at the Headquarters did include the 18 Group maritime aircraft, so that I was familiar with the general concepts of strategy and tactics which formed the basis of the Groups operations. The faithful old Shackeltons had quite recently been phased out of service in the maritime patrol role and had been replaced by the Nimrod – a much modified development of the famous de Havilland Comet. The Nimrod was a big aircraft, was packed with advanced electronic surveillance and detection equipment, carried a very large crew of electronic specialists and flew long sorties – just the sort of aeroplane I liked. I had never actually flown one, but I had flown the Comet – and liked it. Taken all in all, the maritime role seemed to offer exactly what I was looking for. A new experience and a new challenge. I made up my mind that, if the opportunity arose, I would opt for a role change at the end of my Headquarters tour.

In due course, I had another chat with Air Marshal Lageson when I had the opportunity to discuss the matter with him. As it happened, it seemed that my newly arrived at idea of changing roles and expressing a preference for the maritime role, fitted in rather neatly with a policy which the Ministry had recently been considering to try to get one or two people with extensive jet experience into posts at the 18 Group flying units. Most of the middle ranking officers in the Group had a very considerable background in the maritime role, but the bulk of their flying experience had been accumulated in piston-engined aircraft – the Shackelton and the Neptune. Few had had the opportunity to get very much experience in modern jet aircraft and, with the conversion of the front-line squadrons to the Nimrod, it was felt that a measured injection of jet-experienced Squadron and Station Commanders into the Group could be of value. So it was that, when my tour of duty at the Headquarters came to an end – very much sooner than I had anticipated – I found myself packed off again to the School of Refresher Flying, carrying the somewhat impressive sounding appointment of Station Commander (designate), Royal Air Force, St Mawgan. I could hardly believe my luck. Just over eighteen months in post at the Headquarters and then off again back to the front-line. Back to flying – and on a new aircraft – and back to command. What more could anyone have asked for?

CHAPTER 48

WHEN I CLIMBED BACK into the cockpit of the Jet Provost for my first re-familiarisation flight at the School of Refresher Flying, I did so with the somewhat depressing realisation that I was embarking on what would probably prove to be the last tour of flying duty of my career. So far, I had been incredibly lucky in having managed to get a flying appointment in every rank which I had held, but I was very conscious of the fact that, beyond Group Captain, there are only one or two very specialised appointments which offer any chance of flying to the holders. Many people – and, in particular, young pilots – assume that this situation stems from the fact that older aviators can no longer cope with the stresses and strains involved in operating high-performance aircraft. Among the young – and particularly among young pilots – it seems to be the generally held view that incipient senility sets in somewhere around the age of thirty-five. I often suspect that my own son regards it as something of a source of wonder that I can still manage eighteen holes of golf without a qualified medical practitioner in attendance. Obviously, I accept that flying modern operational aircraft in the front-line squadrons of the RAF is a demanding business, both physically and mentally. But lots of older pilots have managed to do it – and, moreover, do it outstandingly well. What you lose over the years in razor-edged reactions, you compensate for in experience, judgment and well-founded confidence in your own ability. Given reasonable physical condition, there is no reason why a pilot should not continue flying well into his fifties. Many very distinguished pilots in the world of civil aviation have, in fact, gone on well into their sixties.

The basic reason for the lack of flying opportunities at higher ranks in the service is simply that it is not a cost-effective proposition to pay a Group Captain, Air Commodore or Air Marshal to do a primary job which can be done just as effectively by a junior – and, hence, less expensive – practitioner. By the time the average officer reaches senior rank, the Air Force has made a pretty massive investment in his professional and staff training – and they get a better return for their money by having him do the jobs in the command, staff and administrative fields for which his expensive training and experience have fitted him, than by having him spend the rest of his career enjoying himself in a cockpit. If the service didn't take this somewhat 'commercial' view, we could all look forward to having the time of our lives, driving aeroplanes all over the place, on an Air Marshal's salary. A lovely thought, which many Air Marshals would support enthusiastically – but, regretfully, not one that the Treasury would take to very kindly. In any case, one has to view the situation philosophically. To prevent the stultification of the higher rank structure, there is an evident requirement to have a continuous flow of operationally capable, front-line experienced, officers moving upwards through the various rank levels to the very top. There is always room at the top for those with the application, skill, experience and personal qualities to fit them for the higher levels. Hence, it is crucial continuously to provide room at the bottom to allow the 'new boys' to get the chance to develop the skills and personal qualities which they are going to need as they progress.

As the system works, Wing Commander is generally the last rank at which the balance of a pilot's responsibilities are tilted primarily towards his flying duties. Beyond Wing Commander, while you may as a Group Captain command a flying station and even get quite a few hours into your log-book, there is always the consideration that any flying you might be fortunate enough to get is likely to be very much on a part-time or opportunity basis. You will not be a part of a crew or a squadron and you will not be rated as operationally qualified. You simply have to accept the hard fact that, from now on, flying is not and will never again be your primary function. Like it or not, you are now an executive and that is what you are going to be for the rest of your career.

There is also the point that, with increasingly demanding responsibilities outside the cockpit environment, it becomes more and more difficult to maintain the very high standards of professional knowledge and familiarity with procedures, which are so much an essential part of the pilot's job. In fact, to be brutally honest, it becomes downright impossible. I could understand and sympathise with, many of the senior officers who were desperately keen to keep themselves in close touch with front-line flying, but I never did have a lot of admiration for those who did their flying only when they had an experienced squadron pilot or instructor along to hold their hand. They may have been able to delude themselves that they were still able to 'cut the mustard', but they seldom, if ever, deluded anybody else. I always felt very strongly that when the time came when I didn't have the opportunity, or the time, to do the job professionally – and unaided – I wouldn't want to do it at all. I loved and respected flying too much ever to want to play at it.

I should, perhaps, make it crystal clear that these weighty considerations didn't exactly overburden me as I launched off on my refresher flying course. I had been away from a cockpit for just over five years and I couldn't wait to get back to it again. If I was starting off on my last real flying tour, then I was bound and determined to enjoy every single minute of it. Fortunately, my time on the ground didn't seem to have affected my ability to drive an aeroplane. Once I had become familiar with one or two new procedures and got a couple of hours in the air under my belt, it felt as if I had never been away. On the refresher course, with no responsibilities other than to polish up the old skills again, it was sheer bliss to feel the aeroplane 'talking' to me again through the feel of the controls and to coax it through all of the basic exercises in stalling, spinning, aerobatics, formation flying and instrument flying. I suppose that the ease with which most RAF pilots come very quickly back to a high level of competence after a spell on the ground is the most eloquent testimony possible to the standards of training that the RAF provides for its pilots right from the very first time they take to the air as *ab initio* students. They train you so well that the mechanics of flying really do become second nature. Some people, I know, allege that the RAF overtrains their aircrew, but I have never accepted that contention. I would unhesitatingly claim that the average RAF aircrew member is more capable, more self-reliant and more adaptable than any other aircrew in the world. They ought to be – their training is rigorous enough and expensive enough. But, at the end of the day, when you assess their operational competence, discipline and resourcefulness, every penny spent on their training can be regarded as money very well spent.

In the interests of complete accuracy, I should perhaps be entirely honest and admit that my return to flying did present me with one minor problem. After five years on the ground – most of it spent sitting behind a desk – my stomach had got out of the habit of putting up with the stresses of the job and it took me quite a few sorties before I 'hardened up' again sufficiently to get over the queasiness which attended my first few aerobatics and spins. I had never been airsick in my life – and I had no intention of starting at Leeming – but I did, at first, experience mild twinges of discomfort when the sky started whirling around again.

Inevitably, when you develop an Achilles Heel – however temporary – someone can be guaranteed to happen by to aggravate the affliction. In my case, it turned out to be John Parker, Station Commander at Leeming and an old friend. On the evening before my final handling test, John and his wife had me round to their home for dinner, at which occasion I wined and dined most pleasurably. During the evening, John, ever the most hospitable of hosts, listened most sympathetically and understandingly to my complaints about the effects of spinning on my over-sensitive tum, the while he urged his wife to help me to "just another soupçon" of a most delicious dessert which, as I recall, seemed to have been constructed very largely out of thick whipped cream.

Next morning, at the Refresher Squadron office, I found that John had most courteously arranged to take my Final Handling Test himself. Still more than somewhat bloated from my excesses of the previous evening, I was relieved to find that I would be flying with one of my own contemporaries rather than with one of the young 'tigers' who would be likely to try to turn me inside out – and enjoy every minute of it. At least, John understood the sensitivities of middle-aged re-tread aviators and would probably confine himself to a quick 'once round the pattern' and easy on the aerobatics. After all, he had been stuffing himself the night before, too. Well, we did go once around the pattern and we did go easy on the aerobatics – but for all the wrong reasons. The trip lasted one hour and thirty-five minutes, of which, in my admittedly jaundiced recollection, something like an hour and twenty minutes was spent in spinning. Straight spins and inverted spins followed one another in an apparently never-ending sequence of lurching, wallowing, spirals earthward. What with the earth spinning violently around under the nose and the aeroplane pitching up and down under me like a bucking horse, I had to fight a constant battle with my stomach which seemed to be under a strong compulsion to leave me – and quite violently, at that. Fortunately, for my personal pride, I won but – as the Duke of Wellington remarked on another occasion – there were times when it was a damned close run thing.

When John Parker signed me off as competent to be returned to front-line flying, he could have added that he had tested me to the limit and not found me wanting. For my part, I resolved to stay away from rich feeding and to embark on a course of rigorous exercises to get myself – and, in particular, my abdominal region – thoroughly well hardened-up again.

Immediately on completion of my Jet Provost refresher flying, I went straight down to St Mawgan to start my conversion on to the Nimrod. As it happened, I arrived there on the day when the annual Easter leave break was starting. The bulk of the station personnel, other than those on essential duties, were going off on leave, so that I had a few days of peace and quiet in the Mess to get myself organised and to become acquainted with the place, before I had to start work on the Nimrod conversion course in earnest.

CHAPTER 49

ST MAWGAN IS THE MAJOR RAF maritime flying base in England, located just outside Newquay, in Cornwall and very close to the delightful little village of St Columb Major. This is a very picturesque part of the country, right on the dramatic Cornish coastline, and in summer it was thronged with tourists – referred to locally as 'Emmets'. The local roads could perhaps more properly be described as country lanes and when the tourists were out in force, it could be something of a nightmare trying to move about in the local area. I can remember one occasion when Jean tried to get into Newquay during the height of the tourist season. The place was less than five miles away but, after dawdling about in the car for something like forty five minutes, she still hadn't even reached the main road. Sometime later, when I had to cope with major exercises and 'no-notice' Tactical Evaluations, I used to dread having to order a station recall during the hours of daylight in the summer months. With a great many of the station personnel living off-base, the traffic chaos around the base was appalling and could – and frequently did – result in inordinate delays in getting some of the key personnel back on to the station. Somewhat unusually, the station executives used to pray that all exercises would be called in the middle of the night – hard on the families, perhaps, but at least you could move on the roads.

The importance of easy movement on the roads around the base stemmed from the fact that less than twenty per cent of the station strength actually lived on-base at St Mawgan. This odd situation came about from the original disposition of the RAF's maritime force flying units in the South West. In the days of the Shackleton, there were two major flying bases in Cornwall – St Mawgan and a sister station, St Eval, situated some six or seven miles to the North. When the Nimrod was introduced into service, it was found that the runway at St Eval couldn't be lengthened sufficiently to accommodate the new aircraft – one end was practically in the sea and the other end abutted on to non-Ministry of Defence property. At the same time, the housing area at St Mawgan couldn't be extended to cope with the increased numbers of personnel required to operate, service and support the Nimrod force. As a result of these circumstances, the somewhat unhappy solution was arrived at whereby the aircraft would operate from St Mawgan and the bulk of the married personnel would be accommodated at the Married Quarter sites at St Eval. At St Mawgan, accommodation was provided only for unmarried personnel in the various messes and Barrack Blocks and for seven families in Married Quarters assigned to the key station executives who, by the nature of their responsibilities, were required to be on immediate call at all times. Even at that, St Eval couldn't cope with the number of families involved when the station came up to full strength. Additional Married Quarter sites at Padstow, Newquay and St Merryn had to be brought into use and other families had to be 'farmed out' to Air Force hirings scattered virtually throughout the length and breadth of Cornwall. When one adds to that the number of families who had bought their own homes in the local area, it can be realised why it was that contacting the off-base personnel and getting them back on to the station at very short notice, presented major problems which were never easily resolved.

St Mawgan itself was a very sizeable base which actually embraced two airfields within its boundaries. There was the modernised St Mawgan proper, from which all operations were conducted and there was also the wartime airfield of Treble-zue which had long been out of active use, but which was used for glider flying and as a storage facility. The main base supported the operations of Number 48 Squadron, one of the Nimrod force front-line squadrons, Number 236 Operational Conversion Unit, the unit which handled the conversion training of all aircrews assigned to the Nimrod force and Number 7 Squadron, a target facilities squadron equipped with the Canberra TTl8, which operated in support of the air defence squadrons and fleet units to provide targets for air firing and gunnery practice. I should, of course, make it quite clear that the Canberra aircraft weren't the targets themselves. They towed a banner target at a safe distance astern for the fighters or ships to fire at. Come to think of it, though, there were times when the fighter pilots or ship's gunners got sufficiently enthusiastic to make it FEEL as if the aircraft was the target. Target towing may not be the most glamorous job in the flying world, but it calls for a lot of precision in the air – and fairly steady nerves!

As well as a major RAF maritime base, the station was also a major NATO facility, used routinely by maritime and other aircraft of the NATO powers. As a consequence of the NATO role and because many of the NATO countries used either American aircraft or American equipment – ourselves included – there was an on-base facility operated by the United States Navy to provide extremely valuable in-theatre specialist support. The US Facility was operated by personnel of both the United States Navy and the United States Marine Corps.

On top of all this, the Station was designated as a UK Master Diversion Airfield, operational twenty-four hours a day, three hundred and sixty five days a year, to provide emergency facilities to deal with either weather or flight hazard diversions. Moreover, the airfield also served as a civil airport, utilised both by British Midland Airways and by Bryman Airways, a small West Country airline operating Islanders down to the Isles of Scilly and elsewhere. Airport terminal buildings and Customs facilities had been constructed on a part of the North side of the airfield released to the local authority for the use of these airlines, occasional air charter services and private aircraft.

All in all, in the few days that I had to myself prior to starting work after the Easter break, I was impressed by the size of the organisation and by the complexity of the various responsibilities involved in its day-to-day operations. I was already well aware that, quite apart from the work on the base, I would inevitably be involved in a fair amount of activity off-base in contacts with the various local authorities and civic groups. The station was the largest single employer of contractors and labour in the immediate area and constituted a very important element in the local economy. Altogether, I formed the early impression that I wouldn't have to look too hard to find enough work to keep myself fully occupied when once I was in the chair.

I had, however, some way to go before I got myself into the chair. I had been allocated some forty hours or so of flying to convert on to the Nimrod and I had to get the ground school and flying exercises completed – and, at the same time, learn everything I could about the tactical flying side of maritime reconnaissance, anti-submarine and Air/Sea Rescue operations – before I could be considered qualified to assume command. In one way, the location of the UCU at St Mawgan could have been regarded as less than ideal when changes of command were in the offing, in that it meant that both the current Station Commander and his designated replacement, were serving on the same base at the same time. No base can have two commanders but, quite plainly, it is difficult for station personnel to treat the 'new boy' as just another hand about the place. I have always felt that the ideal solution was to have the new man converted somewhere else, so that he arrived fully qualified and ready to take over command. In the case of St Mawgan, this ideal solution simply wasn't possible, because the specialist conversion unit was already located there. Fortunately, Don Arnott, my predecessor in command, accepted the situation philosophically and did everything he could to see that I was well settled in prior to the actual hand-over of command. At the same time, I did all I could to confine myself to the business of my conversion course which, fortunately perhaps, didn't allow me a lot of spare time to get in anyone's way during the period of transition.

Throughout my entire flying career, I have been very lucky with my instructors and I was to find that St Mawgan would be no exception to the rule. When I had completed the ground school phase of the conversion programme, I was handed over to Squadron Leader Freddie Fielding to look after me in the air. I couldn't have asked for a more capable or agreeable mentor. Freddie was himself a very experienced maritime pilot, instructor and one who had the precious knack of being able to pass on his very wide experience of both the aircraft and the role easily and humorously. The more I came to know him, the greater became my admiration and respect for him. In some ways and although he was rather less rumbustious, he reminded me a lot of Jack Allavie. Although he was a bit older than I was myself, he had enthusiasm, drive and commitment in everything he did. He flew hard, he played soccer with gusto and he was generally among the last to leave any party or social occasion. He had a zest for doing things that kept him young in spirit and in outlook. In my time, I have known many 'young' air-crew members whose attitudes made them seem to be like old men. Somehow or other, they lacked the spark of sheer enjoyment in the job which they were doing. Maybe and perhaps unhappily, that was the nub of the matter. To some unfortu-nates, flying is simply the job that they do and not – as it should be – an adventure and a way of life that is there to be savoured to the full. Freddie Field-ing was the other side of that particular coin.

With Freddie to hold my hand, I sailed through the conversion on to the Nim-rod, which I found to be a delightful aircraft to fly. Admittedly, I found the various check lists so long as to be thoroughly tedious but, to be fair, the aircraft did carry a very extensive fit of radio, radar and electronic equipment, so that one had to expect that the check lists would be pretty comprehensive. Still, at times, it felt as if you were ploughing through something akin to the Old Testament before you got round to pressing the engine start buttons. And all this before you faced up to the eight or nine hours in the air which was the average operational sortie length.

In view of the fairly long sorties which were standard, it was fortunate that the Nimrod was a very comfortable aircraft to fly in. Developed from the Comet airliner, it was the first land based, all-jet, maritime reconnaissance/anti-submarine aircraft to enter service with any of the world's air forces and its design and equipment fit, reflected the very latest concepts in both roles. It could transit very quickly to its search area, spend more than six hours on patrol at more than a thousand miles from base and react very quickly in a 'dash' to the area of an identified submarine threat. In order to accommodate the new role equipment, the airframe had been extensively modified to incorporate a second 'bubble' fuselage below the pressure cabin to house the ventral weapons bay. The pressure cabin itself had also been modified to house the consoles for the Air Electronics Operators who monitored the diverse sensors that fed information into the computer-controlled tactical navigation and attack system. There was even a 'dinette' on board where the crew could enjoy proper sit-down meals with a knife and fork – a far cry from the sandwiches and coffee in your lap, which was the lot of earlier generations.

The sortie profiles were particularly interesting to me since they involved a method of aircraft operation, which was quite new in my experience. The transit flight from base to the operating area was carried out at high cruising speed and high altitude in order to get the maximum economy from the four Rolls Royce Spey turbo-fan engines. Once in the operating area, when time on-station became an important factor, the aircraft came down to low altitude for the tactical phase of the sortie. The two outboard engines were shut down, so that the two remaining engines could operate at higher thrust settings, but also at lower overall fuel consumption rates. In this economical half-power condition, the aircraft flew just as happily and handled pretty much as crisply, as it did under full power. If, however, it became necessary to respond immediately to a submarine contact, or re-position to another area, it was a matter of only a couple of seconds to re-start the other two engines, so that full maximum speed capability was very quickly restored.

One of the things I found to be very odd about Nimrod flying – at least, initially – was operating without a parachute and flying helmet. For most of my career, I had been used to having a parachute strapped to my rear end – more often than not as part of a singularly uncomfortable ejection seat – and to having my head encased in a helmet and 'bone dome'. There was none of this in the Nimrod. Instead, it was much more like flying a civil airliner – a very comfortable padded seat, a feather-light set of headphones with the microphone on the end of a little boom in front of the lips and a pair of sunglasses to shield the eagle eyes against the glare. All very civilised stuff. After a bit, I just got used to having no parachute with me. After all, the aeroplane had four engines – and it could get along perfectly comfortably on only two of them if required. Moreover, in the event that some catastrophic incident did occur which prompted either a bale-out or a ditching, there was seldom any place to jump into except the sea – and the aircraft would almost certainly be going into the sea very soon anyway. In the circumstances, there seemed little attraction in anticipating the event by baling out – you were going to get just as wet either way.

One issue that I remember particularly from the conversion flying was the sharp difference of opinion that existed between myself and the 18 Group Standardisation Unit on the best technique for operating the flaps during instrument approaches. As I remember the Standard Operating Procedure, it called for some flap to be lowered during the flying of the initial pattern, a bit more as the glide slope was intercepted and the final descent commenced and the final dose at something like two hundred feet when the inner marker was being passed with the runway in sight. Personally, I had never liked this technique for two main reasons. First, it delayed the final flap selection until the aircraft was quite close to the ground, thus giving you something important to do when you were likely to be quite busy sorting yourself out for touchdown -particularly on a dark and dirty night. Second, it delayed a significant change in the aircraft trim until a very late stage in the approach, which meant that you could find yourself chasing the elevator trimmers all over the place as the flaps came fully down, at the same time as the speed was falling off.

Although I didn't like it personally, there was nothing basically wrong with the approved technique, which stemmed historically from the operation of aircraft which didn't have a lot of power in reserve. When you overshoot from the approach in such aircraft, you don't want to be fighting against the drag of full flap, so it made sense to delay selecting the last bit of flap until you were pretty sure of getting down. With modern jets, which have very considerable power reserves, such considerations are not nearly so important – at weights considerably higher than its average landing weight, the Nimrod would overshoot quite happily with two engines out on one side In these circumstances, it always seemed to me that the important consideration was to make the final approach, flare-out and touch-down phases as simple and as un-complicated as possible. My own technique, developed in many types of multi-engined jet 'heavies', was to lower full flap immediately the final descent was started on intercepting the glide path. In this way, I could take out all the trim changes somewhere around five miles from the end of the runway, leaving only very minor corrections to be made as the airspeed was bled off in the final stages of the approach. All I ever had to do at about the 200 foot mark was bring the throttles back and concentrate on the flare-out – to me, at any rate, a much simpler and safer procedure altogether.

I had a great many discussions on the subject with both the OCU Staff and with the 18 Group standardisers, but I could never manage to convince them sufficiently to get them to change the Standard Operating Procedures. That is one of the dangers of specifying Standard Operating Procedures in Chapter and Verse. As soon as techniques are written down in some official document, they become enshrined in tablets of stone as THE way, and, moreover, as the ONLY way, to execute the particular manoeuvre. Any method which is different from THE way must, of necessity, be wrong because it is not the one laid down in the book of rules. A pity, but that's the way the system works. In the end, I gave up. I did it their way, just to prove that I could do it and to keep everybody happy, but whenever I was driving the thing for real, I did it my way – which I still believe to have been the simpler and safer of the two options.

While my conversion to the Nimrod presented no problems – the machine is quite straightforward and easy to fly – trying to master the tactical flying aspects of anti-submarine operations was something altogether different. It was possible to detect the presence of submerged submarines by the use of a variety of passive sensors – sensors, that is, which do not alert the submarine to the fact that it is being tracked. When one went over to the attack phase, however, it was necessary to go active- by dropping sonobuoys which transmit an underwater signal which is reflected from the submarines hull. Just like a small scale version of the ASDIC so beloved by the makers of naval war movies. Once you went active and the submarine became aware that he was being pinpointed, the tactics became something like a three-dimensional game of chess, with each participant trying to double-guess his opponent. You knew where he was and where he was heading and you also knew that, if he stayed on the same heading at the same speed, you could calculate very precisely where to put your weapon so that it came down on top of him. But, at the same time, he knew that you knew where he was and where he was heading – and the average submarine captain wasn't dumb enough to hold course and speed just waiting for your weapon to arrive. So he would change heading, or speed, or depth, or even all three, to try to lose you. I found this type of exercise to be absolutely fascinating, but it is a long way from being something that you pick up in five minutes. Good maritime crews develop a sort of sixth sense about what a submarine is likely to do in any given circumstance – a sense developed over years of first-hand experience in the art. I admit freely that I never did develop this very high level of tactical awareness. Maybe I was too used to bomber flying – in that business, you don't have to go hunting for the target before you attack it.

During the course of my tour at St Mawgan, I got to know quite a lot of the Navy's submariners when they visited the station to see how we operated against them. I found them to be something of a breed apart – highly individualistic, completely dedicated and frighteningly efficient. I have always had an enormous admiration for people who are professionally efficient at their jobs, no matter what that job may be. In my experience, submariners are professionals with a capital P. Frankly, I don't know how they can ever take that sort of a job on – I have always consoled myself that what goes up, must come down, but the reverse is not necessarily true. It must take a special type of courage and commitment to launch yourself under the bounding main in an overgrown sardine tin. I went in a 'submarine' once – at the 30,000 Leagues Under The Sea ride at Disney World – and that almost reduced me to a snivelling wreck. Somehow, I never quite had the courage to try the real thing.

In due course, I completed my conversion on to the Nimrod and was taken under Don Arnott's wing for a week of introductions to various officials of Cornwall Council, Restormel Council, Newquay Council and St Columb Council Then, there were introductions to the officials of various community groups, the Chambers of Commerce, the Hotels and Caterers Associations and many others. When I had a fair idea of our local contacts, we went over the station, checked the books and the petty cash and got on with the handover. I signed for one RAF station in good working order, found my name up outside my office in Station Headquarters, hung up my hat and sat down in the Station Commander's chair. That was it. I was now in command.

CHAPTER 50

THE STORY GOES THAT when Harry S Truman was President of the United States, he had a card on his desk, which bore the legend, 'the buck stops here'. If the story is true, then it is evident that President Truman – in his capacity of Officer Commanding the United States of America – had a very clear understanding of the nature of command. The card on his desk succinctly condensed just about everything that could possibly be said on the subject into one memorably pithy phrase. Whether it comes at the exalted level of the Presidency, or somewhere a lot lower down the scale, command is just another word for responsibility. Be the organisation concerned military or otherwise, the man in command is the man who bears the responsibility. That's why he's there. If the organisation runs smoothly and prospers under his direction, he takes the credit. If it doesn't, he carries the can.

When a new commander takes up his appointment, he has his own ideas on how to set about his job. By that, I don't mean to say that he knows exactly how is going to tackle every single problem that might ever come his way – such an idea would clearly be nonsensical. Rather, I mean that he brings with him a fairly clear concept of which issues are important to him and which carry a rather lower priority. To take a simple example, few service commanders would argue that the operational effectiveness of their unit was their number one priority. But how would you regard their proficiency at ceremonial drill? In the Brigade of Guards or the Queens Colour Squadron, this would undoubtedly be accorded a high priority. At a unit not quite so often called on to perform in the public eye, it might be regarded as rather less important. Not unimportant. Just less important. Like many another serviceman, I have served on units where rehearsal after rehearsal was held before a big occasion -rehearsals when cooks and fitters and radar technicians – yes and aircrew too – have been marched backwards and forwards over and over again in a somewhat forlorn attempt to transform them into a 'showpiece' ensemble. At other times, there have been only a couple of quick 'dry-runs'; one to check uniforms and one to remember the drill patterns. In my experience, there has seldom been much to choose between the end result in either case. Experiences like this tend to determine the sort of priorities you bring with you to a command appointment. However, your priorities have been formed, they determine – either consciously or unconsciously – the way you set about your command role.

First of all, from day one, you are going to be the one called to account for your command. So you may as well ensure that you get it running in accordance with your own ideas as soon as possible. Therefore, the first thing to do is to confirm whether the priorities already in force accord with your own views. If they do, fine; if they don't, you change them – and, if you have any sense, you change them quickly. You don't have all that long in the job and there is no point in carrying on with a set of guidelines that do not accord with your own ideas. Since you are going to be the one called to account for your command, you may as well ensure that you get it running in accordance with your own ideas as soon as possible. Once you have the guidelines laid down and thoroughly understood by all concerned, you have to review your organisational structure to ensure that the chain of command is clear and direct, that areas of responsibility are explicitly defined and that channels of communication are simple and responsive. When you have done that and effected any changes you may have seen to be necessary, then you are in a position to do your job properly. You won't mind having to pay the piper, because you will be calling the tune – and it will be the tune of your own choice.

Sometimes – indeed, most times – a new commander will find that the existing organisation is ticking along perfectly effectively and satisfactorily. Hence, any small changes he has in mind can be implemented with a minimum of disruption. In this way, the day-to-day running of the organisation continues relatively smoothly and unruffled and changes in policies or procedures are effected almost imperceptibly. At other times, however, it can be necessary to adopt rather more of a 'bull at a gate' approach, whereby the newcomer has to go flat out to get his changes implemented and into effect, within a very short space of time after his arrival. Somewhat like the Assyrian of the poem, he descends "like a wolf on the fold," and the organisation goes through a sharp 'culture shock' until the new ways of doing things become adopted as routine.

I have dwelt on this matter of command at some length because I have found that very few people outside the service environment seem to understand what command is all about. They see the saluting and the privileges that the Commander gets and they see all the many personnel of the command apparently dancing to his dictate. What they don't see is that every single event that happens on the unit ultimately ends up on the commander's lap and that he is the one who has to account for it to higher authority. An aircraft misses its scheduled take-off time on an exercise because somebody dropped a spanner or a pencil which had to be searched for. A cook doesn't wash his hands and somebody gets food poisoning. An armourer injures himself and leaves his section short-handed. A signal gets lost in the mass of paperwork in the orderly room. As far as higher authority is concerned, the commander is responsible. He might have been on leave at the time the incident occurred, but he is still responsible. And higher authority is quite right. The commander IS responsible. It is his job to see that incidents like these don't happen. It is up to him to specify and implement policies and procedures to ENSURE that they don't happen. It may be hard on the poor commander if he has a bunch of butter-fingered mechanics and armourers, careless cooks and inefficient clerical staff but, if that is his misfortune, then he ought to have foreseen the likelihood of these events and done something about them beforehand.

It is this ever-present sense of responsibility that makes a command appointment so demanding. It is also why most commanders 'do their own thing' – within limits – in so far as running their command is concerned. If the captain is going to catch it in the neck when the ship goes on the rocks, it is not unreasonable for him to demand that he should be the one to say how it ought to be steered.

I was lucky at St Mawgan, in that, in every one of the really important areas of Base activity – Operations, Engineering and Administration – the key executives were all thoroughly experienced, extremely capable and utterly reliable. Their unstinted support and co-operation during the potentially difficult settling-in period was invaluable and allowed me to implement the changes that I had in mind smoothly and with minimum disruption to the station routine. What turned out to be something of a bonus was the fact that the people who were holding down the key appointments were extremely easy to get on with at a personal level. As I got to know them, I found that I liked them all as individuals – a circumstance which made it very easy to settle into the job in a harmonious working and social environment.

The actual day-to-day working routine of any front-line RAF station follows pretty much of a standard pattern, regardless of the operational role of the base, or of the types of aircraft being operated. This is hardly surprising, since, while aircraft types, sortie patterns and sortie durations, may vary from place to place, the essential function of any front-line station is to support the activities of the flying squadrons based there. The flying task is the justification for the existence of the station in the first place and for the presence there of every single man and woman carried on its strength.

Every flying squadron in the RAF is changed with the responsibility for being prepared to carry out certain specific wartime or peacetime tasks. For example, both 42 Squadron and the Operational Conversion Unit carried the wartime task of operating in the maritime reconnaissance and anti-submarine roles and in general operations in support of naval forces. In peacetime, the Squadron was tasked with maritime surveillance and with Air/Sea Rescue operations. The OCU was tasked with the training of aircrew for the front-line. Seven Squadron's primary role was the peacetime task of providing target facilities support to both air and naval forces and they carried a wartime responsibility to operate in support of the Commander UK Home Forces.

The nature of the tasks that are assigned to the flying squadrons determines the pattern of flying activity at the base which supports them. In addition to flying the sorties required by their peace-time tasks, the aircrews have to maintain their general flying skills – in particular, their instrument flying skills – they have to practice the operational techniques involved in their various war-time roles and they have to undergo regular periodic check flights to confirm their continued ability to meet the flying standards demanded by either flight safety or operational effectiveness criteria.

All of this flying is catered for by the allocation to each flying unit of an annual allowance of flying hours. Within this allowance, a flying programme is drawn up to provide the various types of sortie required to satisfy the operational, training, flight safety and classification requirements. It is the execution of the daily elements of this flying programme which sets the pattern for the day-to-day routine of the station.

Oddly enough, it can, at times, be quite easy to lose sight of the primary objective of the whole exercise, because of the sheer scale of the enterprise. The average front-line flying station represents a very large investment indeed in terms of both equipment and manpower – very expensive equipment and very expensive manpower. The cost of the aircraft and role equipment alone will certainly run into many millions of pounds. Their effective operation demands not only highly skilled and expensively trained aircrew, but also the backing of a maintenance support organisation embracing the services of a very large number of engineering and technical specialists in practically every conceivable branch of modern-day technology. On top of this, you have to take account of the back-up services which are required. Spare parts, fuel, weapons and other expendables all have to be provisioned, stored and accounted. The airfield and its essential services have to be provided and maintained – miles of runways and taxiways, servicing areas, hangers and dispersal areas, Air Traffic Control, Fire and Emergency Rescue services, airfield lighting and power and approach aids and communications.

Then there is the administrative side. People have to be accommodated, fed, paid, looked after medically and spiritually and provided with sporting, educational, cultural and recreational facilities. Every one of them has to be very extensively documented so that details of marital status, promotions, leave, medical history, qualifications and disciplinary matters can be recorded and kept up to date.

You could, if you wished, go on almost indefinitely. You have your own Fire Brigade, your own police and security organisation, your own telephone and telex exchanges, your own power, heat and electricity generating plants, your own builders and construction teams, metal workers, painters and joiners – the list is never ending. At RAF Bruggen in Germany, the Station Commander even has his own railway! When all of these diverse elements are put together, the result is a very large multi-million pound organisation which employs the highly specialised skills of anything up to a couple of thousand people. And every single one of them – from Station Commander to the newest aircraftsman – is there for one reason and for one reason only: to make their individual contribution to the achievement of the station flying task. In the modern vernacular, that's what it's all about.

In most cases, while the flying programme is drawn up – at least in outline – on a fairly long term basis in order to allow for careful integration of the activities of the various organisations involved, it is normally published on a weekly basis. Once published, the flying programme establishes the station operational routine for that week. The aircrews know when they will be flying or on stand-by and when they will be required for other training activities such as emergency drills, flight simulator exercises, survival training, dinghy drills, or whatever. The Engineering Wing will know when aircraft will be required, what fuel and stores loads will have to be provided and when turn-around or post-flight servicing will occur. The support organisations will know exactly what services they have to provide and when they are needed. In a nutshell, the flying programme determines the operational basis for the daily working routine of the whole station for the following week, and, moreover, provides all personnel with a blueprint of what the station will be trying to achieve during that period.

Once the programme is promulgated, the Station gets on with the job of meeting it. Most flying stations are functionally organised into a three wing structure – Operations, Engineering and Administration – the three major 'working' elements of the unit. The Commanders of these three wings, plus the commanders of the flying squadrons, form the nucleus of the station 'Board of Directors' which, under the Chairmanship of the Station Commander, plans, directs and supervises the day-to-day management of the base. Additional members are co-opted to the Board as required, to represent important specialised interests. For example, the Clerk of Works, the Security Officer, the Senior Medical Officer and the Station Warrant Officer, all have important contributions to make. Equally, if the Station employs significant numbers of civilian workers, it can be very helpful to include representatives from the relevant Trade Unions. In this latter context, I might note, in passing, that my experience of Trade Union representatives was almost completely different from what I had been led to expect by media reporting. Almost without exception, I found them to be easy to work with, helpful and genuinely co-operative.

The 'Board' – or, to give it its more formal title, The Station Commanders Committee – met once a week to conduct its business. In broad terms, the agenda normally covered three main areas of interest. First, a review of the past week's activities and events to assess what had been achieved in relation to the planned task, to investigate shortcomings and problems and to review the effectiveness of working procedures as demonstrated by the results achieved. Second, to 'fine-tune' the programme of events for the current week, and, third, to review progress in the planning for longer-term activities and commitments.

Outside the service, it is not generally appreciated that every single station in the RAF is responsible for carrying out a very extensive annual programme of events, quite apart from its flying programme. This 'secondary' programme can embrace a large number of commitments, involving a wide range of diverse activities and it stems from the fact that any station – and, especially, a front-line one – is an important entity on two counts: it is a vital element in the country's defence organisation; and it is an important – and sizeable – economic component in the local community within which it is located. Accordingly, from both the service and community viewpoints, there is considerable direct interest in the place and in its activities. On the service side, this direct interest was manifested by a large number of visits of one sort or another throughout the year. Some such visits might be classified as familiarisation or orientation occasions and could involve members of the Royal Family, political leaders and Ministers of State, parliamentary groups of various types and representatives of the Ministry of Defence, Command and Group Headquarters, the other Services and foreign military forces. Of perhaps more immediate relevance to the station itself, The Commander-in-Chief, Strike Command, the Air Officer Commanding 18 Group and the Commander, Southern Maritime Air Region would all drop in regularly to cast an eye over the place, to discuss problems and to keep the station executives up to date on plans and policies. Once a year, the Air Officer Commanding would conduct his major inspection of the unit and this occasion was invariably preceded by a whole series of visits by his staff specialists to check up on the fine details before the big day.

Again, because the station was actively engaged in both the execution of peacetime operations and in training for wartime operations, there was a fairly extensive programme of visits from service organisations interested in getting first-hand experience of the operational tactics and techniques in use. The RAF Staff College and the Air Warfare College were among our 'regulars' and we had occasional visits from the Imperial Defence College and the Staff Colleges of the other two Services. Moreover, because of our involvement in a wide spectrum of maritime-orientated activities, we had many exchanges and liaison visits with elements of the Royal Navy engaged in the same specialised line of work – the fleet anti – submarine surface units, the training establishments and the submariners themselves.

To add to the programme, on numerous occasions throughout the year the Station plays host to 'lodger' units of various types – air defence squadrons on detachment to practice air firings at the ranges in the South West, University Air Squadrons on summer camps, maritime strike/attack squadrons on forward deployment to cover the area of the Western Approaches, NATO maritime aircraft detachments on routine off-base deployment and service experience camps for pre-service training organisations such as the Air Training Corps.

At St Mawgan, our biggest single commitment of this type was the annual International Air Day, a major flying and static display Air Show on the lines of the Farnborough event. The show featured displays by aircraft from many nations and was one of the biggest holiday attractions of the year in South West England, bringing anything up to fifty or sixty thousand spectators on to the Station on the day. All of the planning and organisation for this major occasion – as well as its control and staging – was carried out by the station personnel at St Mawgan as just another part of their regular duties.

Finally, there were the commitments arising from the station's relationship to the surrounding community in Cornwall. Quite clearly, there were considerable potential problems in the location of a major jet flying air base right in the middle of one of the most popular holiday resort areas in the United Kingdom. By maintaining very close contacts with the local authorities and with local business representatives, we were able to understand the problems that our operations posed for them – particularly in the matter of aircraft noise. When it was at all possible, we did go to considerable lengths to arrange our flying schedule to minimise annoyance to visitors and locals alike. We arranged regular briefings and visits to the station for local authority representatives, business interests, school parties and community groups. In sum, the station did as much as it could to operate as an integral part of the local community, rather than as something quite separate from the world about us. We fostered close links with all sections of the local population and maintained these relationships – whether formal or personal – through participation in a wide range of official, recreational and social activities.

It will readily be appreciated that when the average weekly ration of activities of all of these types was superimposed on top of the weekly share of the flying programme – which, after all, was the primary business of the Station – there was normally not an awful lot of slack left in the station diary. Right throughout the year, the daily programme of events was invariably quite sufficiently full to ensure that everyone on the base was kept fully and productively, employed. At various times, I have heard many views expressed on what life is like in the services. I think that anyone who has ever served on a front-line Station could honestly state that, whatever else may have been the case, their life there involved them in their fair share of plain, old-fashioned, hard work.

CHAPTER 51

WHEN YOU FIRST SIT DOWN in your chair as Commander of a front-line station, it is not at all unusual to find the whole experience somewhat overpowering. The place is so big; so busy, so diverse. There are so many new things to do and to remember; so many people to meet and consult with; so many problems to investigate and to resolve. So many pitfalls and so little margin for error. Damn it all, it is overpowering! All of a sudden, it is brought home to you with awful clarity that it is all yours – it is your responsibility. Yours and nobody else's. And you can't put it off. You can't say, "hang on a bit. I'd like a week or two to get the feel of things before I start to make any decisions, or commit myself on any of these issues." Even as you sit there, a queue is forming outside your door bringing you the daily dose of actions to be agreed, decisions to be made, problems to be solved. The whole place is looking expectantly to you to lead them, to guide them, to encourage them, to support them and to solve their problems. In a way, it can make you feel just a little like God, but it can also make you painfully aware of your many shortcomings in attempting to fill the part.

Inevitably, different people react to the job in different ways. Very, very occasionally, some simply find it impossible to cope with the pressures of the situation and ask to be relieved, or have to be removed, from the post. Some overwork themselves; some overwork their staffs; some are intense; some relaxed; some impose themselves on the job; others allow the job to impose itself on them. Most – and by that I mean the vast majority – simply get on with it to the best of their individual ability and in a style which reflects their individual personality. They draw on their background experience, professional skills and common sense to deal with each issue as it arises and they do their level best to maintain their perspective and sense of humour through all the trials and tribulations that are likely to beset them. They are not afraid of the job, or of the challenges it brings. Certainly, they will make mistakes – the Station Commander hasn't drawn breath yet who didn't. But they will learn from their mistakes, put the situation right and go on to do better next time. Above all, perhaps, they have the capacity, when the pressure is really on, to reflect to themselves – albeit, sometimes rather ruefully – "well, after all, you wanted this job. There was a time when you would have given my eye teeth for it. Nobody ever promised that it would be a bed of roses. So just get on with it the best way you know how and try to prove that you're worthy of it." I sometimes think that it is as good a testimonial to the RAF as any, that so many are.

For my own part, I brought with me to the job one personal conviction about work in general which had been bred in me all the way through the ranks and in all the appointments I had served in. That conviction was that, in any organisation, rank, or status, or position in the hierarchy, is no more than a reflection of the holders capacity – in experience – to make the decisions that are appropriate to that particular level of operation. You don't ask a Flying Officer to run a station, because he hasn't had the chance to develop the ability and gather the experience for that type of job. Long experience has taught the RAF that the decisions which have to be made in running a station call for the sort of ability and experience levels normally associated with Group Captain rank. Having accepted that, I did not then and I do not now, believe that the number of 'rank-level' decisions which have to be made in the routine running of a station are numerous enough to keep any normal Group Captain fully occupied for more than, at the very outside, three days in an average working week. In my view, any Station Commander who winds up chained to his desk, beavering away industriously for all the hours that God sends is, frankly, either over-working, over-acting, or just plain incompetent. For much of his time, he is simply doing work which should properly have been delegated to one or other of his subordinates. And, more importantly, he is missing out on the most important single part of his responsibility, which is to keep his finger on the pulse of his unit so that he can actually get out there and lead it.

With this lofty concept firmly in mind, I set about organising my working week in such a way as to give me ample opportunity to get out and about. I made a very determined effort to get in one Nimrod flight every week so that I could keep my hand in on the operational side of our activities. It wasn't always possible to do so, because the normal Nimrod sortie involved two or three hours of pre-flight preparation followed by eight or nine hours in the air – that's virtually a full day written off just to get in one flight. Because of other commitments, this wasn't always feasible, but I did try. Certainly, I always tried to make myself available for any of the shorter duration sorties being flown by the Squadron or by the OCU. It was always rather easier to fit in a Canberra trip and I could generally manage to get in one or two sorties with 7 Squadron during the week. Most of 7 Squadron's TT18s had started life as either B2s or B6s in Bomber Command and had been converted to the target-towing role after the Canberras had been retired from the front-line. It was odd, at times, when entering up a trip in my log-book, to find that I had flown the same aircraft some twenty years previously, when I had been serving with 27 Squadron.

Away from the flying side, I made a point of taking at least one day a week simply to drive about the Station and drop in to the various workplaces to meet people and to see, at first-hand how things were going. I found this exercise to be absolutely invaluable – it provided the opportunity to make personal contact with the people who were actually doing all the work on the base, to find out what they were thinking, to find out what was irritating them, or worrying them and to find out how the policies which we were implementing were affecting them in their daily working lives. I have always been strongly of the view that the greatest asset of any Service is its people. I believed that it was my job to get to know them as well as I possibly could and to give them a chance to get to know me. I had to know what issues were important to them and they had to know what issues were important to me – and why!

At first, it was something of an uphill struggle. When I dropped in on a section unexpectedly, the atmosphere tended to be somewhat formal, or even strained. Gradually. however, as people got used to my 'no-notice' visitations and realised that I was simply there for a cup of coffee and a quick chat, rather than for an inspection of the place, things became a lot more relaxed. I can honestly say that I learned more about the morale and general condition of the station during these informal visits than I ever did on the occasions when I conducted my routine formal inspections of the various wings.

Incidentally, I was lucky in bringing with me one lesson which I had learned the hard way in squadron life and which I commend unhesitatingly to any 'manager' on a tour of the shop floor. If you are given a cup of coffee – and you will be – make a point of always washing your cup or mug before you leave. That way, you stand a fair chance of being offered another cup next time you drop by.

As I settled down into the job at St Mawgan, I think that the overriding impression that was borne in on me was of the value and quality of the people with whom I had the good fortune to be serving. Somehow or other, in the services, the shirkers, the layabouts, the incompetents and the uncommitted get themselves slowly but surely weeded out. What you are left with is a very professional body of men and women, well trained, well-motivated, with genuine pride in themselves, their unit and their service. Give them a job to do and explain why it has to be done and they will give you the results you want, no matter how difficult, dangerous, or unpleasant it may be to accomplish. They are self-disciplined, cheerful, loyal and dedicated. I readily admit to being thoroughly biased, but I simply don't believe that you could assemble a finer group of people anywhere in the world.

On every front-line RAF station, regular participation in operational training exercises was very much part of the normal working routine. When such exercises were conducted on a single-service basis, they were originated and controlled either by Command or Group Headquarters and they were undertaken with three major fundamental objectives in mind. First, to exercise the operational command and control system – including the appropriate communication links – between the originating authority and the operating unit. Second, to exercise the capability of the station to generate aircraft to operational readiness in accordance with the requirements specified for various states of preparedness. And third, to exercise the station's capability to meet its commitments under current operational plans by mounting simulated war-time operational sorties as required and by maintaining the flying effort at either sustained or intensive operating rates for the duration of the exercise period.

The single service exercises served to keep the stations at a high standard of capability to react to crisis situations, by rehearsing the procedures that would be implemented in such circumstances and they also served to assure the Commanders at Group and Command level of the continued operational effectiveness and responsiveness of the forces under their command.

In addition to the single-service exercises, most front-line stations also participate regularly in very large-scale major exercises, which might involve all of the forces in co-ordinated operations to test national contingency plans, or which might be undertaken on a NATO-wide basis to test Alliance responsiveness to a variety of potential threat situations In all of these different types of operational exercises, the emphasis of the effort, at station level was very much on the preparation of aircraft in accordance with the specified generation schedules and on the flying of the exercise sorties.

Because they were so very much flying-orientated occasions, there were quite a number of the sections of the station whose involvement with and participation in, the exercise situation was relatively minimal. At least, that had largely been the case in the past. I was soon to find, however, that things had changed – and changed very significantly.

When I began to become involved in the straightforward types of exercise at St Mawgan, I found that the general procedures were not all that much different from those with which I been familiar in Bomber Command. Certainly, the operational plans, the equipment and the sortie profiles were all new to me, but the over-all station responses, the generation procedures and the launching and control of the operational sorties were and not surprisingly, conducted along very similar lines. Accordingly, I felt quite at home in the new environment and found that managing the station activities during the various exercises didn't really pose too much of a problem.

What did pose something of a problem – in fact, a veritable hornet's nest of problems – was a completely new type of exercise system which Strike Command had introduced to make possible the rigorous and minutely detailed assessment of the operational effectiveness of its front-line units. The new system was called Tactical Evaluation – TACEVAL for short – and it was, without question, the finest tool ever made available to any Commander to satisfy himself that his force was operationally capable – not only in respect of meeting the flying task, but in every single aspect of preparedness, response and mission execution imaginable. It was also, from the viewpoint of the station personnel, an unmitigated nightmare.

TACEVAL was a once – occasionally, twice – a year event. It was a 'no-notice' exercise which could be sprung at any hour of the day or night throughout the year. Invariably, the first indication that a TACEVAL was on, was the unheralded arrival on the station of a team of up to ninety specialist assessors – every one of them an expert in one or other aspect of station activity. As they arrived at the main gate, an exercise signal would be received by the Operations Room advising that a state of emergency had arisen and that the station was to implement immediately the laid-down procedures to move progressively through the various transition readiness states to a fully operational war footing. In effect, the station then went to war – with every single step of the procedures being recorded for future analysis by the members of the TACEVAL team. From a completely 'cold' start, the station had to initiate three major activities immediately and effectively.

First – and crucially important to all subsequent activities – all station personnel had to be recalled to duty on the station as quickly as possible. As I have noted earlier, this could be a heartbreaking operation to set about in Cornwall, particularly in the summer, with the majority of station personnel living off-base in a large number of dispersed locations and the roads absolutely crammed with holidaymakers. At the Station PBX, we had something like six external telephone lines available to start the recall operation off – not a lot when you have something over a thousand people to contact. We used a 'pyramid' telephone contact system, whereby each person contacted directly had the responsibility of contacting three or four others; we used the alert warning sirens at the major Married Quarter sites; we sent siren-equipped vehicles to the smaller Married Quarters areas; we contacted a very co-operative local Police Force to root out personnel living in isolated communities. Using any and every means at our disposal, we contacted every single person on the station strength to get them back to work as quickly as possible.

At the same time as the recall was in full swing, the duty administrative staff already on base were starting to set up the extra accommodation, catering and car parking facilities which would be needed to cope with the larger numbers who would be arriving to live on-base for the duration of the exercise. The gymnasium, the cinema and various other locations were converted into additional dormitory facilities and all Messes -and the NAAFI – went over to what was virtually an all-ranks, round-the-clock, cafeteria feeding system. To the general delight of all drill-shy personnel, the station parade ground was used as the main car park for off-base residents.

The second major activity which had to be initiated right from the off was the implementation of the Station Ground Defence and Security Plan. Protection had to be provided against enemy air action – key installations to be sandbagged, anti-aircraft defences set up and damage repair parties and their equipment brought up to immediate readiness. Protection also had to be provided against infiltrators, assault groups, saboteurs and demonstrators. Security patrols had to be augmented, key points guarded and defensive positions manned. Access to sensitive areas such as the aircraft flight line and main servicing areas and to the Operations and Communications Centres had to be strictly controlled.

In a real-life crisis situation, most front-line stations would have their strength augmented by reserve forces specifically allocated to provide the manpower required to take on the bulk of the ground defence and security tasks. In TACEVAL, you made do with what you had – and it was never enough. The security force was made up of every man and woman on the unit who was not actually working at the time – mechanics, clerks, cooks, medical orderlies, storekeepers,- yes and aircrew too. Even the Padres had a security role to fill. For everyone on the base – officers and airmen alike – there was no such thing as off-duty time during TACEVAL. If you weren't actually working or sleeping, then you were either out on security patrol, or you were guarding one or other of the essential installations.

Security of the station and ground defence was everybody's business and it was taken deadly seriously. The TACEVAL team could be guaranteed to present you with a wide variety of threat situations and you had to be prepared to cope with all of them. If you didn't, then you would almost certainly wind up with half of your Station 'blown up' and most of your aircraft destroyed, before the exercise was even properly underway. To give yourself any chance at all, you had to have your procedures absolutely cut and dried and put into effect, right from the off.

The third major activity that you had to get on with from the very start, was the preparation of the aircraft to meet potential tasks at rates of effort higher than we normally used in peace-time. That meant recovering aircraft from fairly major servicings, when the aircraft might well be scattered about the hanger in a million pieces, as well as rapidly rectifying every aircraft's list of unserviceabilities and equipment malfunctions. The aircraft 'generation' schedule was very tightly controlled so that specific numbers could be produced, fully serviced and prepared for operations, within defined time-scales from the start of the exercise. And this at the very time when you were trying to get your servicing crews back on to the unit and when you had to use your engineering wing personnel to provide the major contribution to your security force. When you have your OC Engineering fighting to keep his manpower on the job of producing serviceable aircraft to meet the generation schedule and, at the same time, have your OC Ground Defence screaming for more men to meet his security commitments, you are continually being presented with nice problems in setting your priorities. Right from the very start, the TACEVAL Team would introduce 'incidents' to ensure that the pressure went on early and stayed on for as long as the exercise lasted. Using personnel from other units, or from other services, they would test your preparations to deal with every conceivable type of security threat. You could find yourself faced with assault groups, saboteurs, fifth columnists, infiltrators, or political demonstrators. Among the favourite ploys was the use of demonstrators to lie down in the access roads to block traffic – how do you cope with that in a recall situation, with a hundred or so demonstrators littered across the one and only main access road to the station and only a couple of young airmen on guard at the main gate? Another favourite was the infiltration of young – and, generally, pretty – WAAFs with forged identity cards in their hands and 'explosive devices' concealed about their persons. There is an understandable – but potentially fatal – reluctance to regard any young girl as a serious security threat – a reluctance which cost us dear on one miserably wet night when a WAAF intruder was arrested and considerably taken into a maintenance line hut out of the teeming rain for questioning. Once inside, she produced an explosive package which had been strapped to her thigh and we lost that facility for the duration of the exercise. Following this incident, every intruder ~ whether man, woman, or child – was held face down in the mud at the business end of a gun until they could be strip searched by a security specialist on the spot. Embarrassing and unpleasant maybe, but TACEVAL is not a game. You do what you would do in a real life situation and you do it properly – otherwise, your security lapses will certainly lose you the war before you have even got started.

We could also find ourselves having to cope with directly offensive operations by trained saboteur teams of Army, Royal Marine or RAF Regiment cut-throats. They absolutely revelled in this sort of clandestine, stealthy, operation and they were frighteningly skilled and determined. Moreover, this was their sort of game and they were a lot more used to playing it than we were. When you were subjected to an intrusion by, for example, a team from the Royal Marine Commandos, you could very easily wind up with part of your security force wiped out and many of your facilities destroyed, before you even knew that they were on the place. These people were experts at this sort of business and we weren't, so that it was very tempting to complain that it was all very unfair. The TACEVAL team's irrefutable response was invariably to ask politely what sort of group you thought might be sent against you by a potential enemy – a pack of Brownies? They were giving you a realistic threat to deal with and if you didn't know how to set about countering it, then you had better learn – and quickly, too!

What made security such a nightmare during TACEVAL was that if your defensive system fell down and a facility was 'destroyed', that was it – you didn't get it back again. You just had to carry on as best you could without it. And even if your security and ground defence system stood up to the test, the TACEVAL team could always contrive 'enemy air action' or some other disaster to lose you a few of your essential services. Try running an operational station on a war footing some-time without an operations Room, without a maintenance control centre, without a communications centre, a hospital, or a telephone exchange. Try it without your Wing Commander Operations – 'killed' by a letter bomb: without fifty skilled aircraft servicing tradesmen – food poisoning: or without your intelligence staff and all their records – victims of an 'air raid'.

Inevitably, no matter how good your security and defence systems, you lost fa-cilities. The average base was so big and covered such a huge ground area, that all-round defence was simply not a practicable proposition – particularly when the infiltration and sabotage threat was posed by groups who were well trained and professionally skilled. What you had to aim to do was to limit your losses to pe-ripheral resources and progressively bring in your security and defence cordon to provide an effective inner ring around the really essential elements – the aircraft, the servicing facilities and the command and control network.

Because you could be quite certain that you would lose certain key facilities, you had to be prepared to come up with some alternative way of continuing to operate effectively without them. This meant prior planning to provide stand-by and fall-back options. If the telephone exchange was lost, we lost all of the prima-ry internal communication links on the unit. In this event, we could still carry on operating using a 'squawk-box system linking our essential control centres. Throw in a power failure and we lost the 'squawk-box' system. In that case, it was back to pre-laid, land-line links connecting hand-cranked field telephones. If, for some unforeseeable reason, we lost that system too – land lines can he cut or damaged – we could fall back yet again to battery powered walkie-talkies. After that, it was back to real basics – virtually a system of runners with cleft sticks. For external communications with higher authority, we could fall back progressively on tele-printer links, then to the Air Traffic Control radio network, then to radio links set up in an aircraft on the ramp and finally to a system using lovingly repaired old world war 2 radio sets, reclaimed from the scrap heap and about thirty years out of date.

The same general principle applied to just about every aspect of station activity. During the average TACEVAL, you had to be prepared to lose practically any facil-ity on the unit and have a back-up and a further stand-by facility, ready and prepared to go into operation immediately. You lose a Mess or a dining hall and you have a couple of hundred people due for a hot meal in the next ten minutes. How and where, do you feed them? You lose Station Sick Quarters – where do you treat your casualties? You lose part of the main runway through bomb cratering – are you prepared to continue flying off and recovering sorties from the taxiways or grass surfaces until repairs can be effected? You lose a Barrack Block – where do you provide beds and toilet facilities for the shift due off duty twenty minutes from now? How do you let them know where they now have to go to wash and sleep and how do you replace all the personal clothing that has also gone? Even in a war, people have to wash and shave and change their clothes. If you haven't thought about and prepared for these and a hundred other similar problems, well in advance of the event, you are going to find that even a short TACEVAL will reduce your station to absolute chaos in next to no time. And TACEVALS can last for anything up to a week or eight days.

In many ways, TACEVAL constituted a no-win situation. When the team reported that your operations centre was a vulnerable target to either air attack or to sabotage, there was no point in arguing reasonably that it wasn't your fault that it wasn't built underground. When you were told that your bright, shiny, fuel storage tanks stuck out like a sore thumb and ought to be 'toned-down', you couldn't come back with the excuse that they were built that way and that, anyway, you weren't allowed to paint them dark green because of the evaporation problem. In TACEVAL, there was only one rule – you coped and coped effectively, or you failed. Alright, we accepted that some of the situations were deliberately pressurised. It was no more than a realistic recognition of existing circumstances to acknowledge that, in the real life situation, you could well be subjected to air and ground attack, to sabotage, to infiltration and to demonstrations: and any of them could occur while you were trying to prepare for, or execute, operations at maximum intensity. But it might be considered stretching it a bit to postulate that you would be likely to get everything at once – plus an influenza epidemic, earthquake, communications breakdown, power loss and God knows what else. Presumably, it could happen. In any event, if you happened to be running a frontline Station in Strike Command, you had to be prepared for it to happen and you had to be prepared to cope with it.

CHAPTER 52

I MAKE NO BONES about it: I absolutely dreaded TACEVAL. So, I believe, did practically every other Station Commander in the service. It was a truly harrowing experience to undergo. But having said that, I still believe that it was the best system ever introduced by a military organisation to keep itself in condition to react effectively to the sort of situations which could well occur in times of tension or war. The acid test was that the system worked. When you earned a 'satisfactory' assessment overall, you knew, beyond any doubt, that your organisation could cope with practically every possible contingency which might occur and still continue to carry on with the primary task efficiently. I have no doubt that both the Army and the Navy carried out readiness and effectiveness assessment exercises on their own operational units, but, to the best of my knowledge, only the RAF went to such lengths to test the capability of its front-line force. A nightmare it might have been, but it certainly ensured that the Strike Command forces could do their jobs.

I remember, with particular pain, an occasion when I was hosting a dinner party to entertain my senior station executives and quite a large number of local dignitaries. While we were contentedly sipping our pre-dinner sherries, the station alert hooter blasted off. The poor local guests must have wondered what had hit them. My staff officers and I and the stewards, all immediately dropped everything to race off to change and report in to our posts, leaving Jean and the other station wives to cope as best they could with the wreckage of the evening. All the guests cars – unregistered on the station – were being turned upside down for bomb searches and all of the guests had the utmost difficulty in getting off the station. They had to be escorted to the main gate by the wives and, without any sort of official identification, everyone must have been stopped and interrogated a dozen times before they could get off the place. I really sympathised with their unfortunate situation – there's nothing like coming out to dinner and finding yourself knee-deep in a full-scale war before you've even got round to the soup – but I had my own hands full at the time.

Thankfully, life at St Mawgan wasn't all TACEVALS. Once or twice a year was more than enough. For the rest of the time, it was a matter of routine station activity, getting on with our normal flying and visit programmes and with the ceremonial, social, recreational and sporting occasions that made up our diary of non-flying events. We participated a lot in the local fairs which are such a feature of life in Cornwall. We had a strong pool of good quality athletes to provide high-calibre competitors in individual events and we also provided various display teams such as our Police Dog Team and our group of Tae-Kwan-Do enthusiasts, who invariably made a very considerable impression with their demonstrations of how to demolish a brick wall in seconds with their bare hands.

As Station Commander, I was involved in a fair amount of off-station activity, some of which got me into situations that were quite new to me. I remember once being on board the Trevose Head lifeboat when it was let loose down the slipway in a demonstration launching. No wonder the lifeboat crews seem to take their hazardous duties so calmly – after the excitement of the spectacular launching, everything else must seem like a fairly dull anti-climax. I remember, too, being invited once to go down the Wheal Jane tin mine to let me see what it was like underground. I didn't want to go underground: in fact, to be brutally honest, I was scared stiff of going underground. But when the invitation comes, you accept gracefully: it's all part of the job. Well, I went down ONCE: down into an absolute hell-hole of noise, dripping water and claustrophobia. Everyone else seemed to think that it was absolutely splendid and they kept telling me how fine it all was compared to the old days. I swallowed hard and tried to give the impression that I was enjoying it all. When, blissfully, I was allowed to get back to the surface, I headed straight for the nearest bar and tried to put it all firmly out of my mind. I vowed silently that the next time anyone gets me to go underground, it's going to be for keeps. I won't ever do it again as long as I'm drawing breath.

On the Station we organised some activities that were very successful and which provided welcome breaks in the daily routine. With apologies to Mr Morley and Miss World, we ran our own Miss International Air Day beauty competition. The WAAFs were tremendous in the way they entered into the spirit of the thing and it proved a howling success. When the girls were all done up in their evening dresses, they would have given any chorus line a very good run for their money. Each competitor, inevitably, was accorded unstinted and vociferous support from her working colleagues and the winner was appointed to act as the station 'hostess' for all of the public events of the International Air Day for that year.

One activity that came our way proved to be something right out of the ordinary as far as normal RAF station routine was concerned. It all started with a phone call from the Public Relations Branch at the Ministry of Defence to advise me that a visiting American film producer was looking for a world War 2 sort of airfield to 'shoot' some scenes for a forthcoming film. In due course, Mr John Sturges arrived at St Mawgan to discuss the matter at rather greater length. I knew him by reputation and by some of his previous film productions. He had made quite a lot of westerns – a brand of movie to which I have always been somewhat childishly addicted. Good or bad, I always enjoy a horse-opera. Mr Sturges, I might say, made extremely good ones – 'Gunfight at the OK Corral' and 'Last Train from Boot Hill' were only two of a long string of successes for which he was responsible.

On this occasion, so he told me, he was planning to make a film of Jack Higgins's bestseller 'The Eagle has Landed'. For reasons which are probably quite clear to people in the film industry, but certainly were not to me, he was planning to shoot the St Helier scenes in Cornwall and the Norfolk scenes in Berkshire. Now, he was looking for some place to film the scenes that took place on a run-down Dutch airfield. I was almost tempted to suggest Holland as a good starting point, but that was probably too obvious and anyway, MOD had suggested that Treblezue might just possibly fit the bill. When we went out to have a look over the place, it was obvious, from his reaction, that Mr Sturges had found his 'location'. I must admit that, with its somewhat shabby hangers and buildings and its overgrown runways, the old airfield really did look the part. So it was that the film-makers moved in on us in some force. Other than liaising with them on their requirements and trying to schedule the flying programme so that they weren't faced with a Nimrod howling by in front of the cameras, or getting a very non-wartime roar of jet engines on their sound track, I tried to keep myself and the rest of the station out of their hair. They had a job to do and it wouldn't help them to have too many spectators getting under their feet. Quite a lot of the station personnel were roped in at weekends as extras or for crowd scenes and it was odd to see so many of them wandering about the place in German Army uniforms. I remember that they all had to submit to the director's concept of German Army haircuts – right down to the bare wood – but they got a daily meal on the set and something like £10 or £20 a time for their efforts.

Mr Sturges seemed to appreciate the co-operation which we provided and, towards the end of his shooting schedule, he set aside one morning so that the station WAAFs and the wives and families, could visit the set and get to meet the stars. Michael Caine, Donald Sutherland, Robert Duval and Jenny Agutter were all on hand and were very patient with their visitors.

I remember particularly being much impressed by watching one scene being filmed. In this scene, Donald Sutherland was supposed to be boarding his aircraft to parachute into England and the script called for Michael Caine to shake him by the hand and wish him good luck. After what seemed like an inordinate amount of preparation, there came the cries of "Lights," "Camera, "Action," and the actual filming of the scene got underway. At this point, the two principals entered, shook hands briefly as Michael Caine muttered "Good Luck," and Donald Sutherland turned away to mount the aircraft ladder. As soon as he put his foot on the first step, somebody yelled "cut," and the scene was over. The whole thing hadn't taken more than about twenty seconds. After a couple of re-takes during which the same brief scene was re-enacted, the whole unit started to dismantle their gear preparatory to packing up for the day. I couldn't believe it. John Sturges seemed to sense my bewilderment and he leaned over to remark, quietly, "in this business, Harry, it's a good days work if we get thirty seconds worth of useable footage in the can." I began to wonder whether I wasn't in the wrong line of work.

One particularly pleasurable by-product of the filming was that I was afforded the opportunity to get my hands on the aircraft which were being used in the film. One was a Dakota – a type which I had flown before – but the other two, a Feisler Storch and a Messerschmitt Me 109, were both genuine 'one-offs'. The Storch, a very early Short Take-Off and Landing Army Co-operation/observation aircraft was fitted with all-metric instrumentation and had a broken Air Speed Indicator. The film unit's pilot laconically advise me to "feel it out a bit before you land." In the air, I found that it could be flown very slowly indeed. It had full length leading edge slots and slotted flaps and by comparing my rate of progress with cars on the roads below me, I reckoned it could trundle along quite happily at something like twenty to twenty five miles an hour. When I brought it back in to land, it must have stopped rolling in about the length of a tennis court.

The Me 109 was a very different proposition. It had apparently started life as a Bf109E and had passed to the French at the end of the war. It had been converted into a two-seater and back again on a number of occasions. Thereafter, it had passed into private ownership, fitted with a down-rated engine of about only half the power of its original power plant. Even allowing the tribulations that it had been through and the shortcomings of the down-rated engine, the machine had the unmistakable stamp of a pure thoroughbred. Initially, I was just a little wary of its very narrow track, conventional tail-wheel undercarriage – I had become very used to tricycle landing gear – but a couple of minutes in the air was more than enough to banish every emotion except sheer pleasure in the feel of a really superb aircraft. It was as close as anyone is ever likely to come to the sensation of having a personal set of wings. The controls were beautifully harmonised and the aircraft almost seemed to sense what you wanted to do with it. Even when I brought it round the final turn for the landing, it seemed to be saying, "just you sit there and relax and I'll get us down alright." Imaginative maybe, but I hardly had to touch it as it whispered on to the runway in a soft as silk touch- down. I only flew it once, but I will always remember that aeroplane with real affection. It had genuine class welded into every rivet. When I reluctantly climbed out of the cockpit, I discovered that a group of the St Mawgan 'extras', all impressively at- tired in their German uniforms, had prepared an honour guard for a formal ceremony at which Warrant Officer Charlie Lusty gravely invested me with an enormous cardboard 'Blue Max'. A bottle of champagne was produced to mark the occasion and a genuinely good time was had by all – the champagne helping more than a little. It was all a lot of fun and, for me, the perfect end to a flight that I enjoyed as much as any other I ever made.

When I started out on my tour of duty in command at St Mawgan, I was con- scious, as I remarked earlier, that it might well prove to be the last flying assignment of my career. In this circumstance, I was keenly motivated to take every opportunity that came my way to get into the air whenever I could find the time to do so. While the majority of my cockpit hours were accumulated in our own Nimrods and Canberras, I was delighted to discover that the flying opportu- nities at St Mawgan were by no means limited exclusively to these two types. Somewhat to my surprise, I found that opportunities did, in fact, crop up from time to time to fly other aircraft which came on to the base on visits or on de- tachment. I tried very hard never to miss out on any such opportunity which came my way, because I always found that I got a great deal of pleasure and genu- ine satisfaction from the challenge of getting to grips with a type of aircraft which I hadn't flown before.

Many pilots, I know, take a rather different view and much prefer to limit their flying time to the type of aircraft with which they are currently familiar. For me, I suppose that it was a legacy of my time in the test flying business that I always enjoyed trying my hand on something new. I liked the experience of a new and different cockpit, a different set of controls, different handling characteristics, different response rates. In one sense, aeroplanes are a bit like motor cars – if you can drive one, you can drive them all. But, at the same time, every one is just that little bit different from every other one. Some of them, in fact, are a whole lot different. In much the same way as I wouldn't recommend anyone to jump straight from the driving seat of a Mini into a Grand Prix Ferrari, so I wouldn't seriously recommend anyone to leap straight out of a Tiger Moth into the cockpit of a Jumbo Jet or Concorde. It can be done, but you want a fair bit of type flying experience under your belt before you try. And the only way to get type experience is to go out and fly different types of aeroplane.

At St Mawgan, the Air Traffic Control Staff knew that I was keen to try my hand on different types, so that they always kept me informed whenever something of interest was due to arrive. That gave me the chance to have a word with the visitor and see if I couldn't persuade him let me have a go at his particular charge. A surprising number did. In particular, I found that the period around International Air Day was a very fruitful time to try to wangle trips, because there was always a large influx of other people's aeroplanes arriving on to the base for either the flying or the static displays. Additionally, I was very lucky in that I had a lot of friends and former colleagues who knew that I liked to try my hand in something different. From time to time, they would drop in for lunch, or for a weekend, the price of which was usually a quick sortie in their particular piece of hardware. Visiting RAF and NATO units on detachment were also generally quite happy to provide some cockpit time to anyone who took a direct interest in their activities while they were on the base.

Incidentally, it was a visiting Lightning fighter squadron which gave rise to my most depressing experience at St Mawgan. On base for an air-firing detachment, they very generously posted a notice in the mess that any visitors would be welcome to ride with them on some of their sorties in the dual-control T4. I did two or three rides with them and, to his eternal credit, a young navigator from 42 Squadron also went over to join the 'Thousand Miles an Hour' Club. Apart from we two, not one other aircrew member on the unit took the offer up. To say that I found that hard to understand would be something of an understatement. We had plenty of young pilots on the place and it seemed to me, at the time, quite inconceivable that they wouldn't leap at the opportunity to get their hands on a Mach 2 fighter. It may have been just a manifestation of the price we pay for increased specialisation but, if it is, then we have lost something very valuable in the sense of fun, exhilaration and adventure in our profession.

Anyway, I suppose I was pretty set in my ways by then. If it came my way and it had wings on it, then I wanted to try it out. And I did, too. During the time I was at St Mawgan, I got my hands on something like twenty-one types which I hadn't flown before – and I enjoyed every one of them. In fact, I did fly rather more than that number of aircraft which were new to me, but I believe that a pilot has to be realistic about the types which he records in his log-book. If they are simply 'one-off' trips, you have to set some sort of honest criteria for yourself to justify entering it up as a 'type flown'. For myself, I only ever 'logged' an aircraft if I had done the flying from either the front seat or the left hand seat and if I had been able to fly the whole mission myself – take-off, full sortie profile and landing. Sometimes it could be quite difficult to get all of it in. I remember one time when I had to fly a full formation aerobatic rehearsal sortie in the number four slot of the Patrouille de France display team just to get the Fouga Magister into my log book. And when I flew the Lancaster of the Historic Aircraft Flight, the Captain's hands were very nervously hovering around the controls as I brought it in to land. Understandably, too – that particular aircraft is quite irreplaceable.

One aircraft which I didn't get to fly, but which I saw occasionally during Nimrod patrols was the Russian Tupolev Tu-95 'Bear'. This was a very big, four engined, turbo-prop bomber/reconnaissance aircraft which we would run across from time to time over the Atlantic or the Northern Seas, engaged in very much the same sort of business as we were ourselves. Occasionally, we would fly close enough together to wave to each other and to take photographs – the Intelligence Staffs at Murmansk were probably just as interested in the aerials and antennae on our aircraft as the Staff at 18 Group were in the bits and pieces on the Bear. All part of the game, but it was odd to reflect that your grinning face would be appearing on some Russian Intelligence Officers desk first thing tomorrow morning.

What invariably depressed me about these encounters was to have a close-up look at the very business-like 23 millimetre cannon with which the Bear was generously equipped. Every time I looked down the barrel of one of their cannon, I was very forcibly reminded that the Nimrod carried no defensive armament whatever – a fact which, for the life of me, I was never able to understand. I could see some operational justification for sending out Mosquitos unarmed during the war – they flew higher and faster than most of the opposition fighters of that time. In the early 1950s, the Canberra were in very much the same situation. But an unarmed maritime patrol aircraft always seemed to me to be a nonsensical concept. During the war, the Sunderland, the Hudson and the Catalina had all been quite adequately provided with defensive firepower to give them a chance to defend themselves against long-range fighters or enemy patrol aircraft.

Now, here we were, forty years on, operating one of the most complex and comprehensively equipped aircraft of its type in the world, in a number of vitally important operational roles – and we couldn't have defended ourselves effectively against a world War 2 fighter. If our activities really did pose a problem for the potential enemy – and that was the primary justification for our existence – then one might reasonably suppose that he would be moved to do something about it. If he ever did, then the pilots sent out to intercept us were in for an absolute field day. Oh yes, there was a procedure to be followed if the aircraft was ever engaged in air combat. I can't remember the details now, but I do recall feeling very strongly, at the time, that a much more realistic procedure would have been for the Captain to lead the crew in a devout recitation of the Lord's Prayer, so that, when they were all blown to Kingdom Come, at least they would depart in a suitably pious frame of mind. I did spend a lot of my time trying to persuade 18 Group that even one little machine gun – on a mounting similar to the one designed to be fitted in the Hercules transport – would have been of considerable value. To be fair, they did take the idea seriously but, at the time I left St Mawgan, the Nimrod was still, effectively, a flying 'clay pigeon'.

Defensive armament or not, the Nimrod patrols were always interesting – and occasionally quite exciting when we ran across units of the Russian Fleet on exercises or on deployment. The modern Russian warships were very fine looking craft and some of their submarines were quite staggeringly big boats. Very formidable looking indeed. We also used to see quite a lot of their fishing fleets, generally operating around one or two factory ships and almost invariably accompanied by a 'spook' electronic eavesdropper done up to look just like any other trawler. I don't know why they bothered. The spook always stood out like a sore thumb – it was the only one in the fleet which wasn't surrounded by seabirds trying to get at the fish scraps.

CHAPTER 53

IN THE MIDDLE OF 1975, I was caught up in the celebrations attending the 199th anniversary of the formation of the United States Marine Corps. I had always had a very high regard for the Marines. They have a long history of service of which they are justifiably proud and they maintain consistently high standards of discipline, physical fitness, turn-out and general behaviour. I knew Frank Busam, the young Captain who commanded the St Mawgan detachment very well. A veteran of multiple combat tours of duty in Viet Nam, he was a very personable individual, very professional, very dedicated and – as I found to my cost – a pretty fair country poker player.

When the Marines 199th birthday was coming up, Frank very kindly invited me to be guest of honour at the celebration dinner, an invitation which I felt privileged to accept. When I confirmed that a few words from me were expected on the night, I set about putting together a few thousand well-chosen words to fit the occasion. Thus equipped for what I presumed would be my after-dinner speech, I looked forward to the event with keen anticipation. It is always a pleasure to be accorded the opportunity to participate in the formal social occasions of another Service – one of my golden memories is of a naval dinner in the Painted Hall at Greenwich, during which my table companion, a saturnine captain of submarines, drew my attention to the precise number of naked breasts on display in the paintings on the walls, pillars and ceilings. While I was struggling to think of some suitable rejoinder, he commented, moodily, "It's all a bit much with your kippers in the morning."

On the night of the Marine's celebrations, I very quickly discovered that the Anniversary Dinner was not, as I had at first thought, simply a local 'one-off' event. On the contrary, it was probably the most important single occasion in the Marine Corps social and ceremonial calendar and it was conducted along very formal lines hallowed by years of tradition. It was, I regret to have to say, this tradition which almost proved to be the undoing of all of us.

The dinner was held in one of the recreation facilities at St Eval, which the Marines had themselves decorated with multi-coloured panels from old parachutes swathed in folds from the ceiling. Since the occasion was very definitely a formal one, all of the Marines were in full dress ceremonial uniform, all the guests in their appropriate Mess Kit and all the ladies in evening dresses. A very colourful assembly indeed. As Jean and I made our entrance as part of the Marine Commander's party, it was to find all of the company standing and all of the tables set around the centrepiece of the evening – an absolutely enormous birthday cake bearing all of the Marine Corps battle honours on individual plaques of sugar icing and surmounted by one hundred and ninety nine birthday candles – one for every year of the Corps's existence.

When we had taken our places at the top table, an honour guard – complete with swords and colours – was positioned around the central table bearing the cake. At this point and in accordance with the traditions of the evening, one of the officers read to the company a birthday message issued by a former Commandant of the Corps. It was a very good message but, in the context of this particular evening, it had two distinct disadvantages. First, it was fairly lengthy; and, second, it was being read by an officer who was taking it very slowly. As his delivery proceeded, I began to notice, somewhat uncomfortably, that the candles on the cake were blazing away fairly merrily – a hundred and ninety nine candles can generate quite a lot of heat – and the ever-lengthening flames were beginning to lick perilously close to the parachute panels swathed from the roof.

By the time the Birthday Address had ground to its conclusion, bits of the icing on the cake had caught fire and the whole thing was beginning to take on the appearance of a gigantic blow-torch. Everyone in the room was conscious of it, but apparently nothing could be done until the candles were extinguished and the cake officially cut. At this point, I became aware that every face in the room was turned expectantly towards me and I realised, to my unutterable horror, that the speech which I had expected to be delivering after dinner, was apparently due right now. By this time, the parachute panels were very definitely smouldering, the top of the wretched cake was an absolute sheet of flame and the sweat was pouring off the poor honour guard in torrents.

I congratulate myself that I reacted to the circumstances in the only way possible. In an extempore effort worthy of the Guinness Book of Records, I raced through what was probably the shortest speech ever delivered by a Guest of Honour in the entire history of the United States Marine Corps. Even while I was in the process of sitting down, Frank was rushing, with almost indecent haste, into the next part of the proceedings which involved cutting the cake and, thankfully, extinguishing the bonfire on top. For a second or two, it was touch and go whether fire extinguishers would have to be used but, happily, the Marines managed without them. The rest of the evening, I remember, was a roaring success – due in part, maybe, to sheer relief that we hadn't burned the entire building to the ground.

Above my desk now, there is a plaque presented to me by the Marine detachment at St Mawgan – a reminder of an association with the Corps which I remember with pride and affection. But I never look at it without remembering that cake and the inferno raging on top of it. The Corps must now be worth something like two hundred and eleven candles, so that my very serious recommendation to anyone accorded the honour of an invitation to the Anniversary Dinner as Guest of Honour is to prepare a short speech – a VERY short speech – and make sure you know the location of the nearest Fire Exit.

In due course, my time at St Mawgan came to an end and I started to make my preparations to hand over command to my successor, Barry Duxbury. I remember thinking to myself that it seemed as if no time at all had passed since I had been the one arriving to take over the reins. Now, here I was, with my station command tour behind me, waiting to hand over to someone else. In a matter of days, I would be gone, Barry would be in the CO's chair and the station would get on with the job of adapting itself to the new man's way of doing things. I would find myself in a new assignment and, before very long, St Mawgan would be just a collection of personal memories and a few dozen pages of entries in my logbook.

In a sense, changes of command are very representative of life in the service in general. You come to a job, you give it your best shot and then you move on, as someone else comes in to take your place. The part you play in things is very transitory, your triumphs and your disasters alike of little moment overall. Only the service itself has any permanence. In one way always the same, in another, always changing, it continually adapts to new times, new ways and new challenges. You come and you go: it goes on.

CHAPTER 54

WHEN I FINISHED UP at St Mawgan, I was assigned, almost inevitably, back to the Ministry of Defence into the Operational Requirements Staff – but, this time, not to the Air Force Department. Instead, I took the post of Senior Air Adviser to the Deputy Chief of the Defence Staff (Operational Requirements) in the Ministry's Central Staff. The job was a fascinating one, in that the function of DCDS(OR)s Staff was to co-ordinate operational requirements submissions from all three service departments prior to their consideration by the Operational Requirements Committee – which decided whether the submissions were operationally well founded – and by the Weapons Development Committee – which decided whether they could be afforded and fitted into the projects programme. I shared an office with a Captain RN and an Army Colonel and we operated as a tri-service staff to comment on and assist in the preparation of, project submissions from all three individual Service Departments. I was generally lucky in my staff appointments, in that the jobs which I was given to do always seemed to turn out to be full of interest and, perhaps more importantly, always very closely associated with either the equipment or the operations side of things. In my Central Staff role, I had the opportunity to become very familiar with a whole range of up-coming projects from all three service departments and to see the practical difficulties involved in getting them approved and funded. There is simply never enough money available to do all that you want to do, or even to do all that you know you need to do. Inevitably, hard – sometimes agonisingly hard – decisions on relative priorities have to be resolved and some projects have to be axed from the programmes. Nobody likes it – especially not the sponsoring department – but there is simply no other practicable alternative.

Even today, people still comment to me on the 'vast' sums of money spent by the services, as if a considerable proportion of the country's wealth were being squandered on shiny, new, aircraft, ships, guns and tanks, largely for the personal satisfaction and aggrandisement of the Air Marshals, Admirals and Generals. What nonsense! I honestly question whether any other organisation handling comparable sums of money pinches its pennies quite as hard as the services do. The fundamental – and painful – truth is that defence costs. If the country wanted to do without defence at all and was seriously prepared to face up to the realistic possible consequences, it could save a fortune overnight. What it can't do – not nowadays – is get defence on the cheap. Either defence is credible, or it is not worth having. And, to make it credible, you have to pay for modern, effective, equipment. Bows and arrows are fine – cheap, too – but they are not a lot of use against an armoured troop carrier or a tank. So the choice is a simple one: either don't defend against the tank, or be prepared to pay for something which will be effective against that sort of threat. Nowadays, you won't buy that sort of 'something' for the price of a bow and arrow!

Certainly, nobody could dispute that situations do arise when very large sums of money are effectively wasted. TSR2 – millions spent and not a single aircraft to show for it. Nimrod AEW – much the same story. Off-hand, I can think of quite a number of such apparent debacles. But before people rush in to pick on these instances, they might just reflect that the service departments are not, for the most part, buying kit for today. They are provisioning for ten, fifteen, twenty years ahead. You don't do the research, development, testing and production of a modern weapons system in a matter of weeks – particularly when the requirement itself and all of the associated technologies, are continually evolving and changing right up to the time when the system actually goes into service. How many people would be prepared to sit down right now and come up with a design for a television set, a computer, a motor car, or anything else, which they could guarantee would precisely and cost-effectively, meet the needs of twenty years from now? Not easy is it? Yet projects such as these are small-scale exercises compared with the problems of producing an effective aircraft, or ship, or battle vehicle in the same sort of timescale. When you really think about the magnitude of the task, the wonder is not that the services, or Industry, do sometimes get it wrong. The miracle is that they so frequently get it right.

When I finished my time in the Central Staff, I moved back to the Air Force Department on to the Staff of the Assistant Chief of Air Staff (Operations). My post was very much the Ministry equivalent of my previous appointment at Strike Command and was concerned with the Strike/Attack and Maritime aspect of Air Force offensive operations. Again, it was interesting and challenging work and I enjoyed every minute of it. But, at the same time, it was a continuation of the commuter regime which I heartily detested and which seemed to involve almost as much time in getting to and from Whitehall as was actually spent behind one's desk. Quite a lot of the Whitehall brigade put their wives and families into houses in their home areas and themselves moved into flats or bed-sitters in London. I could never see myself adopting that particular option. Home life, to me, was what being part of a family was all about, and, anyway, I couldn't see it as much of a practicable proposition to dash up to Edinburgh every other week-end just to have the chance to spend a few hours with the wife and children. It might work for some, but I was quite clear in my own mind that this particular route was definitely not for me.

Fortunately, I still had my golf activities to keep me in touch with the world outside the Ministry. On my return from Cornwall, I had been able to renew my membership at Sonning and I managed to get in a game there during most weekends. At the same time, I had taken over the appointment as Chairman of the RAF Golf Association, a post which kept me very closely involved with Air Force golf generally. As a matter of policy, I was not a member of the Selection Committee, but, somehow or other, I usually managed to scrape into the RAF Team – invariably, in the number eight position, and, in all honesty, probably only after every other possible option had been exhaustively reviewed and reluctantly rejected.

One of the golfing initiatives which gave me a great deal of pleasure was the institution of an annual challenge match between the RAF Team and a Team representing Tactical Air Command of the United States Air Force. That the initiative ever got off the ground at all owes a great deal to the then President of the RAFGS, Air Marshal Sir Peter Terry, to General William Creech, then Commanding General, Tactical Air Command and to Air Commodore Peter Scott, then Chairman of the RAF Sports Board. Without their wholehearted and enthusiastic support, the project would never have got beyond the concept stage. But the support was forthcoming and the series was duly launched, with the inaugural match being held at MacDill Air Force Base, near Tampa in Florida and the first return fixture at RAF Bruggen in Germany and St Andrews.

I was very pleased to have had the opportunity of playing a part in setting up this exchange which is still going strong – one year in the United States and one year in Europe. So far, I believe that honours are just about even – normally the TAC Team wins in America and the RAF Team on this side – although the Americans may just have taken the lead by recording their first win on our home ground at Fulford. While it has always been the case that the result of the match was kept in perspective, it is, nonetheless, a very important issue to those who take part. And rightly so: the whole point of competition is competing to win. If the winning becomes unimportant, then there is no point at all in taking the trouble to compete in the first place. It would be true to say, however, that, while winning was always important to both teams, it was never allowed to become regarded as all-important. Getting to know your hosts and to learn something of their home country and their way of life, was always one of the primary objectives of the exercise. I can think of no better way to do that than to get together over a beer in the clubhouse after a well-fought game. Certainly, there are now quite a few young Americans and Brits who have a greater understanding and respect for each other than they might have done had they not had the opportunity to meet and get to know each other, during the series of matches.

As I got well into my second successive staff appointment in the Ministry, I found that it was becoming increasingly difficult to reconcile myself to the commuting life. Even though my flying was now confined to a desk, I enjoyed the work and I would probably have been quite happy to go on doing it, if I could only have got away from London and the daily grind of getting backwards and forwards between Caversham and Whitehall. I had never liked the lifestyle of the typical London commuter from the very first day when I had to try to adjust to it and I was finding out daily that the older I became, the less appealing I was finding it to be. No matter whether the journey to town was made by car or by train, it came down, in the end, to two hours to get there in the morning and two hours to get back at night. By the time I got back to Caversham in the evening after work, cleaned up, changed and had a meal, it was too late to think of doing much except get ready for bed, so that I could be ready to face the same sort of drag tomorrow. I hated every minute of it. Even the weekends, when it was at least possible to get out to the shops on to the golf course, began to feel as if they were only very inadequately short breaks in the otherwise unrelieved monotony of the commuters lifestyle.

Somehow, I just couldn't resign myself to carrying on in this way for the next three years to the official retiring age of fifty five. I might have had one more promotion left in me, but, even so, my background specialisations would have almost certainly kept me in London in one Ministry appointment or another. Rightly or wrongly, I felt that there had to be a bit more left in life than the 7.35 to Town in the morning and the 6.05 back again at night.

Eventually, after a great deal of agonised consideration, I came to the conclusion that I really didn't want to carry on in the way that I had been doing for the past four or five years. It wasn't in any way a case of disenchantment with the service: it was simply that I was no longer enjoying my working life as much as I had been used to – and for no other reason than the location of the Ministry in Central London. Had I been anywhere else, I would probably have soldiered on perfectly happily until it was time for me to hand in my blue suit. But the chilling prospect of another three years of commuting was simply more than I could bring myself to face up to.

Having arrived at a firm decision, I took the plunge and submitted my application to be permitted to leave the service on Premature Voluntary Retirement. Even though I knew that it was the right move to make and the right time to make it, I found that putting my signature on the application form was the most difficult thing I ever had to face up to. Effectively, I was electing to cut myself off from a service and a way of life, which I had loved and been proud to be a part of, for my working lifetime, and, when it came down to the moment of decision, I found it to be very hard to put my name on the dotted line.

Once the paperwork had been formally submitted, the administrative machinery ground around until the day arrived when I reported to the Discharge Centre at RAF Uxbridge to be formally mustered out of the service. I turned in my identity card, signed the appropriate forms and walked out of the office a civilian again. As I drove out through the gates of RQF Uxbridge, I was very conscious that I was leaving behind me thirty of the best years of my life – thirty years of doing one of the most challenging, demanding and rewarding jobs conceivable and thirty years of association with some of the finest people one could ever be lucky enough to work with. The young airman on guard duty gave me a typically smart salute, little realising that his routine courtesy was to be my last formal contact with the service which had been virtually my whole life. As I swung into the traffic beyond the gates and made my way away, my days as a member of the Royal Air Force were over and I was no longer privileged to count myself a part of it.

Now, when I look back on it all, I think mostly of how incredibly lucky I was. For thirty years of my life, I was given the opportunity to do a job that I wanted to do more than anything else in the world and which so many others would have given anything and everything to be allowed to do. Even today, I still have the feeling of being in touch with it. As I write, my son Graham is starting his flying training at Cranwell, on the same base where I started myself so many years ago. For him, as it was for me, it is what he wants to do. In many ways, his Air Force will be vastly different from the one I knew, but it will still offer the same chance of one of the best and most satisfying careers to be had anywhere. I only hope that he gets half the fulfilment, half the pleasure and half the fun out of it as I did. If he does, he will truly be able to count himself as fortunate as I feel myself to have been.

There are times when I can't help thinking back to those very far-off days when, as quite a small child, I dreamed my dreams of aeroplanes and of flying as a way of life. I suppose that, when we're young, all of us have our dreams, whatever they may be. The pity of it is that, all too often, they never get the chance to come to pass. Circumstance, or luck, or whatever, shapes the pattern of our lives and the early, precious dreams fade and are forgotten. That didn't happen to me. I carry with me today and I will carry with me always, the feeling that I was one of the lucky ones – one of the one-in-a-million really lucky ones – for whom the dream didn't fade and for whom it didn't get forgotten. Quite simply, for me, the dream came true.